Father Miller's Daughter

Father Miller's Daughter

ELLEN HARMON WHITE

Donald Edward Casebolt

WIPF & STOCK · Eugene, Oregon

FATHER MILLER'S DAUGHTER
Ellen Harmon White

Copyright © 2022 Donald Edward Casebolt. All rights reserved. Except for brief quotations in critical publications or reviews, no part of this book may be reproduced in any manner without prior written permission from the publisher. Write: Permissions, Wipf and Stock Publishers, 199 W. 8th Ave., Suite 3, Eugene, OR 97401.

Wipf & Stock
An Imprint of Wipf and Stock Publishers
199 W. 8th Ave., Suite 3
Eugene, OR 97401

www.wipfandstock.com

PAPERBACK ISBN: 978-1-6667-9799-2
HARDCOVER ISBN: 978-1-6667-9798-5
EBOOK ISBN: 978-1-6667-9800-5

JULY 15, 2022 8:40 AM

"We are all tattooed in our cradles with the beliefs of our tribe; the record may seem superficial, but it is indelible."

OLIVER WENDELL HOLMES

Contents

Preface | ix

Acknowledgements | xv

I   Introduction: EGW's Dependence on Miller's Erroneous Allegorical Historicism | 1

II   Test Case of the Ottoman's Empire's Failure to Collapse | 21

III   Hosea, Luke: The Day = 1,000 Years Principle | 33

IV   Prophecy of Moses = Seven Times of Gentiles | 52

V   Potpourri of Fanciful and Arbitrary Prophetic Interpretations | 69

VI   Snow's Explanation of Miller's March 21, 1844 Failure | 76

VII   Crosier's Extended Atonement | 102

VIII J. Turner's Bridegroom and Shut Door | 115

IX   EGW Saw Sabbath, High Priest, and Censor in Late 1847 Vision Only after These Were Ideas Taught Her by Bates, Crosier, Turner. They Are Missing "behind the Veil" in December 1844 Vision. | 146

X   "Then I Saw in Relation to the 'Daily' (Daniel 8:12) That the Word Sacrifice Was Supplied by Man's Wisdom and Does Not Belong to the Text." | 162

XI   1851 Chart Perpetuates Erroneous "Daily" Concept | 179

XII Waldenses: Poster Children for Historical Sabbatarians | 192

XIII "Enslavement of the Papacy" (Caspar)—or "Supremacy" of the Papacy (White)? | 213

XIV I Saw "Solitary Vice Is Killing Tens of Thousands." | 268

XV   Summary of Evidence | 285

Epilogue: Love not Algorithms | 291

Bibliography | 295

Index | 303

Preface

"We are all tattooed in our cradles with the beliefs of our tribe; the record may seem superficial, but it is indelible."

OLIVER WENDELL HOLMES

IN MY BOOK *Child of the Apocalypse: Ellen G. White*, I document the fact that Ellen Harmon (White) was a mere twelve years old when Father Miller converted her with his fifteen mathematical, biblical proofs that the second coming of Christ was predicted to be in 1844; that Miller's hellfire preaching exacerbated her preexisting, morbid fear of hell; that she was exposed to William Foy's ecstatic hellfire preaching just days prior to a predicted date for the second coming; that her severe prefrontal-lobe brain injury caused her to drop out of school just weeks prior to her first personal interaction with Miller; and that she, therefore, did not have the mental capacity to judge Miller's convoluted chronological proofs. Furthermore, she was surrounded by persons having ecstatic out-of-body prostrations by what they thought was the Holy Spirit. Moreover, she was sociologically isolated in a semicultic environment which dismissed critics of Miller's speculations as being the "synagogue of Satan." Due to Foy's model of out-of-body visions and Miller's numerous biblical proofs, Ellen dismissed all criticism of Miller's speculations as Satan inspired. Even more stunning, in her later prophetic pronouncements, she said she "saw" that God and his angelic messengers inspired Miller with divine insights of "last days" biblical prophecies which God had hidden away for eighteen centuries—but had now revealed to Father Miller. These factors predisposed Ellen to accept Miller's interpretations. But, aside from factors such as Ellen Harmon's age and mental capacity, was Miller merely allowing Scripture to interpret itself? Was his methodology literal and commonsensical? Contrary to Miller's self-conception and SDA historiography—no.

Thus, I will shift focus away from Ellen Harmon and toward what Miller wrote and preached. The present book now examines, text by text, Miller's purported proofs in Miller's own words (and those of his chief imitators such as Snow, Turner, Crosier, and Bates), via primary sources of the 1830s and 1840s. Most of his "proofs" were so far-fetched that one must see/read them to believe it. Thus, there are multiple block quotations taken from Miller's verse-by-verse commentary so that readers can see them in context and judge for themselves. This book demonstrates that Miller's "divine insights" were *not* based on a literal, commonsense interpretation of Scripture. Christ warned his disciples that they would not know the "day and hour" of his coming. How could a commonsense interpretation of these words mean that Miller's method could predict the very day? No. Miller utilized a fanciful, arbitrary, allegorical-typological-historical "methodology" noted to be "far-fetched" even by Seventh-Day Adventism's most famous apologist, F. D. Nichol.

Not only are many of Miller's "biblical math" results demonstrably false, but he was consistently and *systematically* erroneous. Miller's fifteen proofs are dissected textually and historically. Many of these fifteen proofs have been repudiated explicitly or implicitly. (For example, even Uriah Smith repudiated the so-called 2,520-year prophecy. This is one of the prophetic periods included in the 1843 chart that Ellen White said God preserved from error. Today it has been forgotten and lies decomposing in the dustbin of history). In addition, a potpourri of other minor Millerite interpretations is demonstrated to be without merit.

I also document how Ellen Harmon White was also immensely influenced by several of Miller's lieutenants. Most famously, S. S. Snow, Joseph Turner, and O. R. L. Crosier continued using Miller's fanciful methodology to salvage Miller's failed predictions of March 21, 1844 and October 22, 1844. Unfortunately, today most apologists still using and defending Miller's failed allegorical-typological-historicist methodology do not know the basics historical facts of Miller's own arguments. By endorsing Miller, by approving Snow's "midnight cry," Turner's bridegroom theory, and Crosier's "extended atonement" hypothesis, Ellen White immortalized Miller's erroneous speculations concerning last days events, even as these events are relics of a bygone age now over a quarter of a millennium old.

> But of that day and that hour knoweth no man, no, not the angels which are in heaven, neither the Son, but the Father. (Mark 13:32 KJV)

> But of that day and hour knoweth no man, no, not the angels of heaven, but my Father only. (Matthew 24:36 KJV)

To understand Father Miller's daughter, Ellen Harmon, one must first separate the hagiographic conception of Miller from the historical Miller. Father Miller's most notorious claim was that he had scores of texts and fifteen prophetic calculations that proved that the exact date for the second coming would be October 22, 1844. S. S. Snow, Miller's successor and protégé, surpassed him and asserted: "God is an *exact time keeper*." Miller claimed that the interpretive system he used to make this prediction was based on a literal, commonsense methodology. Simply put, he asserted that "of that day and hour knoweth no man" literally meant that he and *all* sincere Christians must know the day. On the face of it, this is an oxymoronic assertion. Yet this was and remains the cornerstone of Millerism. Miller claimed that he only used his Bible and a concordance, that he had set aside all commentators, and that in divinely inspired dreams God had commissioned him to proclaim his fifteen proofs to the entire world. Father Miller's spiritual daughter, Ellen Harmon, accepted Miller's self-conception at face value. Then she enhanced and disseminated Miller's system and self-perception, going so far as to claim that Father Miller had been prefigured by Elijah, Elisha, and John the Baptist, and that God had given Miller individualized, divine insight into prophecies that had been shrouded in mystery for centuries. Miller's spiritual daughter, upon assuming the prophetic role of God's special Messenger, perpetuated this hagiographical conception of Miller. More importantly, she endorsed his nonliteral methodology. As a result, the church that Ellen White founded retained the vestigial remains of many of Miller's purported proofs as well as his nonliteral methodology—all the while imagining that Miller's method was literal and commonsense. Ironically, Miller's original writings prove that he did not exhibit any special prophetic insight. In fact, Miller's speculative interpretations were consistently fanciful and erroneous. Ellen Harmon-White was mistaken in concluding that Miller's methodology was based on a commonsense, literal interpretation with solid textual support.

Obviously, a religious movement whose *central* claim is that it possesses a method capable of predicting the very day of the second coming—in direct contradiction to Christ's clear warning that "of that day and hour knoweth no man"—cannot simultaneously claim that it is promulgating a literal, commonsense interpretation of the Bible. Furthermore, abundant documentation that Miller's actual method was an arbitrary allegorical-typological historicism will be provided below.[1]

In my book *Child of the Apocalypse: Ellen G. White*, I argue that when in 1840 twelve-year-old Ellen Harmon encountered Father Miller, her prefrontal cortex had been seriously damaged, she had been forced to drop out of a female seminary due to mental incapacity, and she did not have the mental capacity to judge Miller's fifteen proofs and his allegorical-typological-historicist method.[2] Despite Ellen White's later evaluation that even a child could comprehend Miller's simple, textually based arguments, it is simply not true that Miller's interpretative method was literal or simple. Indeed, Miller's argumentation was *complex, convoluted, and often incomprehensible*. The evidence for this assertion is obvious if one carefully reads the primary sources of Millerism.[3] When the reader has finished studying the first six chapters of the present work, I expect the candid reader to be puzzled and perplexed by Miller's reasoning, saying to themselves: "I cannot comprehend how Miller got that interpretation out of that text!" Likewise, the reader will be stumped by how S. S. Snow reached his conclusions about the "midnight cry" and the "tarrying time." So, when you tire of the tough schlepping through Miller's interpretive labyrinth, ask yourself: Was Millerism really so simple that twelve-year-old Ellen Harmon could be expected to comprehend and rationally evaluate his assertions? Was he rightly dividing the Word of God?

An outstanding case of how outlandish Miller's method was is illustrated by James White's use of it in making his interpretation of

---

1. Nichol, *Midnight Cry,* 507–10, Appendix L. Thus, the dean of SDA apologists found Miller's method far-fetched, fanciful, and hoary with age.

2. Casebolt, *Child of the Apocalypse*. White, *Life Sketches*, 26.

3. Reading only Miller's *Evidence* (1842) and Snow's "Behold" would be sufficient to confirm that Millerite exegesis was anything but literal, commonsense, and simple.

the four watches of the night.[4] This example of how James White utilized Miller's method is revealing because White was Ellen Harmon's closest associate and husband; because it illustrates how James White, while travelling and collaborating with Ellen Harmon, used Miller's nonliteral *"method"* to predict the second coming for October 1845. It demonstrates that Ellen Harmon-White was oblivious to the faults of the method. Crucially, it is contemporaneous written documentation of how Ellen Harmon, James White, and many disappointed Millerites were predicting the second coming for October 1845. Even a superficial study of how James White constructed his proof that Christ would return during October 1845 demonstrates how fallacious his method was. James White would later claim that just a few days prior to his predicted date, Ellen Harmon said she had a vision that he would be disappointed. But by the time of this *fourth* disappointment, it hardly took prophetic insight to disavow yet another erroneous result. Ellen White never had a vision in which she was shown that *the Millerite allegorical-typological-historicist method was fatally flawed.* Consequently, Ellen White's endorsement of Miller's method resulted in the fact that the church she cofounded retained both specific disconfirmed dates/events and Miller's nonliteral method.

If I demonstrate that Miller's method was fatally flawed (and not merely his numerous erroneous results), then it follows that Miller's failures had a wider influence beyond Ellen Harmon. Through her voluminous writings she perpetuated an inaccurate paradigm of William Miller's methodology and results. Miller's sincere self-conception was that he was merely letting the Bible interpret itself. In effect, *when Miller spoke, God was speaking.* Additionally, he felt that God gave him dreams which irresistibly required him to communicate his biblical interpretations. Ellen White immortalized and strengthened this paradigm when she claimed that she "saw" that God regularly sent angels to supply Miller with his conclusions—insights which the Christian world had overlooked for centuries. She engraved upon the collective consciousness of proto-SDAs the teaching that Miller's

---

4. See the section in chapter 8 dedicated to James White's interpretation of the four watches. See particularly Damsteegt's discussion in "Early Adventist Timesettings." Damsteegt labels the disappointments of spring 1845 and October 1845 the third and fourth disappointments. He also documents the extreme reliance of James White and other Millerite thought leaders like W. Thayer, Jacobs, J. Hamilton, R. G. Bunting, and Samuel Pearce on fanciful typological-chronological arguments. See his footnotes 45–54.

method was literal, commonsense, and supported by numerous biblical texts. Thus, all Miller's faulty conclusions became the collective intellectual property of Ellen White's church. It retains a historically and hermeneutically inaccurate paradigm of Miller, his method, and his interpretations.

Acknowledgements

THE FOLLOWING INDIVIDUALS HAVE been kind enough to read this manuscript and provide me some oral and/or written feedback: Esdon Bacchus, Scott A. LeMert, James Hamstra, Larry Geraty, Gilbert Valentine, Jonathan Butler, Paul Lee, Calvin Hill, James Hayward, and Douglas Morgan.

Ellen White's "messages from God" were "emanating from the Divine Mind."

NOVEMBER 1855 GENERAL CONFERENCE

I

Introduction: EGW's Dependence on Miller's Erroneous Allegorical Historicism

> But of that day and that hour knoweth no man, no, not the angels which are in heaven, neither the Son, but the Father. (Mark 13:32, KJV // Matthew 24:36)

Ellen Harmon encounters Father Miller

Father William Miller made an indelible imprint on twelve-year-old Ellen Harmon[1] when she initially attended his evangelistic lectures in the spring of 1840. Although it would be an exaggeration to say that Ellen Harmon-White was wholly Miller's creation, nevertheless, she was Father Miller's spiritual daughter and most important convert. Both his results and his methods became the cornerstone of Ellen

---

1. Ellen Harmon became Ellen G. White when she married James White in 1846. I refer to her at times with her married name, at times with her maiden name, and at times with the hyphenated Ellen Harmon-White. Although Millerism imploded with the Great Disappointment, Ellen White would organize its remnants into what eventually became the Seventh-Day Adventist (SDA) church, which, as of 2021, has about twenty million members.

White's beliefs.[2] Ellen White's conception of history and interpretation of Scripture cannot be understood without a solid understanding of Miller's conception of the nexus of Scripture and history.[3] William Miller taught that God had revealed to him a long sequence of fifteen datable prophetic periods ending with Christ's second coming and the first resurrection "about 1843."[4] In turn, Miller cannot be understood without understanding that he himself was profoundly indebted to an already discredited and falsified historicism[5] that had blossomed in the Reformation Era. Historicism's credibility had been severely undermined by the fact that scores of Protestant commentators had employed historicism to calculate exact dates for the second coming and premonitory signs just preceding the end of the world. Three centuries before Miller's historicist predictions, scores of historicist predictions had been disconfirmed. That is, like Miller, they had predicted multiple sequences of events linked with Revelation's seven churches, seven trumpets, seven vials, and seven seals, etc. Nonetheless, Miller imagined that his predictions were based on a literal, commonsense interpretation of Scripture, and that he had laid aside all commentaries and relied solely on the Bible and his concordance.[6] Additionally, Miller envisioned that God had communicated with him via dreams and given him a divine imperative to warn sinners that the earth would be cleansed with fire in 1843. By 1843 Ellen Harmon believed that she too was receiving divinely inspired dreams that ratified Miller's claim that the second coming could be dated to a precise year, if not an exact day and hour. By late 1844 she believed that she had received visions confirming Miller's date-setting, conferring upon her a Messenger status with the command to spread the light of

---

2. See Knight's *Millennial Fever* for broad description and historical context of Millerism's critical years 1840–45.

3. See Rowe's God's *Strange Work* for an excellent biography of Miller himself.

4. Arasola's *The End of Historicism* is the most comprehensive, scholarly, and balanced analysis of the origins and contents of Miller's fifteen exact proofs that the "time of the end" began in 1798 and would end "about 1843."

5. "Historicism" is the shorter term for the more accurate appellation, "allegorical-typological historicism." Ellen White did not employ a simple historicism. Rather, as documented below by Burt, the critical Parable of the Bridegroom of Matthew 25 was interpreted allegorically.

6. Ironically, Froom's, 4-volume work, *The Prophetic Faith of Our Fathers*, exhaustively documents Miller's massive dependence on the hoary tradition of historicism.

the "true midnight cry"[7] outside her hometown, Portland, Maine. She had confidence in Miller's date-setting since she believed that she received visions in which God communicated to her the fact that he had regularly communicated with Miller and given him repeated angelic instruction concerning the prophecies of Leviticus, Daniel, Revelation, and Matthew which nearly two millennia of Bible students had not been able to comprehend. As Ellen G. White, the SDA Messenger, she prophetically endorsed Miller's calculations, stating that he had been divinely and angelically inspired in arriving at his conclusions. White likened him to Elijah and John the Baptist. She stated that just as John the Baptist was Christ's forerunner at his First Advent, William Miller was Christ's forerunner at his Second Advent.[8]

So, what did the forerunner of Christ's second coming predict? In most SDA histories it is recounted that Miller first predicted the world would end on or about March 21, 1844. When this prediction failed, an initial disappointment occurred, and a "tarrying time" commenced. But this was not Miller's first failed prediction of the end. He first predicted that history would end in 1839, not "about 1843." Muslims had made a profound impression on Western Christianity at least since their siege of Vienna, the capital of the Austro-Hungarian Empire, in 1529. They had made such a profound impression on Martin Luther that he identified the Muslim empire as the little horn of Daniel—not the papacy. Since then, Muslims figured prominently in Christian apocalypses. Miller mimicked numerous learned historicists when he predicted that an Armageddon event resulting in the collapse of the Ottoman Empire and the second coming would occur in 1839.[9] Miller found the Muslim hordes predicted not only in the trumpets of Revelation, but also in Daniel.[10] Miller later altered the year of this last great battle to 1840, then one of his disciples eventually dated the Ottoman Empire's collapse to August 11, 1840. This never happened but Millerites rejiggered the data to claim that it did. Recall that Ellen Harmon was only twelve in the summer of 1840 when Millerites made this claim. Until her death, she persisted in her

---

7. The midnight cry was also known as the "seventh-month movement." It was the climactic phase of Millerism originated by S. S. Snow, and most notable for his prediction that October 22, 1844 would be the second coming.

8. White, *Spiritual Gifts*, 1:128–29, 131, 133–35.

9. Miller, *Evidence from Scripture*, 70–75.

10. Miller, *Evidence from Scripture*, 60–67.

inaccurate claim that the Ottoman Empire collapsed on August 11, 1840. See chapter 2 for details.

Chapter 3 documents two of Miller's most bizarre proofs that the second coming would occur "about 1843." Most SDAs are familiar with Miller's principle that a prophetic day equals an historical year. Virtually none know that with equal certitude Miller asserted that two of his exact predictions employed his interpretive rule that a *prophetic day* also equals a *thousand years*. His manner of using his concordance resulted in his "biblical" interpretation that two prophetic intervals of two thousand years existed. In his concordance he found that Luke 13:32 used the word "day" (Jesus said: "I do cures *to day* . . . and the third *day* I shall be perfected" [KJV]). Miller reasoned that any "today" or "third day" could signify a thousand years just as well as it could signify only one historical year. This allowed him to transform the synoptic Gospel of Luke into a prophetic book. Miller confidently asserted that this interval had to start in 158 BC because the Jews made a league with the Romans that year. Similarly, the word "day" occurred in Hosea 6:1–3 ("After two days will he revive us: in the third day he will . . ." [KJV]). The "two days" signified two millennia, Miller confidently asserted. Such was the foundation for his interpretation that Luke 13:32 and Hosea 6:1–3 predicted a prophetic interval of two thousand years from 158 BC to 1843. Can this be considered evidence of the special insights that Ellen White credited him with?

Chapter 4 provides further examples of Miller's insights in inventing several of his prophetic proofs for arriving at 1843 for the second coming. One was his "seven times of the Gentiles," which he claimed was a 2,520-year interval reaching from exactly 677 BC to 1843. The was first known as the "prophecy of Moses" and the text Leviticus 26. He also claimed that the same prophetic interval was found in Deuteronomy 15:1–2 and Jeremiah 34:14, where he entitled it "the year of release." This seven times theory appeared in multiple Millerite books and articles. It was such a pillar of Millerite exegesis that it was included in the notorious 1843 Millerite chart. It was still considered a valid prophetic period in 1851 when Ellen G. White, claiming a vision commanding her to create the 1851 White/Nichols chart, reinforced it. Amazingly, she also said her newly remodeled chart's creation was predicted in the Bible. Nonetheless, in 1897 the stalwart apologist Uriah Smith contemptuously dismissed the 2,520-day-year period as a "supposed" prophetic period.[11] Besides this "supposed" prophetic period, chapter 4 describes a half-dozen of Miller's other means of concocting prophetic intervals all ending in 1843. The Lisbon 1755 earthquake, the Dark Day of 1780, and the 1833 meteorite shower, all considered by Millerites to be supernatural cosmic signs of the end, are also analyzed.

Chapter 5 provides a sampling of other fanciful historicist interpretations. Miller had yet other far-fetched methods of interpreting Daniel and Revelation. Most SDAs are familiar with his assertion that the seven churches of Revelation refer to seven exactly dated, sequential epochs in Christian history. They may be surprised to learn that Miller claimed that the four beasts of Revelation 4:7—the lion, the calf, the man, and the eagle—also represent four grand epochs in church history. The apostolic era, for example, was represented by the lion, because the gospel was boldly proclaimed, like a lion. In characterizing each of these four periods, Miller strained his creative interpretative genius to the maximum.

This brief survey of Miller's so-called literal, commonsense interpretations demonstrates that Miller's exegetical method was far from literal or commonsense. Thus, it was not a surprise to most of his contemporary critics when his third predicted date for the second coming, March 21, 1844, was a failure. Today, no one who has read Miller's several editions of *Evidence(s)* could conclude that his interpretations are literal or commonsense interpretations. But what about the fact that Miller was greatly dependent on Reformation Era historicists? There are so many evidences of this that listing them monotonously, chart after chart, would quickly become tedious. Thus, I cite one churchman as a representative example. Most SDAs who are familiar with the standard SDA charts and dates will immediately note the similarities and discrepancies. One representative illustration of demonstrably falsified historicist interpretation involves Brightman, an English clergyman who was a forerunner of Joseph Mede. Chapters 8–12 of Revelation describe seven trumpets. Revelation 16 describes seven vials. Reformation Era historicists claimed they could identify seven exact, discrete, sequential historical events/epochs for seven trumpets and seven vials. Some asserted that there were only seven events in total, that the seven trumpets and seven vials were

---

11. Smith, *Daniel and the Revelation* (2016), 600–602.

a repetition of only seven discrete events. Others asserted that there were fourteen *separate* events with no duplication.

Brightman's Elizabethan vials, churches, and trumpets

Thomas Brightman (1562–1607), who wrote *A Revelation of the Revelation*, separated the vials and trumpets, claiming that they predicted two different sequences of history. He asserted that he could identify specific Bible verses with specific datable events, whereas Napier, the inventor of logarithms and a historicist in the mold of Sir Isaac Newton, would "synchronize" them, asserting that each vial was duplicated by a trumpet representing a single event. Practically no two of such commentators could agree on the same date or identification! As an example of Brighman's specificity, for instance, he claimed that the Harvest of the Apocalypse] "was in Germany and hath brought us to the year 1530: This Vintage [of the Apocalypse—treading of grapes] was in our Realme of England, being so mervailously jumping with the matters . . . that it is not to be doubted but that the Holy Ghost hath pointed his finger to these Grapes." According to Brightman, Thomas Cromwell was predicted in the Apocalypse as the Revelation's avenging angel; Thomas Cranmer was allegedly the soul from out of the altar (Revelation 6:9); the seventh trumpet blew in 1558; and the vials began under Queen Elizabeth in 1560. All the vials symbolized godly Protestant punishments inflicted on the Catholics. Brightman specifically identified the first four vials with the following historical events/dates.

1. 1563 — Elizabeth dismissed many of the papist clergy.
2. 1564 — The Council of Trent, meeting for many years, confirmed errors which effected the damnation of many.
3. 1581 — Act of Parliament against the treason of papists.
4. His present "this boiling heate of the Sunne is nowe every daye to be loked for, that is, some more cleare opening of the Scriptures, whereby the man of sinne may be more, vehemently scorched."[12]

---

12. Firth, *Apocalyptic Tradition*, 170.

Brightman also proposed precise dates for the seven churches. Note below that the fifth, sixth, and seventh churches were all Reformation Era churches. These "last days" events are now half a millennium in the past. Thus, Miller had to redate Reformation Era calculations.

Brightman's seven churches:

1. Ephesus   31–313, Apostolic to Constantine
2. Smyrna   313–382, Constantine to Gratian
3. Pergamum   382–1300, a type of corrupt papacy[13]
4. Thyatira   1300–1520
5. Sardis   1520, German Reformation
6. Philadel   Calvin's Genevan Reformation
7. Laodicea   Church of England becoming Protestant

Brightman's seventh trumpet brings one to precisely 1588, Queen Elizabeth's 1588 triumph over Catholicism.

Brightman's seven trumpets:

1–4.   313–607, Constantine, when pope takes control
5.   607–1300, Muslim invasions and Pope Boniface's collusion with Emperor Phocas; locusts = Saracens in East and = monks in West
6.   1300–1696
7.   1588, triumph of Elizabeth, Virgin Queen

Scores of self-contradictory, historically falsified, historicist interpretations were made. They all have in common the fact that 1) they obviously were not based on a plain, commonsense, literal interpretation of the Bible; 2) they were stream-of-consciousness, allegorical, arbitrary interpretations; 3) Miller was dependent upon such fanciful interpretations; and 4) Miller and his audience inherited many specific historicist traditions, such as the assertion that the Muslim invasions were a fulfillment of the fifth trumpet. Miller's only

---

13. Since Pergamum was specially associated with a dominant papacy (unlike Wm. Miller's and Uriah Smith's choice of Thyatira), Brightman found it difficult to settle on a definite commencement date. Besides 382, he also estimated that Pergamum may begin in 380, 400, 506, or 607.

original contribution was that he supplied new dates and events for the failed dates and events of the Reformation Era commentators. By Miller's time, Brightman's identifications had been falsified by the passage of three centuries.

Significantly, Miller's chef d'oeuvre is entitled *Evidence from Scripture and History of the Second Coming of Christ*. This was in the historicist tradition of Alexander Keith's 1839 *Evidence of the Truth of the Christian Religion: Derived from the Literal Fulfillment of Prophecy*. The first word in both titles, "evidence," manifests the Zeitgeist's conviction that empirical *evidence* from the Bible could scientifically prove biblical doctrines. William Whiston's 1724 ponderous tome, *The Literal Accomplishment of Scripture Prophecies, Being a Full Answer to a Late Discourse, of the Grounds and Reasons of the Christian Religion*, purported to rationally demonstrate the truth of Christianity via lists of hundreds of fulfilled prophecies.[14] Whiston, Keith, and Miller incarnated a counterattack against deism. They believed they had discovered a mathematical, biblical science which could prove the foreknowledge of a personal God and refute the claims of deism, which Miller had embraced in his youth.[15] What better evidence that deism was bankrupt than a mathematical-historical proof demonstrating a personal God's prophetic foreknowledge? There is a direct line from Keith to S. S. Snow, the former atheist. Keith asserted: "if men do not believe Moses and the prophets, neither would they be persuaded though one arose from the dead."[16] S. S. Snow would climax his proofs of the midnight cry with the clarion call: "If they hear not MOSES and the PROPHETS, neither will they be persuaded, although one arose from the dead."[17] The centuries of tradition that stood behind the hoary historicist method convinced Miller and Snow that the Bible provided empirical evidence, scientific evidence, even mathematical evidence, which proved their assertions about the date of the second coming. Historicists speculated that there existed a one-to-one relationship between Scripture and history. They asserted that a text from Scripture could be exactly matched with an event in

---

14. Whiston, *Literal Accomplishment of Scripture Prophecies*.

15. Similarly, such *Evidence* converted S. S. Snow from atheist to Millerite—before he became Elijah in 1845.

16. Keith, *Evidence*, 19.

17. Snow, " Behold," 1–4.

history. They congratulated themselves as the wise who could discover these one-to-one relationships.

Miller had proclaimed that his fifteen proofs demonstrated that Christ's second coming must occur by March 21, 1844—despite Christ's warning in Mark 13:32: "No man knoweth."

> I believe the time can be known by all who desire to understand and to be ready for his coming. And I am fully convinced that some time between March 21st, 1843, and March 21st, 1844, according to the Jewish mode of computation of time, Christ will come, and bring all his saints with him; and that then he will reward every man as his work shall be.[18]

When Christ did not appear by March 21, 1844, Millerism was thrown into a mix of chaos and despair. The solutions proposed to this existential crisis indicated that Miller was not the most exuberant practitioner of the allegorical-typological-historicist method. Thus, after chapter 6, I transition from examples of Miller's failed method and results to a presentation of how S. S. Snow, using the identical methodology, came up with his concept of the midnight cry and October 22, 1844.

S. S. Snow had already displayed his creativity in inventing historicist solutions prior to this date. In 1844 Snow published a series of articles stressing typology and prophetic intervals.[19] His theory was that God had deliberately planned that the "about 1843" proclamation should fail. God designed that the Millerites should proclaim the March 21, 1844 date, the last day of the rabbinical Jewish year of 1843, as the end of the world. But God also designed and even predestined that the "first angel message" should *fail* in order to *fulfill* prophecy. He postulated that Habakkuk 2:3 predicted that following March 21, 1844 there would be a very brief but indefinite "tarrying time." He also asserted that Ezekiel 12:22-24 predicted the Millerite experience of both 1843 and 1844. He claimed that the phrase "The days are prolonged, and every vision faileth" referred to the vision of Daniel *seeming to fail*.

Snow also pressed Jeremiah 51:45-46 into a historicist mold.

---

18. Miller, "Synopsis of Miller's Views," 145–50.

19. See Turner, *Three Angels' Messages Source Book*, 72–86 for a series of letters by S. S. Snow. This is an internet compilation of Millerite documents, including Crosier's article on the extended atonement.

"a rumor shall both come one year [1843], and after that there shall come in another year [1844] a rumor, and violence in the land, ruler against ruler." What is the rumor here spoken of? It is the Advent message. And what is the first year of the message? It is the Jewish year 1843. And God foresaw the passing by[20] of that year of the rumor, he saw it necessary lest the hearts of his people should faint.[21]

"One year" referred to 1843. "Another year" referred to 1844. Then, "there should come another message, and in another year, after the first." Therefore, Miller's fifteen "periods could not terminate before the seventh month of the Jewish sacred year in A.D. 1844."[22] Thus, the Jeremiah passage referring to events regarding Babylon in Jeremiah's time Snow wrested out of context, brought forward over two millennia, and marshalled in favor of an exact year and season for the second coming: autumn 1844.[23]

Snow's interpretation of Ezekiel 12:22; Habakkuk 2:3; Jeremiah 51:45–46; and 2 Esdras 2:19 demonstrate the capricious nature of the allegorical-typological-historicism employed by Miller and Snow. See chapter 6 for a detailed analysis of Snow's fantastical exegetical feats.

With chapter 7 we transition from pre-Great Disappointment use of Miller's and Snow's methodology to the post-Disappointment exercise of the same speculative method. O. R. L. Crosier and Joseph Turner were the most famous practitioners. Ellen Harmon borrowed from both.

When the Great Disappointment of October 22, 1844 followed the little disappointment of March 21, 1844, Millerism, like Humpdy Dumpty, was shattered irretrievably. Yet Ellen Harmon and other "shut door" adherents continued to utilize the same allegorical-typological historicism to solve their disenchantment. They based their speculation on an *allegorical* interpretation of Matthew 25's Parable of the Bridegroom and the Ten Virgins. This was the foundation of Crosier's

---

20. "Passing by" of the year 1843 is a euphemism for the failed prediction of March 21, 1844.

21. Snow, "Letter from S. S. Snow," June 27, 1844.

22. The "periods" refer to the 1,335-year period, the 2,300-year period, the 2,520-year period, the 2,450-year period, and the 2,000-year periods of Hosea and Luke which Miller and Snow claime would all end in 1843–1844, specifically October 22, 1844, the equivalent to the seventh month in the Jewish calendar.

23. Snow, "Letter from S. S. Snow," June 27, 1844.

1845 and 1846 exposition of an "extended atonement." He claimed that the failure of Christ to come on March 21, 1844 and again on October 22, 1844 constituted two great signs.

> For Bridegroom Adventists their basic theological argument was drawn from the parable of the ten virgins in Matthew 25. They made the parable *allegorical* to their 1844 experience, and believed that on or about October 22, 1844, Jesus had gone into a heavenly wedding. The *Advent Mirror* divided the marriage into *two steps*; the actual marriage and the marriage supper [emphasis added].[24]

The historical underpinnings for Ellen Harmon's reaffirmation of the prophetic significance of October 22, 1844 came into being in stages.

First, centuries prior to her birth, the continuous-historical paradigm burgeoned during the Protestant Reformation. (This paradigm I have also termed the allegorical-typological-historicist method.) Commentators in this tradition proposed numerous historically precise events that they believed had a one-to-one relationship with specific texts in Daniel and the Apocalypse. Because they believed that the last days were in their day, they asserted that specific geopolitical events in the sixteenth and seventeenth centuries were predicted by these biblical books. As time passed, hundreds of their predictions failed. However, certain broad features were reworked and redated by William Miller. Others, like claiming that specific events in the reign of Elizabeth the Great fulfilled prophecies of the vials of Revelation, were discarded and then reinterpreted.

Second, Miller built upon the sands of a historicist foundation with his emphasis that fifteen texts mathematically proved that the Second Advent could come no later than March 21, 1844. When this did not occur, S. S. Snow originated the midnight-cry stage of the Millerite movement. Ironically, all of Miller's lieutenants repeatedly rejected dating the second coming to a specific day as non-biblical until just weeks before October 22, 1844. Snow and his devotees did not manage to stampede Miller into accepting October 22, 1844 until just days prior to the event (October 6). He then repudiated this teaching by the summer of 1845.

---

24. Burt, "'Shut Door' and Ellen White's Visions," 45.

In the third stage, S. S. Snow asserted that the failed date of March 21, 1844 was due to a mere temporary delay, the "tarrying time," and recalibrated the second coming for exactly October 22, 1844. When this did not occur, the stage was set for Joseph Turner, O. R. L. Crosier, Joseph Bates, James White, and Ellen Harmon to recalculate and reinterpret Scripture yet again.

Fourth, Joseph Turner and Apollos Hale speculated that the failure of Christ to come on October 22, 1844 was because there was a two-stage coming. Christ came as bridegroom *invisibly* on October 22, 1844 in the first stage. In the second stage, Christ would come *visibly* to earth as King within several weeks or months. They based their speculation on an allegorical interpretation of Matthew 25's Parable of the Bridegroom and the Ten Virgins.

Fifth, O. R. L. Crosier also contributed to this two-stage speculation. He proposed a two-staged, two-chamber process with Christ mediating for all humanity in the Holy Place from his ascension until October 22, 1844, and then moving to the Most Holy Place as High Priest to enact an extended atonement, for the "wise virgins" *exclusively*, from October 22, 1844 onward. In the first stage, Christ's mediatorial labor was offered to everyone. In the second stage, post-Disappointment, it was available only for the wise virgins inside the "shut door." Until October 22, 1844 Christ had "an important work to do for his enemies with the Father, to make 'intercession for the transgressors,' at the end of which he has a work to do for his saints exclusively before their resurrection; then follows his visible Advent..."[25] The invisible must precede the visible. The several bibliographic items by Burt best sum up the 1845–1846 period. His most important observation is that Turner, Hale, and Crosier consistently employed Miller's allegorical-typological-historicist method for calculating post-Great Disappointment events. Ellen White claimed that Crosier's exposition was "the true light."[26] Crosier and Harmon affirmed the novel doctrine of a two-chambered, "extended" atonement, which morphed into a pre-Advent or "investigative" judgment. On October 22, 1844

---

25. Burt, "Day-Dawn," 320.

26. See James White, 'Word to the "Little Flock,"' for Ellen White's striking claim that: "The Lord shew me in vision, more than one year ago, that Brother Crosier had the true light, on the cleansing of the Sanctuary, &c; and that it was his will, that Brother C. should write out the view which he gave us in the *Day-Star, Extra*, February 7, 1846."

two critical events occurred: Christ 1) shut the door and 2) moved into the Most Holy Place, where he mediated "for his saints exclusively." Ellen White followed Crosier's "true light." For the next six to seven years, Ellen G. White repeatedly insisted that all conversions to open-door Adventism were counterfeit. As late as March 24, 1849 she wrote: "Some appear to have been really converted so as to deceive God's people," but their hearts were "as black as ever. My accompanying angel bade me to look for the travail of soul for sinners as used to be. I looked, but could not see it, for the time of their salvation is passed."[27] Or, as late as December 25, 1850: "Dare they admit that the door is shut? They said the shut-door was of the devil and now admit it is against their own lives. They shall die the death."[28]

The Reformation Era historicists William Miller, S. S. Snow, Joseph Turner, and O. R. L. Crosier all employed the identical demonstrably fallacious methods and obtained historically falsified results. *Their actual allegorical-typological-historicist method was neither commonsense nor literal.* The myriad of scriptural texts they cited impressed Ellen White immensely. The problem was that these texts were consistently wrested out of context; the eschatological and chronological conclusions built on this textual foundation frequently lost all touch with reality. The historical record demonstrates that Miller did not have the special insights into Daniel and Revelation that Ellen White credited him with. In fact, the overwhelming majority of his verse-by-verse commentary is objectively preposterous. This is substantiated by a detailed examination of his own words in chapters 2–5. The undeniable evidence that Snow, Joseph Turner, and O. R. L. Crosier continued to use Miller's failed methodology is demonstrated in chapters 6–8. Chapter 6 is dedicated to Snow's use of the allegorical-typological-historicist method. Chapter 7 is dedicated to Crosier's creation of the extended atonement using the same method. Chapter 8 is dedicated to Joseph Turner's bridegroom and shut-door speculation. This last chapter also documents how Ellen Harmon inherited her shut-door belief from Miller, and how the Ellen G. White Estate finally conceded that Ellen Harmon believed in the shut door for several years and, they believe, misinterpreted her own first vision to accommodate this doctrine.

27. White, *Ellen G. White Letters & Manuscripts*, 160–63.
28. White, *Ellen G. White Letters & Manuscripts*, 273.

Chapter 9 demonstrates how Ellen Harmon's first vision intersects with the concepts of Turner and Crosier, and what she had learned (or not yet learned) from Joseph Bates about the historiography of the Sabbath. In an 1847 vision focused on the Sabbath, Ellen G. White claimed to have seen critical cultic objects in the Most Holy Place behind the second veil. Yet during her tour of the Most Holy Place during her December 1844 vision, these cultic objects were inexplicably missing. Her first vision had about forty lines of text describing specifically what she saw "within the veil" of the heavenly Most Holy Place. She and James White excised these from her 1851 version of this vision, most likely because she did not see the halo around the Sabbath commandment. And this absence was embarrassing. Nowhere in these forty lines does she recount having seen in December 1844 what she now claims to have seen in April 1847. If, as of October 23, 1844, Christ as High Priest with the golden censer had moved into the Most Holy Place to begin the second phase of his mediatorial work, as of December 1844 Ellen Harmon would have doubtless seen him with the golden censer. She did not see the High Priest, the golden censer, or Sabbath halo. These three items were prominently engraved in the 1851 White/Nichols chart. The golden censer with its incense was the crucial symbol of this Day of Atonement ministry, which became the trademark, novel doctrine in SDA theology. As of December 1844, Ellen Harmon had not yet learned from Bates, Crosier, and Turner about the two-chambered, extended atonement and the movement of Christ from the Holy to the Most Holy Place. *Therefore, she did not yet see these concepts in her first vision. Every significant theological teaching that Ellen White said she learned in vision, she first learned from the writings and talks of Miller (multiple prophetic periods and cosmic signs); Snow (midnight cry and tarrying time); Joseph Turner, (bridegroom); and Crosier (extended atonement).* In every case she only had a vision after she had been "taught by man."

The sole burden of her first vision was to assert the validity of the October 22, 1844 date-setting midnight cry. She had not yet been "taught" by Turner and Crosier their theories explaining the delay of the second coming. Neither did she see in her first vision that the first four commandments of the Decalogue were more important than the last six. In her first vision she did not see a bright halo around the Sabbath commandment. She only saw things about the Sabbath in her visions after she had learned them in real life from Joseph Bates.

Chapter 10 discusses aspects about "the daily" and the 1,335-day-year prophetic period which have not heretofore been noted by scholars. This prophetic period is probably considered arcane, obsolete, and nit-picking by most contemporary SDAs, if they have even heard of it. Ellen White said she saw in a vision that the word "sacrifice" was inappropriately supplied by KJV translators, but she was mistaken. Just like many other concepts she erroneously borrowed from Miller, she imbibed this error from him—even if she thought she saw otherwise in vision.

Historically, "the daily" and the 1,335-day-year prophetic period was crucial in Miller's 1843 chart. Miller considered it as equivalent to his 2,300-year prophetic period. His multiple proofs for both 1798 and 1843 necessitated a prophetic *terminus a quo* of 508. Without 508 Miller would lose his 1,335-day-year proof that the end would be "about 1843" and his 1,290-day-year proof that the last days would begin in 1798. Late in her career Ellen G. White would claim to have no light on "the daily." But in 1850 Ellen G. White claimed that she saw that the KJV translators illegitimately and mistakenly appended the word "sacrifice" to the term "the daily," which occurs in Daniel 8 and 11–12. She claimed that before the split between the shut-door and open-door Adventists occurred in 1845 the Millerite movement had been unanimous in their view of "the daily." Very true. In the 1840s all Millerites *were* unified in asserting that "the daily" symbolized pagan Rome's dominance during the 666-year interval of 158 BC to 508 AD. In about 1910 a major controversy arose in the SDA church as to the correct understanding of this critical term. Ellen G. White claimed at this time that she had no "light" from God on the topic. To the contrary, Uriah Smith and S. N. Haskell insisted that the traditional or "old view" of this term had been endorsed by an Ellen G. White vision in 1850. The "old view" unambiguously stated that "the daily" referred to pagan domination or pagan Rome. This is what William Miller preached. Ironically, Kaiser's 2009 MA thesis documents that by 1930–2008 Ellen White's "old view" of "the daily" was considered valid by only a fringe element in the SDA church.[29]

By 1910 SDA scholars such as W. W. Prescott and Louis R. Conradi had convinced high-ranking ecclesiological officials (like General Conference president A. G. Daniells) that this "old" view was based

---

29. Kaiser, "History of the Adventist Interpretation," 137. For an accessible version, see https://digitalcommons.andrews.edu/theses/45/.

on a fundamentally nonhistorical basis. They proposed a "new" view that asserted that "the daily" referred to Christ's sacrificial offering, which had been obliterated by papal Rome. Note: "the daily," which was unanimously proclaimed by Millerites to be a devilish "pagan dominance," now became Christ's supreme sacrifice. In the intervening half-century writers like J. N. Andrews and Uriah Smith had strongly supported the "old view." They, like Ellen G. White writing in 1850, claimed that "the daily" had nothing to do with a literal sacrifice. and were unalterably opposed to modifying that view. (Smith would say he never changed his mind despite being formally coerced into compliance). They, like Ellen G. White writing in 1850, claimed that "the daily" had nothing to do with a literal sacrifice. William Miller had claimed that he had searched his Bible and concordance and could find no relationship whatsoever between "the daily" and sacrifice. Astonishingly, however, it is simple to prove that over one hundred occurrences of "the daily" (*hatamid*) exist in the Old Testament. The Hebrew word for "the daily sacrifice" unambiguously refers to the *literal* twice-daily sacrifices prescribed in the Torah, sacrifices which are to be offered morning and evening, exactly as it is phrased in Daniel.

In short, Ellen G. White could not justifiably claim that she saw that the word "sacrifice" had been incorrectly supplied by KJV translators. This is simply not factually correct. Rather, she received this mistaken concept from Miller, whose eisegesis of this phrase is textually insupportable.

Chapter 11, dealing with the White/Nichols 1851 chart, offers supplementary evidence for this conclusion. This chart had immense theological significance which has since been forgotten. It distills in pictorial form the most salient features of Ellen G. White's 1851 Adventism just as the 1843 Millerite chart represents the core dogmas of Millerism. It was Millerite eschatology's new-and-improved 1851 edition. It corrected the single mathematical error that the shut-door Millerites conceded. It gave a pictorial justification for the delay of the second coming. This was a chart whose necessity Ellen G. White says she saw was vital and whose creation she personally supervised. Like the 1843 Millerite chart, it included several prophetic periods which have meanwhile been disconfirmed: the 1,290-year period, the 1,335-year period, the 2,520-year period, and the August 11, 1840 date. They both refer to the 158 BC Roman-Jewish league and identify the 508 date as marking the end of "pagan dominance." Significantly, Ellen G. White claimed that "God was in" the "publishment" of the 1851 White/Nichols chart, using the same phraseology as when she claimed that "God was in" the midnight cry's date-setting proclamation of October 22, 1844.

Chapter 12 reviews the historiography of the Waldenses, who were the poster children representing "proto-Protestants" for the Protestants, who, however, had never remotely suggested that they were Saturday Sabbatarians. Ellen G. White borrowed the Waldenses from the Millerite literature with all the traditional encomiums heaped upon them by the Protestant world. She made the additional assertion that they were Sabbatarians, the pure, non-Catholic church, persecuted especially for their Sabbath-keeping. Since Ellen G. White originated this assertion, SDA scholars have felt obliged to defend it. This chapter explains how the legend originated and is maintained. Incomprehensibly, one prominent SDA apologist's recent article argues that because the Waldenses only revered Sunday (and not other common Roman Catholic religious holidays), therefore, they were Sabbath keepers.

Chapter 13 discusses the concept of the supremacy of the papacy, which Millerite literature said persecuted the pure church for a 1,260-year interval from 538 to 1798, during which millions of Waldensian Christians were supposedly slaughtered. This chapter documents that this interval was never predicted in advance but rather, after 1798, was generated *ex post facto*; that wholesale persecution did not exist during the interval 538–1798 but rather flared up only with the wars of religion which followed the Reformation; that Sunday worship was widespread long before 538; that several popes who venerated Sunday were martyred prior to Constantine; that dates of both 538 and 1798 were capriciously arrived at. Far from enjoying supremacy, the period following the 538 era was a catastrophic nadir for the papacy. Pope Pius VI's successor in 1800, Pope Pius VII, suffered an imprisonment which was harsher and more catastrophic than Pope Pius VI's 1798 capture and imprisonment. The first thirteen chapters document Ellen White's dependence upon erroneous Millerite eschatological themes. The following chapter addresses her dependence on erroneous biological concepts.

Chapter 14 discusses Ellen G. White's assertion that she saw that "solitary vice is killing tens of thousands." She also states that solitary vice caused innumerable deaths due to scrofula and consumption. Millions were dying of scrofula and consumption but not due to solitary vice. These multitudes of death and disease were due to tuberculosis—obscured by the archaic terms "scrofula" and "consumption." In short, Ellen White mistook tuberculosis for masturbation as the cause of death. The historical apologetic defense trying to substantiate that solitary vice caused mass insanity, and the archaic terms, obscured this fact until I discovered it while proofreading the footnotes in this book. Due to the enormous shame and stigma surrounding sexuality, especially masturbation, this is a topic that is difficult to address with detachment. It goes without saying that any sexual activity which direct revelation asserts will result in mass insanity, cancer, and death will inevitably be steeped in shame and embarrassment. And that is precisely what Ellen G. White asserted she saw via direct revelation. Ellen White's assertions about both "the daily" and "solitary vice" were both founded solely on her "I saw" claims of direct revelation. In both cases she was simply mistaken as to what she thought she saw. She adopted misconceptions popular in her day and then thought she received the information via direct revelation. The missing cultic objects in her December 1844 vision also illustrate this phenomenon.

Ellen G. White never admitted that her first vision taught that probation had closed for all those who rejected S. S. Snow's date-setting midnight cry. From 1845 to 1851 she believed that the midnight cry had divided Christendom into only two camps: the sheep and the goats; the wheat and the tares; the clean and the filthy still. Only later would she and her apologists envision a third group, those who had not had the opportunity to knowingly accept or reject the midnight cry. However, eventually apologists such as G. Damsteegt, Robert Olson, and Merlin Burt all had to concede that Ellen G. White, at minimum, "misinterpreted" her own first vision. She concluded that it meant that the door of probation was shut on all who doubted Snow's midnight cry.

Chapter 14 documents the fact that Ellen G. White's statements clearly echoed several of her contemporaries' fundamentally mistaken idea that loss of seminal fluid via masturbation was not only the *chief* cause of a pandemic of insanity but a whole plethora of "loathsome diseases" which attacked every body system. It documents how apologists strain credulity with obscure, atypical medical speculations that, at best, hint that perhaps in exceptional cases masturbation might cause a zinc deficiency (from loss in the seminal fluid), which, in turn, might cause insanity. They seem unconscious of the fact that Ellen G. White claimed that women were at higher risk for insanity and loathsome diseases because they have inherently less "vital force." They seem also unconscious of the fact that since females do not ejaculate seminal fluid, they are not in danger of zinc deficiency from this quarter. It has been unrecognized that Ellen and her contemporaries imagined females have less "vital force" precisely *because they have no semen*! Ellen White believed the 1840 physicians who informed her that a *single drop of semen has forty times more vital energy* than a drop of blood. She copied contemporary medical authorities who asserted that solitary vice caused tens of thousands of cases of insanity, death, and loathsome diseases. There was *nothing* she said about the disastrous results of solitary vice that her sources had not already said. Additionally, James White wrote a book in 1870 on the same topic, which, like her 1864 book, included a compilation citing medical authorities of that bygone age. In some cases, it is impossible to untangle these sources. (Ellen White concluded that her visions confirmed what her medical authorities told her, evidently.) In a couple cases, both James White's book and Ellen White's book relate what purportedly are their personal experiences (in autumn 1844 at a state insane asylum) with extreme cases of insanity. They may be mere copyists forgetting to credit their sources.

Even more stunning is the fact that a careful reading of Ellen White's assertions concerning solitary vice demonstrates that she (and James and their medical authorities) believed that the pandemic of tuberculosis, which they referred to as "consumption" and "scrofula," was caused by solitary vice. This is now a completely discredited and preposterous belief. It is well known that consumption and scrofula are caused by *Mycobacterium tuberculosis* and have nothing whatsoever to do with solitary vice. To my knowledge, no other apologist or critic has ever noted the significance of Ellen White's assertion of the causal relationship between solitary vice and tuberculosis.

Preliminary conclusions

The predominant paradigm of SDA laity, clergy, and high-level administrators regarding Ellen G. White's authority and fallibility is that she cannot be mistaken to any significant degree. Her "I saw" statements identify "hard facts" that she received through direct divine revelation, which must, by definition, be authoritative. Although formally not said to be inerrant, she is nonetheless held out to be practically inerrant. When textual, empirical, and historical evidence counter to this conclusion is cited, apologetic responses are prepared in isolation without considering the cumulative evidence systematically. I have documented about twenty-five counterproofs where writers preceding Ellen White took erroneous positions which White afterward adopted. Ellen G. White was plainly literarily and/or intellectually dependent on erroneous statements from human sources. Several of these erroneous statements concern non-trivial SDA dogmas. Most such cases originated with Miller and historicist traditions. Others came from hoary nineteenth century "medical" authorities who wrote before the germ theory of infectious diseases was recognized, specifically before the etiology of TB was announced in 1882 by Koch. *It is beyond a reasonable doubt that twelve-year-old Ellen Harmon was massively influenced by Millerite methods, "facts," and results.* It is also irrefutable that William Miller committed multiple major exegetical malpractice while Ellen Harmon credited him with receiving his multiple chronological proofs from repeated direct divine guidance. It is also undisputable that after the Great Disappointment these methods were still copied by writers like James White, Joseph Bates, Joseph Turner, Apollos Hale, and O. R. L. Crosier. These writers, in turn, had a decisive influence on Ellen Harmon's beliefs and paradigms. As a result, according to the Ellen G. White Estate itself, she misinterpreted her own visions.

Even prior to Miller's prediction that the second coming would occur on March 21, 1844, he predicted the end of the world for 1839–1840, concurrent with the fall of the Ottoman Empire. The fact that the world did not end and the Ottoman Empire did not collapse is a significant failure of the Millerite allegorical-typological-historicist method. This failure took place four years before the failure of Miller's fifteen proofs *reoccurred* on March 21, 1844, and well before the climactic failure of S. S. Snow's midnight cry. Twelve-year-old, prepubescent Ellen Harmon was simply too immature to realize Miller's fundamental misconception in 1840; at sixteen her judgment was still not sufficiently seasoned in the autumn of 1844 to realize that Snow's date-setting midnight cry was scripturally bankrupt.

II

Test Case of the Ottoman's Empire's Failure to Collapse

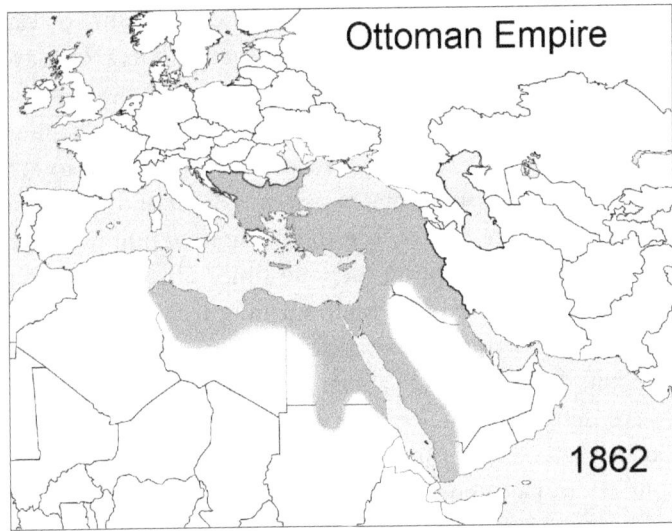

THE ABOVE MAP HAS been imported as a visual illustration of the extent of the Ottoman Empire in 1862, some twenty-two years after 1840, when the empire was to have collapsed according to Miller's eschatological calculations.[1] The above map of Ottoman hegemony flatly disconfirms Millerism's claim that the Ottoman Empire collapsed on August 11, 1840, as also claimed by Ellen G. White.

---

1. For a short dynamic video of the changing land mass of the Ottoman Empire, see https://www.youtube.com/watch?v=KuwanQyGKHw. This is only about one minute long. This animated map showing the growth and decline of the Ottoman Empire 1300–1923 comes from the map images of *Wikipedia* author Esemono. Public domain.

First disappointment: Ottoman Empire does not collapse as predicted

Because Ellen Harmon's central nervous system had been shattered, she had to drop out of a female seminary on about November 26, 1939. She said that continued schooling would have killed her. Nonetheless, from March 11 to 23, 1840 she was much impressed by Miller's Portland, Maine hellfire-and-brimstone presentations combined with his mathematical proofs predicting the second coming. She confided her terror of hell to brother Robert during Miller's March 11–23, 1840 series. Meanwhile, the collapse of the Ottoman Empire and end of the world were recalculated to August 11, 1840. Then, prior to absorbing Miller's second series during June 4–12, 1842, at the Buxton camp meeting, Ellen had her first ecstatic experience. William Foy claimed he had two visions on January 18 and February 4, 1842. In May 1842 the Millerite General Conference endorsed an exact year for the second coming; Miller settled specifically on March 21, 1844; and just two weeks prior to this date Ellen Harmon was exposed to William Foy's apocalyptic expostulations in person. Miller and Foy presented a sharp binary choice: either face the hellfire coming by March 21, 1844 or be saved by accepting "definite time." On June 26, 1842 Ellen Harmon was baptized into Methodism but, she insisted, through Millerism, and had another ecstatic experience. Levi Stockman confirmed Ellen's "special work" about September 1842. These experiences were determinative for both her conception of the midnight cry prior to October 22, 1844 and her visionary interpretation of the midnight cry in December 1844. First, Miller claimed that the close of probation would occur with the collapse of the Ottoman Empire in 1839.[2] Second, he made the same claim for March 21, 1844. Third, he repeated the claim for October 22, 1844. Every time the Millerite predictions failed, the Millerite practitioners of the CH (continuous-historical) scheme of interpretation fell back on the same method to

---

2. . Theoretically, the close of probation could have closed invisibly at any point prior to 1839, 1840, or 1844. However, the first resurrection and the second coming "in power" could not occur invisibly. Thus, had Miller/Litch only predicted the close of probation for these dates, it still might be argued that this prediction was unfalsifiable. Not so for such visibly cosmic events as the first resurrection and second coming. The collapse of the Ottoman Empire could be reduced to a diplomatic note but not these two events.

explain their failures. The initial case of the purported collapse of the Ottoman Empire in 1839/1840 established a pattern.

Insufficient attention has been paid to Miller's failed 1839/1840 prediction that the Ottoman Empire would collapse and the world end. This had great significance on how twelve-year-old Ellen processed information about the reliability of the CH method. Ironically, she thought that events in the Ottoman Empire confirmed Miller and Litch's prediction. The failure of the prediction illustrates a classic example of cognitive dissonance. This set a robust precedent for the tarrying-time disappointment of March 21, 1844 and the Great Disappointment of October 22, 1844.

Ottomans will collapse and close of probation predicted for 1839

Miller initially predicted the fall of the Ottoman Empire in 1831, when Ellen Harmon was only four years old.[3] He had already calculated that the 1,260 years ended in 1798 and that "according to Daniel, forty-five years will complete the whole plan of redemption." He claimed that the "sixth vial was poured out about the year 1822, when the Ottoman power began to be dried up. This is an important sign that we are on the brink of the judgment day." Then the "last great battle" will occur and "will take place at the pouring out of the seventh vial, in the year 1839 or 40. At the pouring out of the seventh vial, a voice from the throne will pronounce the word, It is done." He also already pinpointed the "resurrection at the end of the 1335 days," which he calculated to end in 1843.[4] Miller also wrote that "whoever lives until the year 1839 will see the final dissolution of the Turkish Empire, for the sixth trumpet will have finished its sounding."[5] Then, he said, "the seventh trump and last woe begin," during which all worldly powers will be destroyed and "the world cleansed." This last expression is identical with his interpretation of the "sanctuary" of Daniel 8:14, which he said will be "cleansed" with fire at the second coming. Thus, already in 1839 Miller predicted that there will be "no more time for mercy" because "your day of probation 'should be no longer.'" The

3. Rowe, *God's Strange Work*, 134–39.
4. Miller, "Lecture on the Signs," 6.
5. Miller, *Evidence*, 70–75.

Bridegroom has come, and shut to [sic] the door." With the fall of Turkey in 1839, "the third woe cometh quickly." "The seventh trumpet begins to sound," and when the "last trumpet shall sound, the dead in Christ shall be raised." In other words, with the 1839 fall of Turkey, cosmic events of the last woe and last trumpet would occur "quickly." The collapse of the Ottoman Empire would lead directly to the close of probation and first resurrection. The collapse of the Ottoman Empire in Millerism was not merely a mundane, earthly event but a cosmic event that would end history.

Revelation 9 and Daniel 11–12 parallel "predictions" of end of world and Ottomans for 1839

The purported climax of earth's history triggered by the collapse of the Ottoman Empire in 1839, according to Miller's interpretation of Revelation 9, is paralleled by Miller's year-by-year commentary on Daniel 11:40—12:1. Miller asserted that these verses in Daniel foretold events starting with Napoleon's deposition of the Pope Pius VI in 1798 and *also ending in 1839* during the time of trouble when "Christians will be persecuted unto death, and dens and caves of the earth will be their retreat." "And this, if I am right in my calculations, will begin on or before A. D. 1839," when the first resurrection will occur. Beginning with Daniel 11:40, Miller provided a precise CH day-year description. Verse 40: In 1798 Napoleon wounds the papacy. (Verse 41: In "June, 1800" Napoleon conquers three kingdoms at Marengo. His later retreat to Egypt fulfills "the country once inhabited by the Edomites, Moabites, and Ammonites 'escaped out of his hands.'" Verses 42–43: Napoleon ravishes Egypt, Libya, and Ethiopia. Verse 44: The Holy Alliance confronts him. Verse 45: Planting his "tabernacle" in the "glorious holy mountain" "was *literally fulfilled in May 26, 1805* [emphasis added] when Bonaparte was crowned king of Italy . . ." "Yet he shall come to his end" predicts Napoleon's exile and death. "This was in the latter part of the year A.D. 1815."

Then in Daniel 12:1 Michael stands up. This, according to Miller's CH scheme, refers to the large-scale conversion of sinners because "in the years 1816, 17, 18, more people were converted to the faith of Jesus than had been for thirty years before." This process lasts "for 20 years," i.e., until 1839, when there will be a "time of trouble," the four angels "now holding the four winds" "shall cease their holding," the angels "shall seal the last child of God," i.e., probation closes, and then there "should be no longer delay" to the Second Advent. And, as mentioned above, "Christians will be persecuted unto death . . ."[6]

In sum, the climaxing event in Revelation 9, the collapse of the Ottoman Empire in 1839, is simultaneous with the climaxing events in Daniel 11–12, the standing up of Michael, the close of probation, the first resurrection, and the time of trouble, all timed for 1839. According to Miller, the cosmic events of the end of history were directly associated with the Ottoman Empire's fall.

Miller's 1839 prediction was taken up by Litch and underwent several alterations. Litch modified the date from 1839 to 1840 because he concluded that a 391-year-day interval (the year, month, day, and hour of Revelation 9) started one year later than Miller. In 1838 Litch said the Ottomans would be overthrown "in A.D. 1840, some time in the month of August." This was a reasonable guess because as Litch was writing in 1838, a war broke out between Egypt and Turkey. Miller's converts took this as a striking proof that prophetic predictions were being fulfilled as they read their newspapers. Their expectations were raised even further in June 1839 when the Ottoman fleet received a "deadly wound" at the battle of Nizip. William Miller's son, William S. Miller, was certain that they were seeing "the entire fulfillment of the prophecies."[7] William Miller himself wrote to pastor Henry Jones, a doubter in definite time, arguing that current events concerning the Ottomans proved Miller's date-setting thesis.[8]

---

6. Miller, *Evidence*, 60–67. Ellen G. White recycled symbols like the four winds, the time of trouble, and the sealing multiple times during the following decades. The midnight-cry phase of Millerism clearly utilized the symbolism of the midnight cry to argue that Christ's second coming was imminent, indeed just months away. In an identical process, Ellen G. White convinced herself and others that symbols like the four winds, the "time of trouble," the "loud cry," and the "sealing" signified the very last of last-days events which were transpiring even as she spoke and wrote. When James White republished Ellen G. White's initial visions on May 30, 1847, he wrote that he and Ellen were firmly convinced that the "'time of trouble such as never was,' is fast coming upon the nations of the earth." Ellen said the "time of trouble" had, in fact, already started. For Ellen and James White's 1847 view of extreme imminence, see http://centrowhite.org.br/files/ebooks/apl/all/JamesWhite/A%20Word%20to%20the%20Little%20Flock.pdf

7. William Miller to Miller, January 24 and November 18, 1839, as cited in Rowe, *God's Strange Work*, 136.

8. Miller to Henry Jones, September 9, 1839, Miller letters cited in Rowe, *God's*

But then European powers intervened and the Ottoman Empire did not collapse as predicted.

Miller's intellectual dependence on Mede for hoary Muslim exegesis

About two centuries earlier Joseph Mede had offered an interpretation identifying the Muslims in prophecy, which Miller merely modified. Indeed, many sixteenth-century Protestant interpreters, doubtless impressed with the Ottoman's penetration to the very capital of the Austro-Hungarian Empire, had begun to see the Muslims in the Apocalypse. Indeed, it may surprise SDA readers to know that Martin Luther said that the little horn was not the papacy but the Muslim power! In his introduction to Daniel, Luther says:

> A little horn shall also come forth from among them and shall pluck out three of the foremost horns of the ten. This is Mohammed or the Turk who today has Asia, Egypt, and Greece in his claws.[9]

Not a few Protestant theologians, like Georg Nigrinus (1530–1602), concurred. He believed that the little horn referred to the "Turk," who had been given 1,260 years from 623, the date of Mohammed's flight from Mecca to Medina, until 1883.[10]

Joseph Mede (1586–1639) published his *Clavis Apocalyptica* in 1627. It projected the end of the world by 1716, possibly in 1654, and identified Muslims as fulfilling the fifth and sixth trumpets. Mede calculated that the year, month, day, and hour of Revelation 9 should equal 396 years. Rather than a 360-day prophetic year, Mede assumed a 365-day solar year. Therefore, the prophetic year (365) + month (30) + a day (1) = 396 historical years. For centuries, Protestants identified Muslims with the fifth and sixth trumpets. There was an unbroken line from Luther, Mede, and Miller/Litch to Ellen Harmon and Uriah Smith.

Strange Work, 136,

9. Froom, *Prophetic Faith*, 2:269. "Asia, Egypt, and Greece," of course, were the three horns plucked up by the little horn.

10. Froom, *Prophetic Faith*, 2:327. One of multiple speculations about an exact 1,260-year period.

Muslims' 391-year rule in Harmon's 1822 KJV Bible

Ellen Harmon's family 1822 King James Bible had explanatory footnotes that asserted that Revelation 9 referred to the Muslims and that 391 years (not Mede's 396 years) fulfills a Bible prediction. In other words, the 391-year (the prophetic year = 360 years, + 30 years for the prophetic month + 1 year for the prophetic day = 391 historical years) "prediction" was a widely known cultural assumption. The fact that it was in an 1822 annotated Harmon family Bible made it doubly believable to Ellen Harmon.[11] Note many similarities to Miller.

A footnote for Revelation 9: 1, 3 reads: "A star—locusts," "A star," "Mahomet, or Mahommed, who began his imposture in Arabia about A. D. 606. He shone with a conspicuous but pestiferous lustre. Locusts. The vast armies of Saracens, resembling locusts in numbers and in desolating effects."

The footnote to Revelation 9:5 reads: "Kill," "Not kill them as a state." This meant that "[t]hey [the Muslims] could not wholly extirpate the Greek and Latin churches. Revelation 9:11's footnote: "Apollyon," "Destroyer." This referred "to the caliphs or chief priests of their religion, in succession destroying both the bodies and souls of men." Revelation 9:16's footnote, "Two hundred," refers to one of the most notorious Millerite predictions. "A large definite put for an indefinite number of men, employed in the conquests of 391 years."

I cite the following as a typical illustration of historicists' contorted treatment of the Ottoman's (Turk's) role in prophecy, and how different it is compared to Miller and Litch. Mede's analysis of the fifth trumpet was complex. He concluded that the core of the time frame covered by the fifth trumpet was the 150 years, 830–980, or prophetic five months. But since this five-month period was mentioned twice, he doubled it to the interval 750–1055, starting with the Abbasid caliphate and ending when the Turkish king captured Bagdad; then he brought the whole period forward to 630 on the basis that that was when the Saracens began to expand their empire.[12]

---

11. This was Joseph Teal's *Columbian Family and Pulpit Bible* (1822) mentioned by Graybill, *Visions*, 45 n. 16.

12. Firth, *Apocalyptic Tradition*, 216–21.

In contrast, Miller and Litch wanted to reserve the 150 years for the period 1299–1449,[13] or several centuries different than Mede and with an entirely different event "exactly predicted."

The interval spanning "an hour, and a day, and a month , and a year, for to slay the third part of men" Mede dated from 1057, and using a 365-day year or a total of 396 years in real time (365 year; 30 month, day), he concluded the period in 1453 with the fall of Constantinople, or 400 years *prior* to Miller's and Litch's calculation! Historicists like Isaac Newton claimed that the fire, smoke, and brimstone of Revelation referred specifically to the new invention and use of gunpower by Mehmet against Constantinople.[14] Trifling details of interpretation were handed down for centuries, eventually to be repeated by Miller. For example, in his commentary on Revelation 9:7–11, Andrew Fuller (1754–1815) claimed: "Their glittering harness and use of gunpowder are both foretold."[15] These were accompanied by wild variations in historicists' "exact" calculations. He also said that the "Turkish Woe,"] or 391 years, extended from 1281 to 1672; the 391 years he calculated from 1281 to 1672, when the Turks had their last victory over the Poles. The five months he assigned to the period 612–762, "when the Saracens ceased to extend their conquests and settled down peaceably in the countries conquered."[16]

Suffice it to say that Isaac Newton differed with Miller, Smith, and Mede.

In sharp contrast to Mede, Miller/Smith used a 360-day year in place of a 365-day year to calculate a 391-year total.[17] Furthermore, Miller started this 391 years in 1449, four years before Mede's endpoint, and claimed an exact end on August 11, 1840. The chief historical reason for this major difference is because Mede had predicted 1736 for the Second Advent and interpreted the final two trumpets and vials with events contemporary with his epoch, the Reformation.

13. These exact dates were in the Millerite 1843 chart and the 1851 White/Nichols chart. In this chart about a third to a fourth of the space is dedicated to dates assigned to Muslim powers. See White, *Ellen G. White Letters & Manuscripts,* 242–44.

14. Iliffe, *Priest of Nature,* 286–87.

15. This minute, obscure detail occurs in the 1851 White/Nichols chart: "Fire arms first used on horseback by the Turks."

16. Froom, *Prophetic Faith of Our Fathers,* 3:352.

17. Discrepancies between assuming a 365-day- versus a 360-day-year complicated being "exact."

However, for Miller, history had already lasted beyond the "end times" of Mede. Explicit in Miller's, and therefore Ellen Harmon's thesis, is that the Reformation churches had become *Babylon*. In a polar opposite interpretation, Reformation era (CH) commentators depicted the Reformation churches as *Christ's victorious church*. For them, the Reformation church was the victorious woman standing on the moon enduring the attacks of the Catholic Church.

In sum, neither Mede nor Miller nor any of the historicists provided a literal interpretation of the Apocalypse. Their identifications were equivalent to arbitrary, allegorical identifications associated with interpreters such as Origen, and their dates were as random and scattered as buckshot.[18] It was Miller's contention that in his prophetic predictions "every word and every particular has had an exact and literal accomplishment."[19] This was far from the case. Indeed, CH practitioners are hard pressed to provide evidence for a single exact and literal case.

When in 1839–1840 Miller and Litch's expositions were falsified by events, they made major modifications in their interpretations to save appearances. Eventually, the cosmic events which were inseparable from their original predictions shrunk down to thin, ambiguous diplomatic notes. Nonetheless, to young Ellen Harmon such predictions seemed exact and impressive; and the elder Ellen G. White never departed from her original impression. In her 1911 edition of *Great Controversy*, Ellen White continued to assert that August 11, 1840 was an example of a "remarkable fulfillment of prophecy." When Turkey "accepted the protection of the allied powers of Europe," according to Mrs. White, Litch's 1838 prediction was "exactly fulfilled."[20] Not that there was any dishonesty on Miller's or other Millerites' part. Cognitive dissonance made them artlessly unaware that they were moving the goalposts to arrive at *post hoc* rather than predictive interpretations.

There was a disappointment that the Ottoman Empire had not collapsed as predicted in 1839/1840; there was a disappointment that the Second Advent did not occur by March 21, 1844; there was a

18. Bates, *Seal of the Living God* is an excellent illustration of the strained allegorical-typological-historicist methods shut-door Adventists employed in determining whether a given symbol in Revelation was literal or nonliteral.

19. Miller, *Evidence*, 2.

20. See Anderson, "Millerite Use of Prophecy," 78–91 for a textbook example of a disconfirmed "exact" continuous-historical calculation.

third disappointment on October 22, 1844. Each time the movement's religious leaders asserted that the failure of their prediction was necessary to "test" the true believers. Thus, after each failure a reflexive rationalization explained away the failed prediction by applying the same CH *presumptions* and by either giving a different definition to a biblical symbol or choosing a different CH event.

Miller's euphemistic expression "about the year 1840" recalled his similarly euphemistic expression "about 1843." In both cases he attached an exactitude to his calculations which belied the word "about." In any case, when Ellen Harmon was only about eleven in 1839, she would have witnessed that the Ottoman Empire had not "come to an end in 1839." When she was only about twelve, she would have witnessed that the Ottoman Empire had still not collapsed on August 11, 1840, as Josiah Litch had predicted. She could hardly have missed the intense speculation about the predicted fall of the Ottoman Empire as news of the "Eastern Question" filled Millerite periodicals in virtually every issue, or at least monthly, for several years both before and after August 11, 1840. Meanwhile, meticulous Bible expositors, even ones friendly to Miller, pointed out that Miller's prediction had failed miserably. Not only had he predicted the collapse of the Ottoman Empire, but he had also predicted that the collapse would be simultaneous with the close of probation, the last woe of Revelation, and the first resurrection. Isaac Fuller, "Miller's longtime mentor and defender," frankly chastised him for settling on a specific date for this event and said that "the falsehood of your whole system is already provd by your failure in this particular."[21] Nonetheless, Millerites and then SDAs would go on predicting the re-collapse of the Ottoman Empire clear up to and past the First World War.[22] Twelve-year-old Ellen Harmon was convinced by Miller and Litch that the Ottoman Empire collapsed on an exact day. The mature Ellen G. White would write that this prediction, exact to the very day, was a model for other predictions of exact days in prophecy. In short, she never abandoned this "exact" fulfillment of prophecy even after it was falsified by the event.[23] Neither did many Millerites between September 1840 and Oc-

21. Rowe, *God's Strange Work*, 135–37, 139, 201.
22. McArthur, *A. G. Daniells*, 333–96.
23. The *Ellen G. White Encyclopedia* cites both the 1,260-day/year and Ottoman Empire calculation as evidence of exactly fulfilled prophecy according to the day-year hypothesis. See Damsteegt, "Prophetic Interpretation," 1061–63.

tober 22, 1844. Indeed, both they and Ellen G. White would note that the August 11, 1840 prediction was a powerful impetus persuading their audience that Christ would reappear on March 21, 1844 and then October 22, 1844.

Prelude: Miller's first failed prediction of the second coming: the Ottoman Empire

An examination of Miller's first failed prediction of the second coming is very instructive. It contains all the facets of his methodology. It sheds "light" on Miller's and Snow's prediction that the world would end "about 1843," and then exactly on October 22, 1844.

Thus, the question arises: Was there any "light" or truth in the midnight cry's proclamation of an exact date for the second coming? When William Miller, S. S. Snow, and Ellen Harmon asserted that texts like Matthew 25, Daniel 8, and the Synoptic apocalypses demonstrated that God was in the date-setting midnight-cry movement, were they correct?

Properly interpreted, all the texts they relied on to preach "definite time" actually taught the opposite. "No man knoweth the day or hour." How did such zealous Christians so misinterpret Scripture and then insist that it was "the true light"?

The historian can trace a long line of misguided historicists who repeatedly asserted that the end of the world was imminent and that events in their lifetimes were foretold in Scripture as end-time events. The historicists' method, so popular during the Reformation and from about 1517 to 1817, generated many predictions similar to Miller's. All of them had been falsified by history. Nonetheless, Miller, a voracious reader, absorbed both the general assumptions of historicism and many, many of its specific elements. The apologetic depiction of Miller is as a *tabula rasa* who merely used his concordance to let the Bible interpret itself. Nothing could be further from the truth. He asserted that he had discovered fifteen proofs that the second coming was mathematically certain to be, as he euphemistically expressed it, "about 1843." History proved that Miller and Snow were simply wrong—however sincere they may have been.

Miller's two most bizarre proofs: based on the day = 1000 years principle

A few of Miller's most curious proofs were his assertion that Hosea 6 and Luke 13:32–33, combined with Revelation 13:18's mention of the number 666, proved that he had discovered fifteen mathematical proofs that the second coming would occur "about 1843." They are the two of the most striking empirical indications that Miller's actual method was a sort of whimsical allegorical procedure—completely opposite of the commonsense, literal methodology he is apologetically credited with. It also documents the credulity his audience had to exercise in order to believe in him. Historically, the most influential member of that audience was Ellen Harmon.[24]

---

24. Following these two proofs there is also a section demonstrating how Miller's lax interpretation of the personal pronouns in Daniel 10–12 violates the elementary rules of grammar.

III

Hosea, Luke: The Day = 1000 Years Principle

"Leave men a moment to their own judgment in the interpretation of prophecy, and we immediately have the most sublime exhibitions of human fancy."

URIAH SMITH, *DANIEL AND REVELATION* (1897)

ELLEN G. WHITE GAVE very powerful endorsements of William Miller's divinely inspired insights into the prophecies; likening him even to John the Baptist and Elijah, the greatest of the Old Testament prophets.

She further stated that Miller "dwelt upon the [fifteen] prophetic *periods*, and *piled up proof* to strengthen his position [emphasis added]."[25] These were "clear and conclusive" proofs and "plain and startling facts."[26] Specifically, "Calculation of the time was so *simple and plain* [emphasis added] that even the children could understand it."[27] To the contrary, this book provides evidence that Miller completely miscalculated scores of biblical passages. Yet Miller insisted that any sincere person with common sense, a Bible, and a concordance could understand even the most obscure apocalyptic symbols. Below the reader will find several of Miller's legendary lost prophecies. These will be presented in several block quotations which will provide *prima fascie* evidence of several things: 1) they are convoluted, abstruse, and

---

25. James and Ellen White, *Life Sketches: Ancestry,* 137.

26. White, *Life Sketches of James White and Ellen G. White,* 149. See accessible online 2017 version at https://egwwritings-a.akamaihd.net/pdf/en_LS80.pdf.

27. White, *Christian Experience,* 49.

virtually impossible for even an adult to understand; 2) they violate elementary principles of grammatical interpretation; and 3) they have nothing to do with prophecy. Two of Miller's "proofs" relied upon Miller's most bizarre rule of interpretation (his number X): this states that *a biblical "day" can just as easily be a thousand years as a single year.*

We find Miller's first legendary lost "prophecy" in Luke 13:31–33, a passage which has no Synoptic parallel in either Mathew or Mark. He asserts that the words "today and tomorrow, and the third day" constitute a prophecy of three millennia whose commencement he could date precisely to 158 BC. He quotes the KJV of Luke:

> At that very hour some Pharisees came, and said to him [Jesus], "Get away from here, for Herod wants to kill you." And he said to them, "Go and tell that fox, 'Behold, I cast out demons and perform cures today and tomorrow, and the third day I finish my course. Nevertheless I must go my way today and tomorrow and the day following; for it cannot be that a prophet should perish away from Jerusalem.'"

He proclaims this as a proof text, on par with Daniel 8:14's 2,300 days, to prove that Christ's Second Advent would occur in 1843. Ellen Harmon was influenced by Father Miller and his many such proofs to an incalculable degree. She believed that they were so conclusive and obvious that even she, a child of twelve, could understand them.[28] Miller believed that he had discovered these proofs by faithfully applying the Protestant principle of *sola Scriptura*; by affirming that the Bible was the supreme epistemological authority; by using what is today called a grammatical-historical interpretation of the Bible; by assuming that all the apocalyptic symbols could be interpreted in a univocal manner; and, most critically, by assuming that *"every word and every particular has had an exact and literal accomplishment..."*[29] He called his experience with the Bible "a feast of reason."

However, Miller did not actually practice these principles. Rather, he utilized a variant of the allegorical, stream-of-consciousness method, which allowed free reign to his imagination. He brought

---

28. This is what is called the doctrine that the Bible is perspicacious. The fact that Ellen Harmon was only twelve years old, and quite ill when she first heard Miller lectures, was doubtless an immensely pivotal, existential event which convinced her that even a child like herself could understand Miller's proofs.

29. Miller, *Evidence*, 2. Emphasis added.

preconceived ideas to Scripture rather than gathering data inductively from Scripture.[30] This is called eisegesis rather than exegesis.

Miller's 666-Year prophecy from 158 BC to 508 AD based in three texts

Miller asserts that Revelation 13:18's mention of 666 is sufficient to establish 158 BC as the *terminus a quo* for Luke 13:32–33's "prophecy," Hosea 6's "prophecy," and Revelation 13:18. First, he presumes to know the identity of the number 666.

He asserts: it is specifically pagan Rome that must be "numbered" 666. For this he relies on a hoary historicist tradition that identifies seven sequential forms that the Roman government was claimed to have adopted through the centuries. He enumerates the seven forms, including "decemviral," imperial, republican, consular, tribunitial, imperial, etc., and says that five of the seven had passed away when John wrote, and thus it must be the sixth or pagan power that is identified by the number 666. Then he addresses a potential query:

> But the querist may ask by what rule I apply the number 666 to time.[31] I answer, first, because the time the other beast was to reign 42 months is given in the same chapter, and it would be perfectly reasonable that John should see the end of this beast in order to count the number of the antichristian. The word, 'numberer or wonderful numberer,' is used in reference to time, as in Dan. 4: 36; also marginal reading in Job 16:32; Dan. 8:13.[32]

> Thus from the considerations mentioned, I have come to the conclusion that this beast called Pagan Rome began when Rome became connected with the Jews, by league 158 years

---

30. According to the Teachers Sabbath School Bible Study Guide, "How to Interpret Scripture" (April–June 2020, 73), 61, "Interpreters of the Bible cannot completely divest themselves from their own past, their experiences, resident ideas, and preconceived notions and opinions." It also cautions against that "we do not indiscriminately string together various passages to prove our opinion." Yet this is exactly how William Miller operated.

31. Indeed, which of Miller's rules did he use to "apply the number 666 to time?" His *ad hoc* explanation follows.

32. In other words, the papal aspect of Rome would reign a specific number of years—1260, according to Father Miller; therefore, the pagan aspect of Rome must also reign a specific number of years—666.

B. C. and lasted 508 years after Christ, making in all 666 years. Then by adding Daniel's 1335 years bringing us down to A. D 1843.[33]

He argues that the Jews made a "league" or treaty with Rome in 158 BC, and makes this date a pivot point for two of his proofs taken from Luke 13:32-33; Hosea 6: 1-3; and Revelation 13:18. He asserts that when any nation comes into contact with the "people of God," at that time the Jewish nation, they are mentioned in biblical prophecy. Thus, he concludes that "when the fourth kingdom, [pagan Rome], became connected by league with the Jews or people of God, in the year B. C. 158,"[34] this is the exact date which must be the commencement of the 666 years. Then the *terminus ad quem* of 666 years, or 508, becomes simultaneously the *terminus a quo* of the 1335 years, which, per Miller, would also end with the second coming in 1843, since 508 + 1335 = 1843. As early as 1833 Miller interprets Luke 13:32-33 as a textual proof that the second coming would occur in 1843.[35]

Luke 13:32, "The third day I shall be perfected," or 158 BC-1843 AD

The key to this particular Millerite interpretation is that he uses his day = thousand years principle to reach 1843 for the millennial Sabbath. (While reading Miller's dense block quotes and convoluted chronology below, remember Ellen White's claim that Miller's speculations are so plain and clear that a child could understand them easily). The following provides the reader the unexpurgated Father Miller and his actual principles of interpretation.

> We have another prophecy of Christ himself, agreeing with one in Hosea.[36] "And he said unto them, go ye and tell that fox behold I cast out devils, and I do cure, to-day and to-morrow, and the third day I shall be perfected. Nevertheless,

---

33. Miller, *Evidences* (1835), 36.
34. Miller, *Evidences* (1835), 39.
35. Miller, *Evidences* (1833), 39-40.
36. Miller alluded to the biblical admonition of establishing the validity of any fact from a minimum to two witnesses, in this case Hosea and Luke. Additionally, he stressed that this is a prophecy spoken by Christ himself—claims highly persuasive to Ellen Harmon.

I must walk to-day and to-morrow and the day following, for it cannot be that a prophet perish out of Jerusalem," Luke 43:32-33 [sic].[37]

In this passage, three days are again mentioned in similar language to the one in Hosea,—to-day and to-morrow the same as two days. The only difference is, Hosea spake of them as future; Christ as living in the first day; and these two days in Luke were to be employed by Christ in casting out devils, and doing cures, and the third day he should be perfected; that is, as I humbly believe, the third day, the church or body of Christ would be perfect,[38] and 'presented a glorious church without spot or wrinkle' like unto Christ a glorious body, united to him, and made one with him. And then the Lord Jesus Christ will have accomplished his mediatorial work on the earth of casting out devils and doing cures. *That this passage means literal days, no one can believe* [emphasis added], for Christ himself destroys that explanation in the same passage by saying, 'Nevertheless, I must walk to-day, and to-morrow, and the day following,' plainly indicating that he did not mean common days.[39] That he meant phrophetic [sic] days is equally evident; for the spirit of God has done cures, and cast out devils more than two years—so that literal or prophetic days cannot be the time designated. And I know of no other construction that can be put upon this passage, except the same I have fixed to that in Hosea.

In this passage in Luke, they came to Christ and told him that Herod sought his life; and Christ answered and said, 'go tell that fox', as much as if he had said; although he is cunning as the fox, and 'understands dark sentences,' as Daniel had long before prophesied of him; and although he, or the fourth kingdom, under which he exercises his authority, is permitted to punish the transgressions of my people; yet I will cast out devils and do cures to-day and to-morrow, and the third day my kingdom shall be perfected. That is *two thousand years*, my gospel shall be proclaimed [emphasis added],[40] my

---

37. In an evident misprint the citation is given as Luke 43:32-33, rather than Luke 13:32-33.

38. That is, by the millennium the church of Christ will be perfect.

39. Was Miller really justified in choosing this spot to abandon literal interpretation?

40. Given that Miller's two thousand years starts at 158 BC, it is incongruent that Christ's "gospel shall be proclaimed" for two thousand years when he would not be

grace perform its work, and children shall be regenerated and adopted into my kingdom, and in the third thousand it will be complete, in spite of all opposition.[41]

Then, through page 40 Miller goes on a homiletic reverie imagining the glorious third day and millennium. Thus, he concludes that

> we have only to apply these days the same as we did those in Hosea, and we are again brought down to the year A. D. 1843, which is the commencement of the day of rest, [millennial Sabbath], the year Christ will come in the clouds of heaven, ... resurrection of the righteous dead, the sanctuary be cleansed, and the church made perfect ... All these things will take place in the commencing of the last day, which if I am right in my calculations of the times, (that have been thus far examined,) will come to pass in the year A. D. 1843, that is, if our chronology since the crucifixion of Jesus Christ is right; if not, then it will vary accordingly. Some say we have lost four years; if so, then we may look for the fulfilment in 1839[42]—but I believe we may not expect it until, 1843, which I have strong reason to believe is the true time, from the events that happened in 1798.[43]

Note that simultaneously, in 1843, Luke 13:32–33 *proves* that Christ will come, the righteous dead will be raised, "the sanctuary be cleansed, and the church made perfect."

Next note that Miller also interprets Hosea 6:1–3 to mean that the text " After two days will he revive us; in the third day he will raise us up" is yet again interpreted by his day = thousand years principle. That is, the "two days" equal two thousand years stretching from 158 BC and ending in 1842, when the second coming and the first

---

born nor his ministry start until about 158 years later.

41. Miller, *Evidences* (1835), 39-40.

42. This is a critical chronological date because it was exactly 1839 that Miller originally predicted for the collapse of the Ottoman Empire in his interpretation of Revelation 9. The second coming and first esurrection were predicted for 1839 on the basis of a prophetic period of 391 years, per Miller's calculation.

43. 1839 does not fit into Miller's system as neatly as 1843. See Miller, *Evidences* (1835), 40. Miller much preferred 1798 as a pivot point for the end of the 1,260 years but equally for the 1,335 years, which he obtained by first subtracting the 1,290 years to arrive at his critical 508 date for the abolishment of paganism; then added 1,335 to 508 to arrive at 1843 for the end of the world and added 1,290 also to 508 to arrive at 1798, which marked the beginning of the last days.

resurrection would occur "about 1843" with the beginning of the "third day."

Hosea 6:1–3 or 158 BC to 1843 and the resurrection

> We will now examine a prophecy in Hosea 6: 1–3 'Come let us return unto the Lord: for he hath torn and he will heal us; he hath smitten, and he will bind us up. After two days will he revive us; in the third day he will raise us up, and we shall live in his sight. Then shall we know, if we follow on to the Lord, his going forth is prepared [page 37] as the morning, and he shall come unto us as the rain, as the latter and former rain unto the earth.' In this prophecy, there are a number of prominent things plainly brought into view. 1st, an exhortation to repentance. 2nd. the church in a state of tribulation and trial two days.[44] 3d. the power of gospel grace to heal and bind up. 4th the resurrection in the third day revived and raised up. 5th the knowledge we shall then have of his first coming, and 6thly our reign with him the 3d day.
>
> 1st. Repentance, "come let us return unto the lord." This was preached by John the forerunner of Jesus Christ. "The voice of one crying in the wilderness, saying repent ye." Also by Christ himself, "except ye repent ye shall all likewise perish . . ."
>
> Secondly. That the church were to be in a state of trial for a season, here called "two days," cannot be doubted, when Christ himself has said, "in the world ye shall have tribulation . . ."[45]

In the following few paragraphs Miller makes the argument that this "trial" and "tribulation" must be that inflicted by the Roman dragon with its "great iron teeth" for "two days." These prophetic "two days" are equal to a historical two thousand years. Meanwhile, Miller cites *Scripture after Scripture*, not repeated here. Ellen Harmon took special note of Miller's extensive citation of Scripture. Snow's midnight-cry interpretation contained the same massive citation of Scripture. Miller now arrives at his fourth point:

---

44. Per Miller these two days are two thousand years in which the devil persecutes the church, from 158 BC to 1843.
45. Miller, *Evidences* (1835), 36–37.

4th. The resurrection, "After two days will he revive us: in the third day he will raise us up, and we shall live in his sight." This can mean nothing less than the resurrection.[46] The word revived is used in the same sense in Romans 14:9; Psalm 88:6, "And he will raise up," is used many times in the word of God in reference to the resurrection, as in John 6:39, 40, 44, 54.

He cites multiple other texts. He insists that this is a prophecy, a prophecy with a "definite," not "indefinite," starting and stopping point. This prophecy "ends in the year 1843."

But this third day they would live in his sight, in his personal presence. This brings us to consider what these three days mean. Are we to understand any definite time?[47] And if so what? Is it expressed as definite time, by saying two days, and in the third day, &c? And it would require some stretch of faith and more evidence to believe it indefinite[48] than I can find in the word of God, unless our minds were swayed by prejudice, and then we believe almost anything to get rid of a conclusion which we fancy it is not our interest to believe.[49]

That common days is meant, is improbable, or even years,[50] for facts are stubborn things; for the church has been more than two days, or even years in this third state, and three days, and even years, have long since passed away,

46. Note how categorically absolute Miller was even though this obviously has nothing to do with the resurrection and Judgment Day. This is a perfect demonstration of how egregious Miller's proofs were and how tightly his proofs were linked to the resurrection and the end of history. This makes them impossible to reinterpret as a change in Christ's location from the Holy to Most Holy Place.

47. "Definite time" is a key phrase in Millerism's setting specific dates like March 21, 1844 and October 22, 1844. Here Miller was setting a precedent for such a practice. He believed Hosea 6 taught that Millerites would experience the personal presence of God in 1843.

48. Miller believed he had more evidence to support the conclusion that his definite dates of 158 BC to 1843 were correct. He pointedly rejected any "indefinite" interpretation. This is clear evidence that the essence of Millerism was date-setting—not the classic, orthodox teaching of the second coming as Ellen White routinely implied.

49. He accused anyone doubting his 2,300-day calculation of the worst motives just as he impugned the motives of those who doubted his calculations here.

50. Here Miller built his case not for a day=year principle but for a day=thousand-year principle. Historicists' day-year paradigm was expressly created because literal days did not provide them with sufficient time for their preferred interpretation. Here Miller argued that even employing years for days is insufficient. Each "prophetic day" must be a thousand years.

and Christ has not yet come the second time; and yet, this is promised in the third day in the text.[51] There remaineth, therefore, but one bible way to explain day, and that is a thousand years; which is the meaning I am forced to attach to the passage we are considering, not only because it is our last resort for a scripture rule, but the third day spoken of in the passage, is evidently the same day John mentions in the 20th of Rev. "And they lived and reigned with Christ a thousand years." Also in 2d Peters 3:8, we are commanded not to be ignorant, "That one day is with the Lord as a thousand years [emphasis added], and a thousand years as one day." And again 90 Psalm, a thousand years is said to be as one day in the sight on the Lord.[52]

It is very evident that Peter and John were talking about the same day, that Hosea calls the third day, and would it not be reasonable and more than probable, that the prophet Hosea, had a view of this thousand years' reign, when he said 'and we shall live in his sight.' and if so, then *the other two days, being coupled with this thousand, must be understood to be of the same length each*, which brings me to the following conclusion: That the church, or people of God, would be wounded, smitten and persecuted by the Roman, or fourth kingdom, with his great iron teeth, two thousand years, and the third thousand would be the [p. 39] reign of Christ with his people. *The two thousand would begin, when the fourth kingdom became connected by league with the Jews or people of God, in the year B. C. 158, which added to 1842 after Christ makes the 2000 years, the year 1843 being the first in the third thousand, agreeing with the 2300 in Daniel*,[53] and the 666 added to 1335 makes 2001 and ends in the year 1843—and the reader will now perceive that *we have witnesses all agreeing with the same point of time*.[54]

51. In short, by the 1830s Miller needs to fill a gap of almost two thousand years. A day-year calculation was not sufficient. Too much time had "long since passed away, and Christ has not yet come the second time." Therefore, Miller felt forced to use the principle that a day = a thousand years to attain the needed time.

52. These are the multiple biblical proofs that impressed Ellen Harmon so much. These texts from 2 Peter and Psalm 90 are the basis for his principle that when Hosea and Luke say "day," it means a thousand years.

53. It was very important for Miller to have multiple prophetic time period proofs that simultaneously ended in 1843. He found nine such proofs. This was a critical aspect of his intellectual, mathematical appeal—in addition to persons being prostrated by the Spirit, like Ellen Harmon.

54. Miller, *Evidences* (1835), 38–39. Emphasis added.

Miller uses the same methods of interpreting Hosea 6 and Luke 13 as he does in interpreting Daniel 8:14 and his other fifteen proofs. Is Miller a reliable guide to a plain, literal, grammatical sense of the text?

Even the dean of SDA apologists, F. D. Nichol, who wrote the classic defense *The Midnight Cry*, concludes that these "so-called proofs that 1843 was the climax year of prophecy are plainly fanciful." He also characterizes them as "begging the question," "farfetched," and "hoary with age." Moreover, he goes on to say:

> In fact, we are tempted to believe there was a [good] deal of truth to the charge of some of his opponents that after Miller had decided on 1843 as a result of his study of the 2300-day prophecy, he worked backward from that date to secure certain of the dates that he employed as the starting point of some of the secondary lines of proof.[55]

Daniel 11:40—12:13 per the 1835 version of Miller's *Evidences*

Miller seriously contravenes other rules of the grammatical-historical method in his treatment of Daniel 11–12. His most glaring offense is the cavalier manner in which he treats pronouns. From the 1840s to the present, one of the most glaring Achilles heels of SDA interpretation of Daniel has been its interpretation of the "king of the north" and "king of the south" in Daniel 11–12. It has been incoherent and contradictory because it was based on Miller's patent stream-of-consciousness mode of interpretation, in which he violates the plainest rules of interpretation.

Miller's 1835 version of *Evidences from Scripture* is slightly different from his 1833 edition and 1842 edition. In this chapter, I have referred mostly to his 1835 version. I begin with Miller's explanation as to how he identifies the king of the north and king of the south. His manner of treating the pronouns "he or him" in this prophecy is critical. If Miller can insert any antecedent at will, a completely arbitrary interpretation foreign to the plain, literal, grammatical sense of the text was possible. The *April–June 2020 Adult Teachers Sabbath School Bible Study Guide*, page 61, admonishes that we must "carefully take

---

55. Nichol, *Midnight Cry*, Appendix L.

into consideration the context of each passage. Besides the immediate context before and after a passage under investigation, we should take into consideration the context of the book in which the passage is found." This Miller fails to do. If the reader takes any version of the Bible and read the entire text of Daniel 10-12, the reader will easily comprehend that the king of the north and the king of the south are unchanging entities throughout, and that they are the clear antecedents of "he or him." Miller's interpretation in these passages requires him to give changing identifications as he marches through the years/verses prior to and after Daniel 11:40.[56] But there the change and his explanation is most striking. He identifies these entities by his own peculiar, presumptive, prophetic chronology. That is, first he establishes by fiat that the "time of the end" must be be 1798 with events in France. Therefore, the "he or him" must be France, and in particular Napoleon Bonaparte.

> Therefore I understand the pronouns in the above named 40th verse and those following in the chapter to refer to the same kingdom, or principle ruler in said kingdom[57], and that the Angel has reference to the principal kingdom[58] of the 10 kingdoms into which the Roman was divided when anti-Christ arose, Which 'shall hate the whore and shall make her desolate and naked, and shall eat her and burn her with fire.' Rev 17:12-16.[59] If this is correct then France is intended by he or him in this prophecy. In order then to give my view, the reader will permit me to paraphrase these few remaining verses.[60]

---

56. Uriah Smith, mostly dependent on Miller, also proposed changing identifications of these antecedents. The overwhelming number of subsequent SDA exegetes have echoed Smith with virtually no original exegesis. But whereas Miller assigned all the verses after Daniel 11:40 to Napoléon, Uriah Smith at this point switched and replaced the French Napoleon with the Turkish Empire.

57. Miller baldly asserted that the text must refer to Napoleon Bonaparte and the kingdom of France. Therefore, great portions of Daniel had to have been fulfilled by events of the French Revolution and the Napoleonic Wars. That these events, purportedly events comprising the "time of the end [1798 especially]," are now a quarter of a millennium in the past is yet another cogent reason to doubt the Millerite paradigm.

58. Elsewhere Miller argued that France was the most dominate of the ten kingdoms which followed the fall of Rome. Therefore, it must be France here.

59. The anti-clericalism and dechristianization of France as illustrated in the Vendean battles is the burning with fire.

60. Miller, *Evidences* (1835). See the verse given in text rather than page

(This use of pronouns, and assumptions regarding 1798 and contemporaneous and notorious events in France, inspires Miller to circumvent any actual grammatical, contextual treatment of the text. Miller's allegorical treatment replaces a literal, commonsense interpretation.) In the block quotations below, *parentheses marking Miller's interpolations are original*, not supplied.

> 40. "And the time of the end (of Antichrist,) shall the king of the south (Spain) push at France (Vendean war)[61] and the king of the north (Great Britain) shall come against France, like a whirlwind, with chariots, and with horsemen, and with many ships; and the French (of Bonaparte the principal ruler;) shall enter into the countries, and shall overflow and pass over."

This is literally reading into the text (eisegesis) with parentheses bracketing whatever entities come to Miller's mind. Miller abruptly inserted Spain as the king of the south without any textual warrant. Second, in the original context the entity that the king of the south "pushes" at must be the king of the north. Since Miller asserts that Spain pushes against France, to be consistent, France in this verse must be the king of the north. But in the next phrase Miller informs us that the king of the north, for his interpretation, is Great Britain. Thus, there is a tripartite chaotic muddle. Where the text only has two combatants, Miller has gratuitously inserted a third combatant. In his 1842 edition Miller modifies the above to be even more specific. In the chaos, Spain "pushing" as an enemy against France becomes its ally. He says:

> This is a description of an alliance entered into by the king of Sardinia, Italy, and Spain, in the south , and Great Britain, in the north, for six years. England engaged, in this treaty,

---

number. I transcribed all the text cited from this 1835 edition from a smudged, difficult-to-visualize copy assessable at https://adventistdigitallibrary.org/islandora/object/adl%3A22250850?solr_nav%5Bid%5D=40dd0ec4dbof19263e6b&solr_nav%5Bpage%5D=0&solr_nav%5Boffset%5D=1.

61. This term and the enclosing parentheses and brackets were original with William Miller. The War in the Vendée (1793) was a counterrevolution in the Vendée region of France during the French Revolution. From January to May 1794, twenty thousand to fifty thousand Vendean civilians were massacred by general Louis Marie Turreau. Pregnant women were especially targeted for their potential of providing counterrevolutionary babies. In museums in the city of Nantes I personally have seen massive painted canvasses documenting the slaughter with heaps of bloody corpses.

to pay the king of Sardinia 200,000. per annum to furnish an army of horse and a large fleet. The command of the fleet was given to Lord Nelson. Various was the success of the allies in the south. Spain had to recede, and finally joined the French. The king of Sardinia had to leave his territories on the continent, and shut himself up in the island of Sardinia. The king of Naples fled to the island of Sicily, after making a vigorous push[62] [note Miller's attempt here to borrow a two-word phrase from the text to make his eisegesis appear more likely.] at the French, in November, 1798, and getting possession of Rome . . .]

41. "Bonaparte shall enter also in the glorious land (Italy) and many countries shall be overthrown; but these shall escape out of Bonaparte's hands, even Edom and Moab, and the chief of the children of Ammon," Ottomans and eastern nations.[63]

Miller gratuitously inserts Italy here when "glorious land" obviously refers to Israel for any historical-grammatical interpreter.[64] Miller gratuitously identifies the "Ottomans and eastern nations" as Edom, Moab, and Ammon with no explanation or justification.

42. "Bonaparte shall stretch forth his hand also upon the countries, and the land of Egypt shall not escape.

[page 28 begins here] 43. But Bonaparte shall have power over the treasurers of gold and of silver, and over all the precious things of Egypt: and the Sybians [sic][65] and Ethiopians shall be at his steps.

44. But tidings out of the east and north [holy alliance] shall trouble Bonaparte: therefore he shall go forth with great fury (to Moscow) to destroy, and utterly to make away many."[66]

---

62. Miller, *Evidence* (1842), 55.

63. Miller, *Evidences* (1835), 27.

64. He asserted that in Daniel 11:16 it is the history of "Pompey the Roman general" who conquered the "glorious land," which Miller implicitly defined as Israel, not Italy. *Thus, Miller assigned two contradictory identities to a single, very well-defined geographical term.* See Miller, *Evidences* (1833), 16. Another key instance is that he argued for two different meanings to be assigned to a single word, "sanctuary," that occurs in Daniel 8:11–14.

65. Misprint for Libyans.

66. Miller, *Evidences* (1835), 28.

The Holy Alliance was a coalition linking the monarchist great powers of Austria, Prussia, and Russia to oppose revolutionary France. Miller has gratuitously inserted the Holy Alliance here. He has abruptly started inserting Bonaparte into the original quoted text without even bothering with parentheses. He has gratuitously inserted Moscow also. This is not a translation; it is not even a paraphrase. Miller is infringing on the warning in Apocalypse 22:18-19.[67]

> 45. "And Bonaparte shall plant the tabernacles of his palace (be crowned king) between the seas[68] [Milan] in the glorious holy mountain (Italy)[69] yet Bonaparte shall come to his end and none shall help him." In this passage of holy prophecy, the history of the times from 1798 for twenty years are so clearly delineated, especially that of Bonaparte and the French nation, that it seems as though *we cannot be mistaken*, in the application to these events.[70]

Miller's insertions of "be crowned king," "Milan," and "Italy" are without justification. In the original text they clearly refer to other entities and events. Yet, with his typical overweening confidence, he finds the history from 1798 to 1818 to be "so clearly delineated . . . that it seems as though *we cannot be mistaken* . . ." Such was the level of *absolute certainty* to which twelve-year-old Ellen Harmon was exposed. And Uriah Smith, whose *Daniel and Revelation* was warmly recommended by Ellen G. White, largely merely parroted Miller's interpretation of Daniel 10–12. Generally, later SDA commentators of Daniel 10–12 merely echo Uriah Smith. In the following paragraph Miller

---

67. In the KJV translation: "For I testify unto every man that heareth the words of the prophecy of this book, If any man shall add unto these things, God shall add unto him the plagues that are written in this book: And if any man shall take away from the words of the book of this prophecy, God shall take away his part out of the book of life and out of the holy city, and from the things which are written in this book." Miller has inserted additions corrupting the sense of the text. Thus, he is subject to this curse.

68. "Between the seas" is an expression referring to the area between the Mediterranean and Jerusalem, not Milan in Italy.

69. Miller, *Evidence* (1842), 56. In this later edition Miller was even more categorical. He quoted: "He shall enter also into the glorious land," (or land of delight, as it might have been translated.) This, *I have no doubt*, means Italy [emphasis added]. Bonaparte fought some of his most brilliant battles in this delightsome country . . ." One observes the loose associations and stream of consciousness with which Miller operated here.

70. Miller, *Evidences* (1835), 27. Emphasis added.

gives a protracted historical overview of Bonaparte's exploits—sufficiently protracted that the reader is distracted from noting that all this granular history has no textual basis.

> After the French Revolution in 1793-4, the Vendean war broke, out, in which the papal States, Spain and England combined against the French; yet the French conquered and subdued almost all the nations of Europe, in a very short time; except Great Britain, and the success that followed the armies of the French, is without a parallel in history; after humbling Spain, and conquering Italy, Bonaparte went into Egypt, and as is supposed with an intent to press his way through to the British East India possessions, 'but these,' said the Angel 'even Edom, Moab, and the chief of the children of Ammon, shall escape out of his hands.' After the conquest of Egypt, Bonaparte marched into Syria, where, after gaining some advantages he was defeated before St. John d'Acre. The combinations of the holy alliance, as it is called, his campaign into Moscow, the loss of a large share of his troops, his being crowned king of Italy at Milan, the total defeat at Waterloo, his captivity and death, are all foretold with that precision[71], that the *fulfilment of this prophecy is but very little doubted by skepticism itself.*[72] We will now review the 12th chapter of Daniel.
>
> 1 verse, "And at that time shall Michael stand up, the great prince which standeth for the children of thy people;'" This part of this verse has been fulfilled in the pouring out of the Spirit of God' and in the conversion of many, to the faith of the gospel of Jesus Christ;[73] in this passage called Michael the great prince, since A. D. 1798, "And there shall be a time of trouble, such as never was since there was a nation even to that same time." This prophecy is a parallel to that in Rev. 16; 18-21, also . . . [several more citations are given] and has already begun. Witness the convulsions, in the political world;

---

71. The precision Miller referred to does not exist in the text. The precision is in his predetermined chronology which he brought to the text.

72. Emphasis added. Miller the skeptic himself was convinced by such "evidences" and logic.

73. In later editions Miller would fill out this assertion, claiming that more persons were converted to Christianity in the two to three decades after 1798 than during the many years previously. He would also refer to the foundation of Bible societies as a fulfillment of Michael standing up.

and the divisions and subdivisions of the churches,[74] also the pestilence that is spreading terror and dismay through our world. "And at that time thy people shall be delivered, every one that shall be found written in the book." The people of God will at these troublous times be delivered, from the grave, the power of death, the thralldom of sin, the force of temptation, and the persecution of the world . . .[75]

(These last five phrases are clear references to the first resurrection, the second coming, and the end of sin; all of which Miller believes will happen in 1839 when he wrote this in 1835.)

2 verse "And many of them that sleep ... everlasting contempt."

This brings us to the resurrection, and Miller mentions two resurrections, beginning with a quotation of verse 3 on page 29 and then follows this with his commentary from Daniel 12:3–7, where the figure 1260 is mentioned. Then he quotes to verse 11, where "the daily sacrifice" is mentioned (p. 30) as being taken away and says that from the time the "'abomination that maketh desolate is set up, there shall be a thousand two hundred and ninety days.'"

158 BC + 666 years = 508 and the taking away of "the daily"

By this verse I understand that from the taking away of the first abomination, which may properly be called "the daily sacrifice[76] abomination," to the end of the last abomination that maketh desolate, should be 1290[77] years, being 30 years more than the last abomination, should reign over the kings of the earth [or Roman government] and tread the church

---

74. The "time of trouble," per Miller, was the multiplication of schisms in the Christian church resulting in many denominations, many of which he specifically enumerates.

75. Miller, *Evidences* (1835), 27–28.

76. In 1835 Miller did not hesitate to supply the word "abomination" to fit his paradigm.

77. Note that Miller introduced yet another one of his fifteen proofs, the 1,290 years. Miller created an intertwined meshwork of exact prophetic intervals.

under foot. The said 30[78] years being the vacancy between the taking away the one, and setting up the other. This taking away the first, agrees with what Paul says in 2 Thess. 2:7. "For the mystery of iniquity doth already work; only he who now letteth (or hindereth) will let, (or hinder,) until he be taken out of the way . . ."

. . . It has likewise been proved that the Antichrist should reign 1260 years, of which from the taking away pagan Rome to setting up papal, would be 30 years, making the 1290 years, and if pagan Rome was to continue 666 years; as has been mentioned, and which we shall endeavor to prove hereafter; then pagan Rome becoming the fourth kingdom in 158 years before Christ would cease,[79] 508 years after Christ to which add the 30 years, will bring us down to the rise of Antichrist A.D. 538. Then add the length of his reign 1260 years would end in 1798 or add the 1290 to A. D. 508, would be the same 1798. Now add the remainder of the 1335[80] over and above 1290 which is 45 to A. D. 1798, and it will end in A. D. 1843 or add 1335 to A. D. 508 when pagan Rome was destroyed, or the [p. 31] daily sacrifice abomination was taken away, and you have the same A.D. 1843.

2300 years from 457 before Christ, Daniel's vision will end. 490 years from the same 457 B. C. Christ was crucified and the 70 weeks ended. The fourth kingdom and the last of all earthly kingdoms, was divided into two parts,[81] *The last number given in Daniel (viz.) 1335 carries us down to the resurrection and will end A. D. 1843.* In this last number is included the reign of Antichrist, 1260 years beginning in

78. Here Miller created a movable thirty units of time to fit into his interlocking prophetic gears. One might expect that the 1,260, 1,290, and 1,335 figures would all commence at the same time. However, Miller's system required that he first establish 1843 for his end date and then *calculate backwards*. Hence, both 1,290 and 1,335 must start thirty units of time before the 1,260 figure in order for the 1,290 figure to end at 1798 with the beginning of the last days, and the 1,335 figure must reach until the resurrection in 1843. The forty-five years between 1798 to 1843 were critical to Miller's analysis of Michael standing up. It would also provide a prophetic pedestal for the 1840s' purported fulfillment of the three angels' messages of Revelation 14:6–12.

79. Here Miller began his argument that there is an exactly fulfilled prophecy extending from 158 BC until 508—666 years. He added 1,335 years to this to arrive precisely at 1843.

80. The 1,335 years is yet another of Miller's fifteen proofs enmeshed in his narrative here.

81. It was critical for Miller to present Rome as having two aspects, pagan and papal, the first of which stretched from 158 BC to 508.

A. D. 538 and ending A. D. 1798 also the 1290 beginning A. D. 508,[82] and ending A. D. 1798. The remaining 45 years are for the spread of the gospel; the resurrection of the two witnesses; the church to come out of the wilderness, the troublous times; the last great battle; and the second coming of Christ, to raise his people; and reign with them personally the thousand years following.[83]

Miller is completely fanciful in his treatment of the text and selective in his use of history. He violates the most basic rules of interpreting language and using pronouns. He brings very peculiar chronological assumptions and circular logic to his treatment of the text. He takes a single word in the text and assigns multiple *ad hoc* definitions to it. Miller's method of determining the prophetic periods (2000) 158 BC to 1842 from both Hosea and Luke is just as reliable as his method for calculating the intervals (666) 158 BC to 508 AD; (1335) 508 to 1843, (1290) 508-1798, and (1260) 538-1798. His method and paradigm for establishing the interval 457 BC to "about 1843" is no different than all his multiple other calculations.

Miller may have believed that his method was literal and based on common sense. However, the actual process that Miller employed in interpreting the texts of Daniel, Revelation, Hosea, Leviticus, and Luke was, as F. D. Nichol described it, "farfetched." Moreover, the empirical instances examined here are but a small, representative sample. The quotation of multiple biblical citations, however "farfetched," was what convinced the twelve-year-old Ellen Harmon that Miller's conclusions were conclusive and so easy that she could understand them. She was convicted by Miller's 1840 sermons that "Christ was coming in 1843, only a few short years in the future. The preacher traced down the prophecies with a keen *exactitude* that struck conviction to the hearts of his hearers. He dwelt upon the prophetic periods, and *piled up proof* to strengthen his position."[84] She repeatedly characterized Miller's many proofs as "clear and conclusive" proofs, "plain and

---

82. See chapter 10, where Ellen G. White's prophetic treatment of "the daily" is highlighted.

83. Miller, *Evidences* (1835), 29-31. Emphasis added. Note that this critical forty-five-year period of 1798-1843 includes the last great battle (collapse of the Ottoman Empire), the second coming, the first resurrection, and the beginning of the millennium. This makes it impossible to retroactively reinterpret the nine exact prophetic periods to refer to an invisible movement of Christ in a heavenly sanctuary.

84. James and Ellen White, *Life Sketches: Ancestry*, 137. Emphasis added.

startling facts...."⁸⁵ "Calculation of the time was so simple and plain that even the children could understand it."⁸⁶

However, given the hindsight that Nichol enjoyed, one must agree with the august dean of SDA apologists that Miller's methods and results were indeed "fanciful" and "farfetched." Did God "open his understanding" to Daniel 8:14 but not Hosea 6:1–3; Luke 13:32–33; or Daniel 11:40?

The next of Miller's fifteen proofs that will be described is called the "prophecy of Moses" or the "seven times of the Gentiles." This was the first of three of Miller's fifteen proofs that he asserted started in 677 BC and extended 2,520 years until "about 1843." Miller maintained these *three* identical periods based on *three separate biblical texts*. (This is the most striking example of the purported textual proofs which so impressed Ellen Harmon.) He considered these three separate biblical proofs. Significantly, this 2,520-year period is found on both the 1843 Millerite chart and the 1851 White/Nichols chart, both of which Ellen G. White asserted had divine sanction.

---

85. James and Ellen White, *Life Sketches: Ancestry*, 149
86. White, *Christian Experience*, 49.

IV

Prophecy of Moses = Seven Times of Gentiles

> "Age will not make error into truth, and truth can afford to be fair. No true doctrine will lose anything by close investigation."
>
> ELLEN WHITE, "CHRIST OUR HOPE," 785

MILLER LOCATED THIS PROPHECY in Leviticus 26: 18–28. He dedicated the entire seventeenth lecture of his 1842 book *Evidence* to proving that this prophetic interval lasted from 677 BC to 1843. Ironically, although the interval is prominent in both the 1843 Millerite chart and the 1851 White/Nichols chart, one indication of the credibility of such a "prophetic period" is Uriah Smith's evaluation of such a claim. In 1897 Uriah Smith dismissed Miller's and White's claim that it was a time prophecy. He called it a "supposed prophetic period," saying, "there is no such prophetic period in the Bible." He contemptuously asserted that if it really was a prophetic period, "then we would have four of them, amounting in all to 10,080 years, which would be rather a long time to keep a nation under chastisement."[1] The following is Miller's textual basis. Notice that Miller discovered supposed prophetic periods even in Leviticus:

> And if ye will not yet for all this hearken unto me, then I will punish you seven times more for your sins. And I will break the pride of your power; and I will make your heaven

---

1. Smith, *Daniel and the Revelation* (2016), 600–602.

as iron, and your earth as brass: And your strength shall be spent in vain; for your land shall not yield her increase, neither shall the trees of the land yield their fruits. And if ye walk contrary unto me, and will not hearken unto me; I will bring seven times more plagues upon you according to your sins. I will also send wild beasts among you, which shall rob you of your children, and destroy your cattle, and make you few in number; and your high ways shall be desolate. And if ye will not be reformed by me by these things, but will walk contrary unto me; Then will I also walk contrary unto you, and will punish you yet seven times for your sins . . . I, even I, will chastise you seven times for your sins (Lev 26:18–24, 28, KJV).[2]

In this passage the phrase "seven times" is used four times as Uriah Smithly noted. According to Miller, this does not mean that Yahweh would punish them sevenfold for their sins. Seeing prophetic time in each expression, Miller asserted that each "time" was equivalent to 360 years. Multiplying this figure by seven times resulted in 2,520 years. Miller further asserted that Yahweh would punish Israel for 2,520 years, during which the Gentiles would dominate Israel. Thus, this prediction became popularly known as the "seven times of the Gentiles." According to Miller, the Bible could prove that the 2,520 years spanned the interval from 677 BC to "about 1843." How did Miller prove that this interval started in 677 BC? Almost certainly, Miller simply subtracted 2,520 years from 1843 to arrive at 677 BC.[3] He then tried to assemble some evidences that that supported this calculation. He found it in the KJV's marginal note (based on Ussher, whom he accepted in this case, though not in the millennial-Sabbath proof) for 2 Chronicles 33. This text was associated with Manasseh's arrest by the Assyrians. Miller asserted that when Jeremiah 15:4 spoke of Israel being punished for Manasseh's sins, these were the very sins mentioned in Leviticus. Miller also asserted that although

---

2. Miller, *Evidence* (1842), 153–61.

3. Nichol, *Midnight Cry*, Appendix L and 507–10. Nichol characterizes Miller's calculations as "begging the question," "farfetched," and "hoary with age." Moreover, he goes on to say: "In fact, we are tempted to believe there was a [good] deal of truth to the charge of some of his opponents that after Miller had decided on 1843 as a result of his study of the 2300-day prophecy, he worked *backward* from that date to secure certain of the dates that he employed as the starting point of some of the secondary lines of proof" (emphasis added).

the northern ten tribes *began* to be exiled in 722 BC, this was not completed until 677 BC.[4] And therefore Miller chose to calculate his 2,520-year period starting in 677 BC. He based this on another marginal note in the KJV where Isaiah 7:8 was dated to 742 BC. And, since this text prophesied that "within three score and five years shall Ephraim be broken," he simply subtracted sixty-five from 742 BC to arrive at 677 BC. Quite a tenuous chain of reckoning.

It is significant that Miller recorded that he found the seven times of Leviticus 26 *prior* to making his calculations about the 2,300 day-years of Daniel 8. "In a sermon, recorded by Litch, Miller says: 'I was satisfied that the seven times terminated in 1843. *Then* I came to the 2300 days; they brought me to the same conclusions."[5] In short, the dubious 2,520-year calculation was the decisive basis which led Miller to his 2,300-year calculation.

This convoluted reckoning requires that one transmute a sevenfold degree of punishment into a precise chronological prophecy while totally ignoring the original context and using dubious marginal notes.

Year of release proof of 1843

Another mode of Miller's arriving at the identical prophetical prediction of 2,520 years may be termed the "Year of Release." Again, Miller found "prophetic periods" far from Daneil and Revelation. Deuteronomy 15:1–2 constituted the proof text for this prophetic prediction:

> At the end of every seven years thou shalt make a release. And this is the manner of the release: Every creditor that lendeth ought unto his neighbor shall release it; he shall not exact it of his neighbor, or of his brother; because it is called the LORD. (KJV)

Here again Miller asserted that each of these seven "prophetic" years contained 360 historical years; he then multiplied by seven to get 2,520 years. These "seven years" were an allegory of Israel's history.

---

4. In an identical manner, shortly after 1798, when historicist commentators subtracted 1,260 years from 1798 to obtain 538 for the commencement of the 1,260 years, they cited an imperial decree dated 533 but argued that it could not go into effect until 538.

5. Arasola, *End of Historicism*, 97. Emphasis added.

He asserted that this period also started in 677 BC and said that 1843 represented the "year of release" when the chosen (the Millerites) would be liberated from their worldly oppressors at the dawn of the great antitypical sabbatical millennium.

Miller found yet another proof text for his 2,520 years in Jeremiah 34:14:

> At the end of every seven years let ye go every man his brother a Hebrew, which has been sold unto thee, and when he has served thee six years, thou shalt let him go free from thee; but your fathers hearkened not unto me, neither inclined their ear. (KJV)

Yet again, ignoring the context and original intent, Miller asserted that the law which limited Hebrew slavery to seven years was a predictive prophecy. He also asserted, without any particular justification, that this 2,520 years also began in 677 BC and ended "about 1843."

Leviticus 26:18-28; Deuteronomy 15:1-2; and Jeremiah 34:14 constituted the scriptural basis which so greatly impressed the young Ellen Harmon. Three proof texts for one prophetic period of 2,520 years could not be wrong. Such were the proofs that Miller piled up.

Gog and Magog proof of 1843

The Gog and Magog proof was based on Ezekiel 39:9-12, which describes the aftermath of Gog and Magog's apocalyptic invasion of the chosen people.

> And they that dwell in the cities of Israel shall go forth, and shall set on fire and burn the weapons, both the shields and the bucklers, the bows and the arrows, and the handstaves, and the spears, and they shall burn them with fire seven years: So that they shall take no wood out of the field, neither cut down any out of the forests; for they shall spoil those that spoiled them, and rob those that robbed them, saith the Lord GOD.—And seven months shall the house of Israel be burying of them, that they may cleanse the land. (KJV)

It describes a seven-year period during which Israel would reap the spoils from their victory over the defeated forces of Gog and Magog. Miller stood this on its head and interpreted it as a period in which God's chosen would be oppressed. Once again, he asserted that this seven-year period equaled 2,520 literal years; once again, he asserted that it must commence in 677 BC. The text also refers to a "seven months" period during which Israel would bury the pagans' bodies. Miller claimed that these prophetic months consists of thirty literal years each (7 x 30= 210 years).[6] He further asserted that this subsidiary period was nested within the 2,520 years and that it extended from 1588, when the Edict of Nantes was enacted and Henry IV, king of Navarre, was turned against the papal power, until 1798 when papal supremacy was ended. Miller justified his allegorical-historicist interpretation by saying that during this 210-year period from 1588 to 1798 the "people of God" were "putting away the rotten carcass of papal power." Additionally, for Miller, this seven-month (210-year) period conveniently coincided precisely with the 1,260 years which he had already determined to end in 1798, the last days. But Miller was confused. The Edict of Nantes did not occur until 1598.[7] Again, it is likely that Miller arrived at his date for commencing the 210 years by simply subtracting it from 1798 to arrive at 1588.

1,335-year prophecy

Miller derived this prophecy from Daniel 12:11–12:

> And from the time that the daily sacrifice shall be taken away, and the abomination that maketh desolate set up, there shall be a thousand two hundred and ninety days. Blessed is he that waiteth, and cometh to the thousand three hundred and five and thirty days (KJV).

From the text itself, there is no clear means of determining when either the 1290 or 1335 figure should commence. Thus, Miller established this by a very circuitous reasoning. First, he presumed that he had already proved that the 1,260-day-year interval extended from 538 to 1798. By fiat he asserted that 1,290 must be subtracted from 1798 to establish its *terminus a quo* as 508. Then, also by fiat, he

---

6. Miller calculated these seven months exactly as he calculated the five months of Revelation 9. Just as these 150 years had to be nested within some historical period which has some presumed relationship to the text, so Miller had to find some significant event at the commencement of this 210 years.

7. Arasola, *End of Historicism*, 104–5.

asserted that 1,335 must be added to 508 to arrive at "about 1843" for the second coming.

The calculations Miller made to arrive at 1843 for his 1,335-year prophecy are identical to what would be S. S. Snow's third proof in his midnight-cry message. Here the pivotal nature of the 1,260 years is most obvious. The 1,260 day-years, the 1,290 day-years, and the 1,335 day-years all interlock precisely with each other.

Miller had already argued that "the daily" of Daniel 8 and 12:11 must represent the power of pagan Rome, which was replaced by the power of papal Rome during the interval from 508 to 538. According to the 1843 Millerite chart, 508 marked the crucial transition from pagan Rome to papal Rome. In 538, "the daily," or pagan Rome, was taken away.[8] He said the "reign of the ten kings 'one hour,' or 30 years" occurs; then "the abomination that maketh desolate, or Papal Rome, was set up." (One prophetic hour should be only 15 historical years according to the day = year principle, 1/24th of 360 being 15. This is how Litch figured the prophetic hour of Revelation 9). Adding these 30 years to 508, he arrived at 538, and 538 became Miller's the *terminus a quo* for a prophetic period of 1,260 years. Miller asserted that adding this prophetic period to 538 brought him to 1798, when Napoleon ended the temporal power of papal Rome, which marked the beginning of the last days. Simultaneously, Miller subtracted 1,290 from 1798 to again arrive at 508, "the time that the daily sacrifice shall be taken away" (Daniel 12:11). His math was simple. The second jigsaw puzzle piece, 1,335 years, was simply added to 508 (508 +1335 = 1843), bringing one to precisely 1843 for the end of the world.[9]

---

8. Ellen White endorsed the 508–538 "the daily" interpretation that said this meant that pagan Rome ended on this date. She said: "Then I saw the 'daily,' that the Lord gave the correct view of it to those who gave the first angel's message. When union existed before 1844, nearly all were united on the correct view of the 'daily,' but since, in the confusion, other views have been embraced and darkness has followed." However, both White and the Millerites erred. See chapter 10, which documents in detail this error.

9. Miller, *Evidence* (1842), 186–88.

Multiple synchronous proofs prove the exact last year ends March 21, 1844

Miller had so many proofs he could seldom give his entire opus in the limited space of one article or book. Other Millerite writers packed in multiple proofs into single articles. One such writer compiled eight exact prophetic periods.[10] On January 25, 1843 Miller issued a multipoint synopsis of his views. This was Miller's most succinct, comprehensive summary of his proofs. This comprehensive masterpiece and S. S. Snow's August 11, 1844 *Midnight Cry* article are probably the two most influential Millerite articles ever written.[11] These two foundational Millerite documents contain the "powerful reasons" that moved Millerites from "of that day and hour knoweth no man" (Matthew 24:36) to "the wise" who *must* know the day. Miller's major points were given in capital Roman numerals, each followed by his list of proof texts. Point XIV stated:

> I believe the time can be known by all who desire to understand and to be ready for his coming. And I am fully convinced that some time between March 21st, 1843, and March 21st, 1844, according to the Jewish mode of computation of time, Christ will come, and bring all his saints with him; and that then he will reward every man as his work shall be.[12]

Nine of Miller's fifteen proofs all ended precisely in 1843. Miller asserted that these proofs "*all harmonized and come out in one and the same year.*[13] (Froom's four-volume *Prophetic Faith* provides extensive documentation for a very curious phenomenon: as he catalogues precursors on whom Miller is dependent, he approaches Miller's lifetime. The closer he approaches Miller's lifetime, the more one notes that multiple commentators display a marked penchant for providing multiple definite-time proofs that the second coming is going to occur on various dates, particularly 1840–1866.).

On June 14, 1843, in *Signs of the Times* (vol. V, no. 15, p. 115) a chart of nine prophetic periods mathematically demonstrating that the second coming would occur in 1843 was produced.

---

10. Jacobs, "Prophetic Time," 1–8.
11. Snow, "Behold, the Bridegroom Cometh," 1–4.
12. Miller, "Synopsis of Miller's Views," 145–50.
13. Arasola, *End of Historicism*, 90–91, 220. Emphasis added.

In fact, this irresistible, comprehensive mass of biblical proofs was so convincing that even after the March 21, 1844 Millerite prediction failed, on July 17, 1844, J. V. Himes wrote:

> The above was written in the Jewish year 1843, which has now expired. According to the best chronologers the captivity of Manasseh, the commencement of the seven times, or 2520 years of Levit. 26th. was B. C. 677; also the captivity of Jehoiakim, the commencement of the Great Jubilee, or 2450 years, was B.C. 607; also the decree to rebuild Jerusalem in the seventh of Artaxerxes, the commencement of the 70 weeks and 2300 days, of Dan.8th and 9th was given B. C. 457; and also the taking away of Paganism in Rome, the commencement of the 1335 days of Dan. 12th, was about A.D. 508. Reckoning from those several dates, the respective periods can extend only to about the Jewish Year 1843. This being ended, our published time is now past; but as we can find no new dates for the events from which we have reckoned those periods, we cannot extend them beyond the time specified, which has been our only time; and yet our faith is as strong as ever, that at the end of those periods the Lord *will surely come* . . .[14]

Note that several of the fifteen long-neglected Millerite predictions that the world would end "about 1843" are included in what J. V. Himes labeled as "Fundamental Principles on which the Second Advent Cause is Based." According to Miller, in addition to his nine mathematical proofs all ending "about 1843," six additional exact prophecies, although not ending in 1843, did end precisely in other specific and eschatologically critical dates. For example, he claimed that five separate textual proofs (Daniel 12:6–7; Daniel 12:11–13; Revelation 11:3; Revelation 12: 6, 14; and Revelation 13:5), demonstrated that prophecies of either 1,260 years or 1,290 years all ended in the critically important year of 1798. He concluded: "These several ways of prophetic chronology *prove the end in 1843.*"[15] In Miller's address to the Second Advent Conference in 1841, he explicitly listed many of his arguments—6,000 years, 2,520 years, 2,450 years, 2,300 years, 2,000 years, and 391 years and 15 days—and then challenged his listeners:

---

14. Himes, "Fundamental Principles," 185–92. Emphasis added.
15. Miller, "Synopsis of Miller's Views," Appendix V. Emphasis added.

> You will next inquire, How shall we know when these times will all end? I answer, when you or any other man can show by scripture rule that they all harmonize and come out in one and the same year, they cannot be far from the truth.[16]

These fifteen exact mathematical proofs were the textual and exegetical basis for Ellen G. White's assertion that God had opened Miller's understanding to the calculation of the Parousia, and that he could therefore "unfold the mysteries of the kingdom of God" "down through the prophecies to the second advent of Christ."

After Miller came to the firm conviction that multiple separate biblical prophetic periods all reached until "about 1843," Miller concluded that the Bible necessarily taught the doctrine of definite time. The tipping point for the movement came during the May 1842 General Conference, which asserted that "*God has revealed the time of the end of the world and that that time is 1843.*"[17]

Thus, many Millerites would sneeringly dismiss their coreligionists' protests that no man could or would know the day or the hour. For example, by May 1, 1843 Apollos Hale had written an entire book subtitled *The Objections to Calculating the Prophetic Times Are Considered.*

After Hale considers "the principal objections and difficulties which have been presented against calculating the termination of the prophetic periods, especially that view of them which supposes that they bring us to the end in 1843," he says the argument that "No man knoweth the day or the hour" is ludicrous. Its weakness is "*so very palpable, that nothing but the most obsequious bigotry, or the most unpardonable ignorance could ever*" consider it. He concludes that it is not even probable that Jesus "meant to say that 'man' should never know the day or the hour of his coming in the most literal sense..."[18]

2,300-day prophecy only one of "main pillars"

He then goes on to list the many proofs that Millerites had gathered to buttress this conviction. He states that the 2,520-year (seven times) period is a "main pillar" of Millerism. The "proofs that the end will

---

16. Arasola, *End of Historicism*, 91.
17. Knight, *Millennial Fever*, 128. Emphasis added.
18. Hale, *Second Advent Manual*, 30. Emphasis added.

come at the end of this period are found in Dan. 12:1–7, Luke 21:24, 27," he says. The 1,335-year period was a "fundamental part of Mr. Miller's Calculation" and the 1,290-year period was "intimately connected" with it, because at the end of the 1,335-year period the reign of Christ would commence, the judgment would be pronounced, the resurrection would occur, and the glorification of the righteous would be evident. Moreover, the 1,335 years and the 2,300 years would "terminate together."[19] White continued to make the identical argument in the 1850s.

Multiple exact prophetic periods and miraculous apocalyptic signs convince Harmon

At a very young and impressionable age, Ellen Harmon was inculcated with all these signs and prophetic periods, and thus she concluded: "The Bible testimony in support of their [the Millerites'] position seemed *clear and conclusive*. Signs[20] *which could not be mistaken* [emphasis added] pointed to the coming of Christ as near." These were the "plainest statements of Bible facts, which could not be controverted." To those who disputed Miller's pretension to predict exact dates, Ellen G. White, mirroring Apollos Hale's example,[21] distainfully said: "'No man knoweth the day and the hour' was heard from hypocritical minister and the bold scoffer." To the contrary, she asserted, no honest Christian desirous of "understanding" definite time could maintain such a position.[22] Ellen G. White and other Millerites made a point of asserting that even the "most learned of their opponents" were forced to confess that "[y]our [the Millerites'] reckoning of the prophetic periods is correct," such were the "powerful reasons offered."[23] "Neither [minister or scoffer] would be instructed and corrected on the use made of the text by those who were pointing to the year when

---

19. Hale, *Second Advent Manual*, 34, 59, 95.

20. These unmistakable signs were the 1755 Lisbon earthquake, the 1780 Dark Day, and the 1833 Meteorite shower, which are analyzed just below.

21. Per Hale, only "obsequious bigotry or the most unpardonable ignorance" stood behind objections to Millerism's claim to know the exact day of the second coming.

22. White, *Spirit of Prophecy*, 212, 217, 228, 241, 250.

23. White, *Spiritual Gifts*, 1:139.

they believed the prophetic periods [plural] would run out, and to the signs which showed Christ near, even at the doors."[24]

"We were firm in the belief that the preaching of the definite time was of God"

This was the spiritual crucible which convinced thirteen-year-old Ellen Harmon to say: "We were firm in the belief that the *preaching of the definite time was of God*. It was this that led men to search the Bible diligently, discovering truths they had *not before* perceived."[25]

What were these "clear and conclusive," incontrovertible, "powerful reasons"?

The Millerites touted three categories of proofs: 1) prophetic, day-year biblical texts, 2) matching historical events, and 3) cosmic signs. Historicism rested on the hypothesis that there existed a one-to-one relationship between text and historical event. Therefore, Miller entitled his work *Evidence from Scripture and History*. Cosmic signs purportedly predicted in Revelation were proofs that Ellen Harmon copied from Miller. For example, Miller asserted that the 1755 Lisbon earthquake was a fulfillment of the earthquake predicted in Revelation 6:12.

The great Lisbon earthquake of 1755 predicted in Revelation 6:12

While Protestants like Ellen G. White and William Miller interpreted the Lisbon earthquake of 1755 as marking the last days, Catholic Jesuits claimed that it was divine retribution on the king of Portugal.[26] Ellen Harmon unambiguously identified the Lisbon earthquake as the fulfillment of Revelation 6:12.[27] She asserted that this was the

24. White, *Spiritual Gifts* 1:135.

25. White, *Life Sketches*, 189–92. Emphasis added. These "truths" were the prophetic periods which ended in 1843 and 1798, and the multiple apocalyptic signs which occurred in 1755, 1780, and 1833.

26. Burleigh, *Earthly Powers*, 33.

27. Significantly, while the earthquake in Revelation 6:12 was identified with a *literal seismic event*, the earthquake in Revelation 11:13 was identified as a *political event*, namely, the French Revolution. The KJV translation reads: "And the same hour was there a great earthquake, and the tenth part of the city fell, and in the earthquake

first in a sequence of apocalyptic, cosmic signs. She noted that earthquakes were listed as a sign of the last days in the Synoptic apocalypses. She asserted that this earthquake marked a pivotal point in her 1,260-day-year calculation (538–1798). Because of the biblical phrase that the days of persecution will be shortened (Mathew 24:22 and Mark 13:20), she stated that this referred to the fact that shortly prior to 1798 the earthquake of Revelation 6:12 would occur.

In other words, the standard SDA interpretation of the peculiar relationship between the Lisbon earthquake of 1755 and the end of the 1,260 years in 1798 was that although the interval 538–1798 was purportedly the predicted period of papal persecution, persecution allegedly ended a bit early, in 1755. An earthquake in 1755 fit nicely. White further listed it as a specific last-days event and the "most terrible earthquake that has ever been recorded." This fails on both accounts. Almost three hundred years have passed. This alone makes it a rather incredible candidate for being the earthquake mentioned in Revelation 6:12. And it is indisputable that she has borrowed this directly from Millerite teaching. She was "taught it by man" years prior to her first vision. There is no evidence that this was the worst earthquake up until 1755; however, there is more evidence that shows that since then several more powerful earthquakes have occurred. Given that the Lisbon earthquake is a quarter of a millennium in the past, that eliminates it as a fulfillment of Revelation 6:12. Yet this did not deter Ellen White from asserting:

> The revelator thus describes the first of the signs to precede the second advent: "There was a great earthquake; and the sun became black as sackcloth of hair, and the moon became as blood." Revelation 6:12.
>
> These signs were witnessed before the opening of the nineteenth century. In fulfillment of this prophecy there

---

were slain of men seven thousand: and the remnant were affrighted and gave glory to the God of heaven." See Smith, *Daniel and the Revelation*, (1897), 503, who argued that "the city" is papal power, the "tenth" of that city is France, the "collapse" is the French Revolution, and the seven thousand people who died represented seven thousand titles of nobility that were eliminated with the French Revolution. See White, *Great Controversy* (1988), 286, 269, where she claimed: "France was shaken as if by an earthquake." "This prophecy has received a most exact and striking fulfillment in the history of France."

occurred, in the year 1755, the most terrible earthquake that has ever been recorded.[28]

The *Wikipedia* article on the Lisbon earthquake states: " Seismologists today estimate the Lisbon earthquake had a magnitude in the range 8.5–9.0 on the moment magnitude scale, with its epicentre in the Atlantic Ocean about 200 km (120 mi) west-southwest of Cape St. Vincent."[29]

Currently, an article listing the ten worst earthquakes in history does not even contain the Lisbon earthquake.[30] The first five listed are above 9.0 on the Richter scale. The most intense was Valdivia, Chile, May 22, 1960 (9.5).

Supernatural Dark Day of 1780

Immediately following the Lisbon earthquake in the sequential prophetic scheme of Ellen White is the Dark Day of 1780. She states categorically:

> Twenty-five years later appeared the next sign mentioned in the prophecy—the darkening of the sun and moon. What rendered this more striking was the fact that the time of its fulfillment had been definitely pointed out. In the Saviour's conversation with His disciples upon Olivet, after describing the long period of trial for the church,—the 1260 years of papal persecution, concerning which He had promised that the tribulation should be shortened[31],—He thus mentioned certain events to precede His coming, and fixed the time when the first of these should be witnessed: "In those days, after that tribulation, the sun shall be darkened, and the moon shall not give her light." Mark 13:24. The 1260 days, or years, terminated in 1798. A quarter of a century earlier, persecution had almost wholly ceased. Following this persecution,

---

28. White, *Great Controversy* (1988), 304.

29. *Wikipedia*, "Lisbon Earthquake," at https://en.wikipedia.org/wiki/1755_Lisbon_earthquake.

30. Phillips, "Earthquakes."

31. In other words, E. G. White, following Miller, asserted that papal persecution had largely ceased prior to 1798. This concept of shortening papal persecution was a standard Millerite interpretation.

according to the words of Christ, the sun was to be darkened. On the 19th of May, 1780, this prophecy was fulfilled.³²

Ellen G. White asserted that it was significant that only twenty-five years separated the 1755 Lisbon earthquake from the Dark Day of 1780. Both the 1755 and 1780 dates are chronologically close to 1798. It is now conceded in official SDA church papers that this was not a supernatural event but the effect of smoke in the air following a forest fire.³³ Ellen White made the same argument regarding the timing of the event: namely, that the date 1780 is prophetically linked to 1798, a central date in the day-year prophetic scheme of William Miller. Since supposedly "the tribulation should be shortened," Ellen White said that the persecution of 1,260 years, which ended precisely on 1798, had "almost wholly ceased." Therefore, precisely on May 19, 1780, "this prophecy was fulfilled."

In her discussion of both the Lisbon earthquake and the Dark Day of 1780, the bulk of her homiletical discussion is made of multiple references to various sources which speak of the events as if they were singular, supernatural events.

She was categorical regarding the wondrous nature of the Dark Day:

> May 19, 1780, stands in history as "The Dark Day." Since the time of Moses no period of darkness of equal density, extent, and duration, has ever been recorded. The description of this event, as given by eyewitnesses, is but an echo of the words of the Lord, recorded by the prophet Joel, twenty-five hundred years previous to their fulfillment: "The sun shall be turned into darkness, and the moon into blood, before the great and terrible day of the Lord come." Joel 2:31.³⁴

Miller, followed by Ellen White, asserted that the 1780 Dark Day was a stupendous cosmic event. However, this is impossible because the event was not supernatural, nor in any way a fulfillment of prophecy. Yet the "fulfillment of this prophecy on May 19, 1780" is still so central to SDA eschatology and identity that it is cited in the 28 Fundamental Beliefs.³⁵ In this document, the 1755 Lisbon earth-

---

32. White, *Great Controversy* (1888), 306.
33. Casebolt, "Is Ellen White's Interpretation," 2–9.
34. White, *Great Controversy* (1988), 308.
35. Ministerial Association, *Seventh-Day Adventists Believe*, 378–79.

quake and the 1833 meteorite shower are also cited as eschatological signs validating the midnight-cry date-setting of October 22, 1844. Even during the event, eyewitnesses noted that smoke and soot in the atmosphere greatly obscured vision and precipitated on the ground, covering it in a layer of ash. Local witnesses noted that the Dark Day "was accompanied by 'thick, dark and sooty' rain and the smell of burnt leaves." Yet many attributed the event to supernatural rather than natural causes. In 2007 researchers from the University of Missouri "discovered signs of a massive, centuries-old wildfire in the Algonquin Highlands of southern Ontario. 'Fire scars' in the rings of the affected trees allowed the team to date the blaze to the spring of 1780." Similar "dark" or "yellow" days caused by forest fires have been recorded. A "similar phenomenon also occurred in 1881, when the haze from fires in Ontario and Michigan reduced sunlight in New England by as much as 90 percent."[36] These researchers noted that "great wildfires burning in the Lake States and Canada can affect atmospheric conditions several hundred miles away." Researchers as early as Plummer in 1912 have documented several "dark" or "yellow" days. Just as ancient primitive peoples, not comprehending the nature of eclipses (or meteorite showers), attributed them to supernatural sources, in 1780 "people were technologically unable to confirm the source of such a phenomenon."[37] Just as Millerites and Shakers attributed the Dark Day of 1780 to divinely predicted supernatural events, Millerite journals also described the aurora borealis, or northern lights, as supernatural signs of the last days. Thus, the purported supernatural character of the 1780 Dark Day was an eighteenth-century version of an urban legend. Miller adopted this legendary account from others and Ellen White adopted it from the common fund of Millerite folklore. Her credulous appropriation of such a thoroughly discredited legend provides strong disconfirmation of common SDA claims that Ellen G. White's prophetic authority can authenticate historical events. Conversely, it strongly supports the theses enunciated by several SDA scholars, like George R. Knight, that Ellen G. White did not intend to be used as an authority regarding historical matters.

However, given that SDA eschatology is so dependent on continuous-historical assumptions, the attempt to differentiate

---

36. Andrews, "Remembering New England's 'Dark Day'"

37. See: McMurry et al., "Fire Scars Reveal Source," 266–270. For an accessible abstract see https://www.fs.usda.gov/treesearch/pubs/41025.

historiography and history from biblical chronology and eschatology is virtually impossible operationally.

Falling of the stars in 1833

> In 1833, two years after Miller began to present in public the evidences of Christ's soon coming, the last of the signs appeared which were promised by the Saviour as tokens of His second advent. Said Jesus: "The stars shall fall from heaven." Matthew 24:29. And John in the Revelation declared, as he beheld in vision the scenes that should herald the day of God: "The stars of heaven fell unto the earth, even as a fig tree casteth her untimely figs, when she is shaken of a mighty wind." Revelation 6:13. This prophecy received a striking and impressive fulfillment in the great meteoric shower of November 13, 1833. That was the most extensive and wonderful display of falling stars which has ever been recorded...[38]

That event was hardly "the most extensive and wonderful display of falling stars which has ever been recorded." It has been demonstrated elsewhere that this was a periodic meteor shower which has been occurring for thousands of years and was by no means a supernatural event as indicated by the Millerites and Ellen G. White.[39]

For hundreds of years people had had superstitious beliefs about meteorites. Some meteors became religious objects. Like beliefs about solar and lunar eclipses, meteorites and comets were thought to portend special messages from the gods. Thus, in Hebrew thought unusual phenomenon related to the sun, moon, asteroids, meteorites, and the fixed stars were thought to be supernatural events rather than the naturalistic phenomena we now understand both eclipses and meteorite showers to be. In Ellen Harmon's childhood, meteorites were just being started to be studied scientifically. In the natural history museum in Angers, France there is an interpretive exhibition of meteorites. The exhibition explains that in the early 1800s when the peasant folks reported to the Enlightenment scientists of France that they had observed rocks falling from the skies, scientists initially considered these reports to be preposterous, superstitious reports of

---

38. White, *Great Controversy* (1988), 332.

39. Casebolt, "Is Ellen White's Interpretation," 4. See also Jenniskin, "Meteorite Showers and Their Parent Comets," 4–11.

ignorant peasants. Rocks do not fall out of the sky! It was only upon actual field study that scientists confirmed that rocks really did fall from the skies.

Given the primitive comprehension of scientists during Ellen Harmon's childhood, and since she was only six years old when the 1833 meteorite shower occurred, it is not surprising that a large number of persons participating in the Millerite movement, including the ill-educated Ellen Harmon, would associate this meteorite shower with a biblical verse about stars falling from the shaking heavens.

V

Potpourri of Fanciful and Arbitrary Prophetic Interpretations

BESIDES MILLER'S FIFTEEN MAJOR proofs, he applied his allegorical-typological-historicist methodology to the entirety of Daniel and Revelation. He forced broad swaths of these two books into a sequential continuous-historical framework. A representative sample will be displayed directly below to document that Miller's interpretation was far from literal and commonsense. It was unfailingly allegorical and fanciful. For example, in his lecture on the "new song" of Revelation 5:9-10 he took the four beasts, gave them a precise sequential historical application, and arbitrarily gave each beast symbol an allegorical identity:

Four beasts are four epochs of church history per Miller

The four beasts [lion, calf, man, eagle] he insists "represent the four grand divisions of the gospel church. The first represents the church in the apostolic age, when the church went forth, bold as a lion, preaching and proclaiming the gospel among all nations. The second state or division of the church was the times of persecution and slaughter by the Roman emperors, represented by the calf. The third state of the church was in Constantine's day, when the church enjoyed privileges as a man, and became independent, and like a natural man,

> proud, avaricious, and worldly. The fourth and last state of trial was when the anti-Christian beast arose; and under the scourge of the abomination, the church having two wings given her, like the wings of an eagle, she flew into the wilderness, where a place being prepared for her, she is nourished from the face of the serpent a thousand two hundred and threescore days, Rev. xii. 6, 14.[1]

This illustrates the lengths to which Miller went in imposing his historicist sequence on the text; it also illustrates the tenuous relationship between a symbol and its interpretation. A calf represents the Roman emperors' persecution? And one can date this calf epoch after the apostolic age and prior to Constantine? Miller never explained how his four-beast scenario fit with his seven-church sequence of the same period. Did the man epoch last from 313 until 538, and the eagle epoch last from 538 until 1798?

He repeated this error in his arbitrary assignment of specific historical periods to the seven churches.[2] His historical periodization of the seven churches was followed by Uriah Smith.[3] For example, he assigned to the church of Pergamos the period "A.D. 312 until A.D. 538." The scant or virtually non-existent textual support for such a procedure is unmistakable. The same judgment applies to all the dates he assigned the seven churches. Many historicists prior to Miller assigned similarly exact dates to their speculative periodizations. Such speculative periodizations were invariably mutually contradictory and have been disconfirmed by history.[4]

Multiple identities for the two witnesses

Miller's thirteenth lecture on the two witnesses of Revelation 11 provides more examples. Initially he identified the two witnesses as "the Old and New Testament." But for Miller the witnesses' identity was

1. Miller, *Evidence* (1842), 98.
2. Miller, *Evidence* (1842), 70–88.
3. Ellen G. White strongly endorsed Uriah Smith's book on Daniel and Revelation. She endorsed Smith in such a fulsome manner, saying something to the effect that angels stood by his side as he wrote it, that a traditional faction of the SDA membership interpret her stamp of approval as rendering Smith's commentary nearly inspired.
4. See Firth, *Apocalyptic* for examples.

sufficiently malleable that they could take on multiple personalities. After an extended explanation of how the Old Testament and New Testament were in "sackcloth" for 1,260 years, he explained how the expression "fire out of their mouth" was fulfilled by the carnage of the French Revolution. Where the text says that the two witnesses could "turn water into blood," Miller asserted that "waters" means "people" and "blood" means "wars." This he asserted was fulfilled when Europe had religious wars. He asserted that verse 8, which says the "dead bodies" of the two witnesses "shall lie in the streets of the great city," transforms the two witnesses from the "Old and New Testament" into the literal bodies of dead Huguenots because "the people of God are called Christ's spiritual body." "Crucifying our Lord, that is, in a spiritual sense" was literally fulfilled in the St. Bartholomew's Massacre, "when 50,000 Huguenots were murdered in one day."

He asserted that the verse 11 reference to "and after three days and a half, the spirit of life from God entered into them" now transforms the literal 50,000 Huguenots bodies into "the Bible [which] would be dormant three years and a half." Earlier Miller had said that the beast coming from the abyss, which would attempt to kill them, the two witnesses, was exactly fulfilled when the French government warred on the Bible. This campaign he also conflated with the 1,260 years of the papacy's war on the Bible because, according to Miller, the principles of papal Rome and French deism were the same. "This will apply to France in particular." The text in Revelation 11:8 which says that the nations will look at the dead bodies for three and a half years, per Miller, means that the Protestant nations would "prevent the Scriptures from being buried, or put out of sight." Thus, the Bible would merely be dormant for three and a half years, after which it would be resurrected in the form of Bible societies. Further, when verse 12 says "they ascended up to heaven," it means that the Bible would be translated into many languages. "Here we have a *plain* [emphasis added] and distinct prophecy of the Bible societies."

> ... the slaying of the witnesses; their lying in a dead state three years and a half in the street of the great city; the revolution spoken of in this prophecy—all happened in the French revolution between the years 1793 and 1798.[5]

---

5. Miller, *Evidence* (1842), 118–21. No such precise campaign existed.

EGW copied Miller's Bible society concept, already present in her 1822 KJV Bible

Ellen White copied from Miller his interpretation that the formation of Bible societies fulfilled Revelation 11 after the Bible had been dormant for three and a half years. She said:

> Concerning the two witnesses the prophet declares further: "And they heard a great voice from heaven saying unto them, Come up hither. And they ascended up to heaven in a cloud; and their enemies beheld them." Revelation 11:12. Since France made war upon God's two witnesses, they have been honored as never before. In 1804 the British and Foreign Bible Society was organized. This was followed by similar organizations, with numerous branches, upon the continent of Europe. In 1816 the American Bible Society was founded. When the British Society was formed, the Bible had been printed and circulated in fifty tongues. It has since been translated into many hundreds of languages and dialects.[6]

Seven thousand French titles abolished: Smith copied Miller, who copied Priestley

Copying far-fetched, obscure allegorical interpretations in the guise of literal, commonsense interpretation is strikingly documented. The symbolic number of seven thousand slain was morphed into a claim that it referred to seven thousand French titles of nobility being abolished in the "earthquake" of the French Revolution. Ellen G. White copied the concept that the earthquake of Revelation was not literal but figurative of the French Revolution.

In Revelation 11:13, the earthquake in which a tenth of the city falls and seven thousand are slain means, per Miller, that "one of the ten kingdoms,[7] which had given their power and support to the Papal

---

6. White, *Great Controversy* (1988), 287.

7. Elsewhere, Miller, in *Evidence* (1842), 27 precisely defined each of these ten kingdoms. They were "the Goths, Huns, and Vandals, 'France, Britain, Spain, Portugal, Naples, Tuscany, Austria, Lombardy, Rome, and Ravenna. The three last were absorbed in the territory of Rome,' (E. Irwin,) and became the States of the Church." Miller, followed by Uriah Smith and the many anti-Trinitarian SDA pioneers, would make a major issue that three of these ten kingdoms were Arian and therefore plucked up by the Trinitarian Roman Catholic Church. Also on this page is Miller's gratuitous

beast would fall; and seven thousand names, or titles of nobility, in church and state would be destroyed. . . ." "Here we again see exactly depicted the French revolution and its effects; and we cannot but see that the whole of this prophecy has been literally fulfilled."[8] This is a striking example of a very obscure but specific interpretation "discovered" by Joseph Priestly and then copied by Miller. In February 28, 1794 Joseph Priestley (1733-1801), the discoverer of oxygen, repeated others' assertion that the "late revolution in France" was predicted under the symbol of an earthquake in Revelation 11:13. Then he added this minute detail: "And the same hour there was a great earthquake, and the tenth part of the city fell, and in the earthquake were slain of men (or literally, names of men) seven thousand. . ."[9] William Miller copied Priestley's concept, stating: ". . . and in the earthquake were slain of men [names or titles] seven thousand . . ."[10] Uriah Smith copied Priestley and Miller's interpretation that the seven thousand persons slain were not literally killed. Rather, it meant that seven thousand French titles of nobility were abolished during the French Revolution.[11] This is a striking example of how Miller, far from getting his interpretations from only his Bible and a concordance, was strongly influenced in the minutest detail by the hoary traditions of historicists. Ellen G. White's *Great Controversy* chapter on revolutionary France was largely borrowed from William Miller and Uriah Smith, as documented by Ron Graybill.[12] Miller asserted that "the earthquake spoken of is the French revolution." He further insisted that multiple prophecies had been "accomplished literally, and in the time specified. Many events have been foretold, the times given, and not one failed. How can you disbelieve? How can you shut

---

identification that "'eyes' means faith," which in turn meant that the Catholic Church made a pretense of being in "the faith." Whether in broad themes or minute details, Miller had no hesitation in making arbitary, evidence-free assignations of hermeneutical interpretations to word after word and phrase after phrase of biblical text.

8. Miller, *Evidence* (1842), 120.

9. Froom, *Prophetic Faith of Our Fathers*, 2:746.

10. Miller, *Evidence* (1842), 106.

11. Smith, *Daniel and the Revelation*, (1897), 503, quoting Revelation 11:13, stated: "'And in the earthquake were slain of men [margin, names of men, or titles of men] seven thousand. France made war, in her revolution of 1793-98 and onward, on all titles of nobility. It is said by those who have examined the French records, that just seven thousand titles of men were abolished in that revolution."

12. Graybill, "How Did Ellen White Chose," 49-53.

your eyes against so much light?"[13] Neither Miller, Smith, nor Ellen G. White offered a commonsense explanation of why an earthquake in one location of Revelation should be a political revolution and not a literal earthquake, whereas other descriptions of earthquakes elsewhere in Revelation are actual earthquakes, most notably the Lisbon earthquake. Why such arbitrary inconsistencies? Clearly because they had an *a priori* attachment to a chronological scheme that made dates like 1798 critical.

Miller then enumerated a long series of arbitrary equivalences. Revelation 11: 14: "The second woe began by the civil wars in France and Germany, and ended in the French revolution."[14] This is a baseless assertion. Revelation 12:12, "Woe to the inhabitants of the earth," per Miller, means "those who live under the Roman government," "and of the sea" meaning "the principal kingdom among the ten kingdoms. France is generally meant by sea in this prophecy".[15] There is no basis for identifying the earth's inhabitants with Roman citizens; no basis for identifying France with the sea. Miller's entire commentary on verse 14 is similarly baseless. Two wings are hardly the "Arian and Papal controversy," or the western-versus-eastern division of the empire, as Miller asserts. Nor are there any grounds for Miller claiming that a controversy over the saints or the infallibility of the popes took place at the time he stated. But especially baseless is his contention that during said controversy certain groups withdrew, "settled in the north-west part of Asia," and then sent colonies to the "Piedmont and valleys of the Alps, where it is supposed the true worship of God was retained during the dark ages of Papal ignorance, bigotry, and superstition. (See Milner's Church History, and Benedict's History of the Baptists)."[16] This is an allusion to the Waldenses and/or Albigenses. Inaccurate assertions about the Waldenses made by Miller and Ellen G. White are discussed in chapter 12.

Miller claims of Revelation 12:16 that the "earth helping the woman" was fulfilled by "the German princes [who] helped their subjects against the armies of the Pope, and destroyed and swallowed up many of the Papal armies, from the thirteenth to the fifteenth century."

13. Miller, *Evidence* (1842), 122.
14. Miller, *Evidence* (1842), 121.
15. Miller, *Evidence* (1842), 128.
16. Miller, *Evidence* (1842), 128. Note that even Miller qualified his assertion, saying, "it is supposed."

Of verse 17, Miller is "constrained to believe" that "this battle of the dragon's last power will be in America." This was likely the nucleus for the later SDA identification of the geopolitical role of the USA as the two-horned beast in biblical prophecy. Yet, there is no evidence for this geopolitical identification any more than there is for Miller's assertion that the "fowls" mentioned in verse 17 must be "warriors in favor of liberty" who will fight "papal Rome, or [the] false prophet."[17] Ellen G. White did not copy *all* of Miller's fanciful schemes, sequences, and assertions, but she was intellectually dependent on Miller for the overwhelming majority of them. In sum, Miller was unfailingly fanciful in his allegorical-historicist identifications, and Ellen G. White routinely mirrored Miller's interpretations. Miller did not use angelic insight and commonsense to generate his interpretations. His interpretations regularly demonstrate a lack of commonsense.

In these initial five chapters I have dealt exclusively with the evidence that Ellen White was the spiritual daughter of William Miller. She was dependent on Miller for dozens of her allegorical-typological-historicist interpretations, just as Miller was dependent upon centuries of flawed historicist interpretations. But Miller had other progeny who also had an outsized influence on Ellen White. Chief among these was S. S. Snow, whose midnight-cry date-setting message superseded Miller and was the proximate cause for White's first vision, whose central burden was the validity of the date October 22, 1844. The following chapter will demonstrate how Snow eclipsed Miller in the interval between March 21, 1844 to October 22, 1844.

---

17. Miller, *Evidence* (1842), 129–30.

VI

Snow's Explanation of Miller's March 21, 1844 Failure

ALTHOUGH MILLER GAVE HIS name to the movement, he began losing control of it March 21, 1844 when Christ did not come on the date he predicted, and a period called the "tarrying time" began. The certainty of Miller's spring definite time was shattered and this uncertainty created a vacuum which S. S. Snow filled with a definite time in the autumn of 1844.

What the tarrying time reveals about the core of SDA theology and hermeneutics

Miller had proclaimed that his fifteen proofs demonstrated that Christ's second coming must occur by March 21, 1844—despite Christ's warning in Mark 13:32: "No man knoweth."

> I believe the time can be known by all who desire to understand and to be ready for his coming. And I am fully convinced that some time between March 21st, 1843, and March 21st, 1844, according to the Jewish mode of computation of time, Christ will come, and bring all his saints with him; and that then he will reward every man as his work shall be.[1]

Ellen Harmon repeatedly characterized Miller's proofs as "clear and conclusive," "plain and startling facts," "so simple and plain that

---

1. Miller, "Synopsis of Miller's Views," 145–50.

even children could understand it." She concluded that since "[h]e supported his statements and theories by Scripture proof," the calculations contained in his proofs must be correct.[2] Speaking of her eye-witness experience of Miller's March 1840 preaching in the Casco street church in Portland, Maine when she was only twelve years old, she stated that Miller "traced down the prophecies with a keen exactitude... [and] dwelt upon the prophetic *periods* [plural: emphasis added], and piled up proof to strengthen his position."[3]

When Christ did not come as predicted on March 21, 1844, a decisive crisis in Millerite history occurred. For the first few days many were convinced that Christ was still on his way. But as days passed into weeks new explanations were required. They only had two options: 1) they could conclude that their continuous-historical method was mistaken, that God never intended to have them proclaim a specific date for the second coming, and cease their efforts to calculate a specific date for the second coming; 2) they could reaffirm definite time and conclude that they had simply made a minor chronological miscalculation. Within days after the March 21, 1844 failure, Millerite thought leaders generated biblical reinterpretations still retaining definite time. Two variants of the second option existed. The first was only a temporizing option. This one substituted a Karaite form of reckoning the Jewish year such that it ended about April 21, 1844 rather than March 21, 1844. When Christ still did not come by late April, this obviously lost its utility. The second variant of the second option was to assert that a minor miscalculation left open the potential to find a new and improved specific date. But a new definite time was not yet calculated. Thus, they labeled this interim of uncertainty, the interval when the virgins "slumbered and slept," the "tarrying time." S. S. Snow generated biblical proofs that the tarrying time itself was predicted.

His interpretation of Ezekiel 12:22; Habakkuk 2:3; Jeremiah 51:45–46; and 2 Esdras 2:19 demonstrates the quintessential allegorical-typological-historicism inherent in Millerism and Snowism. Although the Millerites may have imagined that they were promulgating a literal interpretation, this is simply not the case. The possibility of a new and improved autumn date already had been suggested by S. S.

2. White, *Christian Experience*, 49.
3. James and Ellen White, *Life Sketches: Ancestry*, 137.

Snow just shortly before Miller's initial spring date failed.[4] Deference to Miller prevented Snow's initial autumn calculations from gaining traction, but once Miller's spring date had been disconfirmed, Snow would persevere in advocating for an autumn date as determined by Karaite reckoning.

Just as there would have never been a Millerite movement without Miller, *there never would have been a midnight cry without S. S. Snow*. And without Snow's midnight cry, Ellen Harmon's first vision would not have had his midnight cry as its focal point. The midnight cry should be labelled the "Snowite movement." His series of letters from February to August 1844 and his preaching at the Exeter, New Hampshire camp meeting gave birth to the "tornado" of the midnight cry. It eclipsed a reluctant Miller, who never would have endorsed October 22, 1844 without being stampeded by Snow and the tornado he generated.[5] Snow's crowning written contribution came in August 22, 1844. In it he retained, with an autumn modification, what Apollos Hale[6] called the major pillars of Miller's fifteen proofs so as to provide to his breathless audience a specific date for the second coming which they yearned to embrace.[7] Snow's autumn version of Miller's proofs was the midnight cry. Just as the United States was born with the Declaration of Independence, Snow's August 1844 modification of Miller's chronological calculation gave birth to the midnight cry. The psychological and sociological setting of the Exeter camp meeting where S. S. Snow gave his oral rendition of the midnight cry contributed to the Millerites' conviction that a "tornado" of the Holy Spirit had struck them at Exeter. Since March 21, 1844, when the tarrying

---

4. Snow, "Letter from S. S. Snow," February, 22, 1844. It is well known that Miller, Himes, and other well-known Millerite lecturers endorsed the midnight cry date of October 22, 1844 only very late and reluctantly after *repeatedly* asserting that setting the exact "day" was not biblical. It is not well known that prominent Millerite preachers, like George Storrs, did set other exact dates. In one peculiar interpretation they reasoned as follows: The text of the Bible does not say that the exact year cannot be known; in fact, we know that the last year ends by March 21, 1844. On March 20, 1844, if Christ has not come by then, we will know the exact day of the second coming. It must be March 21, 1844.

5. Knight, *Millennial Fever*, 203. Miller and Himes refused to endorse the October 22 date until October 6, 1844 when they capitulated to Snow. Less than eight months later Miller categorically disowned the central propositions of the midnight cry.

6. See Hale, *The Second Advent Manual*. Hale was a major Millerite spokesman.

7. Snow, "Behold, the Bridegroom Cometh," 1–4.

time began, they had been in the doldrums. From March through about July–August of 1844 they conceived of the tarrying time as a brief but indefinite period. But they had a deep yearning for a definite date. At Exeter, there were meetings that continued "nearly all night, and [were] attended with great excitement, and noise of shouting and clapping of hands, and singular gestures and exercises." Some had shouted themselves speechless. "Others had 'literally blistered their hands' through much clapping."[8] Snow was quite literally the very man which "the day and hour" demanded. He eclipsed Miller and stampeded Miller and his chief associates into reluctantly giving their belated blessing to October 22, 1844. As slavery was the cornerstone of the Confederate economy and identity, so was Snow's August 22, 1844 exposition the cornerstone of the midnight cry and its quintessential date-setting nature. This provided energy to the tornado. Yet despite Ellen Harmon's first vision, which gave her unqualified endorsement to Snow's midnight cry, *no SDA theologian has ever defended Snow's scriptural basis for the midnight cry*—because of what F. D. Nichol himself characterized as Miller's "farfetched" and "fanciful" proofs.[9]

In any case, by summer 1844 the Millerite explanation of the failed March and April 1844 dates was that a definite time for calculating the date of the second coming was yet possible; they just did not know what it was. Jesus was "tarrying" for a brief but indefinite period. *God intended for the proclamation of March 21, 1844 to fail.* In fact, Millerites would conclude that the prediction of March 21, 1844 was biblically predicted to fail. Puzzlingly, the failure of March 21, 1844 was somehow proof that God was in the 1843 message of time.

The initial disappointment of March 21, 1844 was paradoxically quite large. The Millerites had amassed such a mountain of textual evidence which they believed proved that they could predict a specific date that it was psychologically impossible to alter their thinking. After a temporary hesitation from April to July 1844, Millerites, like poker players who had just bet their entire paycheck on a losing card, doubled their bet on the new definite time, October 22, 1844.

Already by May 1842, the tentative expression "about 1843" was an obsolete euphemism. In the May 1842 Millerite General Conference, this ecclesiological authority affirmed that the Bible necessarily

8. Knight, *Millennial Fever*, 177.
9. Nichol, *Midnight Cry*, Appendix L.

taught the doctrine of definite time. It solemnly asserted that "*God has revealed the time of the end of the world and that that time is 1843.*"[10]

Ellen White endorsed Miller's first "proclamation of the time in 1843," saying:

> I saw that God was in the proclamation of the time in 1843. It was his design to arouse the people, and bring them to a testing point where they should decide.
>
> The most devoted gladly received the message. They knew it was from God, and that it was delivered at the right time. Angels were watching with the deepest interest the result of the heavenly message, and when the churches turned from and rejected it, they in sadness consulted with Jesus. He turned his face from the churches, and bid his angels to faithfully watch over the precious ones who did not reject the testimony, for another light,[11] [Snow's midnight cry of 1844], was yet to shine upon them.[12]

The "proclamation of the time in 1843" she entitled the "First Angel's Message," as chapter 23 in her book *Spiritual Gifts*.

Many of Miller's (and later Snow's) exact proofs and "figures" found their way into the legendary 1843 chart. Ellen White wrote:

> I have seen that the 1843 chart was directed by the hand of the Lord, and that it should not be altered; that the figures[13] were as He wanted them; that His hand was over and hid a mistake in some of the figures, so that none could see it, until His hand was removed.[14]

---

10. Knight, *Millennial Fever*, 128. Emphasis added.

11. Ellen G. White asserted that she saw that God was in 1) the prediction of March 21, 1844 and 2) the prediction of October 22, 1844. However, one only has her extrabiblical authority to substantiate her claim that both Miller and Crosier were directed to their conclusions by God.

12. Ellen White, *Spiritual Gifts* 1:133–36. In this chapter she makes six references to "prophetic periods" being the foundation of a "saving message."

13. Thus, God must have ordained the following chart "figures," since they all were prominently displayed on the 1843 chart: the 2,520 years of the seven times of the Gentiles; the 1,335 years; the 1,290 years; the 158 BC and 508 AD dates, which were the foundation of Miller's 666-year interval, the 1,290-year interval, and the 1335-year interval; and the 1299, 1449, and August 11, 1840 dates associated with the Muslim empires.

14. White, *Early Writings*, 74.

She also saw that Miller had divine and angelic guidance in composing his multiple proofs concerning the second coming. Ellen Harmon was convinced that William Miller was divinely guided by angels. For example, she said:

> I saw that God sent his angel to move upon the heart of a farmer who had not believed the Bible, and led him to search the prophecies. Angels of God repeatedly visited that chosen one, and guided his mind, and opened his understanding to prophecies which had ever been dark to God's people.[15]

She even likened him to three of the greatest prophets in the Bible: Elijah, Elisha, and John the Baptist. Indeed, William Miller was a modern-day John the Baptist, a pivotal personage whom Jesus said was greater than a prophet:

> As John the Baptist heralded the first advent of Jesus, and prepared the way for his coming, so also, Wm. Miller and those who joined him, proclaimed the second advent of the Son of God.[16]

She then gives a homily on how angels guided John the Revelator prior to a segue on how the same angels guided William Miller as he interpreted the Revelation of Saint John. "God led the mind of Wm. Miller into the prophecies, and gave him great light upon the book of Revelation."[17]

Thus, when Miller's fifteen proofs failed, Miller and his followers were befuddled and disappointed. Miller was bewildered and said: "Christ did not come in 1843—but I can't see where I'm wrong." J. B. Coles drew the lesson that "a certain limited year, should never have been set." And, he continued, "to continue to fix the time upon any definite point in [the future], is the consummation of folly."[18] But the majority of Millerites, still convinced of both their assumptions and their results, continued to think, like Ellen Harmon, "that God was in the proclamation of the time in 1843." Indeed, Ellen G. White, during her entire lifetime, would continue to assert that "calculation of the time was so simple and plain that even the children could understand

---

15. White, *Early Writings*, 128.
16. White, *Spiritual Gifts*, 1:133-35.
17. White, *Spiritual Gifts*, 1:131.
18. Knight, *Millennial Fever*, 171.

it." "Therefore the vision of time did not tarry, though it had seemed to do so."[19] March 21, 1844 still had prophetic significance. S. S. Snow convinced Ellen Harmon that Ezekiel 12:22; Habakkuk 2:3; Jeremiah 51:45–46; and 2 Esdras were biblical proofs that supported her lifelong belief in the tarrying of several months beginning on March 21, 1844. Ellen White endorsed Snow's interpretation of Ezekiel 12:22; Jeremiah 51:45–46; and Habakkuk 2 with these words: "With clearness they explained their mistake, and gave their reasons why they expected their Lord in 1844."[20] These reasons were biblical proofs of a new definite time, October 22, 1844. Examination of Snow's "biblical proofs" demonstrates their capricious character. Snow allegorically interpreted the three canonical texts in a seminal article arguing that Miller's failure in predicting March 21, 1844 was itself predicted in the Bible.[21] This made another date-setting prediction inevitable. The ensuing movement was called the "midnight cry." In addition to Ezekiel 12:22; Habakkuk 2; and Jeremiah 51:45–46, Snow's articles recycled several of Miller's fifteen proofs with an autumnal, Karaite modification.

Ezekiel 12:22–24 proves that "God was in" the 1843 movement

According to Snow's letter of June 27, 1844:

> It was necessary that a mistake should be made in regard to the ending of the days, and that this mistake should be general among the expectants of the kingdom, in order that their faith might be tried... Had not such a mistake been made, there are some prophecies which could never have been completely fulfilled. Such for instance as Ezek. 12:22, "Son of man, what is that proverb that ye have in the land of Israel, saying, The days are prolonged, and every vision faileth?" Also Hab. 2:2,3.[22]

19. White, *Ellen G. White: The Early Years*, 85.
20. White, *Spiritual Gifts*, 1:139.
21. Snow, "Letter from S. S. Snow," June 27, 1844.
22. Snow, "Letter from S. S. Snow," June 27, 1844. Ellen White repeated and endorsed Snow's application of this passage in Ezekiel as late as her 1884 edition of the *Great Controversy*.

Snow was asserting that Ezekiel 12:22 "could never have been completely fulfilled" without the failed prediction of March 21, 1844. But Ezekiel 12:22 contains no prophecy. Ezekiel 12:23-24 is a statement about what Yahweh is going to do about the observation of Ezekiel 12:22—namely, that in Ezekiel's time this proverb will no longer be quoted in the geographical limits of Israel. "The days are near"— not the days are two millennia in the future, in 1844—"when every vision will be fulfilled," and "they will no longer quote it in Israel."

Ezekiel 12:22 is a narrative in which Yahweh accosts Ezekiel, citing a proverb that was popular in Israel at the time. In the KJV version it states: "Son of man, what is that proverb that ye have in the land of Israel, saying, The days are prolonged, and every vision faileth?" Yahweh attacks this cynical attitude, saying: "I will make this proverb to cease, and they shall no more use it as a proverb." Ezekiel's vision specifically referred to, according to Snow, the vision of Daniel 8:14 and the March 21, 1844 date, which seemed to have come to nothing by March 22, 1844. But, contrary to Snow, within a very short period during Ezekiel's career, Yahweh intended to stamp out the Israelites' cynical proverb. It has nothing to do with a mistaken prediction of "the day" in 1844 during Snow's lifetime. Nonetheless, the Millerite paradigm was that specific events in the Millerites' 1843-1844 experience were predicted in several texts, including, most famously, Revelation 14:6-12 in addition to Ezekiel 12:22-24; Habakkuk 2; and Jeremiah 51:45-46. Indeed, the three angels' messages of Revelation 14:6-12 is the equivalent of an SDA trademark.

Yet, according to Snow's attempt to explain the delay, Ezekiel 12:22 "could never have been completely fulfilled" if Miller had not erroneously stated that March 21, 1844 was the date for the second coming. To follow Ellen Harmon's analysis, God would have had to have given divine guidance to Miller to pick the wrong date just so he could be wrong and thus fulfill prophecy—and test Millerites and their opponents.

In short, Snow implied that although the Millerites understandably were discouraged and were tempted to believe that their explanation of the vision of Daniel 8:14 had failed, in reality God was still in the 1843 movement and it would be fulfilled. The tenacity and significance of this peculiar interpretation of Ezekiel 12 as proof that God was in the 1843 movement, later defined as the first and second angels' messages of Revelation 14:6-12, is evidenced by the fact that Otis

Nichol, as late as April 20, 1846, founded his chief argument in favor of the authenticity of Ellen Harmon's visions on this interpretation of the same text. In a letter to William Miller on this date, he argued that he "fully believe[s] them [Ellen Harmon's visions] to be from heaven" because "many now say that every vision has failed. Well this is fulfilling Eze 12:22–28. That proverb has been used to perfection for a few months past in the land of Israel saying the days are prolonged and every vision faileth. But God says 'I will make this proverb to cease' with 'the effect of every vision.'" He then went on to argue that the "first vision of E. G. H. [which he enclosed]" has "had as perfect a fulfillment as could possible be . . ."[23] Ellen White herself in 1884 endorsed Snow's interpretation of this passage in Ezekiel.[24]

Immediately following his analysis of Ezekiel, Snow pivoted to Habakkuk 2, the most popular textual citation which Millerites used to prove that God was in the March 21, 1844 date-setting, "about 1843" movement. Snow, along with many others, asserted that Habakkuk 2 predicted Miller's failed prediction of March 21, 1844. However, here Snow only briefly referred to Habakkuk 2 before treating Jeremiah 51:45–46.

Jeremiah 51:45–46 means divine "light" was in both the 1843 and 1844 messages

Before discussing Snow's use of Jeremiah to explain the delay of the Second Advent, some historical and textual background regarding these two verses in Jeremiah is important. These verses come almost at the very end of Jeremiah's book after the fall of Jerusalem. They occur as part of a section from chapters 46 to 51, which is a collection of curses against the foreign nations that have oppressed Judah. These include Egypt in chapter 46; the Philistines in chapter 47; Moab in chapter 48; Ammon in 49:1–6; Edom in 49:7–22; Damascus, Arab tribes, and Elam in 49:23–39; and finally Babylon in chapters 50–51. Each of these nations will be the object of Yahweh's boiling wrath; Babylon especially will be scourged without pity. "Babylon's walls so

---

23. Otis Nichol, "Letter to Brother Miller," April 20, 1846, cited in Levterov, *Development*, 41.

24. White, *Great Controversy* (1998), 205–7.

broad shall be razed to the ground," says Yahweh.²⁵ Thus, Snow's citation from these verses mentioning that "in another year a rumor, and violence in the land, ruler against ruler," refers to the physical violence of battles involving the Babylonians of the sixth century BC.

But in Snow's interpretation, this historical *Sitz im Leben* is entirely ignored and replaced by an 1840s *Sitz im Leben*. Snow introduced his commentary with the note that the Millerites were facing an "emergency." The certainty that Christ's Second Advent would occur by March 21, 1844 had been dashed and Millerites faced an existential crisis. But he said God

> has provided for this emergency. He has not left us at this critical and trying time, without promises in his word... Of the class of passages contained in the blessed book, that are peculiarly applicable to this trying time, there is one particularly striking and encouraging in the 51st chapter of Jeremiah...²⁶

It is ironic that he stated that these verses were "peculiarly applicable to this trying time," because they have nothing to do with the 1840s. But it is revealing that Snow conceded that the Millerite interpretation was facing an "emergency," and that it was a very "trying time." The only greater emergency would occur on October 23, 1844.

Indeed, the tendered explanation for the delay after March 21, 1844 was just as critical as the proffered explanation for the delay following October 22, 1844. The assumptions and hermeneutics to face the emergency were identical in each instance. The allegorical-historicist-typological method was used on each date. A common-sense, literal method was not used.

First, Snow asserted that the phrase in Jeremiah "My people, go ye out of the midst of her" was an exact parallel to Revelation 18:4: "Come out of her my people." This phrase in Revelation 18:4, Millerites asserted, was fulfilled by Fitch's July 26, 1843 "comeouterism" sermon and the movement it provoked as Millerites split from their churches of origin. Second, he asserted that the texts in both Jeremiah and Revelation were chronologically linked to their lived experience, specifically in 1843 and 1844.

---

25. Bright, *Jeremiah*, 353.
26. Snow, "Letter from S. S. Snow," *Midnight Cry*, June 27, 1844.

To link Jeremiah 51:45–46 inextricably to the specific years of 1843 and 1844, Snow quoted it with his commentary:

> "a rumor shall both come one year, and after that there shall come in another year a rumor, and violence in the land, ruler against ruler." What is the rumor here spoken of? It is the Advent message.[27] And what is the first year of the message? It is the Jewish year 1843. And God foresaw the passing by[28] of that year of the rumor, he saw it necessary lest the hearts of his people should faint.

"One year" referred to 1843. "Another year" referred to 1844. Then "there should come another message, and in another year, after the first." Therefore, "the periods could not terminate before the seventh month of the Jewish sacred year in A. D. 1844."[29] Thus, the Jeremiah passage referring to events regarding Babylon in Jeremiah's time was wrested out of context, brought forward over two millennia, and marshalled in favor of an exact year and season for the second coming: autumn 1844.[30] Snow's bald assertion that "one year" referred to 1843 and that "another year" referred to 1844 was entirely without contextual or historical basis.

The reliance on Ezekiel 12:22–24 and Jeremiah 51:45–46 was far surpassed by Millerite reliance of Habakkuk 2 in explaining the failure of their March 21, 1844 prediction of the second coming. No more than two weeks after this failed date, an April 13, 1844 edition of *The Western Midnight Cry!!!* cited Habakkuk 2:3 as the textual basis to explain the delay of the Second Advent.[31] But instrumentalization of Habakkuk 2:3 was merely the most recent example of century upon century of continuous-historical proofs as illustrated by Miller's fifteen proofs.[32] Miller's methodology presumed that the Bible con-

---

27. Snow's assertion that "the Advent message" was the "rumor" is an assertion without any textual or historical basis.

28. "Passing by" of the year 1843 is a euphemism for the failed prediction of March 21, 1844.

29. The "periods" refer to the 1,335-year period, the 2,300-year period, the 2,450-year period, the 2,000-year periods, and the 2,520-year period, which Miller and Snow asserted would all end on October 22, 1844.

30. S. S. Snow, "Letter from S. S. Snow," June 27, 1844.

31. Jacobs, "If the Vision Tarry," 33–40.

32. See Firth, *Apocalyptic Tradition* for multiple examples of failed historicist predictions and identities from 1530 to 1645.

tained a series of unbroken, continuous historical sequences, right up until the first and second angels' messages of Revelation 14:6–12, which purportedly were fulfilled in the 1840s. Thus, the "vision" that "tarried" was simply the latest exact prediction that set on the pinnacle of the mountain of Miller's fifteen proofs, stretching exactly six thousand years from creation in 4157 BC to 1843/1844.

Thus, there could be no doubt that the vision that "tarried" had to occur precisely after March 21, 1844. God, they said, is an "exact" timekeeper."[33] Thus, ironically, the Millerites claimed that the very failure of their prediction that March 21, 1844 would be the end of the world was foreseen and predicted in Habakkuk 2:3.[34] This apologetic *modus operandi* remained universal in the exegetical universe of Millerism even after the Great Disappointment, most notably in the allegorical interpretation of the Bridegroom Parable in Matthew 25. But as Miller paradoxically noted, "Men often explain parables by fancy, to suit their own notions, without any evidence but their own ingenuity; and by this means there will be as many different explanations as there are ingenious mean."[35] Two of Crosier's major proofs or "great signs" that the Bridegroom Parable was a description/prediction of the Millerite movement were the tarrying time which began on March 21, 1844 and the midnight cry of July–August 1844. In 1847 the newly wedded Ellen G. White became convinced that God showed her that

---

33. Arasola, *End of Historicism*, 151, 157. Before and after October 22, 1844 Millerites like James White and Josiah Litch employed their continuous-historical method in calculating exact times, even including fractions of prophetic day-years. For example, the "hour" in Revelation 9 was calculated to be exactly fifteen historical days to arrive at August 11, 1840 for the fall of the Ottoman Empire. Even parables were "historicized" mathematically. Thus, the famous midnight of the midnight cry was calculated to be three historical months, lasting from July/August 1844 to October 22, 1844 on the hypothesis that the nighttime portion of a prophetic day-year must be six months and therefore midway through the six months of night would be midnight. After October 22, 1844 James White made mathematical calculations based on the four watches of the night and determined that Jesus would certainly come by October 1845.

34. E. G. White cited this text multiple times throughout her life as an explanation for the delay. It continues to be central in SDA chronological theology.

35. Miller, *Evidence* (1842), 142. Crosier was merely repeating Miller, but on this same page Miller also said: "But if we apply the parable wrong, if we put on a false construction, it will serve to lead us into an error, and blind us, instead of producing light..."

O. R. L. Crosier received "the true light" regarding an extended, two-chambered, two-phased atonement.

> The Lord shew me in vision, more than one year ago, that Brother Crosier had the true light, on the cleansing of the Sanctuary, &c; and that it was his will, that Brother C. should write out the view which he gave us in the *Day-Star, Extra*, February 7, 1846.[36]

Ellen G. White's endorsement of Crosier's "true light" virtually ensured the immortality of both his treatment of the tarrying time and his conception of an extended atonement.

Habakkuk 2:3 says: "For the vision is yet for an appointed time, but at the end it shall speak, and not lie: though it tarry wait for it; because IT WILL SURELY COME, it will not tarry." This bold, capitalized declaration was the subtitle for an article in the April 13, 1844 edition of *The Western Midnight Cry!!!* whose title was "IF THE VISION TARRY, WAIT FOR IT."[37] Ellen G. White characterized the interval between March 21, 1844 and the midnight cry of July–August 1844 as merely an "apparent" tarrying of the vision—"apparent" signifying that the tarrying delay was not genuine but merely a problem of perspective.[38] "Therefore, the vision of time [Daniel 8:14] did not tarry, though it had seemed to do so," wrote EGW.[39] God's exact timepiece was still meticulously precise.

---

36. James White, "Word to the 'Little Flock'" (1847), 12.

37. Jacobs, "If the Vision Tarry," 33–40. This article is conveniently accessible at http://watchtowerdocuments.org/documents/1844_Western_Midnight_Cry_vol_3.pdf.

38. In *Testimonies*, 1:53 Ellen G. White recounted: "In the joyful expectation of the coming of Christ the apparent tarrying of the vision had not been taken into account, and was a sad and unlooked-for surprise. Yet this very trial was necessary to develop and strengthen the sincere believers in the truth. Our hopes now centered on the coming of the Lord in 1844. This was also the time for the message of the second angel, who, flying through the midst of heaven, cried: 'Babylon is fallen, is fallen, that great city.' That message was first proclaimed by the servants of God in the summer of 1844."

39 White, *Testimonies*, 1:52.

Habakkuk 2:3's vision was Habakkuk 1:1 Vision, not Daniel's vision seventy-seven years later

Ellen Harmon asserted that the tarrying vision referred to in Habakkuk 2:3 was the vision of Daniel 8:13-14.[40] In identical fashion to Crosier's apology of March 1845, Ellen White claimed to have "signs which could not be mistaken."[41] She did not specify exactly what signs she was referring to, but doubtless these were the same signs that Crosier referred to. Crosier referred specifically to two "great signs": 1) the failed March 21, 1844 prediction, or tarrying time, and 2) the failed midnight-cry prediction of October 22, 1844. That two stunning failures could be transformed into two "great signs" is remarkable. He also counted the Dark Day of 1780 and meteorite shower of 1833 as "signs which could not be mistaken."[42] The Millerite conflation of the "vision" of Daniel 8:14 with the "vision" of Habakkuk 2:3 was inevitable. Their concordance told them that the word "vision" occurred in both Daniel and Habakkuk, but it could not inform them about actual history. This fact highlights a fatal flaw in historicism. The vision of Habakkuk 2 cannot be the vision of Daniel 8. This is impossible

---

40. This is a prime example of bibliomancy and concordancomancy wherein any occurrence of "vision" is conflated with any other occurrence of "vision" regardless of historical or linguistic context.

41. The 1884 (1998 reissue) *Great Controversy* version stated: "As early as 1842, the Spirit of God had moved upon Charles Fitch to devise the prophetic chart, which was generally regarded by Adventists as a fulfillment of the command given by the prophet Habakkuk, 'to write the vision and make it plain upon tables.'" See White, *Great Controversy* (1884/1998), 205-7. The 1888 version weakened this to: "As early as 1842, the direction given in this prophecy, to 'write the vision, and make it plain upon tables that he may run that readeth it,' had suggested to Charles Fitch the preparation of a prophetic chart to illustrate the visions of Daniel and the Revelation." The 1884 edition *categorically* states that "the Spirit of Go had moved upon Charles Fitch to devise the prophetic chart..." The "Spirit of God" is the active subject in a declarative sentence in which Charles Fitch is the direct object. In the 1888 edition Fitch's perusal of Habakkuk "suggested" to him that he devise a chart. Thus, in addition to ascribing divine/angelic inspiration to William Miller, S. S. Snow, and O. R. L. Crosier, Ellen G. White also attributed *divine causation* to the fact that Charles Fitch devised the 1843 chart. He also preached the famous "Come Out of Babylon" message, which Ellen Harmon firmly believed. Probably, this is why Ellen G. White saw only Charles Fitch and Elder Stockman in heaven during her first vision. The 1884/1998 version can be found at http://www.great-controversy.org/Whole-GCspdf/GC84-all.pdf. Thus, the 1843 chart fulfilled Habakkuk 2 in being written, while the failure of Christ's Second Advent to come by March 21, 1844 was further fulfillment.

42. Burt, "Day-Dawn of Canandaigua," 317-30.

chronologically. An online version of the *SDA Bible Commentary* on Habakkuk dates it to 630 BC. Daniel's vision was non-existent when Habakkuk wrote. According to the earliest dating of Daniel 7:1, "the first year of Belshazzar" was about 553 BC.[43] So, Habakkuk's vision preceded Daniel's vision of chapter 8 by approximately 77 years (630 to 553 = 77 years). Further, a common-sense, literal, contextual reading of Habakkuk shows that the "vision" of Habakkuk 2 refers to the "vision" of Habakkuk 1:1.

Habakkuk 1:1 begins: "The burden, [oracle, vision, or prophecy], which Habakkuk the prophet did see." The vision which "is yet for an appointed time," mentioned in Habakkuk 2:3, is the vision preceding it in Habakkuk 1:1. Certainly not the vision of Daniel 8, since Daniel had not even been born yet. In the verses prior to Habakkuk 2:3, the prophet dialogues with God complaining and asking: how long must he cry before God listens? How long will God allow oppression and injustice to prevail? Why do the wicked triumph over the upright? God answers that it is he who has stirred up the Chaldaeans (Nebuchadnezzar) to lay siege to Jerusalem (1:6). Then Yahweh goes on to describe the military prowess and ruthlessness of the Chaldaeans (1:5–11). The prophet complains once again and awaits an answer (2:1). At this point God answers, ordering Habakkuk to write down the vision mentioned by 1:1. Yahweh assures Habakkuk that the events that he has described in the vision concerning the Chaldaeans (1:5–11) will be fulfilled quickly—without delay. Yahweh's prediction concerning the Chaldaeans is the vision describing them that will not tarry.

Nonetheless, Millerites asserted that the vision referred to in Habakkuk 2:3 was the vision of Daniel 8:13–14. Asserted Jacobs in typical categorical language:

> The language *unquestionably* [emphasis added] settles the character of the vision, to be identical with that of Daniel 7:9–11, 26, 27, who also gives the "appointed time" referred to in the text. Dan. 8:13,14.[44]

Originally, the Millerites were certain Daniel 8:14 predicted the end of the world by March 21, 1844. Now, they inserted a very brief tarrying time prior to the end. Furthermore, they believed that

---

43. Hartman and Di Lella, *Book of Daniel*, 211.
44. Jacobs, "If the Vision Tarry," 33.

Habakkuk 2:3's vision could only refer to a time thousands of years after Habakkuk's lifetime, specifically only after 1798, when "the Papal power is clearly brought to view." Therefore, Habakkuk 2:3, in their opinion referred to a period between 1798 to 1843. The April 13, 1844 article in *The Western Midnight Cry!!!* gave another unique reason why Habakkuk 2 could not be fulfilled until the 1840s. This was the assertion that Habakkuk 2:15 refers to a "species of 'drunkenness'" "that is peculiar to the present, and two or three of the past generations." Namely, "it [alcohol] is carried in 'bottles,' and people 'made drunken' with it."[45] Since they expected the 2,300 days of Daniel 8:14 to terminate on March 21, 1844, they asserted that:

> The expression, "Though it tarry," supposes time beyond the period when it would be expected to terminate [March 1844]. It however supposes nothing more than a slight error on the part of the expectants, when taken in connexion with the declaration, "IT WILL NOT TARRY."[46]

They imagined that God intended that they should predict that the vision of Daniel 8:14 was to end on March 21, 1844 for the express purpose that such a prediction was predicted to fail. This was to test them to see if they could "wait for it."

Failure of March 21, 1844 prediction = fulfillment of Habakkuk 2 prediction

Thus, the very failure of their prediction that March 21, 1844 would be the end of the world was foreseen and predicted in Habakkuk. Moreover, the text reassured them that there had only been a "slight error on the part of the expectants." Therefore, they assured themselves that their continuous-historical approach was still correct. The prophet Habakkuk was addressing the very doubts of 1844 Millerites in Jacob's imagination.

---

45. Jacobs, "If the Vision Tarry," 33. It is unclear what modern aspect of alcohol this is referring to. Distillation of alcohol was unknown in biblical times. Perhaps this refers to the higher percentage of alcohol that was possible to achieve with advanced distillation techniques. The beer or wine known in biblical times had a low percentage of alcohol and one had to drink a much greater volume to become drunk compared to highly distilled hard liquors of the 1800s.

46. Jacobs, "If the Vision Tarry," 33–40.

> The prophet seems to be solving the doubts[47] that would naturally rise with those who should see "the appointed time." What if, after all the clearness with which the time of the termination of the vision presents itself to my mind the expected period should finally pass by? The answer is, WRITE IT, and make it plain. But Lord, I am a frail erring mortal and I only came upon the watchtower to get instruction relative to the plain practical duties of religion. I pray thee let me be content with these; for after all, the vision may be involved in mystery. Still the answer is, write it, for it "is for an appointed time,"—he can get no other answer. But Lord, if thy word show "the time of the end," it will be wrong for me to encourage any one that it will last a moment longer. If there should be any error in consequence of my misapprehension, "what shall I answer if reproved" for the definiteness with which I must have proclaimed the "appointed time?" Continue to write it, and if it tarry, wait for it. The error can be but small, as it is to be unsealed by divine appointment.[48]

In this imagined dialogue between a doubting Millerite and an imperative God, the chagrined Millerite is reinvigorated to reassert the "definiteness" of his proclamation. All reservations are to be brushed aside with the prophetic proof that God was in the proclamation despite a "slight" error. This reading of Habakkuk is buttressed with the bald assertion that the saying "the days are prolonged, and EVERY vision faileth" never had such appropriate application in the entire history of the people of God.

One of the outstanding aspects of many of the Millerite apologists' writings is what is colloquially expressed as "whistling loudly while walking past the graveyard." Often, they asserted their faith in such a non-negotiable way with such ostentatious certainty that one thinks they "protest too much." Within less than a week before October 22, 1844, George Storrs, for example, wrote an article insisting that it was "Beyond a doubt" that Christ would arrive *within a few days.* Every paragraph is full of such expressions insisting that "God has given us the year as well as the *month and day* [emphasis added] in which our Great High Priest will come forth, and the Trump of

---

47. The Millerite struggle with doubt was repeatedly denied and repressed by emphasizing the certainty that they had about their dogma of definite time.

48. Jacobs, "If the Vision Tarry," 33–40.

Jubilee will sound."⁴⁹ This even though so many of the most well-known Millerite preachers had just recently protested that they would never make such a preposterous claim as to know the "month and day."

> The end of time has been proclaimed, and the vision has been pointed to as our authority. The time generally looked to, for its termination has but recently passed by, and *never, till within the few past weeks*, has this scripture been fulfilled [emphasis added]. ALL your times have now gone by. EVERY vision faileth."⁵⁰

To paraphrase, only in the last few weeks of 1844 did their predicted day fail, thus fulfilling the scripture that "ALL [the Millerite] times have now gone by." The author goes on to reassure wavering Millerites that: "For yet a LITTLE WHILE, and he that shall come will come, and will not tarry. If he came within the limits of the time generally expected, by those that looked for him, Where would be the tarry? There is to be a little while of tarrying, but at the same time, no tarrying beyond the true time 'appointed,' for he 'shall come.'"⁵¹ In other words, Miller's prediction of March 21, 1844 had to have failed—in order for the Bible to be true. Otherwise, "Where would be the tarry?"⁵²

Ellen Harmon's affinity for 2 Esdras because it had a hastening vision also

In addition to the three canonical passages which justified and explained the delay of the second coming, Millerites also utilized the pseudepigraphal 2 Esdras to fortify their apology.

Millerite interpretation of Habakkuk 2 was as precious as water in the Sahara to them. The fact that 2 Esdras had a key phrase

---

49. Storrs, "'Go Ye Out to Meet Him,'" October 16, 1844.

50. Jacobs, "If the Vision Tarry," 33–40. In other words, only since March 21, 1844 did the "time generally looked to" for the end of the world get "passed by." March 22, 1844 to April 13, 1844, when Jacobs wrote these words, constituted the "past few weeks." Paradoxically, only after March 21, 1844 was the predicted failure of the "end of time" proclamation considered fulfilled prophecy.

51. Jacobs, "If the Vision Tarry," 33–40.

52. Jacobs, "If the Vision Tarry," 33–40.

identical to Habakkuk 2 explains why 2 Esdras was so popular with Ellen Harmon and the Millerites. In the same April 13, 1844 edition of *The Western Midnight Cry!!!*, 2 Esdras is quoted to precisely the same effect: "'For now hasteth[53] the vision to come.' Esdras." This was the punchline for three extracts from Esdras included in this number. The first (immediately below) is entitled simply "Extract."

> Let go from the mortal thoughts, cast away the burdens of man, put off now the weak nature, and set aside the thoughts that are most heavy unto thee,[54] and flee from these times; for yet greater evils than those which thou hast seen happen, shall be done hereafter, for look how much the world shall be weaker through age, so much the more shall evils increase upon them that dwell therein, for the truth is fled far away, and learning is hard at hand, for *now hasteth the vision to come*.[55]

Quite significantly, the second extract is entitled "A Glimpse of Paradise." This was the place that they all imagined they would inhabit by April 1844. This was their new heavenly home "within the veil" that Ellen Harmon described in her first vision. And perhaps reading this passage in Millerite literature as well as in her 1822 KJV family Bible was what determined the fact that it was this precise passage that Ellen Harmon paraphrased to describe what she saw in her tour of paradise (2 Esdras 2:19).[56]

> I have sanctified and prepared for thee twelve trees laden with divers fruits and as many fountains flowing with milk and honey, and seven mighty mountains whereupon there grow roses and lilies, whereby I will fill thy children with joy. ESDRAS.[57]

"Extract from Esdras" is the title given to the third citation of 2 Esdras, one following immediately after the other with bold titles

---

53. Miller's concordance method is indiscriminately employed. Any occurrence of a vision which "hasteth" is said to be the same as a vision in any verse of the Bible. Not only do Millerites say that the vision in Daniel is the same as the vision in Habakkuk, they also say that both visions are the same as the Esdras vision.

54. The discouraging thoughts that their prediction of March 21, 1844 for the second coming failed.

55. Jacobs, "Extract [of 2 Esdras]," 33–40. Emphasis added.

56. Casebolt, "'It Was Not Taught Me by Man,'" 66–73.

57. Jacobs, "Glimpse of Paradise," 33–40.

breaking the flow of text.[58] Millerites learned from the pseudepigraphal 2 Esdras just like they learned from Habakkuk that their "everlasting rest" was "nigh at hand."

> Look for your Shepherd, he shall give you everlasting rest, for he is nigh at hand, that shall come in the end of the world. Be ready to the reward of the kingdom, for the everlasting light shall shine upon you for evermore. [59]
>
> Adds the editor: "How beautiful and appropriate is this prophetic[60] exhortation to the Advent children who are now looking in the end of the world for him who shall come. How important that we should flee the shadow of the world, seek of the Lord the glorious garments of holiness, and be of the number of those who are sealed,[61] that we may receive the joyfulness of this hope, and be ready to the reward of the everlasting kingdom."[62]

The essence of the continuous-historical interpretation is that it presumes multiple specific historical dates/events can be unambiguously linked with specific texts. It is on this basis that the three angels of Revelation 14:6–10 were assigned specific historical periods.[63] The entire suite of precise dates in the Apocalypse's churches, trumpets, seals, vials, and the exact periods of 1,260 years, 1,290 years, 1,335 years, 391 years, 150 years, etc. were are founded on the same assumption and specific one-to-one links. The dates in the 1840s for both the tarrying time of Habakkuk 2 and the three angels of Revelation 14:6–12 were clones of this methodology.

---

58. The Millerite esteem for Esdras was also documented by Jacobs, "Tour to New York", 89–96: He added: "Take a little advice from Esdras. Be not curious to know how and when the wicked are punished, but be more curious to know how and when the righteous are rewarded."

59. Jacobs, "Extract [of 2 Esdras]," 33–40.

60. Note how the editor, like Ellen Harmon, James White, and Joseph Bates, considered 2 Esdras to be a scriptural prophet.

61. The "sealing" would soon become a critical element in Ellen Harmon's eschatology, closely associated with the mark of the Beast and the Sabbath.

62. Jacobs, "Extract [of 2 Esdras]," 33–40.

63. According to the White/Nichols 1851 chart, the first angel began in 1837, the second angel in 1843, and the third angel in 1844—even though Ellen and James White did not themselves begin to observe the Sabbath until fall or winter of 1846. See chapter 11 for more details.

Three angels exactly predicted for the 1840s by an "exact timekeeper"

According to the sequential interpretation that Joseph Bates, James White, and Ellen Harmon read into Revelation 14:6–12, the "first angel (verses 6, 7) announces 'the everlasting gospel at the hour of God's judgment. This without any doubt represents all those who were preaching the second Advent doctrine since 1840.' Thus, the first angel symbolizes the Millerite movement."[64] According to Ellen G. White, the second angel (verse 8) was precisely fulfilled in the "summer of 1844."[65] The third angel of verses 9–11 took place "at Midnight in the fall of 1844," according to Bates's original calculation. Then Bates, James White, and Ellen White, upon Bates's becoming a Sabbatarian, recalculated. The "preaching of Revelation 14:12 did not begin until after October 1844," when the three cofounders of the SDA church became "Sabbath and shut door" believers.[66]

Rev 14:6–7	= first angel, Millerite movement in 1830/1840s
Rev 14:8	= second angel, "summer of 1844" (EGW)[67]
Rev 14:9–12	= third angel, October 22, 1844–2022
Hab 2	= tarrying time, March 21, 1844 to August 1844
Matt 25[68]	= midnight cry, August 1844 to October 22, 1844

Ellen Harmon adopted the presumptions of Millerism at the tender age of twelve when she had just been forced to drop out of school for a second time because her central nervous system was

---

64. Knight, *Millennial Fever*, 113–14.

65 White, *Testimonies*, 1:53.

66. Knight, *Millennial Fever*, 113–14. The Whites adopted Sabbath about August or September 1846.

67. Knight, *Millennial Fever*, 153–54, points out that July 26, 1843, when Charles Fitch preached the "most famous [of] Millerite sermons"—"Come Out of Her My People"—would be a more precise date. Although Millerites like Ellen White asserted that there were exact dates for these three angels, they proposed a number of contradictory dates.

68. Burt, "Day-Dawn of Canandaigua," 317–30 gives considerable detail on how O. R. L. Crosier historicized the Parable of the Bridegroom and the Ten Virgins into four discrete historical segments which he considered fulfilled by events in the Millerite movement of the 1840s.

"shattered." [69] According to Damsteegt, White believed that "God directed the mind of William Miller to the prophecies and gave him great light upon the book of Revelation." She wrote that she saw that "angels of God repeatedly visited that chosen one, to guide his mind and open to his understanding prophecies which had ever been dark to God's people."[70] Therefore, "she strongly recommended the use of his principles of interpretation (GC 320), 'searching the Scriptures upon the same plan that Father Miller adopted,' (RH, Nov. 25, 1884)."[71] Damsteegt is among those SDAs who are adamant that Miller's allegorical-typological-historicist method *must* continue to be used. They fail to see that Miller (and White) did not use a literal, common-sense method. Therefore, they are inextricably wed to his "farfetched" interpretations even though as certain events and dates fade into a distant past, such fulfillments become more and more unbelievable. They recognize that Ellen White's eschatology depended on Miller's use of this method, and they are unwilling to concede that Miller was mistaken. Why? Because Ellen White said he had divine guidance.

Thus, Damsteegt confirms that White used Miller's method. White's strong recommendation to use Miller's rules of interpretation constitutes a corporate straitjacket on SDA hermeneutics. But can Miller's principle of a prophetic day = a thousand years really be taken seriously?

As has been demonstrated, the "plan that Father Miller adopted" resulted in the fact that many of his fifteen "proofs" were characterized by F. D. Nichol, the dean of SDA apologists, as "farfetched" and "fanciful."[72] Nichol, who wrote the classic defense *The Midnight Cry*, concluded that these "so-called proofs that 1843 was the climax year of prophecy are plainly fanciful." He also characterized them as "begging the question" and "hoary with age." Moreover, he went on to say:

> In fact, we are tempted to believe there was a [good] deal of truth to the charge of some of his opponents that after Miller had decided on 1843 as a result of his study of the 2300-day prophecy, he worked backward from that date to secure

---

69. Casebolt, *Child of the Apocalypse*. White, *Life Sketches*, 26.
70. White, *Early Writings*, 229–31.
71. Damsteegt, "Prophetic Interpretation," 1061–63.
72. Nichol, *Midnight Cry*, Appendix L.

certain of the dates that he employed as the starting point of some of the secondary lines of proof.[73]

His candidly unguarded and therefore especially reliable characterization of these proofs has great weight.

For almost two centuries, SDA apologists have spent virtually all their energies in explaining the Great Disappointment while the disappointment of March 21, 1844 has suffered from inadvertent neglect. Even critics of unique SDA dogma, like Desmond Ford, focus almost exclusively on October 22, 1844 and Daniel 8:14[74] Yet the explanation for the failure of the first predicted date of the second coming set a *monumental and fateful precedent* for the explanation of the failure of the second predicted date of the second coming.[75]

Ironically, S. S. Snow's tarrying-time explanation for the failed March 21, 1844 date inevitably caused an even more catastrophic disappointment on October 22, 1844. Whereas Miller's original formulation maintained a fig leaf of ambiguity in its "about 1843" form, S. S. Snow unabashedly championed a literal "exact" day and hour, which swept the entire Millerite movement like a tornado.

The same "method" was used by Millerites in explaining the tarrying as would be used by Ellen White to explain the Great Disappointment. Even after the Great Disappointment, the eventual cofounders of the SDA church, Joseph Bates and the Whites, continued to assume that "the day" was still imminent and could be calculated. James White calculated that since the Bible referred to the night having four watches, he could historicize the four watches of the night. He figured that the fourth watch would end in the autumn of 1845 and the second coming would occur about October 22, 1845.[76] One can observe in granular detail the excesses of such a method from 1844 to 1849 in Burt's dissertation[77] and in O. R. L. Crosier's March 1845 article regarding an extended judgment.[78] The fundamental flaw

---

73. Nichol, *Midnight Cry*, 507–10.

74. Ford, *Daniel 8:14*.

75. Technically, the 1839–1840 prediction of the collapse of the Ottoman Empire, simultaneously with the first resurrection, the second coming, and third woe was the first of Miller's failed shut-door events. March 21, 1844 and October 22, 1844 were the second and third failed predictions of the second coming.

76. James White, "Watchman," 25–26.

77. Burt, *Historical Background*.

78. Burt, "Day-Dawn of Canandaigua," 317–30.

in the paradigm which was the cornerstone of their approach was in presuming that the Bible was designed to provide exact mathematical calculations. A mathematical, scientific, literal reading of Scripture is a post-Enlightenment fixation. Both Catholic and Reformation churches made a fundamental error in evaluating the findings of Galileo, Copernicus, and Kepler. Scripture never intended to inerrantly teach a geocentric, geostatic theory of the solar system. Just so, it is highly dubious that Scripture ever intended to supply multiple, exact mathematical proofs culminating in specific dates for either the second coming or an invisible movement from a heavenly holy to most holy place in initiating an extended atonement. Ellen G. White insisted that Snow's exact date was correct while the predicted event was erroneous. The thrice-repeated error in the predicted date was repeatedly explained as God testing the faithful. This seems very unlikely. Because what could be the point of fifteen mathematical biblical proofs predicting an invisible and unverifiable movement from the holy place into the most holy place?

By clutching with a death grip to a traditional, "literal" reading of the Bible to sustain a geocentric solar system, the Catholic and Reformation churches inflicted a "deadly wound" on biblical authority. Similarly, fighting a desperate rearguard action attempting to reinforce the crumbling historical and textual foundations of the traditional allegorical-typological-historicist interpretations, given the capricious and skewed eisegesis of Father Miller and S. S. Snow, is a losing effort.

First, in March 1840, twelve-year-old Ellen Harmon's judgment was that God inspired Miller's calculations that March 21, 1844 was the very day of the second coming. Second, when this failed, she became convinced on the basis of Snow's exegesis of Ezekiel 12:22; Habakkuk 2; and Jeremiah 51:45–46 that a tarrying time explained the delay. Third, Snow's midnight cry convinced her that October 22, 1844 was the very day of the second coming. William Miller could never quite comprehend how he could have been wrong in making such predictions, but by the summer of 1845 he wrote a categorial repudiation—Miller renouncing Millerism.

> I have no confidence in any of the new theories that have grown out of the [seventh-month][79] movement, viz., that

---

79. The label "seventh-month movement" was a synonym of the midnight cry,

Christ came as the Bridegroom, that the door of mercy was closed, ... or that it was a fulfillment of prophecy in any sense.[80]

If one proceeds on the basis of *sola Scriptura* and analyzes the original "founding SDA fathers'" documents' treatment of Ezekiel 12:22; Habakkuk 2; and Jeremiah 51:45–46, one is constrained to conclude that they, including Ellen Harmon, were mistaken. There is no intelligible biblical evidence to support either their presuppositions or their results. One is left with only the extra-biblical pronouncements of Ellen G. White that Miller, O. R. L. Crosier, and S. S. Snow received "the true light" regarding both the tarrying time and the midnight cry.

Summary of tarrying in Habakkuk, Ezekiel, and Jeremiah

For several years Miller had proclaimed that the world would end "about 1843." As 1843 approached, he settled on a more "definite time." He asserted that the last day of 1843 according to Jewish reckoning was March 21, 1844 and that the second coming would occur by then. Miller's fifteen proofs not only failed historically; *Miller did not employ a commonsense, literal methodology as is traditionally claimed.* When Miller's calculations were disconfirmed, S. S. Snow reinterpreted the allegorical-historicist-typological method with more (Karaite) precision. According to the allegorical-typological-historicist method employed by Snow, Ezekiel 12:22; Habakkuk 2; and Jeremiah 51:45–46 proved that Christ would come exactly on October 22, 1844. Like Miller, Snow did not use a literal, plain, commonsense method of interpreting Scripture. When the historicist-typological-allegorical method failed for the third time, an even greater existential crisis shattered the Millerite community. But this time, rather than turning on external foes and anathematizing them as Babylon, a civil war broke out between shut-door Millerites and open-door Millerites. But they both *shared* a commitment to apply the allegorical-historicist-typological method to explain the delay of the second coming. This can be observed in the written polemics exchanged between the two

---

so-called because the Jewish Day of Atonement fell in the seventh month of their calendar.

80. Knight, *Millennial Fever*, 241–42.

factions between 1845 and 1851. Ellen G. White expressly advised her husband to republish articles written by "first-day Adventist 'shepherds' [who] had rejected the first two angels' messages, which, prior to 1844, had been central to their very identity." She said: "I saw the [false]shepherds would soon be fed with judgment."[81] Chief among the false shepherds was William Miller, who said:

> I have no confidence in any of the new theories that have grown out of the [seventh-month] movement, viz., that Christ came as the Bridegroom, that the door of mercy was closed, ... or that it was a fulfillment of prophecy in any sense.[82]

His statement typified the position of the open-door Adventists. On the other hand, Ellen White's August 4, 1850 statement typified the position and tactics of the shut-door Adventists:

> The Lord showed me that he, James Springer White, must take the testimonies that the leading Adventists published in 1844 and republish them and make them ashamed.[83]

Ellen G. White could be contrasted to Miller and paraphrased thusly: I have the greatest confidence in the new theories grown out of the Midnight Cry, viz., that Christ did come as the Bridegroom, that the door of mercy definitely closed, and it was a perfect fulfillment of prophecy in every sense.

---

81. See White, *Ellen G. White Letters & Manuscripts*, 190–91. Roland Karlman, the annotator of this collection of *Letters & Manuscripts*, explains in a footnote: "As James White expressed it, these Adventists now refused 'to acknowledge that the great leading movements in our past experience, such as the proclamation of 1843, the fall of the churches or Babylon, and the midnight cry in 1844, were the work of God, and a perfect fulfilment of his pure word."

82. Knight, *Millennial Fever*, 241–42.

83. White, *Ellen G. White Letters & Manuscripts*, 211.

VII

Crosier's Extended Atonement

Actual historical Millerite/SDA hermeneutic versus current apologetics

"Men often explain parables by fancy, to suit their own notions, without any evidence but their own ingenuity; and by this means there will be as many different explanations as there are ingenious mean.[1]

WILLIAM MILLER, *EVIDENCE* (1842), 142

ELLEN G. WHITE'S ENDORSEMENT of William Miller's "about 1843" and S. S. Snow's "definite" midnight cry was continued in her endorsement of O. R. L. Crosier and Turner. Ellen G. White had anointed William Miller with a status approaching John the Baptist. In 1847 she anointed O. R. L. Crosier with something very nearly approaching special revelation.

> The Lord shew me in vision, more than one year ago, that Brother Crosier had the true light, on the cleansing of the

---

1. It is deeply ironic that Miller was completely oblivious to how this epigraph applied so wondrously well to himself. On the same page Miller also said: "But if we apply the parable wrong, if we put on a false construction, it will serve to lead us into an error, and blind us, instead of producing light . . ."

Sanctuary, &c; and that it was his will, that Brother C. should write out the view which he gave us in the *Day-Star, Extra,* February 7, 1846.[2]

Historically, what was the biblical basis for Ellen G. White's assertion that God was in the date-setting midnight-cry assertions of the Miller and Snow? These Millerite leaders proclaimed that the midnight cry was predicted by an allegorical/chronological paradigm applied to the Parable of the Bridegroom of Matthew 25. The midnight cry was an allegorical fulfillment of Matthew 25. When Matthew 25's "prophecy" failed, Ellen G. White asserted that the Bridegroom Parable of Matthew 25 was still a prophecy; it simply needed to be reinterpreted. Crosier fulfilled this function. According to Crosier, it still contained a detailed chronology of the 1840s, especially the years 1843-1845. Echoing Crosier, Ellen Harmon also asserted that Matthew 25 contained a detailed chronological history of the Millerite movement and its post-Disappointment aftermath. Her prophetic authority imprinted this on her nascent movement.

On February 7, 1846 O. R. L. Crosier explained the failure of the October 22, 1844 date by a complicated schematic of an extended atonement, which he believed started on October 22, 1844 and reached to the millennium.[3] This was an extended development of concepts and proofs he initially published in March 1845. No extant version of this earlier, original document was known to contemporary scholarship until Merlin Burt discovered a copy in April 1995.[4] Crosier's core idea was that Christ's coming had two phases: 1) coming as High Priest and 2) coming as King. He hypothesized that Christ had indeed come on October 22, 1844 but only *invisibly* as High Priest. He would come *visibly* as King within a couple of months or years in phase two. Crosier initially thought this would occur in 1847. Crosier also expressed this two-phased coming in other symbols. For example, he hypothesized that Christ came as bridegroom to the marriage, but this marriage had two chronological phases: 1) an *invisible* marriage ceremony in heaven on October 22, 1844, followed by 2) a *visible* marriage feast, the second coming, on earth, "soon." Similarly, a two-phased, two-chambered sanctuary ministry was proposed. Ellen

2. James White, "Word to the 'Little Flock,'" 12.
3. Crosier, "Law of Moses," 37-44.
4. Burt, "Day-Dawn of Canandaigua," 317-30.

G. White contended that the ascended Christ remained restricted to the holy place until October 22, 1844. He then moved into the most holy place afterwards.

Historicized parable with multiple exact chronological markers?

With typical Millerite certainty regarding dates, Crosier summed up his explanation of the delay thusly:[5] "There in Mat. 25.10 is the chronology of the marriage or setting up of the kingdom *clear as noonday*..."[6] O. R. L. Crosier built his extended-atonement edifice on the methodological presumption that the Parable of the Ten Virgins of Matthew 25 was designed to contain a "chronology of four important events, viz: (1) The Tarrying time, (2) The midnight cry, (3) The marriage, and (4) shutting of the door..."[7]

As Burt notes, Crosier's "exposition of the earthly and heavenly sanctuaries became a *major foundation* of Seventh-day Adventist theology."[8] Because Ellen G. White's endorsement of Crosier's exposition made it foundational to SDA identity and ideology, it is critical to examine the allegorical-typological-historicist details of Crosier's eisegesis.

His interpretation was founded on a minutely detailed historicization or allegorical interpretation of the parable of Matthew 25. He was persuaded that the date-setting failures of March 21, 1844 and October 22, 1844 could be explained by applying a four-part chronology to the parable of Matthew 25. Ironically, the *two failed predictions* were transformed into what Crosier labeled *two "great signs."*

The Achilles' heel of this mode of argumentation is simply put: there is no warrant for presuming that any parable was intended to provide a chronological history. All current reference works on the proper exegesis of Christ's parables confirm this assertion. For example, one conservative theologian, Mark L. Bailey, wrote an article entitled "Guidelines for Interpreting Jesus' Parables," in which

---

5. Crosier and Hahn, reprint of 1845 *Day-Dawn* issue published on last page of *Ontario Messenger*, March 26, 1845.

6. Burt, "Day-Dawn of Canandaigua," 326. Emphasis added.

7. Burt, "Day-Dawn of Canandaigua," 319.

8. Burt, "Day-Dawn of Canandaigua," 317.

he suggests five steps for obtaining a general understanding of Jesus' parables. One of the principles he mentions is that parables "are narrative in form but figurative in meaning." His first principle is that one must understand the setting of the parable and that "conservative hermeneutics proceeds on the premise that language is meaningful . . ." He states that at times the "key to interpretation" may be found in the prologue to a parable or at times "the epilogue gives a clue to the proper interpretation (Matt. 25:13)." "Sometimes Jesus supplied the interpretation (e.g. 22:14; 25:13)."[9] All three of these basic principles apply to Crosier's mishandling of the exact text (Matthew 25:13) which Bailey happens to cite. In the epilogue of the parable in question Jesus supplies the interpretation. If language is meaningful, it cannot bear the interpretation which Crosier attempts to impose upon it. It says: "Watch therefore, for ye know neither the day nor the hour wherein the Son of man cometh." Yet, Crosier's two "great signs" presumed that Millerites did and must know the exact day of the Second Advent. This parable occurs in a suite of parables all of which repeatedly emphasize the same point: humanity would never be able to predict the date of the second coming. Jesus emphatically makes exactly this point in the epilogue of this parable. This single objection to Crosier's theory is fatal.

For Crosier, necessity really was the mother of invention, namely, his invention of an extended atonement. When he wrote his 1845 article, he remained convinced of the validity of Miller's fifteen proofs and the significance of October 22, 1844, but believed that Christ's visible earthly coming would occur in 1847.[10] He believed that a "successive series of prophetic events" down to "the end" had been fulfilled in a manner that was as "clear as light." Celestial signs such as the 1780 Dark Day and the 1833 Meteorite shower were cosmic proofs for Crosier.[11]

---

9. Bailey, "Guidelines for Interpreting Jesus' Parables," 29–38. See https://biblicalstudies.org.uk/article_parables_bailey.html for an accessible version.

10. Burt, *Historical Background*, 243.

11. Burt, "Day-Dawn of Canandaigua," 323.

Shut door integral to both Miller's and Crosier's theories

Even if one grants the general validity of using symbolic parables to provide detailed historical prophecies, Crosier's argumentation remains dubious at multiple points. He asserted that in phase one of the marriage Christ became King. Because this took place "before his visible appearing," this explains why Christ did not appear visibly on October 22, 1844. Crosier believed that the door of probation was shut on October 22, 1844. This was because before he became King he had a function as Mediator for all; specifically, he had "an important work to do for his enemies with the Father, to make 'intercession for the transgressors,' at the end of which he has a work to do for *his saints exclusively* before their resurrection; then follows his visible Advent..."[12] Thus, as Mediator and Priest in the Holy Place until October 22, 1844, Jesus mediated for enemies or transgressors; after this date, as high priest in the Most Holy Place and king, he mediated, or atoned, "for his saints exclusively." He and Ellen Harmon were in accord that as of October 22, 1844 the door (of probation) was shut.

Jacob's forty-day extended atonement becomes 177 years or Crosier's millennium

This brought Crosier to his pivotal extended-atonement proposal. Enoch Jacobs had already attempted to buy Millerism more time by asserting that Miller's fifteen proofs were all still correct and that Christ was still coming very soon but that he was currently performing a work of judgment that would last only the symbolically important interval of forty days.

As early as November 1844, Jacobs conjectured that beginning on October 22, 1844 Jesus began "sitting in judgment." He believed that this would last forty days:

> Definite time for the personal appearing of our Lord is certainly contained in the Bible, and if it lies not at the end of forty days from the "tenth day," it most assuredly does between that time and the end of the Jewish year [April 1845].[13]

12. Burt, "Day-Dawn of Canandaigua," 320. Emphasis added.

13. Jacobs, "Time," 3, 4. Jacobs and other shut-door Millerites set April 1845 as another date for the second coming. The April date typologically paralleled the March 21, 1844 date originally set by Miller. They considered that these dates around the

By March 1845, Crosier needed more than forty days. He began establishing his explanation of an extended atonement by attacking the traditional concept of atonement. He noted that the "prevalent opinion is that he [Christ] made the atonement on the cross." He argued that atonement cannot be made for "sins of an individual before he was born." Therefore, "atonement cannot be made until the last sin is pardoned that ever will be pardoned."[14] Thus, he moves [full historical] atonement to the end of earth's history and *not* "on the cross." Here he tied atonement and the jubilee trumpet (the forty-ninth) together. One of Miller's fifteen proofs was that the forty-ninth jubilee trumpet, ending an interval of 2,450 years from 607 BC to 1843/1844, would sound in 1843/1844. Crosier tied this to the "antitype of the jubilee trumpet (Rev. 10. 7: 11. 15)," and then followed his crucial argument for an extended atonement rather than the single twenty-four-hour-day atonement period which S. S. Snow proposed in 1845.

Crosier argued, since "the antitype of the jubilee trumpet (Rev. 10. 7: 11. 15) occupies more than a literal day [,] may not the atonement also occupy more than a literal day? 'But in the days, [note that "days" is plural not singular] of the voice of the seventh angel when he shall begin to sound the mystery of God should be finished.'" A common post-October 22, 1844 Millerite belief was that October 22, 1844 did see the jubilee trumpet sound at the beginning of this Jewish year and that it would continue until October 22, 1845; and then the second coming would occur. He emphasized the plural "days of the voice of the seventh angel" as his chief justification for arguing that "more than a [or one] literal day" was programmed by God for an extended atonement.

He also made a lengthy argument that an extended atonement could not end until "the mystery of God should be finished," and said that this would occur only when Christ as King, not mere Inheritor, had received his kingdom and God had "made Christ's enemies his footstool."

---

spring equinox were typologically significant in the Jewish calendar, be it rabbinic or Karaite. In 1845 James White picked an autumnal date in 1845 for its typological parallel with the failed October 22, 1844 date. He claimed certainty for this date until about three weeks prior to October 22, 1845.

14. Burt, "Day-Dawn of Canandaigua," 321. Ellen White's adoption of Crosier's position here established the basis for the controversial SDA position that the atonement on the cross was incomplete. There would be a "last generation" who would have to obtain a perfection that would not need Christ's mediation.

Crosier, based on his allegorical and typological assumptions, asserted that the lived Millerite experiences of 1843–1844 proved his point. He asserted: "A chronology founded on a consecutive order of events is of the strongest and safest kind. We have such a chronology from the signs in the 24 & 25 of Mat." Crosier chided Miller's opponents with having shut their eyes to Millerism's "lovely light and madly rushed to ruin." He said, "The lamplight we have followed has not been a tantalizing phantom ... No, the truth of God has lit our entire pathway and still sheds its light around us." Ellen Harmon's first vision's thoughts mirrored Crosier's sentiments exactly. She also stated that the midnight cry was a light which shed its bright beams on the 144,000's steep pathway all the way until the second coming. She said: "They [the Millerites] had a bright light set up behind them at the beginning of the path, which an angel told me was the midnight cry."[15]

Miller's "prophetic periods" simultaneously fulfilled in "about 1843"

Crosier argued that the parable of Matthew 25 was uniquely fulfilled by the events of the Millerite movement and that the 1780 Dark Day, the 1833 meteorite shower, the March 21, 1844 tarrying time, and the fall 1844 midnight cry all had to occur at those exact times for them to fit the chronology of the parable. Specifically, "the tarrying time and the [Midnight] cry are the two great Signs involved in the parable." He argued that the "two great Signs involved in the parable" "serve two important ends: 1. To prepare God's people for the marriage; 2. To give us its chronology."[16] Ironically, the very parables whose moral is that humanity is *not* to know "the day and hour" were contorted into the claim that their purpose is to provide a detailed eschatological *chronology*. Croiser acknowledged that other historical predictions of Christ's coming had been made, had been disconfirmed, and then the disappointed had to tarry, but that 1843/1844 was unique. Alluding to Miller's fifteen proofs, he assertd that "the prophetic *periods* [plural] met their harmonious, i.e., *simultaneous*, termination *in that year* [1844]." He also claimed that Miller's chronological calculations were "proved nearly if not quite correct by the fulfillment of several

---

15. Burt, "Day-Dawn of Canandaigua," 322–23.
16. Burt, "Day-Dawn of Canandaigua," 323.

prophetic periods."[17] He asserted that the parable "is confined to them [the Millerites], because while Christ tarried, "[w]e were lost as to definite time." He equated being "lost as to definite time" as a fulfillment of the parable's description of the time when all the virgins "slumbered and slept." In other words, the fact that Millerites for a period of about three months after March 21, 1844 lost their emphasis on a definite date for the second coming was a fulfillment of the parable. "We now admire the wisdom of Providence in turning our eyes for a few months from definite time to examine the sea we were in." "Is it not a general truth that in that tarry the believers in '43 'slumbered and slept,' became rather indifferent on the time of the Advent?" In other words, the befuddlement they experienced from April to July 1844 occurred as the result of direct divine intervention. "Were not all of the features of the true tarrying time found in the first 3 or 4 months[18] of the present Jewish Sacred year?" He then went on to argue, essentially, that every little jot and tittle of the parable's language had been literally, historically fulfilled in the experience of the Millerites. Because, for example, "we have had an awakening [Midnight] cry following the tarry, and at about midnight of the present prophetic day or Jewish year."[19]

He then argued that the Millerite midnight cry had to be the "cry" of the parable. It was one of the "chronological signs in Mat. 24 & 25." It was given to "prepare those who had been affected by the previous truths for the marriage and *fix its chronology*. Again, the time at which the cry was made proves it correct." About July or August of 1844, "God's time came, the present was incontrovertibly [*sic*] proved to be the year for the sounding of the jubilee trumpet."[20]

17. Burt, "Day-Dawn of Canandaigua," 327. Emphasis added. In short, Daniel 8:14 was just one of nine prophetic periods that Miller calculated would end exactly in "about 1843" or 1844.

18. April–July of 1844.

19. Burt, "Day-Dawn of Canandaigua," 324.

20. Burt, "Day-Dawn of Canandaigua," 325–27. Emphasis added. Again, note the certainty that Millerite preachers and writers seemed to evince repeatedly even after their previous exact dates were disconfirmed. Examples are liberally distributed throughout Crosier's article and Millerite evangelical literature in general. For example, Crosier (327) asserted: "If the jubilee trumpet sounded or began to sound on the tenth day of the seventh month—of which we have not a doubt—on that day our great High Priest made, or began to make, the grand and final atonement. That is the act that married Christ to his people and kingdom."

Midnight cry "incontrovertibly proved" —in minute detail

Crosier even plombed obscure minutiae of Millerite history in order to support his central thesis that the Millerite movement was a remarkable fulfillment of the prophetic parable found in Matthew 25. For example, because the text says all the "virgins arose and trimmed (searched) their lamps (Bibles),"[21] Crosier stated this was fulfilled by the fact that "such an intense interest on the subject of the Advent was never before known. That of '43 was entirely eclipsed by this [of 1844]." He even went so far as to parse the midnight cry's quality and intensity of sound. Purportedly, it was significant that during the period immediately following the tarrying, the cry that had been but a "feeble whisper assumed the character of a stern (Rev. 10. 5–7) and enthusiastic cry at midnight."[22] This resulted in "astounding peals [that] reverberated throughout our land."[23]

In critical chronological points in dealing with the intricacies of his extended-atonement model, Crosier appeared to trip himself up. In his key chronological sequence of "four important events," "viz: (1) The Tarrying time, (2) The midnight cry, (3) The marriage, and (4) shutting of the door," one would imagine that marriage (3) would precede and must terminate before the door is shut (4). Yet elsewhere he sad: "When is the door shut? Of course *before* the marriage proceeds. . . ."[24] So the shut door (4) preceded the marriage (3)?

The open-door Adventists asserted that they were converting sinners. Shut-door believers like Ellen Harmon and Crosier asserted that these were all counterfeit conversions. Crosier mocked these fake conversions, saying: "We need not be surprised at Babylonish revivals."[25] Both Crosier and Ellen G. White argued that fake conver-

---

21. Burt, "Day-Dawn of Canandaigua," 325. This is a textbook example of motivated reasoning. The two glosses in parenthesis, (searched) and (Bibles), are original. Introducing these specific words into the text to make them appear similar to the historical events of 1843/1844 illustrates the length Crosier was willing to go to make his point.

22. This references the beginning of the sounding of the seventh trumpet. Crosier conflated the seventh trumpet with the midnight cry and imagined that this transformed the "feeble whisper" into something with cosmic gravitas.

23. Burt, "Day-Dawn of Canandaigua," 325.

24. Burt, "Day-Dawn of Canandaigua," 329. Emphasis added.

25. Burt, "Day-Dawn of Canandaigua," 329.

sions were predicted in the parable of Matthew 25. After the door was shut, the foolish virgins unsuccessfully knocked on the door for admittance. Between 1844 and 1850 Ellen G. White would repeatedly insist that all conversions to open-door Adventism were counterfeit.[26] Or, as late as December 25, 1850: "Dare they admit that the door is shut? They said the shut door was of the devil and now admit it is against their own lives. They shall die the death."[27]

Crosier would eventually extend his extended atonement even further. He wrote:

> The antitype of the tenth day of the seventh month is not one literal day nor year, but must be *many years* [emphasis added]. The law was precise about the time of this yearly work; it could only be done on the tenth day of the seventh month, hence its antitype must begin on that day of some year. The antitype of this day is not identical with the thousand years' "day of the Lord," but includes it; the former [Day of Atonement] being on the tenth of the seventh month when our great High Priest entered the Holy of Holies, but the latter [thousand years] will not begin till the first resurrection; before which the sanctuary of the second covenant must be cleansed.[28]

In conclusion, Crosier was typical of the great majority of the Little Flock after the Great Disappointment. In their befuddlement and desperation, they were like survivors of a shipwreck, being tossed about by waves of doctrine, frantically trying to clamber aboard fragments of flotsam. Their uncertainty was virtually always associated with strident claims of certainty; certitude that they had finally unlocked the right combination of the continuous-historical code. As one piece of flotsam after another disintegrated, their purchase on reality disintegrated and they floated off into various forms of fanaticism or finally experienced a radical paradigm shift.

Crosier and his colleagues could not conceive that their basic presumptions needed to be altered, that it was folly to conceive of God as "an exact timekeeper," and that God had not liberally distributed throughout history many exact prophetic intervals with the specific

26. White, *Ellen G. White Letters & Manuscripts*, 160–63. White made repeated statements to this effect.

27. White, *Ellen G. White Letters & Manuscripts*, 273.

28. Crosier, "Dear Bro. Jacobs," 23.

objective of making Millerites wise as to specific dates in the last days. Crosier desperately needed more time to rejigger his continuous-historical presumptions. With a great deal of creativity, he imaginatively reconstructed a set of invisible theological events that fit the bitter reality that Christ's literal and visible Second Advent had not occurred on October 22, 1844.

Like Miller and Snow, O. R. L. Crosier did not use a commonsense, literal method of interpreting Scripture. Ellen Harmon did not use a commonsense, literal method of interpreting Scripture. Rather, all four used highly allegorical-typological-historicist methods which *repeatedly* produced predictions which were disconfirmed. These Millerite erroneous results not only falsified their prophetic predictions; they are fatal to the credibility of the allegorical-typological-historicist method. Ellen G. White had no authentic biblical evidence for her claim that God had given Crosier "the true light." Neither Miller, Snow, Crosier, nor Ellen White had a genuine biblical basis for their assertions. They were reading unsupportable presuppositions into the text. They were doing eisegesis, not exegesis.

Visible undated coming bridegroom versus invisible dated coming king

After October 22, 1844, there were only two choices left to Millerites: They could not retain both a literal, visible second coming simultaneously with a specific date. They had to give up one or the other. Some kept the date but changed the event (Christ came spiritually, or Christ came invisibly as bridegroom—the distinction between spiritually and invisibility is difficult to see). Others gave up the date but retained a literal, visible second coming for a later (specified or unspecified) date.

Crosier built his edifice upon faulty premises. Chief amongst these was the premise that Christ's parables had a built-in sequence of precisely timed, continuous-historical events that could be discovered. Second was his premise that the datable historical events he cited (1755 Lisbon earthquake, 1780 Dark Day, 1833 falling of the stars) were biblical, apocalyptic signs. Third, the very concept of definite time is untenable. Even F. D. Nichol recognized that Miller's multiple periods were "farfetched" and "fanciful."²⁹ It would have been inconsistent for God to have led Miller to produce "farfetched" interpretations in fourteen of his calculations while giving him a reliable, direct revelation regarding his fifteenth calculation. How could it be that God gave Crosier "the true light" when he was performing an allegorical interpretation of the Bridegroom Parable and claiming it was literally fulfilled in the events of the 1840s?

In this age of supercomputers that can calculate billions of operations in a nanosecond, how is it that God and other celestial intelligences could take 177 years to investigate the heavenly accounting books of individuals to determine who should be saved in the process of an investigative judgment? This is the current SDA explanation for the delay. The life records of the dead and then the living must be reviewed and judged before the second coming can occur. Millerism initially used the apocalyptic symbol of the midnight cry and shut door to make their argument that the second coming was ultra-imminent. But as a few years past uneventfully, new apocalyptic catchphrases were used to renew a flagging sense of imminence.³⁰ For example, the Latter Rain and the Sealing were used. It was asserted that the Latter Rain or Sealing were now current events, and that once SDAs had received the Latter Rain or been Sealed, the end could come. Another example was the reinterpretation of the Laodicean church, the last of Revelation's seven churches. Ellen G. White continued using such imminence techniques until she was very old. On November 22, 1892 she declared that the long-anticipated "loud cry" had begun. As a result, W. W. Prescott endorsed the testimonies of Anna Phillips and A. T. Jones promulgating the "selling time." Following the example of the 1843–1844 Millerites, promoters of the "selling time" advocated that

29. . Nichol, *Midnight Cry*, Appendix L.

30. In 1856 James and Ellen White came up with an additional typological event that had to occur before the second coming. This was the message to the Laodicean church of Revelation (the last and seventh in a series of seven historicist churches). Pre-Disappointment Millerites claimed this symbolized the non-Millerite Christian churches. Post-Disappointment proto-SDAs claimed it represented open-door or nominal Adventists. After exhausting other symbols of extreme imminence from 1844 to 1856, a new apocalyptic symbol was needed to maintain this imminence. Thus, the Whites came up with a novel interpretation of the Laodicean church. Now, they said, it symbolized a lukewarm SDA church. This Laodicean message had to be preached first, and *then* the end would come. See White, *Ellen G. White Letters & Manuscripts*, 499, 514, 554, 629, 633. For the 1856 Ellen White, the Laodicea symbol functioned identically to the midnight cry of 1844.

SDAs quickly sell their real estate and possessions because the second coming was extremely imminent.[31]

Crosier attempted to salvage the Disappointment by asserting that one could allegorize parables to provide a precise chronology of contemporaneous events from 1840 to 1845. This method, explicitly identified as such by Burt in his introductory article on the shut door in the *Ellen G. White Letters & Manuscripts*, is an indefensible method of interpreting Scripture.[32] Nonetheless, Ellen White's endorsement of Crosier has permanently shackled the SDA church to Crosier's method and interpretations.

Crosier's modification of the Snowite midnight cry permitted the proto-SDA faction to concede that God never did intend to give them a mathematically definite time for the Second Advent—but rather a specific date for the beginning of the pre-Advent judgment on October 23, 1844. Tacitly they dropped the Millerite claim that there was a biblical basis for eight of Miller's nine prophetic periods ending in 1843/1844, defending solely the 2,300-year argument by relating it to an entirely different event. This was the sole vestigial relic. Otherwise, Miller's other "exact" fulfillments have been abandoned. Because Miller's other proofs originally ended with the first resurrection and the second coming, they cannot be reconciled with the alleged event fulfilling the 2,300-day-year interval, an invisible movement of Christ from the Holy to the Most Holy Place in a heavenly sanctuary. The 2,300-year interpretation is the only one of Miller's prophetic periods now claimed to end with a different event.

Ellen G. White's assertion that Miller, Snow, and Crosier had some species of direct divine guidance in effect elevated Ellen G. White to the "greater light" who, by means of three "lesser-lesser lights," authoritatively, if not quite inerrantly and canonically, determined the interpretation of the Bible.

---

31. Valentine, *Prescott*, 54, 84–91.
32. Burt, "'Shut Door' and Ellen White's Visions," 41–61.

VIII

J. Turner's Bridegroom and Shut Door

> "I have no confidence in any of the new theories that have grown out of the [seventh-month] movement, viz., that Christ came as the Bridegroom, that the door of mercy was closed,... or that it was a fulfillment of prophecy in any sense."
>
> WILLIAM MILLER (1845)

CROSIER HAD CONCLUDED THAT Christ's new High-Priestly ministry in the Most Holy Place was exclusively for the saints and that probation had closed for all others. Joseph Turner's January 1845 bridegroom hypothesis preceded Crosier's March 1845 *Day-Dawn* and February 7, 1846 *Day-Star Extra* exposition. But Miller had anticipated both Turner and Crosier by years. As early as Miller's 1835 *Evidences from Scripture* he had argued that Matthew 25 and Revelation 22:11 indicated a close of probation. On October 12, 1844 Miller concluded that "probation had already closed." Joseph Turner merely appropriated his shut-door position from Miller. Then Ellen Harmon founded her own shut-door teaching on the prior works of Miller, Turner, Crosier, and Snow. Although White apologists for many years denied that Ellen White advocated a shut-door doctrine, even White Estate authorities, faced with the overwhelming evidence in primary sources of the 1840s, have finally conceded that she did. Initially, in this chapter the flaws of Turner's bridegroom hypothesis will be analyzed. Then the parallel errors of Ellen White's shut-door teachings will be described based on her earliest statements. When

Miller renounced his shut-door position in the summer of 1845, Ellen White broke with Miller but blamed Himes for Miller's apostasy.

In January 1845 Joseph Turner and Apollos Hale published in the *Advent Mirror* the "seminal and definitive paper on the shut door that first defined the Bridegroom view."[1] Turner's (and then Harmon's) method of explaining the Disappointment was founded on "an allegorical interpretation of the parable of the ten virgins in Matthew 25 . . ."[2] Bridegroom Adventists like Harmon and Turner modified Miller's shut door by "adding post-1844 details to the Matthew 25 parable."

> For Bridegroom Adventists their basic theological argument was drawn from the parable of the ten virgins in Matthew 25. They made the parable allegorical to their 1844 experience, and believed that on or about October 22, 1844, Jesus had gone into a heavenly wedding. The Advent Mirror divided the marriage into two steps; the actual marriage and the marriage supper.[3]

Additionally, they used another parable, from Matthew 22:1–14. In this parable the wise virgins were also shut into the guest chamber awaiting the Parousia. These guests consisted exclusively of Millerites who had accepted the light of the midnight cry and were now shut away in the guest chamber awaiting Christ's coming to earth. "Their [only] work was to keep their garments and wait." "The foolish virgins, who were not ready, were shut out."[4] Only *after* Turner and Hale had published their bridegroom explanation for the delay of the second coming did Ellen Harmon have a vision called the "bridegroom vision" because it included all the significant elements of Turner's paradigm.

Ellen Harmon's intellectual dependence on Turner has elements similar to her intellectual dependence on other non-inspired sources, as has been previously documented regarding 2 Esdras, Milton's *Paradise Lost*, and various health reformers.[5] In all these cases she

---

1. Burt, "'Shut Door' and Ellen White's Visions," 42 n. 3.
2. Burt, "'Shut Door' and Ellen White's Visions," 45.
3. Burt, "'Shut Door' and Ellen White's Visions," 43.
4. Burt, "'Shut Door' and Ellen White's Visions," 44.
5. For Esdras see Casebolt, "It Was Not Taught Me by Man," 66–73. For *Paradise Lost* see Burgeson, "Comparative Study" and Dirk Anderson's "Paradise Lost's Themes Found in Ellen White's Books." The latter is available at https://www.nonegw.

was adamant that her concepts came directly from God without any intervening human influences. Yet she clearly had been influenced by, in this case, Turner and Hale. Paradoxically, she seemed to have been unaware that she had been influenced.

Ellen's solo sleigh ride and Joseph Turner's bridegroom concept

Joseph Bates noted Harmon's dependence on Turner and Hale. Whether Ellen Harmon was personally acquainted with Hale is not clear. However, she had a very close, if contentious, relationship with Turner. Thus, discussion regarding her intellectual dependence on Hale and Turner's bridegroom concept centers on Ellen Harmon's personal interactions with Turner. In a letter to Joseph Bates, she claimed that even though she knew a copy of Turner's bridegroom explanation was in her house, she had never read it; nor had she had any conversation regarding it. This even though it was *the* most critical existential dilemma of her life. Moreover, her admission that she knew that Turner's bridegroom article existed suggests that she must, at minimum, have had a general idea of its contents. In any case, there is no doubt whatsoever that Turner and Hale *published* their bridegroom hypothesis well before Ellen Harmon *even claimed* she received a bridegroom vision. She said she was unaware of its specifics because she had been too ill to read. Simultaneously, she recounted that she was well enough to take a sleigh ride for several miles and be out of her house the entire day until late at night.

Ellen G. White stated that at the time of her first vision she had given up the idea that the midnight cry was a past event, i.e., that October 22, 1844 was a critical day in salvation history, and "thought it future, as also most of the band had."[6] Exactly when in the future she and the band imagined the midnight cry would occur was not stated. But we know from the account of the Israel Dammon trial in Atkinson that those surrounding Ellen Harmon expected the second coming any day, and that Ellen Harmon urged some to be baptized in frozen waters immediately, so imminent was the emergency.[7] Quite a

---

org/egw102.shtml. For borrowed health concepts see Numbers, *Prophetess of Health*.

6. White, *Ellen G. White Letters & Manuscripts*, 124–28.

7. Hoyt, "Trial of Elder I. Dammon," 29–36.

large number of Millerites believed that a biblically symbolic day in April 1845 must be the actual future date for the second coming. To explain to Bates that she was not dependent on Turner, she went on to say that although "God gave me light" on the bridegroom circa February 1845, and "bade me deliver it to the band," she played a reluctant Jonah role. Despite her account that the band in Portland, Maine had immediately accepted her first vision, and even though she had already travelled to multiple locations in New England where other little bands had also accepted her as a visionary, she thought "they would not receive it from me." "I disobeyed the Lord, and instead of remaining at home, where the meeting [where Turner would explain his bridegroom concept] was to be that night, I got into a sleigh that morning and rode three or four miles and there I found J. T(urner)."[8] Incredibly, she claimed that Joseph Turner told her nothing of his views and she told him nothing of hers. He left and only then Ellen "told those around me" that if she attended the meeting and told her vision, she would have to come out against his views. But she has just claimed that she had neither read his views nor talked to him about them. So, why would she come out against his views? Given that their ideas were practically identical, her presumption of the opposite is counterintuitive. Also, it seems incongruent that she could discuss her imagined difference between herself and Turner with the "others" after Turner left, but could say nothing to Turner himself. She offered no explanation for how her views may have contradicted any bridegroom concepts she imagined he had. Clearly, both Turner and Ellen were well known to the "others around me [Ellen]." Ellen arrived at her destination and felt free to spend the entire day. Turner's presence also demonstrates that this was a Millerite band intensely interested in both Ellen's visions and Turner's writings. Are we also to believe that Turner had just spent time there *not* discussing his bridegroom views and then Ellen Harmon spent the entire day there with the same group and did not discuss her views and visions? Certainly, she must have picked up some clues as to Turner's views from the day she spent there. What better subject did they have to talk about from morning until late at night? It also is remarkable that Ellen could have suddenly left her home by sleigh in the morning to avoid a nighttime meeting. Indeed, it is highly unusual that she would have been permitted to

---

8. White, *Ellen G. White Letters & Manuscripts*, 124–28.

leave by sleigh, unchaperoned, alone, and that she would not return until late that night after the "meeting had been done some time." She was an unchaperoned seventeen-year-old female. Had she disappeared the entire day until late at night with or without her father's permission? Secondly, she claimed that she had been deathly ill for several weeks, so it is astonishing to conceive of her gallivanting across the snow in a one-horse open sleigh. Finally, as events unfolded, the band did not doubt her vision but immediately received it.

Allegorical interpretation of parable foundational to extended-atonement doctrine

The two critical keys to this narrative are that 1) both Turner's and Harmon's explanation for the delay were based on "an allegorical interpretation" of Matthew 25, and 2) that Turner's written account preceded Harmon's late oral account.[9] Finally, multiple aspects of Harmon's account effectively denying Turner's priority are highly unusual.

Confabulation: the key to comprehending Harmon's psychology

Ellen Harmon's unawareness of her dependence on Turner is probably explained by a neurological unawareness that the lay person may have heard about in relationship to two medical conditions. For example, after a person has suffered a cerebrovascular attack affecting half of their body, hemiplegia results and if a parietal lobe is involved, a person is unaware that half of their body exists and is also unaware that objects on that side of their body exist. They may be physically unable to, for instance, raise their right arm at the request of their neurologist yet insist that they have complied with that request. They may also confabulate, claiming that the examiner tied their arm down. Similarly, in cases of schizophrenia there is a condition known

---

9. See White, *Ellen G. White Letters & Manuscripts*, 279 for Ellen G. White's explicit instruction to pastor Samuel Rhodes and his partner J. N. Andrews. After Rhodes had spoken on the "subject of the [bridegroom] parable," Andrews was commanded to "watch carefully" and drive the point home. For years, this parable was a crux of their preaching as evidenced in this May 18, 1851 letter to Rhodes, Andrews's mentor.

as anosognosia. This may manifest itself clinically when the person diagnosed with schizophrenia who is experiencing delusions and hearing non-existent voices is entirely unaware that they have a mental illness. Indeed, they will insist that they themselves are sane and that their examiner and others are insane. In neither of these cases is the person prevaricating or denying a reality *that they are aware of.* At times when a person is describing a past memory, they may not be aware that their description of events is not accurate. This results in confabulation. Confabulation occurs when a person generates details of a past memory that can be shown to be objectively false. This classically occurs with persons having dementia, Wernicke-Korsakoff syndrome, traumatic brain injury (TBI), schizophrenia, PTSD, and other pathologies. But, "The literature is replete with examples of memories held by normal, non-pathologically affected individuals, to be firmly and confidently held as true and veridical to the putative prior event, that are simply false." Brown's abstract states:

> *Confabulation is the creation of false memories in the absence of intentions of deception. Individuals who confabulate have no recognition that the information being relayed to others is fabricated. Confabulating individuals are not intentionally being deceptive and sincerely believe the information they are communicating to be genuine and accurate.* Confabulation ranges from small distortions of actual memories to creation of bizarre and unusual memories, often with elaborate detail.

Brown continues: one of the possible reasons an individual may confabulate is because "the individual may possess an unconscious motive to alter the memory."[10] In the case of Ellen Harmon, she had a nearly fatal traumatic brain injury to her prefrontal lobe when she was nine years old. This resulted in a shattered central nervous system, which was life altering. Additionally, she suffered from PTSD. Of equal importance is the fact that for four years she had been totally committed to the belief that Christ's second coming would occur on a specific date. *She had been convinced she was going to hell, until she accepted Millerism. She had had out-of-body experiences which she felt confirmed S. S. Snow's date-setting midnight cry.* The Great Disappointment of 1844 caused her severe psychological trauma. Due to

---

10. Brown et al., "Confabulation," abstract. Emphasis added. See also Loftus and Pickrell, "Rormation of False Memories," 720–25.

her combined physical and psychological trauma, she recounted that her family thought she might die. She also related that in early 1845 she was so stressed that her mind wandered for two weeks at Elizabeth Haines's house. During Ellen Harmon's two weeks of confusion, Ellen also revealed that Elizabeth Haines herself was also suffering from great confusion of mind. The *Ellen G. White Encyclopedia*, a friendly source, documents that:

> In the spring of 1845, it was also in Haines' home that Ellen had her "new earth" vision ... After this vision Haines cared for Ellen in her home for two weeks during a bout with illness. During her illness *Ellen experienced mental confusion.*[11]

Ellen herself described her delirium as having been caused by an existential conflict with Joseph Turner. He attempted to turn her friends "and even my relatives against me, and he succeeded in a measure." Thereafter, she "sank in discouragement, and *my mind wandered for two weeks.* My relatives thought I could not live."[12] This recalled to her relatives her unconscious, "stupid state" which followed her traumatic brain injury a few years earlier.

Ellen Harmon was existentially so committed to her out-of-body experiences and her role as prophetess that early in 1845 she described being struck speechless by what she considered to be divine retribution for doubting her prophetic calling.[13] Her first vision occurred

---

11. Burt, "Elizabeth Haines," 393–94. Emphasis added. The written account of this vision did not appear until much later, January 24, 1846 in the *Day Star*. In the same Haines household Ellen Harmon had other visionary prostrations.

12. White, *Ellen G. White Letters & Manuscripts*, 765, 766. Emphasis added.

13. White, *Sketch of the Christian Experience*, 8, 35–42. In about 1845 or 1846 Ellen Harmon stated that in one of her initial visions she saw, displayed on a card held up before her by either the Holy Ghost or an angelic messenger, fifty biblical verses written out in golden letters on a card. Ellen's account stated that after she came "out" of her vision, she "beckoned for the slate, and wrote upon it that I was dumb, also what I had seen, and that I wished the large Bible. I took the Bible and readily turned to all the texts that I had seen upon the card." The key phrase is that she wrote "what I had seen." This is typically interpreted to mean that she actually wrote out all fifty texts and/or their references; and that this acted as a check upon her ability to then turn to said texts in the large Bible. However, this is not necessarily correct. She could have just as well written: "I saw fifty golden Bible texts," and then turned to any fifty texts that came to mind. Also supporting such an interpretation is the difficulty of even imagining the "slate" capable of containing fifty entire Bible texts. The typical New England home likely did not have easily at hand a slate that could contain so much handwritten information at once. And it would have taken a significant amount

in the home of Elizabeth Haines. After this "vision Haines cared for Ellen in her home for two weeks during a bout with illness. During her illness Ellen experienced *mental confusion*."[14] Her "delirium" was intertwined with experiences which she described as being prostrated or slain by the Holy Spirit.[15] Thus, she had very strong unconscious motives to produce altered memories. It was difficult for herself and others to differentiate between delirium and prostration. In a normal state of consciousness and health, Ellen Harmon would have been aware of Turner's bridegroom hypothesis.

Another critical instance where Ellen Harmon was dependent on human sources for information was when she thought she received direct divine revelation concerned the historiography of the Sabbath. In short, only after her human sources, Seventh-Day Baptists, Preble, and then Joseph Bates, gave her their history of the Sabbath did she see this in in her later visions. See chapters 9 and 13 for detailed evidences.

---

of time to merely write the textual information out. Given the random order in which the texts are now listed, one wonders: did she turn to all the references in order from Matthew, then Luke, then John then Acts, then Revelation, etc.? Or haphazardly, as written in her account, flipping back and forth from Acts, to John, to Philippians, to Acts, to Revelation, to Mark, back to Acts, then Matthew, etc. The father of John the Baptist had a much easier task. He just had to remember the name the divine messenger had provided for the promised son.

14. Burt, "Elizabeth Haines," 393–94. Emphasis added. It is noteworthy that officially sponsored SDA authorities, not critics, concede that Ellen Harmon had mental confusion during periods when she was having visions formative and determinative of later SDA theology.

15. It is not uncommon for persons having strong psychological stresses to believe that they have been struck dumb by an outside reality when it is a voluntarily self-induced state. Significantly, this experience involved seeing texts in the Bible which textual criticism has determined *were not in the original text* of Mark. This suggests that such texts were not imposed upon her brain by God. Rather, they were self-generated. The diagnosis of elective mutism is given to such behavior by Spitzer et al., "Silent Sister," 158–59. A contemporary case occurred in the life of Maya Angelou. As a child the famous writer was sexually abused and raped by her mother's boyfriend. She revealed the name of her rapist. The rapist was killed. Angelou perceived that her spoken word was directly responsible for his death. As a result, Angelou became mute for almost five years.

Gospel's universal proclamation must precede the close of probation

In any case, in early 1845 Crosier and Ellen Harmon were fully persuaded that probation had closed. They, the wise virgins, had entered the wedding hall and its door had been shut. They, like Noah and his animals, had entered the ark of safety. The door of the ark was shut tight and no amount of pounding on it by the antediluvian scoffers could open it. Their fate was sealed. There had been a division between the sheep and the goats; the filthy remained filthy still.

An integral element of the midnight-cry proclamation was the conviction that the wise had to preach the gospel of the second coming to *all* the world, and only then would the end come. In God's justice, the truth of the midnight cry had to be preached to all the people of all the nations so that they could make their final informed choice of whether to accept the midnight cry. This had to occur before the close of probation, and the close of probation had to occur before October 22, 1844—in the Millerite mind.

Miller had taught the shut door for several years. Thus, for several months after October 22, 1844 he held that his work for the wicked world and the nominal churches was finished. We have no Ellen Harmon dairy with daily entries for 1844–1850 to document her initial conceptions of the Great Disappointment. She likely continued to believe that Christ was still about to appear any day for three or four weeks after October 22, 1844. Then, probably, like Enoch Jacobs, she believed that the second coming would occur in less than forty days. Miller used a ship transit analogy. Miller believed he had correctly calculated when the ship had left port (Christ had left heaven); he just had not calculated the length of time it would take for the ship (Christ's small black cloud) to arrive at its earthly destination. That is, Christ had left heaven on a cloud, but was still on his way through the opening in Orion. It would take him another seven days' transit time to arrive. As one day slipped imperceptibly into another, shut-door advocates had an increasingly difficult time in maintaining that the door of probation had closed on October 22, 1844. At a minimum, for the seven days between October 23–30, 1844, Ellen Harmon supposed that the door to probation had shut on October 22, 1844 and that Christ was in transit. After all, in Ellen Harmon's first vision she claimed that she saw the first resurrection, she heard the

144,000 shout "Hallelujah!," then both the 144,000 and those risen in the first resurrection "all entered the cloud together, and were 7 days ascending to the sea of glass." If it took seven days to ascend to heaven through the Orion, must it not take seven days to descend? Then as several weeks passed Ellen Harmon reluctantly concluded that the October 22, 1844 date was mistaken and that the second coming was in a very near future.[16] Most shut-door advocates predicted typologically important dates in the spring or fall of 1845.

Thus, summarizes Damsteegt: "In general it can be said that first the shut-door views excluded salvation for *all* who have rejected the Advent doctrine...."[17] In contrast, open-door Adventists concluded that they had been mistaken in concluding that *the* door had shut. They believed that non-Millerite believers, those of the wicked world or nominal churches, could yet be converted. Therefore, Miller, J. V. Himes, and the main body of open-door Adventists redoubled their evangelistic efforts to reach the wicked world and nominal churches whom the shut-door Adventists completely discounted and ignored. This was *the* empirically *observable* difference between the two groups from 1844 to about 1850. Open-door Adventists thought their mistake might simply be that fallible chronologists had miscalculated the Parousia by at most several years. Therefore, they no longer believed in the criticality of October 22, 1844. They were open to the possibility of recalculating dates for the second coming, and did this frequently. Conversely, Ellen G. White's first vision convinced her that the Holy Spirit had irrevocably established the October 22, 1844 date.[18]

This potent brew of chaos and disappointment led to acrimonious debates between the open-door and shut-door Adventists, the acute phase of which lasted about seven years. During the first year after the Great Disappointment, Ellen Harmon's travel itinerary is imprecise and the details on what she said and wrote are sketchy. But until about October 1, 1845 she and James promulgated the concept that Christ would return by October 22, 1845. And given that Miller "rashly denied" the midnight cry by the summer of 1845, she had

---

16. White, *Ellen G. White Letters & Manuscripts*, 89.

17. Damsteegt, *Foundations*, 163. Emphasis added.

18. Why God would be in a movement predicting an exact day for the second coming was never adequately explained. Why God would be in a movement predicting the *wrong event but the correct, precise Karaite date* for an invisible movement in heaven is also not well explained.

consigned him to one of those who had fallen off the narrow, steep path to heaven into the wicked world below from, where he would never be able to regain the narrow path.[19]

White Estate says: White "misinterpreted" her first vision!

The shut-door dispute is undoubtedly the most recurrent controversy in SDA historical theology. There are scores of footnotes in Denis Kaiser's 2014 *Trust and Doubt* that address it over many decades.[20] Robert Olson (1982) agreed with Damsteegt (1977) that Ellen G. White's "shut-door views excluded salvation *for all* [emphasis added] who had rejected the Advent doctrine . . ."[21] It is remarkable that two such stalwart, conservative defenders of Ellen White's authority would feel constrained by primary documents to admit this.

On April 11, 1982 Robert W. Olson, then secretary of the Ellen G. White Estate (roughly analogous to Cardinal Pietro Parolin, the Secretariat of State of the Vatican), prepared "The 'Shut Door' Documents: Statements Relating to the 'Shut Door,' the Door of Mercy, and the Salvation of Souls by Ellen G. White and Other Early Adventists, Arranged in a Chronological Setting from 1844 to 1851, Complied, with Occasional Commentary by Robert W. Olson" in an attempt to provide a definitive and authoritative apologetic. Below, I will refer to the documents referred to by Olson by the number he assigned them. He notes in his document 3: "In Common with Most of the Millerites, Ellen Harmon also Believed for a Time that the Door of Mercy Was Shut on October 22, 1844."[22] From "Ellen G. White Ms. 4, 1883; *Selected Messages*, book 1, p. 63," he quotes her stating: "For a time after the disappointment in 1844, I did hold in Common with the advent

---

19. She eventually issued him a special dispensation, saving him from the fate of everyone else who "rashly" denied the cosmic significance of October 22, 1844. She suggested that he had been innocently led astray by associates like J. V. Himes, laid in his grave, and would be in heaven after all. In principle, all the other zealous Millerite leaders like Himes, Storrs, S. S. Snow, and others were consigned to perdition, however.

20. Kaiser, *Trust and Doubt*.

21. Damsteegt, *Foundations*, 163.

22. Olson, "'Shut-Door' Documents."

body, that the door of mercy was then forever closed to the world." In this she mirrored Miller's November 18, 1844 letter, where he said:

> We have done our work in warning sinners, and in trying to awake a formal church. God, in his providence has shut the door; we can only stir one another up to be patient; and be diligent to make our calling and election sure. We are now living in the time specified by Malachi 3: 18, also Daniel 12:10, Rev. 22: 10–12. In this passage we cannot help but see that a little while before Christ should come, there would be a separation between the just and unjust, the righteous and wicked, between those who love his appearing and those who hate it.

In Olson's comments preceding and introducing Harmon's first vision, he states: "In Ellen Harmon's 1st vision, she was shown that the Door of Mercy was Shut for (a) Those Millerites Who Denied God had led them in the 1844 'Midnight Cry' Movement, and (b) 'All the Wicked World' Which God Had Rejected." In short, at this time, *Ellen Harmon had no conception of a third group*, undecided, unreached, who were unaware of the "light" and had neither accepted nor rejected it.

In Olson's sixth document he cites James White. In commenting on J. White's description of Ellen Harmon's first vision's "implications," Olson states, "James White indicates that, on the basis of what she was shown in her first vision, Ellen Harmon reverted to her earlier view that the door was shut on October 22. She apparently believed that the door of mercy was closed."

In commenting on his document 7 Olson says: Ellen G. White "at first *misinterpreted* [her first vision] to mean that her work for the world was done." Then "as the years passed," she realized that this was incorrect. He immediately mitigates this admission by stating that the fact that the "seventeen year old Ellen should misinterpret one of her visions should elicit no surprise..." Since she did misinterpret her vision, and widely promulgated this misinterpretation, it is no wonder that we find her prophetic misinterpretation widely seconded by members of her community.

In his document 10 Olson cites James White's statement in the *Day-Star*, January 24, 1846. He cited Jude 3–4 and then stated: "I conclude no intelligent believer in the shut door doubts the direct application of Jude to us since the midnight cry was finished. So the exhortation to contend for the faith delivered to the saints, is to us alone." In short, the door was shut to nominal Christians and sinners. Since he clearly viewed Ellen Harmon as an "intelligent believer in the shut door," it is obvious that as of January 24, 1846 she was a shut-door advocate.

Miller's repudiation: not "fulfillment of prophecy in any sense"

Document 19 is Miller's August, 1845 categorical refutation of his own movement, which I have cited previously. It is a comprehensive repudiation of the midnight cry. It explicitly identifies several of the specific facets of the shut-door doctrine. Miller flatly denied that: 1) Christ came invisibly as bridegroom, 2) the door of mercy was closed, 3) there was no salvation for sinners, 4) the seventh-month movement was a fulfillment of prophecy.

In summer of 1847 James White admitted: "It is well known that many were expecting the Lord to come at the 7th month [October], 1845. That Christ would then come we [Ellen G. White and himself] firmly believed."[23] In a letter dated September 27, 1845, James White wrote: "we have had the 'True Midnight Cry,' and of course the Bridegroom has come, and the door is shut; if not a true Midnight Cry has told a lie ... We are looking for redemption in the Morning Watch.[24] Amen." This was published in the *Day-Star* on October 11, 1845. On May 30, 1847 Joseph Bates used the expression that "since the closing up of our work for the world in October, 1844," the only duty that he and the other two founders of the SDA church had was to "comfort and strengthen his 'scattered,' 'torn,' and 'pealed people' ..." On August 26, 1848 James White wrote the Hastings (Olson's document 32):

> Here is the standard to rally around. Jesus has left His mediatorial throne [where previously he had ministered to sinners]. He is now claiming His new kingdom ... Well, this is the present 'faith of Jesus.' So the shut door and the Sabbath are the present truth. These truths will form and keep up the

23. James White, "Word to the 'Little Flock,'" (1847) 22.

24. This refers to the fact that James White believed that the three months prior to October 22, 1845 constituted the last watch of the night. On this scriptural basis he and Ellen White firmly believed that the second coming would occur on this date.

same mark of distinction between us and unbelievers as God made in 1844.

Ellen G. White would attempt to mitigate her original shut-door position. She did so by changing the *single* shut door of Matthew 25 to *two* doors of the sanctuary: a shut door to the Holy Place and an open door to the Most Holy Place.

For over eighteen centuries no Christian had ever concerned themselves with making a distinction between whether Christ was physically located in the Holy Place or the Most Holy Place of a celestial sanctuary. Indeed, if they pictured him anywhere, they pictured him at the right hand of God, which could only be in the Most Holy Place. The Millerites had preached that Christ would come *out* of the Most Holy Place on October 22, 1844—not go into it. What might be the practical or theological significance of imagining Christ in one place or the other? Several years later, Uriah Smith would argue that it was necessary for Christians to know in which compartment Christ was located in order to receive atonement from him.

In Olson's "Summary and Conclusions," he states that Ellen G. White's December 1844 first vision

> led her to reaffirm once again her view of a shut door . . . She concluded *incorrectly* that the door of mercy was closed on that day for everyone in the world . . . She *failed* [emphasis added] to recognize, however, that there was a third category . . who had never heard or fully appreciated the Millerite message in the first place.

Paradoxically, Olson still denies that "she at any time taught theological error in her shut-door writings." Yet the third category that Ellen G. White "failed to recognize" is the very same third category which was the foundation of her assertion that her vision never taught that the "door of mercy was closed on that day for everyone in the world."

Ellen Harmon's first vision confirmed her shut-door paradigm

For a few weeks between October 22, 1844 and December 1844, Ellen Harmon was forced to conclude that the door of probation had not shut on October 22, 1844 and that this date did not have crucial significance in salvation history. Her first vision of December 1844 reversed this paradigm. The door had been shut on October 22, 1844 after all. The date-setting midnight-cry movement was still valid in its calculation. Everyone, except for William Miller, who rashly denied the "light" of the midnight cry was irrevocably lost.

Ellen Harmon, Joseph Turner, Apollos Hale, J. V. Himes, and William Miller were all befuddled. A vacuum of authority and comprehension suddenly existed. Miller felt he had made a mistake but was baffled about what his mistake was.

The practical function of Turner's and Harmon's new and improved allegorical interpretation of the Bridegroom Parable was to split a single second coming into two comings, an invisible bridegroom (or high priest) coming precisely on October 22, 1844, and a later, visible kingly coming that Ellen Harmon imagined would be merely days, weeks, or at most months distant. This set the precedent for a whole series of two-phased concepts to explain a chronological delay.

One of these was the transformation of a single shut door on the wedding feast hall of Matthew 25 into two doors of an invisible heavenly sanctuary. This permitted Ellen Harmon to maintain that the shut door of the wedding chamber was identical with the novel concept of a shut door to the invisible, heavenly Holy Place, while a newly envisioned open door was simultaneously present into the heavenly Most Holy place. Thus, for a time, two opposites could be simultaneously maintained: an open and a shut door! Then, gradually as Ellen Harmon's theological concepts developed, the single shut door of the wedding feast and the shut door of the Holy Place could gradually be eclipsed by the newly open door of the Most Holy Place. What meaning did that leave for the shut door of the wedding feast? Can one really conflate both a shut and open door of a heavenly sanctuary with a single shut door of a wedding hall? This was a new rule of faith. But even James White conceded that Ellen Harmon's visions should not be the foundation of a novel doctrine. In May 1848 he wrote:

> True visions are given to lead us to God and his written word, but those that are given for a new rule of faith and practice,

separate from the Bible, cannot be from God and should be rejected.[25]

The Lesser Light says that Crosier got "the true light"

As Burt indicates, the shut door, bridegroom faction itself was split into two camps. One, led by S. S. Snow, contended that on October 22, 1844, in a single day, Christ as High Priest began and finished an atonement for *righteous* Millerites. The second faction, associated with O. R. L. Crosier, promulgated an extended atonement that only began on this date but extended for (now nigh unto 177) years into the future. Crosier said it would last until the millennium was completed. Joseph Bates read Crosier's article before Ellen Harmon was aware of it. He recommended it, saying that it was "superior to anything of the kind extant" and afterwards purchased the copyright.[26] Ellen Harmon, having read Crosier, claimed that God had given him "the true light" on this matter.

The allegorical interpretation of Matthew 25 has been a persistent constant in SDA apologetics since its inception. Burt wrote in 2014:

> The minority group came to be known as shut-door Adventists because they based their initial explanation for the disappointment on the [allegorical interpretation of] Matthew 25:1–13 parable of the Bridegroom, which they interpreted as a heavenly wedding.[27]

Both shut-door and open-door Adventists were convinced that they had already preached the gospel, the midnight cry, to all the world. There was no time left after Midnight for goats to become sheep. Some expressed it this way: to attempt to convert non-Millerites who had rejected the midnight cry would have been comparable to Moses and the children of Israel trying to convert the Egyptians during the exodus. Given this unshakable conviction, shut-door Adventists like Ellen Harmon did not believe there could be any true conversions. Open-door Adventists stated that empirical conversions proved that the door was not shut. Ellen Harmon could not deny

---

25. James White, "Word to the 'Little Flock'" (2014), 38.
26. Knight, *Joseph Bates*, 95.
27. Burt, "'Shut Door' and Ellen White's Visions," 41.

that conversions occurred; she just denied that they were genuine. For open-door Adventists, observable facts determined their conclusions of how to explain the midnight cry; for shut-door Adventists, allegorical-typological-historicist assummptions predetermined how empirical facts must be interpreted.

The debate between open and shut-door groups about whether conversions were genuine or counterfeit was simply an alternative way for expressing their theological dispute over whether the door had been shut or was still open. When open-door Adventists, like William Miller and J. V. Himes, concluded that October 22, 1844 was an error, they simultaneously concluded that probation had not closed and the door was not shut. Shut-door Adventists believed that the midnight cry signified that any converts that the open-door Adventists made were all Satan's counterfeits

Two years a long time to only preach shut door and midnight cry

When one is earnestly proclaiming that Christ's Second Advent will occur in a few days, weeks, or months, two or three years is a very, very long time. Yet from October 23, 1844 to the winter of 1846, Ellen Harmon's sole message was the validity of the date-setting midnight cry, to insist that the door was shut, and to propose an invisible coming of the bridegroom. These items constituted the "final test" that would determine one's salvation. Only two years later did Ellen supplement this gospel with the Sabbath. Thereafter, her burden was "the Sabbath and the shut door," which she considered to be inseparable. She and her shut-door colleagues spent all their energy disputing with open-door Adventists about whether their date-setting proclamation during the midnight cry was a fulfillment of prophecy. As late as August 4, 1850 Ellen White saw that they should attempt to shame their open-door opponents by filling their new periodicals with reprints of articles written by open-door Adventists around 1843–1844.

> The Lord showed me that he, James Springer White, must take the testimonies that the leading Adventists published in 1844 and republish them and make them ashamed.[28]

---

28. White, *Ellen G. White Letters & Manuscripts*, 211.

Miller lost according to logic of Ellen Harmon's first vision

In contrast to William Miller's confession of error, Ellen Harmon insisted that God was in the date-setting midnight cry. She argued that to label the date-setting midnight cry an error was equivalent to heresy. The message of her first vision was that the date-setting midnight cry was a divine light shining on their heavenward path; that the Little Flock was still on the narrow, steep path to heaven; that she'd seen Levi Stockman and Brother Fitch in heaven; that they would soon have a right to the tree of life that she had seen there. Conversely, those who rashly denied the light of the midnight cry were irretrievably lost. Logically, this had to include William Miller. Unnamed associates, like J. V. Himes, were guilty of leading the aging leader astray, according to Ellen White, Emily Clemmons, and other shut-door adherents.

Sabbath and shut door replaces shut door alone after two years

Ellen Harmon's sole focus for about two years, from winter of 1844 to autumn of 1846, was preaching the shut door of Matthew 25. This entailed two things: first, that Christ's second coming was still extremely, extremely imminent; second, that the fate of the wicked world and the fallen nominal churches was already decided; third, that all that remained for the remnant to do was to keep the faith in the midnight cry—for they would be immortal very, very soon.

In her March 24, 1849 open- and shut-door vision she linked the Sabbath and the shut door inseparably, speaking of the Sabbath under the rubric of "the commandments of God."[29] She argued that the door was shut and therefore all so-called conversions were false. Ellen White had seen that "the time of their salvation is passed." She repeated the same phrase in an April 21, 1849 letter addressed to Leonard W. and Elvira Hastings.[30] Ellen G. White's extrabiblical authority was the sole evidence that genuine conversions were impossible.

In framing the shut-door debate, Ellen G. White claimed that all those who rejected the midnight cry were rejecting the second

---

29. White, *Ellen G. White Letters & Manuscripts*, 160, 163.
30. White, *Ellen G. White Letters & Manuscripts*, 166–68.

coming *per se*. It is not true that persons who rejected the date-setting of the midnight cry were rejecting the doctrine of the Second Advent. Indeed, Miller was quite a popular revival speaker in multiple denominations during the years 1835–1842. It was only about 1842, when he settled on a specific year and then a specific day, that his disciples were disciplined for heresy.

Also, it is misleading to call the midnight cry biblical "light" when that proclamation directly contravened Christ's warning that specific dates should not be set. Therefore, for Mrs. White to state in later years that people were guilty of rejecting biblical truth was a mischaracterization of events. Crosier's explanation of an extended atonement, a two-part coming, a two-apartment ministry, and eventually White's investigation judgment as a retooling of what the midnight cry meant, does not indicate that this altered version was the message actually taught in the midnight-cry phase of Millerism.

Extreme imminence = functional date-setting

Another indication that Ellen G. White believed that the door was shut is the multiple extreme imminence assertions she made between 1845 and 1851.

Not infrequently, Ellen G. White's accounts of her visions border on non-grammatical glossolalia. There are disjointed phrases rather than grammatically comprehensible sentences. This makes it virtually impossible to make sense out of them. For this very reason they made a strong impression on her disciples. Cryptic, enigmatic, mysterious, ineffable, and urgent utterances were calculated to make a much bigger impression than dry, logical discourse. Ellen Harmon's style was very different from the expository, logical style of J. V. Himes or William Miller. She did not hesitate to use contradiction and paradox to communicate her top-priority message, a kind of midnight cry after the midnight cry.

Snow's midnight cry was unvarnished, discredited date-setting. Ellen G. White employed functional date-setting instead. For example, in her June 30, 1849 vision at Rocky Hill, she used multiple symbols: "Just about to bathe His sword in heaven. How long? How long? How long? How long?" The first phrase is not a grammatical sentence. But it does fire the imagination. To the rhetorical question "How long?," the unmistakably implied answer was: sooner than you can possibly imagine. Words could not adequately express this imminence. Ellen White held that Jesus would soon put on his kingly robes in phase 2, bathing his sword. She repeatedly emphasized swiftness: "Swift messengers," "speed the messengers" is *repeated four times*. Her diction is compacted still more. The end is super, super, super, super near; it could not be nearer. "The angels are letting go, the sword, famine, and pestilence coming speedily." "The sealing work will soon be done." "Every case fixed" (past tense). "The time of trouble is coming." "The latter rain is coming; a few drops have fallen (healing the sick)." In this last phrase, the latter rain is such an imminent future that its beginning is already past. Can there be any greater imminence? It's like: the Titanic is about to sink; it is already sinking. Similarly, she wrote: "The light is almost gone." "The jewels are almost made up. They are made up but they do not shine." But the jewels cannot be "made up," past tense, and simultaneously be "almost made up." She flouted coherence deliberately to emphasize the extreme imminence of the second coming. And this is but a miniscule representative sample of her extreme imminence rhetoric.[31]

Although she did not explicitly promulgate a fixed date that could be easily falsified, she communicated what may as well be a fixed date. In her September 23, 1849 "Remarks in Vision," she employed similar techniques of repetition, allusion, and creative incoherence. "Closing up, closing up, closing up, closing up. But two things—heaven or hell, life or death, now, now." "Behold ye, pleading that blood and after that work is finished. He will hold out no longer. Girds His sword upon His thigh and rides forth for the deliverance of the captive, the destroying angels!"[32] She used cryptic language, non-grammatical structures, repetition, creative incoherence, and ambiguity to express herself in such a manner that it is impossible to tell what she was really attempting to say. But the message was clear. The second coming was unimaginably imminent.

Repeatedly she used various textual slogans to denote that the second coming would occur within a few months. She claimed that new converts would have to learn in a few months what had taken Millerites years to learn. She employed catchphrases, including "the

---

31. White, *Ellen G. White Letters & Manuscripts*, 177–80.
32. White, *Ellen G. White Letters & Manuscripts*, 181–85.

loud cry," the "sealing," the four angels loosening the winds of strife, Jacob's "time of trouble," and the "time of trouble" (the last two as if they were chronologically discrete apocalyptic events). For instance, on November 18, 1848 she asserted:

> The time of trouble has commenced, it is begun. The reason why the four winds have not let go, is because the saints are not all sealed. It's on the increase, and will increase more and more; the trouble will never end until the earth is rid of the wicked.[33]

The "time of trouble" is a cataclysmic event just prior to the second coming. In the above quotation Ellen G. White was asserting not only that "it is begun," but that it would increase in intensity until Christ's second coming rids the earth of the wicked. According to White, "the time of trouble" had been ongoing since the 1840s which means it has purportedly been growing in intensity for about 170 years.

Ellen G. White described the second coming as so imminent in the 1850s that, of course, the door was shut. With Christ girding on his sword and announcing, "heaven or hell, life or death, now, now," the door must have been shut before "now." Ellen G. White made scores more of such extreme imminence assertions, too many to extensively cite.

Burt (2014), constrained to agree with Damsteegt (1977) and Olson (1982), summarized his discussion of the shut door, stating:

> the tenor of her statements and those closely connected with her suggests that for a time she continued to believe that evangelistic work for the unconverted world had ended.[34]

Yet, simultaneously he asserted that: "Her visions did not require this understanding..."[35] In distinction to this unusual apologetic, the natural interpretation of her first vision is that it did "require this understanding." Both her own account of her first vision and James White's account of it stated that those who rashly denied the midnight cry

---

33. White, *Ellen G. White Letters & Manuscripts*, 136–37.
34. Burt, "'Shut Door' and Ellen White's Visions," 57.
35. Burt, "'Shut Door' and Ellen White's Visions," 57.

fell off the path down in the dark and wicked world below. It was just as impossible for them to get on the path again & go to the City, as all the wicked world which God had rejected. They fell all the way along the path one after another, until we heard the voice of God like many waters, which gave us the day and hour of Jesus' coming.[36]

It is as clear as language can make it that those denying the midnight cry would suffer the fate of the wicked world until the end of time, when they would hear the "voice of God" announcing the day and hour of Jesus' coming.

In Ellen Harmon's 1851 revision of her first vision, she retained her insistence that God would make known the "day and hour." Ellen Harmon was denouncing that: "{Others rashly denied the light behind them}, and said that it was not God that had led them out so far. The light behind them went out {leaving their feet in perfect darkness, and they stumbled and got their eyes off the mark and lost sight of Jesus, and fell off the path down in the dark and wicked world below}. [*It was just as impossible for them to get on the path again and go to the City, as all the wicked world which God had rejected.*][37] "They fell all the way along the path, one after another, {until we heard the voice of God like many waters, which gave us the *day and hour* of Jesus' coming}."[38] James White wrote his contemporary understanding of this vision on August 19, 1845, four months before Ellen Harmon produced a written version of the oral versions of her first vision that she had been giving in house meetings. It was published September 6, 1845 in the *Day-Star*. He stated:

> There is one Sister in Maine who has had a clear vision of the Advent people traveling to the City of God. In her vision she heard the "Midnight Cry"—she saw a mighty host start at the point where the cry was made (finished)—soon she saw [many denying the light set behind them], (which was the midnight cry). By this time [they were in darkness,

---

36. White, *Ellen G. White Letters & Manuscripts*, 86.

37. This sentence in italics was deleted in the 1851 revision. What these words meant, before they were excised without notice or explanation, and why they were excised, is at the core of the debate as to Ellen Harmon's prophetic gift and its reliability. If she "misunderstood" life-and-death aspects of her initial vision, how can one maintain either a thought or a word paradigm of her inspiration?

38. Note how Ellen's words within these symbols {} are paralleled by those of James White's phrases below.

and began to stumble and fall off from the strait and narrow path, down into the dark world below to rise no more]. She saw them continually falling [till the voice of God was heard] as recorded in Ezekiel 12:25[39], which was a number of days before the 'Sign of the Son of Man' appeared—which was the great white cloud. Revelation 14:14.[40]

In both accounts the Millerites who denied the prophetic validity of the midnight cry have fallen off the path to the "City of God" to be counted with the wicked. When James said that they were "to rise no more," it was a paraphrase of Ellen Harmon's "it was just as impossible for them to get on the path again and go to the City." It was self-evident that their probation had closed since they were "continually falling till the voice of God was heard" just preceding the second coming. Levterov, director of the Ellen G. White Estate branch office at Loma Linda University, notes that "[t]he Sabbatarians, including Ellen White, supported this idea [the shut-door belief] for some years after the Disappointment, but then rejected it."[41] And Knight states: "Sabbatarians believed that probation had closed for all who had rejected Millerism."[42] Wheeler concurs, noting that James White wrote: "I have no doubt as to the Advent history, shut door and all, not one."[43] Thus, the consensus of scholars in works published by the Review and Herald and Pacific Press is that Ellen Harmon's first vision described those rejecting the midnight cry as eternally lost.

Many SDA apologists attempt to mitigate the historical reality and the clear import of the primary source documents by claiming that Ellen Harmon did not attempt to make converts from the "lost"

---

39. This unpretentious textual reference is critically important and revealing. This was a *key proof text* in the proto-SDA Little Flock's self-understanding. See chapter 6 for my discussion of Snow's bizarre exposition of this text. James White still comprehended the text via this paradigm *years after* Snow's 1844 midnight cry. See S. S. Snow, "Letter from S. S. Snow," *Midnight Cry*, June 27, 1844. Also, Otis Nichols continued to cite this same text with the same understanding of it in his April 1846 letter to William Miller pleading with him to accept Ellen Harmon's gift. Finally, and most critically, *as late as 1884* White (Great Controversy [1998], 206) cited this scripture as a proof text that substantiated her explanation for Miller's failed March 21, 1844 prophecy and the tarrying time.

40. White, "Watchman, What of the Night?" 25–26.

41. Levterov, *Development*.

42. Knight, *Joseph Bates*, 125.

43. Wheeler, *James White*, 44–45.

because the wicked world was not amenable to their message; so she did not try. They suggest it was just a historical accident that Ellen Harmon's burden was limited to midnight-cry adherents. Further, apologists argue that the term "shut door" changed in meaning and included an open door very soon.

The principle of the analogy of Scripture, cited by Damsteegt, must be applied to the statements of Mrs. White. This requires that unambiguous contemporary statements must be used to interpret late or ambiguous statements. Just such a statement was provided by Otis Nichols on April 24, 1846 in a letter to William Miller. He was Ellen Harmon's biggest financial supporter. At the time, he had provided Ellen Harmon with room and board for about eight months. Eventually, he would spend a large amount of his total net worth supporting James and Ellen White's personal ministry. Thus, he was a very friendly and intimate witness to Ellen Harmon's activities and thoughts. He plainly stated that Ellen Harmon encouraged Adventists to

> hold on to the faith and the seventh month movement and that our work was done for the nominal church and the world, and what remains to be done was for the house hold of faith.[44]

Burt concedes that between the Great Disappointment and December 1844, when she had her first vision, she believed "that the October 1844 date was wrong, . . . that Adventists should look to a future date for the coming of Jesus and resume their proclamation to the world."[45] This was what J. V. Himes, William Miller, and the Albany Conference statements proposed. Then her first vision convinced her to reaffirm the October 22, 1844 date, and she "readopted certain aspects of the shut-door that she had previously believed." Thus, apologists perform damage control in asserting that while Ellen Harmon might have temporarily suffered from the "misconception" that "the time of their salvation [sinners] is past"; her visions never explicitly taught this.[46] Yet in 1851 she said: "I saw that the mysterious signs and wonders, and false reformations[47] would increase, and

---

44. Burt, "'Shut Door' and Ellen White's Visions," 49.
45. Burt, "'Shut Door' and Ellen White's Visions," 49.
46. Burt, "'Shut Door' and Ellen White's Visions," 48.
47. "False reformations" is just a synonym for false conversions, itself a surrogate for the shut-door doctrine.

spread. The reformations that were shown me were not reformations from error to truth … My accompanying angel bade me look for the travail of soul for sinners as used to be. I looked, but could not see it; for the time for their salvation is past."[48]

Such statements cannot legitimately be reinterpreted years later on the basis of subsequent documents and fuzzy memories when such interpretations contradict contemporaneous primary documents. Yet years later she would refashion her earlier statements by asserting that in the 1844–1851 epoch she conceived of a third group, namely, "those who have not heard and have not rejected the doctrine of the Second Advent." This directly contradicts Robert Olson's 1982 conclusion that: "She failed to recognize, however, that there was a third category … who had never heard or fully appreciated the Millerite message in the first place." In 1844–1851 she conceived of a strict dichotomous paradigm. Only two groups, not three, existed: the sheep and the goats, the tares and the wheat, the chaff and the grain. On October 22, 1844 the Millerites were convinced that they had preached the everlasting gospel to every tongue, nation, and island. A fundamental aspect of the midnight cry was that it had been preached "into all the world." Even Damsteegt admits that Miller believed that the accomplishment of Matthew 24:14's command to preach Christ to "all the world" had been accomplished and that this was one of the signal "signs of the time of the end." He cites Miller as claiming that the message had gone out to the "four quarters of the globe," including Asia, Africa, Europe, and the Americas. "There was no doubt in the mind of Miller that this prediction had been accomplished as one of the signs of the time of the end."[49] Since it had been preached "into all the world," every sincere person had had the opportunity to either accept or reject the "light" and their fate had been decided.

According to pre-1844 Millerite proclamations, Christ could only appear on October 22, 1844 under the Millerite presumption that everyone had already been proclaimed either "clean" or "dirty" prior to that date. Yet years later it was always a phantom third group to which Ellen G. White would appeal to absolve her visions of error.

Merlin Burt pleads that we must "allow for correction" "on the part of the messenger." "A common misconception regarding the gift

---

48. Burt, "'Shut Door' and Ellen White's Visions," 53 n. 65.
49. Damsteegt, *Foundations*, 50.

of prophecy is the belief that prophetic revelation does not allow for correction or growth in understanding on the part of the messenger."[50] But correction necessarily involves error, like an apology necessarily involves an offense. Burt also pleads that Old Testament patriarchs, whom Christians consider inspired, practiced polygamy, implying that if Old Testament prophets could practice polygamy and still be considered inspired, Ellen G. White could proclaim theological errors without blemishing her prophetic credentials. But would Burt apply the same criteria to Joseph Smith? More importantly, Ellen G. White herself never conceded an error or misinterpretation for which she needed to make correction. It is not only her latter-day apologists who make maximalist claims regarding her factual and theological reliability. Ellen G. White herself also made categorical, maximalist claims. She repeatedly said she saw or received direct revelations for hundreds of statements (testimonies). When persons questioned her reliability, she responded that she was just as reliant on the Holy Spirit for the form in which she communicated her revelations as she was in receiving direct revelations in the first place.

Visions excised of erroneous concepts?

The consensus of scholars intimately associated with the Ellen G. White Estate is that Ellen Harmon endorsed erroneous concepts about the shut door and close of probation for several years. They explain that she miscomprehended her own visions and assert that canonical prophets did the same. The intellectual and literary source of this error was her dependence upon Miller and his disciples. There is a pattern in Ellen White's habit of borrowing erroneous facts and presenting them as if they were emanating directly from the divine mind. It began with her first vision. In "'It Was Not Taught Me by Man': Ellen White's Visions and 2 Esdras," I documented that Ellen Harmon was dependent on the pseudepigraphical book of 2 Esdras for elements of her first vision.[51] It continued when she copied Miller's many erroneous interpretations and Snow's failed midnight-cry prediction. In this chapter I have documented that Turner's written explanation of the bridegroom theory antedates Ellen Harmon's late

50. Burt, "'Shut Door' and Ellen White's Visions," 53.
51. Casebolt, "'It Was Not Taught Me by Man,'" 66–73.

oral explanation. Similarly, Ellen Harmon endorsed Crosier only after Crosier was endorsed by Bates. Thus, Crosier, followed by Bates and Harmon, established the novel extended-atonement rational for the delay of the Parousia.

Four watches of the night predicts second coming in October 1845

Date-setting by Ellen Harmon's closest collaborator, James White

The Millerites both before and after the Great Disappointment were obsessed with prophetic periods and exact dates. They found prophetic periods and dates in all kinds of biblical texts, and years and thousands of years in any occurrence of the word "day." These included not just Daniel and Revelation, but Hosea, Luke, Matthew, Mark, Ezra, and the books in the Pentateuch, Deuteronomy and Leviticus. These prophetic periods, interpreted via their allegorical-typological-historicist method, established "the essential theological framework for the foundations of the Seventh-day Adventist Church," according to Damsteegt. He documents the continuity between Miller's methodology and that adopted by the founders of the SDA church. James White was among those who predicted the second coming in 1845 on this same foundation. Several Millerite expositors cited Mark 13:35 ("Watch therefore—for you do not know when the master of the house will come, in the evening, or in midnight, or at cockcrow, or in the morning" [KJV])[52] and Luke 12:38 (which only mentions a second and third watch) as proof texts that Christ would come again in the autumn of 1845. They divided the night into four watches including 1) evening, 2) midnight, 3) the cock crowing, and 4) the morning watch. They interpreted these as four *definite* periods of watching for his return. Just as Millerites had assigned three specific dates for each of the three angels of Revelation 14, they continued to historicize their own history. They imagined that they could distinguish four periods of watchfulness, each covering roughly six months, lasting a total of two years. They identified the evening watch with the six months from

52. . Ironically, James White strained out the four gnats ("in the evening, or in midnight, or at cockcrow, or in the morning") and swallowed the camel (—"Watch therefore—*for you do not know when* the master of the house will come").

the autumn of 1843 until the first disappointment on March 21, 1844. They identified the midnight watch with the interval between spring of 1844 and October 22, 1844. They identified the cock-crowing watch with the interval from October 22, 1844 until the Great Jubilee of the spring of 1845. They then imagined that they were "unquestionably in the morning watch."[53] Enoch Jacobs, the *Day-Star* editor, predicted that the morning watch would end in October 1845.[54] Since they generally used the day-year rule, one would assume that they would be consistent. That is, given that the four night watches should be equivalent to half of a prophetic day, that would only cover a historical six months. Why they spread out four watches over two years is curious but clear. It was their subjective sense that their lived experience included four intervals of heightened watchfulness over a period of two years that led them to read back into history the four watches. Then, as if to provide another illustration of the highly subjective interpretations one could obtain by employing the allegorical-typological-historicist method, James White came up with a modification to the four-watches theme. Only about four weeks before the predicted autumn 1845 date, he proposed a new chronology of four watches to the *Day-Star*. He speculated that the four night watches covered a single year from October 1844 to October 1845 and had intervals of only three months each. The first watch began on October 22, 1844 and "reached to January [1845] when we got light on the shut door. The second brought us to the Passover [of spring 1845]. (Midnight, or midway in this watching night.) The third brought us to the supposed end of the 1335 days in July [of 1845], since we have been in the morning watch."[55] Displaying typical Millerite certainty that his typological calculations were exact, he wrote that "all who see this light will receive a certainty that before the 10th day of the 7th month 1845 [October], our King will come and we will watch, and like Noah, know the day (Rev 3:3), Awake, awake! awake!! ye heralds of the Jubilee, and tell the scattered flock. The morning cometh!"[56] James White

---

53. Damsteegt, "Early Adventist Timesettings," 156–60.

54. Jacobs, "Watches," 38.

55. White, "Watchman," 25–26. The light on the shut door was Crosier's "true light" that Christ's mediatorial work after October 22, 1844 was exclusively for the wise virgins who still believed the date-setting midnight cry of October 22, 1844 was God's light.

56. White, "Watchman," 25–26.

published this September 20, 1845. Crosier had published his original exposition of his extended-atonement concept in March 1845. Ellen White's first vision was not published until about four months later, January 24, 1846.⁵⁷ This chronological context is crucial. *There is no documentation that Ellen Harmon wrote or said anything to disabuse them of their belief that Christ would come by Passover or fall of 1845.* Many Millerites began proposing future dates very shortly after October 22, 1844. Ellen Harmon had almost a *year* to inform them that they were arbitrarily finding eschatological times in biblical texts that were obviously being twisted out of all rational context. If they had merely compared the Synoptic passage in Matthew (25:13) which paralleled Mark 13:35, they could have noted that it said: "Watch therefore, for ye know neither the day nor the hour" (KJV). Should it have required supernatural visions to realize that setting October of 1845 as the date for the second coming was likely to disappointment them?

Several typical Millerite characteristics are evident in James White's watches eschatology. He expressed certainty in his calculations. His calculations were all connected to typologically significant dates and prophetic periods. These included the Passover, the Day of Atonement, the midnight cry, the dating of the Great Jubilee, the 1,335 years, and the end of the 6,000 years (or beginning of the millennial Sabbath). He still expected, "like Noah, [to] know the day." Given James White's close association with Ellen Harmon in the autumn of 1845, when he wrote his September 20, 1845 exposition of the four watches, it is not probable that Ellen Harmon had a view that differed from White's. He had started travelling with her regularly months earlier. He had cradled her head during the arrest of Israel Dammon at this time (ca. February 1845). He already believed that she had prophetic authority. *Given his strong, publicized convictions on this critical topic, there is no doubt that Ellen Harmon was aware of James White's views on the four watches. Yet there is not the slightest indication that she expressed a differing opinion.* If she had, James White would never have published his exposition. Damsteegt writes that merely a "few days before the passing of time in October 1845, in Fairhaven, Massachusetts, James White was preaching Christ's return

---

57. Harmon, "Letter from Sister Harmon," 31, 32. Harmon had ample time to harmonize her visions with information she was obtaining from Crosier, Turner, Hale, and others.

in the seventh month . . ."[58] Damsteegt goes on to say that Ellen Harmon warned that she had just had a vision that this October 1845 date-setting would lead to another disappointment. But this is based on a late May 1847 statement of James White's. He stated that "we should be disappointed . . ."[59] He did not then say that they were not disappointed in October 1845. They were disappointed. He did state that it was "well known that many were expecting the Lord to come at the 7th month, 1845." He did not ever give an exact date for his prediction that Christ would come at the end of the fourth watch in autumn 1845. Therefore, saying later that Ellen Harmon had a vision saying they would be disappointed "a few days before the time passed" is vague and undatable. How could anything happen "a few days before" if a precise date was never given before? From James White's account, it is typically inferred that he was stating that "a few days before" the end of October 1845 she warned James that he should abandon using his watches theory. There is no documentation prior to October 1845 that James White publicly repudiated his four-watches speculation.

Even if Ellen Harmon did tell James White towards the end of October 1845 that he should abandon this date, this is very meager evidence in support of the claim that this indicates foreknowledge based on a vision. The vast majority of the public already knew from first principles that James White's four-watches theory was unwise. It was notorious that the Millerites had already mistakenly predicted a half-dozen specific dates. It did not require prophetic visions to recommend avoiding an encore. Is it reasonable to imagine that God would have allowed James White and many other Millerites to propound this non-biblical date-setting hypothesis for months and months, only to clue in Ellen Harmon just a few days prior to the end of October 1845 that this was a foolhardy speculation?

The non-Millerite world had been telling them for years that it was unwise to ignore the warning of Christ that "the day" could not be known. It really did not require a vision to reach this conclusion. Furthermore, the entire tenor of James White's May 1847 booklet (and Ellen Harmon's first vision) was that "the day" would be known, and he still quoted S. S. Snow's categorical statements about an exact date to prove it! Finally, surely Ellen Harmon was aware of the many other

---

58. Damsteegt, "Early Adventist Timesettings," 163.
59. White et al., "Word," (2014), 56.

Millerites (listed in Damsteegt's footnotes) that wrote interpretations of the four watches just like James White's, as well as the many others that wrote expositions proposing a variety of contradictory definite times centered on typologically significant periods, like Passover in the spring of 1845. There is no record in 1845 or even later that Ellen Harmon-White received a vision notifying the Millerites that their *method* of interpreting the Bible was erroneous.

A comparison of her first vision with her April 1847 Sabbath vision in chapter 9 further demonstrates her dependence upon human sources. This comes into sharp focus when one notes the textual excisions that were made to the visions between 1845 and 1851. These changes were due to the human sources which determined Ellen Harmon's changing views on new and foundational doctrines.

IX

EGW saw Sabbath, High Priest, and Censer in late 1847 Vision Only after These Ideas Were Taught Her by Bates, Crosier, Turner. They Are Missing "behind the Veil" in December 1844 Vision

APOLLOS HALE, JOSEPH TURNER, Crosier, and Bates introduced key theological concepts to Ellen Harmon. Regardless of the specific typological symbolisms they used, their concepts all had in common the necessity that Christ *physically move from the Holy Place into the Most Holy Place behind "within the veil"*[1] by October 22, 1844. Those critical of this explanation for the delay have noted that this was an invisible, semi-spiritualizing explanation that was unverifiable because it had no human eyewitness. However, Ellen Harmon claimed to be an eyewitness of what was "within the veil" during her tour there in December 1844. Her observations have been overlooked for 177 years. Indeed, a large portion of her first vision, about forty entire lines, purports to be a vivid eyewitness description of what was "within the veil." Stranger still, exactly these forty lines were excised without explanation by the Whites in 1851.

Ellen sees after she has been first told

The heavenly flora and geography of 2 Esdras 2:19 purportedly seen by the pseudepigraphal Ezra were not objective, external realities. When Ellen Harmon copied these same scenes in her first vision, she

---

1. This was a well-worn expression in Millerism that referred to a veil between the Holy Place and Most Holy Place.

had not seen them as an objective, external reality. Rather, her prior reading of 2 Esdras caused her to experience a virtual reality during an out-of-body experience triggered by her recollections of having *read* such scenes. She did not distinguish between seeing pseudepigraphal scenes from seeing canonical depictions of heavenly geography. Both James White and Joseph Bates considered 2 Esdras just as prophetic as any Old Testament or New Testament prophet.[2] Ellen White followed their lead. The triumvirate, Joseph Bates and James and Ellen White, were united in their high regard for Esdras.

Moreover, there are multiple elements in her initial key visions which were also derived from her previsionary thought world and *brought to* her visionary experience rather than originating from it. These include 1) the concept of a two-compartment ministry; 2) the concept that as a bridegroom Jesus "came" on October 22, 1844, travelling from the heavenly Holy Place to the Most Holy Place; 3) the concept that a high priestly Jesus took a censer and began an investigative judgment/Day of Atonement ministry on October 22, 1844; 4) the view that non–shut-door advocates were the "synagogue of Satan" who would soon see the 144,000 shut-door believers triumphantly exchanging "holy kisses" and washing one another's feet; and 5) the concept that the Sabbath had such a preeminent eschatological significance that its inscription on one of two tablets of stone in the Most Holy Place had a halo of light around it.

Ironically, Ellen Harmon's first vision is eyewitness proof that the event which replaced the second coming in the midnight cry, Jesus moving from the Holy into the Most Holy Place, had not occurred at the time of Ellen Harmon's eyewitness journey to the heavenly Most Holy Place in December 1844.

If on October 22, 1844 Jesus had moved "within the vail" as High Priest with a golden censer, and if he was offering "up the prayers of the saints with the smoke of the incense to His Father," as Ellen White asserted in her April 1847 vision, one would expect this external reality to have been visualized by Ellen White in her December 1844 vision. On the contrary, there is no sighting of Jesus as High Priest in the heavenly Most Holy Place in Ellen Harmon's first vision. Ellen White's sighting of Jesus as High Priest with a golden censer in April

---

2. Bates, *Second Advent Way Marks*, 115–22, says: "The prophecy of Esdras begins to search and burn like fire." James White cited 2 Esdras as a "prophecy which has been fulfilling since Octo. 1844" in his May 1847 "Word to the 'Little Flock,'" 1–3.

1847 was a concept she had learned in the interim and brought to her later version. Forty lines, in which a High Priest and his golden censer were conspicuously absent, were expunged in the 1851 version of the first vision.[3]

The eye-popping singularity of the first vision is *what Ellen Harmon did not see* in the Most Holy Place, "within the veil"—and which was later excised. The context is as follows.

Ellen Harmon has just spoken about seeing "brothers Fitch and Stockman." She and they try to "call up our greatest trials," but given the splendor of the city which they had just seen and the "tree of life" and the "throne of God," they conclude that "heaven is cheap enough." They are singing Hallelujah with their glorious harps when their eyes are attracted by "something that had the appearance of silver. I asked Jesus to let me see what was within there." Shortly they are "entering in." Then Ellen says: "I saw a vail with a heavy fringe of silver and gold, as a border on the bottom; it was very beautiful."[4]

> I asked Jesus what was within the vail. He raised it with his own right arm, and *bade me take heed* [emphasis added]. I saw there a glorious ark, overlaid with pure gold, and it had a glorious border, resembling Jesus' crowns; and on it were two bright angels—their wings were spread over the ark as they sat on each end, with their faces turned towards each other and looking downward. *29 In the ark, beneath where the angels' wings were spread, was a golden pot of Manna, of a yellowish cast; and I saw a rod, which Jesus said was Aaron's; I saw it bud, blossom and bear fruit. *30 And I saw two long golden rods, on which hung silver wires, and on the wires most glorious grapes; one cluster was more than a man here could carry. And I saw Jesus step up and take of the manna, almonds, grapes and pomegranates, and bear them down to the city, and place them on the supper table.[5]

The crucial aspect of this extended section of Ellen Harmon's first vision is that it is describes in great detail what was "within the vail" in the Most Holy Place and that Ellen had pointedly asked Jesus

---

3. Graybill, *Visions & Revisions*, 38–39. The asterisks with numbers have been supplied by James White to mark scriptural references, which his correspondents have asked him to include to bolster Ellen G. White's prophetic claims.

4. James White, "Word to the 'Little Flock.'" 19–20.

5. James White, "Word to the 'Little Flock,'" 19–20.

about what was "within the vail." Jesus, with some solemnity, opened the vail with his own right arm and "bade me take heed." Jesus was not only replying to her direct question but giving her an imperative: "take heed." Clearly the matter was of great import. Most of Ellen's description adds nothing to what is already well-known to anyone who has read Exodus 25:10–16; 37:1–5; Numbers 17:8–10; and Hebrews 9:4. Bible expositors agree that there was but one article of furniture within the Most Holy Place: the ark. That ark was composed, for the most part, of the items which Ellen Harmon saw: the ark had a centerpiece "overlain with pure gold," two cherubim facing each other on each end, two gold-plated rods, and a golden pot of manna that is said in Hebrews to have been placed "within the ark." Ellen scrutinized the manna carefully enough to describe the color of the manna being "of a yellowish cast." Finally, she saw Aaron's rod (with buds of almonds) mentioned in Numbers 17:8–10.

Missing two tablets of stone, but extra-biblical items seen

What is remarkable in Harmon's description is the missing quintessential—the two tablets of stone containing the Ten Commandments. Harmon's forty-line description of items "within the veil" was discarded in the 1851 version. Inexplicably, Ellen could describe the precise color of the manna but was visionless regarding the Ten Commandments and Sabbath. Also notable are the extra-biblical items that Ellen Harmon said that she did see. She reported seeing silver wires hanging from the two golden rods, "and on the wires most glorious grapes; one cluster was more than a man here could carry." In addition to the grapes, there were pomegranates. This scene in the Most Holy Place ended with Jesus taking the foodstuffs of manna, almonds, grapes, and pomegranates and placing them on a supper table in the city, to which the Advent band then proceeded. Now, given SDA insistence on rigid type-antitype parallels, is one to literally believe that there were silver wires, edible grape clusters, and pomegranates in the heavenly Most Holy Place?[6]

6. Alternatively, Ellen Harmon may have conflated the account in Number 13:23–4. Israeli spies cut a cluster of grapes so large two men had to carry them on a rod. Additionally, pomegranates and figs were brought back. Ellen Harmon alluded to this event in her preface. She saw herself, like them, on the borders of the Promised Land, bringing back a good report. "I have tried to bring back a good report, and a

Two years later, in her 1847 Sabbath vision, Ellen White reported seeing a reality allegedly outside her own mind that consisted of several discreet elements. (Since Ellen's body remained on earth, she did not literally see actual physical objects in a heavenly sanctuary. What she experienced was more akin to what we today would describe as a "virtual reality" experience, one conditioned by past experiences). There were two tablets of stone; the Ten Commandments were written on these, the first four commandments had a distinct aura about them, and the Sabbath commandment had a radiance that outshone all the rest. Could all these elements have had an independent reality outside of Ellen White's mind during her first vision whilst she was merely blinded to their sight? Furthermore, not only were the silver wires, grapes, and pomegranates non-biblical; the likelihood of perishable grapes and pomegranates being in the celestial Most Holy Place is doubtful. Lastly, the usual strict parallelism between type and antitype in SDA interpretation would be violated. If the earthly Most Holy Place in all respects reflected a heavenly reality, how was it that these pomegranates and grapes were non-existent in the earthly Most Holy Place?[7]

What Ellen White literally saw or did not see with her visionary eyes is beside the point theologically. She did not see things because they are *there*, external to herself. *She saw things which were theologically important to her*, things in which she was "most deeply interested" and would use to consolidate the Little Flock in their battles against the "wicked world," the "nominal Adventists," and the "synagogue of Satan."

Furthermore, there are other elements which were added to the December 1844 vision in the new and improved 1847 edition. The golden censer and the theological point which it is intended to make was another one of these elements.

---

few grapes from the heavenly Canaan."

7. The SDA teaching regarding the earthly and heavenly sanctuary is dependent upon strict typo/antitype relationship. Revelation states that there is no temple/sanctuary at all in heaven. God is experienced there directly without need for architecture.

The missing High Priest and censer in Ellen Harmon's first vision

The 1847 Little Flock document issued under James White's name was a tightly interlocking coproduction of three authors, James and Ellen White, and Joseph Bates. Like a three-stranded cord, each coauthor reinforced the other. Starting with James White's forty-second annotation where Ellen White says: "Jesus raised the second veil, and I passed into the Holy of Holies," she began an extended depiction about what she saw within the "second veil." She again saw the ark and two cherubs, but introduced a new element before she even got to the tablets of stone and the Sabbath. This was a "golden censer." Its introduction in this vision was theologically critical for the investigative judgment/Day of Atonement rationalization for the delay of the Second Advent. According to Leviticus 16:11–14, on the Day of Atonement the High Priest was to use a censer to take burning incense "within the veil." This golden censer held in the right hand of the High Priest was sufficiently critical to Ellen White that she made certain it was included in the White/Nichols 1851 prophetic chart, whose significance is discussed in detail in chapter 11.

How Ellen Harmon's 1850 visions evolved from her first vision, December 1844

On October 23, 1850 Ellen White had a vision that was fundamental to the theological significance of the golden censer she saw in her earlier Sabbath vision of 1847.

As late as 1884, Ellen G. White insisted that God had inspired the 1843 Millerite chart. Specifically, she asserted that God's Spirit "moved upon Charles Fitch" in 1842 to create the 1843 Millerite chart, and that his creation of the chart fulfilled the prophetic command of Habakkuk:

> As early as 1842, the Spirit of God had moved upon Charles Fitch to devise the prophetic chart, which was generally regarded by Adventists as a fulfillment of the command given by the prophet Habakkuk, "to write the vision and make it plain upon tables." No one, however, then saw the tarrying time, which was brought to view in the same prophecy. After

the disappointment, the full meaning of this scripture became apparent.[8]

Ellen G. White wrote out several other visions similar to her October 23, 1850 vision. The crucial point was that an updated chart was needed, one that incorporated the divinely inspired chart of 1843 but corrected the mistake that Ellen asserted had been hid by God's hand.

The cliché is that a picture is worth a thousand words. The White/Nichols 1851 chart captures Ellen G. White's theology, chronology, and hermeneutical positions in pictorial form. Unfortunately, since I am unable to produce for the reader the original, life-sized chart, my verbal description of the pictorial engravings can never do full justice to its visual nature. I strongly recommend that the reader procure a facsimile of the chart as I did. The most significant change between the 1843 chart and the White/Nichols 1851 chart is that the latter chart tacks on O. R. L. Crosier's two-compartment, extended-atonement hypothesis. Ellen G. White had sacralized Crosier's interpretation by including it in the new 1851 chart under her "inspiration." Adjacent to an engraving of the "third angel" is another engraving entitled "MOST HOLY, HEB. 9.3" This caption in bold capitals is above an engraving of the crowned High Priest[9] girded with a breastplate[10] and holding a golden censer of "burning incense" in his right hand above the ark of the covenant, flanked by two large cherubim hovering over two smaller cherubim kneeling on the ark of the covenant. The golden censer was a new element that Ellen G. White first saw in her 1847 Sabbath vision, which, significantly, she did not see in her first vision.[11] In the White/Nichols 1851 chart, below the Most Holy Place is engraved "2nd Vail Heb 9:3" "Sanctuary or Holy." The explanatory text for the "Sanctuary or Holy" identifies three symbols: "the Golden Candlestick, the

---

8. White, *Great Controversy* (1998), 205–7.

9. Thus, pictorially, Christ is simultaneously the High Priest of the first phase of the coming into the Most Holy and the crowned King of the second phase of the coming out of the Most Holy.

10. The breastplate would be a vital element later for Joseph Bates's soteriology and eschatology. On the breastplate Christ acting as High Priest carried the names of the 144,000 over his heart "within the vail."

11. The golden censer was an important pictorial symbol of the new doctrine of the extended atonement and investigative judgment, just like the bright halo over the Sabbath commandment symbolized the "Sabbath and shut door" slogan adopted by Ellen White at this time.

Table and shewbread, and the Brazen Altar and Laver."[12] Immediately below these three images as part of the pictorial (not explanatory text) is printed "DOOR EX. 26:36."[13] Adjacent is the newly minted three-angels hypothesis with specific dates for each angel: first angel 1837, second angel 1843, and third angel 1844. Since not a "peg" was to be altered "without inspiration," Ellen G. White closely supervised every "peg" of the White/Nichols 1851 chart. If it was so critical that the High Priest and golden censer had to be visual elements in the White/Nichols 1851 chart, how is it that this was missing in Ellen Harmon's December 1844 vision?

Hiram Edson, O.R. L. Crosier, F. B. Hahn, Joseph Turner, and Apollos Hale had contributed to the development that a movement of Christ, the High Priest with a golden censer, to the Most Holy Place "behind the veil"—not the second coming—was the event which happened on October 22, 1844. Crosier printed his findings March 1845 in the *Day-Dawn*. Even earlier, in January 1845, Apollos Hale and Joseph Turner published an article in which they claimed that "the coming of the bridegroom" indicated "some change of work or office, on the part of our Lord," "within the veil." In early 1845 Emily Clemons, who lived near Ellen Harmon and was deemed a visionary by some, published similar speculations on the heavenly sanctuary. G. W. Peavy taught in April 1845 that Christ had "closed the work typified by the daily ministrations previous to the 10th day of the 7th mon, and on that day went into the holiest of all." By February 7, 1846 Crosier had published an extended article on the subject.[14] By the time Ellen White had endorsed Crosier's findings in the May 1847 "A Word to the 'Little Flock,'" she must have been, between December 1844 and May 1847, influenced or "taught by man," and have read Bates' endorsement of Crosier, which preceded hers. But in December 1844 during her first vision, neither Bates's advocacy of the Sabbath nor O. R. L. Crosier's and others' concept of the Day of Atonement/investigative judgment occurred to Ellen Harmon. Given that prior to December 1844 Ellen Harmon could not have read, studied, or had

---

12. The explanatory caption continues: "These are patterns of the SANCTUARY in heaven, and TYPES of the Ministration of our great High Priest in the heavenly holy places. Heb. 8:5; 9:1–5."

13. There is a strong visual element emphasizing that the "2nd Vail" of Hebrews 9:3 is now open while the "Door" of Exodus 26:36 is "shut."

14. Knight, *Bates*, 93–95.

"religious reveries" concerning these future theological speculations, this explains the censer's and Sabbath's absence in December 1844 contrasted with their appearance in the 1847 vision.

The golden censer was utilized by the high priest during the Day of Atonement. When Ellen White later saw it, this helped "prove" that something did happen of salvific importance on October 22, 1844. Jesus, acting in his High Priest role (before putting on his kingly Parousia robes), now moved "within the veil" and "as the saints' prayers came up to Jesus, the incense in the censer would smoke, and He offered up the prayers of the saints with the smoke of the incense to His Father."[15]

The doctrine of the investigative judgment was predicated on Jesus as High Priest with the golden censer being bodily present "within the veil" of the celestial Most Holy Place by October 23, 1844. Astoundingly, he was missing (as was the Sabbath halo) in Ellen Harmon's December 1844 vision. To be consistent with Ellen White's concept that Jesus moved from one compartment to a second compartment of the invisible heavenly sanctuary, she also asserted that the Father's throne had to change locations. Thus, she had the Father move from a throne in the Holy Place to a throne in the Most Holy Place. Then, she saaid, Satan occupied the newly empty throne in the Holy Place.

Theological importance of new location of God's throne

The ark then "appeared like a throne where God dwelt." Before this throne, Jesus employed the censer. The location of the throne of God had taken on a polemical function in Ellen White's visions. She asserted that God's throne moved to the Most Holy Place while Satan sat on a throne, impersonating God, in the Holy Place, which God had vacated. She consigned her open-door opponents to the Holy Place, totally deceived and controlled by Satan. Meanwhile, Ellen Harmon had informed Brother Jacobs that since her first vision she had new visionary information which was of "vast importance to the Saints." In a letter published March 14, 1846[16] from Sister Harmon at Falmouth,

---

15. White, *Ellen G. White Letters & Manuscripts*, 112–13.

16. Considerably postdating the works of Crosier, Hahn, Edson, Hale, Turner, Clemons, and Peavy, whose concepts she copied.

Massachusetts, but composed February 15, 1846, she asserted that "one year ago this month: —I saw a throne, and on it sat the Father and his Son Jesus Christ." There followed a brief theological exposition, clearly influenced by the (Trinitarian/anti-Trinitarian) theological debates at the time (as well as current speculations as to the form or formlessness of Jesus). But the more critical debate concerned other theological disputes between two factions of Millerites. Like in her first vision, she saw three classes of persons: "Before the throne was the Advent people, the Church, and the world." [17] Ellen Harmon continued: "Then I saw an exceeding bright light[18] come from the Father to the Son and from the Son it waved over the people before the throne." This divided the "Advent people" into two groups: the group that agreed with Ellen Harmon and "cherished" the "bright light," and a group that disagreed with Ellen Harmon and "immediately resisted it." "Then I saw the Father rise from the throne and in a flaming chariot go into the Holy of Holies within the vail, and did sit." Jesus also rose from his throne and then took his place before the Father as a "great High Priest." Those agreeing with Ellen Harmon's new doctrine of the investigative judgment/Day of Atonement's function in explaining the delay in the Second Advent followed God the Father and God the Son into the Most Holy Place. Those who did not agree with her she described as left behind, "bowed before the throne," in the Holy Place. Meanwhile, Satan had occupied the empty throne in the Holy Place. "Satan appeared to be trying to carry on the work of God." Those "left behind" in the Holy Place were under the power of Satan, she asserted, because "Satan would breath on them an unholy influence." Due to satanic delusion, Ellen White said, duped ex-Millerites left the (doctrine of) Jesus in the Most Holy Place to rejoin Satan in the Holy Place, where at once "they received the unholy influence of Satan." However, she assured those that stayed in the Most Holy Place that soon the "Synagogue of Satan worshiped at the saints['] feet."[19]

   17. Is one to conclude that there literally are two throne rooms in the heavenly sanctuary? And that Satan is literally sitting on God's throne in the Holy Compartment of the heavenly sanctuary? This seems more likely a literary, visionary device to make a polemical theological point. This is a novel explanation for the delay of the second coming. Namely, an "extended" or centuries-long Day of Atonement/investigative judgment necessitates the Godhead moving from the Holy Compartment to the Most Holy Compartment.
   18. This bright light was elsewhere identified as the midnight cry.
   19. Harmon, "Letter from Sister Harmon," 1–2.

Mysteriously missing the Ten Commandments and Sabbath

In Ellen Harmon's first vision, what took place "within the vail" was so expendable that the entire section was summarily jettisoned in the 1851 revision. In the vision of April 1847, the Sabbath "within the veil" was central and was the immediate focus of attention. More importantly, the crucially missing items from the first vision, the two tablets of stone and the incalculably essential Sabbath commandment, took up the vast bulk of the 1847 vision. Ellen White addressed her central concern quickly in the eighth sentence (as numbered and annotated by J. S. White in his "word to the 'Little Flock'" version of this vision).

> I passed through a door[20] before I came to the first vail. This vail was raised, and I passed into the Holy Place. Here I saw the Altar of Incense, the candlestick with seven lamps, and the table on which was the showbread, etc. After viewing the glory of the Holy, Jesus raised the second veil, and I passed into the Holy of Holies. *42
>
> In the Holiest I saw an ark; on the top and sides of it was purest gold. On each end of the ark was a lovely Cherub, with their wings spread out over it. Their faces were turned towards each other, and they looked downwards. *43 Between the angels was a golden censer. Above the ark, where the angels stood, was an exceeding bright glory, that appeared like a throne where God dwelt. *44 Jesus stood by the ark. And as the saints' prayers came up to Jesus, the incense in the censer would smoke, and He offered up the prayers of the saints with the smoke of the incense to His Father. *45 In the ark, was the golden pot of manna, Aaron's rod that budded, and the tables of stone which folded together like a book. *46 Jesus opened them, and I saw the ten commandments written on them with the finger of God. *47 On one table was four, and on the other six. The four on the first table shone brighter than the other six. But the fourth (the Sabbath commandment,) shone above them all; for the Sabbath was set apart to be kept in honor of God's holy name. *48 The holy Sabbath looked glorious—a halo of glory was all around it. I

---

20. What possible sanctuary "door" could this be? The sanctuary had a first and second vail—not doors. This insignificant, mistaken detail belies the hyper-literality of the entire typological paradigm.

saw that the Sabbath was not nailed to the cross. If it was, the other nine commandments were; and we are at liberty to go forth and break them all, as well as to break the fourth. I saw that God had not changed the Sabbath, for He never changes. *49 But the Pope had changed it from the seventh to the first day of the week; for he was to change times and laws. *50

And I saw that if God had changed the Sabbath, from the seventh to the first day, He would have changed the writing of the Sabbath commandment, written on the tables of stone, which are now in the ark, in the Most Holy Place of the Temple in heaven; *51 and it would read thus: The first day is the Sabbath of the Lord thy God. But I saw that it read the same as when written on the tables of stone by the finger of God, and delivered to Moses in Sinai, "But the seventh day is the Sabbath of the Lord thy God." *52 I saw that the holy Sabbath is, and will be, the separating wall between the true Israel of God and unbelievers; and that the Sabbath is the great question, to unite the hearts of God's dear waiting saints. And if one believed, and kept the Sabbath, and received the blessing attending it, and then gave it up, and broke the holy commandment, they would shut the gates of the Holy City against themselves, as sure as there was a God that rules in heaven above. I saw that God had children, who do not see and keep the Sabbath. They had not rejected the light on it. And at the commencement of the time of trouble, we were filled with the Holy Ghost as we went forth *53 and proclaimed the Sabbath more fully. This enraged the church, and nominal Adventists, as they could not refute the Sabbath truth. And at this time, God's chosen, all saw clearly that we had the truth, and they came out and endured the persecution with us. And I saw the sword, famine, pestilence, and great confusion in the land. *54 The wicked thought that we had brought the judgments down on them. They rose up and took counsel to rid the earth of us, thinking that then the evil would be stayed. *55[21]

Given that Ellen Harmon had expressly asked Jesus to explain what was in the Most Holy Place in her first vision and that Jesus had emphasized that she must "take heed," how could it be that any visionary "within the veil" could have missed that "the fourth (the Sabbath commandment) shone above them all; for the Sabbath was set apart

21. White, White, and Bates, "Word to the 'Little Flock'" (2014), 47–49.

to be kept in honor of God's holy name. *48 The holy Sabbath looked glorious—a halo of glory was all around it"?

Did Ellen fail to "take heed?" Did Jesus neglect to explain? Was the halo of glory around it missing in December 1844? When James and Ellen White produced their revamped 1851 edition of her first vision, the forty lines of what Ellen Harmon did not see "within the veil" in 1844 had entirely disappeared.[22] This excision was restored only in an 1882 revision, when it could more safely be restored.[23]

In sum, the chronology of key theological-visionary events is well documented. When Ellen Harmon had her first vision in December 1844 and was given a detailed tour of the Most Holy Place, 1) she did *not* see the halo around the Sabbath; 2) she did *not* see that the first four commandments were brighter than the last six commandments; 3) she did not see that the pope had changed the Sabbath; 4) she did not see the golden censer with incense in the hands of the High Priest in the Most Holy Place. *She only saw these things in later visions after she had been "taught by man."* Only after Joseph Bates convinced her of the criticality of the Sabbath did she see a halo around the Sabbath in vision. Only after she had been taught the purported historicity of the pope's role in changing the Sabbath did she echo this claim as if she had received this historical information by direct revelation.[24] Ellen Harmon could not have seen the halo around the Sabbath in her December 1844 vision. She had not yet been "taught by man." That man was Joseph Bates. It was not until sometime after August 1846 that Joseph Bates urged the importance of the Sabbath on her. Even then, she "did not feel its importance, and thought that Bro. B. erred in dwelling upon the fourth commandment more than the other nine."[25]

---

22. Graybill, *Visions & Revisions*, 38-39.

23. Graybill, "Under the Triple Eagle," 25-33.

24. See chapter 13, where I have documented that this was not the case. The very early church, circa 150, began to venerate Sunday well before a centralized papal authority existed. Sunday was venerated in a geographic extent considerably beyond the jurisdiction of Rome. Several Sunday-venerating Roman Catholic popes were martyred in the pre-Constantine era, when Ellen G. White depicted the church as still being pure.

25. Knight, *Bates*, 95.

Obsolete seven times of the Gentiles: included in 1843 and 1851 charts

The seven times of the Gentiles or 2,520-year prophecy stretching from 677 BC to 1843 still appears prominently in the White/Nichols 1851 chart created by Ellen G. White. One might have imagined that by six years after the Disappointment Ellen White might have jettisoned the seven-times-of-the-Gentiles calculation. But when Nichols, at Ellen White's express urging, created the 1851 chart, it represented the consensus historicist theology and chronology of Ellen G. White and her followers. In the November 1850 issue of *Present Truth*, James White praised the chart because it was "calculated to illustrate clearly the present truth . . . Those who teach the present truth will be greatly aided by it."[26] Ellen G. White wrote in a June 2, 1853 letter of a vision given at Jackson, Michigan:

> I saw that God was in the publishment of the chart by Brother Nichols [Otis Nichols]. I saw that there was a prophecy of this chart in the Bible . . .[27]

Here Ellen White made an extremely striking claim! She claimed that she had a vision in which she saw that the White/Nichols 1851 chart, which she supervised under inspiration, was foreseen in a Bible prophecy. She previously claimed that God inspired Fitch to create its progenitor, the 1843 Millerite chart, and that God superintended this chart so that accurate figures were included in it, except for one mistake that God hid with his hand. It is significant that Ellen G. White stated that "God was in" the "publishment" of the Nichols chart. For this is the same phrase she used when she stated that "God was in" the midnight-cry movement. Even more astounding is her claim that the Bible contained a prophecy that her creation of the White/Nichols 1851 chart fulfilled! Writing on November 27, 1850 to the Hastings' house, she stated:

---

26. White, *Ellen G. White: The Early Years*, 185.

27. White, *Ellen G. White Letters & Manuscripts*, 358. Roland Karlman, the annotator of these documents, notes that this chart "depicted prophetic symbols from Daniel and Revelation together with time calculations. In October 1850 Ellen White had received instruction in vision that a prophetic chart should be published. During the next few months Otis Nichols supervised the publication of a chart that was advertised for distribution and sale in January 1851."

> On our return to Brother Nichols', the Lord gave me a vision and shewed me that the truth must be made plain upon tables and it would cause many to decide for the truth by the three angels' message with the two former being made plain upon tables.[28]

The phrase "plain upon tables" is taken from Habakkuk 2:2–3 and had been applied earlier by Millerites in regard to their 1843 chart. Recall that this was one of the key texts that S. S. Snow had relied on to explain the tarrying of the second coming after Miller's initial prediction of March 21, 1844 for the Parousia. Just a few days earlier, November 1, 1850, she had written:

> There [in Dorchester Massachusetts where Nichols lived] in the night God gave me a very interesting vison, the most of which you will see in the paper. God shewed me the necessity of getting out a chart. I saw it was needed and that the truth made plain upon tables would effect much and cause souls to come to the knowledge of the truth.[29]

In sum, God was in the 1851 White/Nichols chart; it was present truth. Yet it still contained, according to F. D Nichol, the "farfetched" 2,520-year, seven-times-of-the-Gentiles calculation.[30] Because it appears prominently in both the 1843 Millerite chart and the 1851 White/Nichols chart, it is doubly significant. Further, whereas Ellen G. White asserted that God led Miller to his conclusions regarding Daniel 8:14, historically, it was the seven times of the Gentiles that led him to the 2,300-days text.[31]

The 1,335-day-year prophecy was also part of the 1843 Millerite chart. In October 1850 in "A Vision Given on October 23, 1850" while she was at the home of Otis Nichols in Dorchester, Massachusetts, she argued that the previous six years had been the "scattering time," while currently it had become the "gathering time," when their evangelistic

---

28. White, *Ellen G. White Letters & Manuscripts*, 253–54.

29. White, *Ellen G. White Letters and Manuscripts*, 249.

30. The White/Nichols 1851 chart also contained the discredited assertion that the second coming would be concurrent with the fall of the Ottoman Empire. White not only absorbed and further promoted this assertion, but its details fill about one-quarter of the space in White/Nichols 1851 chart.

31. Arasola, *End of Historicism*, 97 quotes Miller: "I was satisfied that the seven times terminated in 1843. *Then* I came to the 2300 days; they brought me to the same conclusions" (emphasis original).

efforts would become successful. A strategic aspect of this evangelistic effort was the production of the White/Nichols 1851 chart. Just as the 1843 Millerite chart had been central to the dynamic Millerite movement of the 1840s, so this new and improved chart would function in the 1850s.

In sum, in the beginning of 1851 Ellen G. White was still not only strongly endorsing the 1843 Millerite chart, but she was planning an evangelistic strategy based on the new and improved 1851 White/Nichols chart. This chart corrected the error in the 1843 chart which God's hand had covered. Namely, rather than supporting the year 1843, this date was replaced by the year 1844. This new chart did not purport to predict a year for the second coming. Rather, it had images of a sanctuary with two apartments, a Holy Place with a "door," and a Most Holy Place "behind the second veil." In the Most Holy Place was an image of a crowned High Priest, clothed with a breastplate and having a golden censer with incense in his hand. In short, the chart had a pictorial representation of the coming of Christ the High Priest to the Most Holy Place. The chart distilled crucial new doctrines based on the allegorical-typological-historicist assumptions as embodied in the writings of Joseph Turner, O. R. L. Crosier, and Joseph Bates. In creating and designing according to what she saw, Ellen G. White was putting her stamp of authority on the White/Nichols 1851 chart. According to the 1843 chart, "the daily" was prominently featured in Miller's chronological scheme. "Taking away of the daily sacrifice, Dan. 12:11,12" was prominently displayed with the date 508 in large font. This had to follow the date 490, when, according to the 1843 chart, Rome was divided into ten kingdoms. Then, thirty years later the pivotal year 538 is labelled with the comment: "The Heruli, Vandals, and Ostrogoths by this time were plucked up; this is the prophetic period for the rise of the little horn." The identical dates and events associated with the dates are repeated in the White/Nichols 1851 chart concerning "the daily."

X

"Then I Saw in Relation to the 'Daily' (Daniel 8:12) That the Word Sacrifice Was Supplied by Man's Wisdom and Does Not Belong to the Text."

> There is no hope of these old people [adherents of the old view] who lived back in the early days of the Message being converted to this new light, even if they [the new-view proponents] bring volumes of histories to prove it. Because they [the old-view supporters] give more for one expression in your testimony than for *all the histories you could stack between here and Calcutta.*" (emphasis added)
>
> S. N. HASKELL TO EGW, MAY 30, 1910

THIS ASSERTION BY ELLEN G. WHITE is unambiguous and can be empirically confirmed or disconfirmed by the Hebrew text. It will be demonstrated below that Ellen G. White was empirically incorrect; the word "sacrifice" does belong to the text.

The identity of "the daily," from the Hebrew הַתָּמִיד, was a foundational issue in Millerism. It was critical to Millerism to have the Roman power be a two-phased entity. The first phase was asserted to be pagan Rome, which ruled over God's people from 158 BC to 508;[1] then there was a transitional period of exactly thirty years until 538, when the second phase of the Roman power, the supremacy of the papacy, ruled over God's people from 538 to 1798. As discussed previously, 508 was the critical *terminus a quo* for the 1,335-year prophecy.

---

1. This interval of 666 years was one of Miller's prophetic periods.

Thus, Ellen G. White was strongly motivated to defend these dates and identifications. In late 1850, in giving crucial guidance to the Little Flock, Ellen G. White related what she saw in relation to "the daily" (Daniel 8:12).

Ellen G. White and the translation of הַתָּמִיד

Ellen G. White denied the validity of translating הַתָּמִיד as "the daily sacrifice." Ellen G. White, Uriah Smith, and J. N. Andrews were adamantly opposed to associating "the daily" with anything having to do with the Old Testament sacrificial system. They required that anything having to do with "the daily" occur *after* Christ's ministry, half a millennium later in 508. If they admitted that "the daily" was related to events in the Old Testament dispensation, they would also have to admit that the sanctuary envisioned by Daniel was the Old Testament earthly sanctuary—*not* the invisible, heavenly sanctuary. Thus, in line with these interpretive assumptions, Ellen G. White saw:

> ... that the 1843 chart was directed by the hand of the Lord, and that it should not be altered ... Then I saw in relation to the "daily" (Daniel 8:12) that the word sacrifice was supplied by man's wisdom and does not belong to the text and that the Lord gave a correct view of it to those who gave the judgment hour cry. When union existed, before 1843, nearly all were united on the correct view of the "daily"; but in the confusion since 1844, other views have been embraced, and darkness and confusion have followed."[2]

Ellen G. White was here asserting she had direct revelation—"I saw"—which delegitimized the conclusion that "the daily" had anything to do with the Old Testament sacrificial system.

Ellen G. White asserted that before the split between the open-door and shut-door Millerites, nearly all were united in the correct view of "the daily." Thus, it is significant to document what that unity consisted of. It certainly consisted of what came to be known as the "old view" of "the daily"—not the "new view."[3] Miller stated that

---

2. White, *Early Writings: Experience*, 74. In short, Miller had the correct view of דִּימְתָה and the translators of the KJV had an incorrect view.

3. See Valentine, *Prescott: Forgotten Giant*, 214–38 for an account of the conflicting "new" and "old" interpretations of "the daily." For example, on page 236, footnote 6, Valentine stated: "Prescott argued vigorously that there existed absolutely no

"the daily" meant pagan rites and sacrifices; it was phase 1 of what Damsteegt calls a "two-abominations motif." "Miller concluded that 'the daily' also signified paganism which gave way to papal Rome." Damsteegt also cites Hale, who said: "I think it [daily sacrifice] will be seen to be the true application, to Paganism."[4] As Valentine noted, "Joseph Bates, J. N. Andrews, and James White had all followed Miller in adopting the view [that "the daily" referred to Roman paganism]."[5] Thus, when Ellen G. White stated that before the Disappointment all were united on the "correct view" of "the daily," it is undisputable that they were united in believing that "the daily" represented Roman paganism.[6]

> In every language there are words that are so rich and deep in meaning that they are difficult to translate adequately with a single word into another language.[7]

As Ellen G. White's assertions about "the daily" originated ultimately in William Miller's writings and methods, an analysis of these assertions must begin with an analysis of the "method" Miller used to arrive at the conclusion that "the daily" must be Roman paganism.

William Miller reached the conclusion that "the daily"[8] of Daniel 8, 11, and 12 referred to a system of paganism by a very dubious methodology. J. N. Andrews and Uriah Smith, using the same methodology, arrived at the conclusion that "the daily" had to refer to a system of paganism that they asserted was predicted by Daniel 8:11, 12, 13; 11:31; and 12:11. They further asserted that these texts predicted that this system of paganism would be removed by a system of popery between 508 and 538. Ellen Harmon's concept of "the daily"

---

historical evidence that the English were converted in 508 and that therefore paganism was at that date taken away by the Papacy."

4. Damsteegt, *Foundations*, 22, 32, 33, 38.
5. Valentine, *Prescott: Forgotten Giant*, 213.
6. Smith, *Daniel and the Revelation* (1897), 149.
7 *Adult Teachers SS Bible Study Guide*, April–June 2020, 87.
8. הַתָּמִיד (*hatamid*) is the Hebrew form in which "the daily" appears in Daniel. It is a noun preceded by a definite article and occurs in this form numerous times in the Old Testament. This form of the noun preceded by a definite article is the typical form in Numbers 28 and 29. For example, the phrase in Numbers 29:31 is as follows: מִלְּבַד עֹלַת הַתָּמִיד מִנְחָתָהּ וְנִסְכֵּיהָ. This is translated in the KJV as: "a sin offering; beside the continual burnt offering." In Leviticus 24:2 it occurs without the definite article, and refers to the lamp burning "continually."

originated in Father Miller's continuous-historical mode of interpretation, "[w]hen union existed, before 1843" and she was intellectually dependent on William Miller's exegesis of "the daily" (הַתָּמִיד).

Her "I saw" statements concerning "the daily" are 1850 examples of her habitual intellectual dependence on Millerism. Her writing demonstrates a consistent pattern of dependence. She was dependent on Miller's prediction that the Ottoman Empire would collapse and the world would end in 1839/1840; she was dependent on Miller's prediction that the second coming would occur by March 21, 1844, resulting in the tarrying-time apologetic; she was dependent on Snow's midnight cry concerning October 22, 1844; she was dependent on Joseph Turner and Apollos Hale's bridegroom theory; she was dependent on O. R. L. Crosier's extended-atonement theory. Now, in late 1850, incorporated into the White/Nichols 1851 chart, there were multiple dates and purported prophetic fulfillments like the 1,335 years, the 2,520 years, and the 508 "the daily" date, etc. There was an *unbroken pattern* of dependence on persons who employed the allegorical-typological-historicist method of interpretation that had already resulted in them predicting the very day of the second coming.

O. R. L. Crosier continued this flawed "method in the post-1844 period. His solution to the problem of the delayed second coming was an extended atonement.[9] Ellen Harmon endorsed Crosier's attempt to make sense of the midnight-cry experience.[10] Similarly, she endorsed the conclusions about "the daily" reached by Miller.

The terms "the daily," "sanctuary," and "host," in addition to the "little horn," are key terms in identifying the players in the drama of Daniel 8:9–14. Obviously, their proper identifications are semantically and syntactically intertwined, and it is almost impossible to discuss each one separately, but I will try to discuss each one in order. We begin by analyzing "the daily," and the method Miller uses in identifying this entity.

---

9. Burt, *Day-Dawn of Canandaigua*, 317–30. See also Burt, "Extended Atonement," 331–39, and Burt, *Historical Background*, 27.

10. "The Lord shew me in vision, more than one year ago, that Brother Crosier had the true light, on the cleansing of the Sanctuary, &c; and that it was his will, that Brother C. should write out the view which he gave us in the *Day-Star, Extra*, February 7, 1846." See James White, "Word to the 'Little Flock'" (1847), 12.

"The daily"

The original method by which Miller concluded that "'the daily' must mean paganism" takes Scripture out of context, is illogical, and is a textbook example of motivated reasoning. Analyzing the scriptural evidence on the foundation of *sola Scriptura* demonstrates that Miller was incorrect in his conclusion. On the basis of Miller's faulty reasoning, "the daily" was said to symbolize a phase of the dominance of pagan Rome, which was superseded by a second phase of papal Roman dominance during the interval of 508–538. This dogma became an unquestionable SDA tradition because this conclusion was adopted by Ellen Harmon.[11]

Miller's inexplicable method of defining הַתָּמִיד ("the daily")

According to Miller, practically any minimally literate person could interpret the obscurities of biblical apocalyptic better than the most erudite theologian if he just used a concordance and a Bible. He gave a demonstration of this method in the *Second Advent Manual*, edited by Apollos Hale. The following is his explanation of how he used a concordance to find the true meaning of "the daily" in Daniel 8:11. He wrote:

> I read on and could find no other case in which it ["the daily"] was found, but in Daniel.[12]

This is remarkable. Uriah Smith himself noted that in his Hebrew concordance the Hebrew word for "the daily" was found 102 times.[13]

Miller continues:

> I then [by the aid of a concordance] took those words which stood in connection with it, 'take way;' he shall take away, 'the daily'; 'from the time the daily shall be taken away, &c.'

---

11. Knight, *Search for Identity*, 127, 139, 154, 171, 202 has attempted to show that Ellen White did not claim infallibility and that it is improper to use Ellen G. White's statements to support such SDA traditions. Nevertheless, the consensus position is that Ellen G. White enjoys practical infallibility. The majority position is that she never made any substantial errors of fact or doctrine.

12. This is Miller's fatal factual error. It is an inexplicable mystery as to how and why Miller missed such obvious evidence.

13. Smith, *Daniel and the Revelation* (1897), 157, 254.

I read on, and thought I should find no light on the text; finally, I came to 2 Thess. 2:7,8. 'For the mystery of iniquity doth already work; only he who now letteth will let, until he be taken out of the way, and then shall that wicked be revealed,' &c. And when I had come to that text, oh! how clear and glorious the truth appeared! There it is! That is 'the daily!' Well now, what does Paul mean by 'he who now letteth,' or hindereth? By 'the man of sin,' and the 'wicked,' popery is meant. Well what is it which hinders popery from being revealed? Why, it is paganism; well, then, 'the daily' must mean paganism.[14]

Miller is confusing. Miller appears to be quoting word for word from Daniel 8:11, but if the reader compares the specific phrases above with the two verses below, the reader will notice that it is not an exact quotation but a tendentious paraphrase. Miller's convoluted explanation has two layers of impenetrability. However, Miller's critical assertion is that his inexact quote, "take way," "the daily" from Daniel 8:11 is equivalent to two Thessalonian phrases "mystery of iniquity" and "be taken out of the way." Both "the daily" and "mystery of iniquity," he asserts, symbolize pagan Rome. Below, the phrases from Daniel 8:11 and 2 Thessalonians 2:7, "was taken away" and "taken out of the way," are Miller's basis for saying both verses refer to the identical historical event of 508, papal Rome replacing pagan Rome.

> Yea, he magnified himself even to the prince of the host, and by him the daily sacrifice *was taken away*, and the place of the sanctuary was cast down. (Daniel 8:11, KJV)

> For the mystery of iniquity doth already work: only he who now letteth will let, until he be *taken out of the way*. (2 Thessalonians 2:7, KJV)

> And an host was given him against the daily sacrifice by reason of transgression, and it cast down the truth to the ground; and it practised, and prospered. (Daniel 8:12, KJV)

> Then I heard one saint speaking, and another saint said unto that certain saint which spake, How long shall be the vision concerning the daily sacrifice, and the transgression of desolation, to give both the sanctuary and the host to be trodden under foot? (Daniel 8:13, KJV)

14. Hale, *Second Advent Manual*, 66. Brackets in original and in J. N. Andrews citation of the same text. See Andrews, *Sanctuary and the 2300 Days*, 40.

Miller's reasoning is so convoluted that even a person sympathetic to his conclusion that "the daily" must mean paganism finds it difficult to follow. Thus, I will provide a step-by-step explanation. The following are Miller's steps. First, he asserts that his concordance provided no occurrence of "the daily" outside of Daniel. Second, he finds a phrase that is associated with "the daily," namely, "shall be taken away." He then reads the entirety of the Old Testament from Daniel onward; he continues reading until he arrives at 2 Thessalonians and finds the phrase "taken out of the way."[15] Third, suddenly he has a eureka moment studded with exclamation marks and concludes that he has at last found the "glorious" truth. He has already concluded that an entity in 2 Thessalonians must be the papacy. And he has also presumed a chronological scheme in which between 508 and 538 the papacy would eliminate paganism. It is paganism, says Miller, which "hinders popery from being revealed." Fourth, therefore, he can import from 2 Thessalonians his preordained conclusions about the papacy and paganism back into Daniel 8:14 and conclude that "the daily" must be paganism. Thus, Miller's interpretation of "the daily" is another of the myriad instances where his actual process is not a commonsense, literal exposition of the biblical text but rather an allegorical eisegesis of the text, founded on a glaring factual error regarding the critical Hebrew phrase in question.

Paradoxically, Miller gives a different explanation of "the daily" as pagan Rome in one of his principal books. He concedes that "the daily" may be understood to mean "the Jewish rites and ceremonies." He then abruptly asserts that: "It is very evident, when we carefully examine our text, that it is to be understood as referring to Pagan and Papal rites, for it stands coupled with 'the abomination of desolation,' and performs the same acts, such as are ascribed to the Papal abomination, 'to give both the sanctuary and host to be trodden under foot.'" Yet simultaneously, he asserts that "by 'sanctuary,' we must understand the temple at Jerusalem." But he also provides a second allegorical definition of the sanctuary. It is the "true sanctuary which God has built of lively stones," a "spiritual sanctuary," a clear allusion

---

15. This text was the classic Protestant proof text that the "man of sin" was the papacy, or Antichrist. The term "Antichrist" was the favorite pejorative label that Protestants attempted to apply to Roman Catholicism. Ironically, *the word "Antichrist" does not appear in Daniel or Revelation.* Thus, this text, interpreted as referring to Catholicism in embryo, was cited repeatedly.

to the apostolic Christian church. He says this "spiritual sanctuary will not be cleansed until Christ's second coming; and then all Israel shall be raised, judged, and justified in his sight."[16] What is remarkable about Miller's exposition here is that he does not say that the sanctuary is the earth that will be burned with fire.[17] He also does not justify his assertion that "the daily [sacrifice]" must be pagan rites on the basis that "sacrifice" is a supplied word provided by the translators, and that the translators had no convincing basis to do so.

Miller states he could find no occurrence of "the daily" outside of Daniel. This is astounding because the Hebrew הַתָּמִיד (hatamid) occurs frequently, particularly in Numbers, for example. There are many occurrences this term has in various forms, with and without the definite article, הַ, namely: Numbers 4:7, 16; 9:16; 28:3, 6, 10, 15, 23–24, 31; 29:6, 11, 16, 19, 22, 25, 28, 31, 34, 38. We shall return to these texts in relationship to Uriah Smith's claim below that the word "sacrifice" was supplied without warrant. Wrote Smith: "The idea of sacrifice does not attach to the word at all."[18]

If one examines these texts, one can quickly establish that the supplied word in question, "sacrifice," is actually very well supported by the immediate context. Especially since in most cases there is reference to a "perpetual holocaust" involving a twice-daily sacrifice—in the morning and evening, as explicitly mentioned in Daniel 8:14.

J. N. Andrews and הַתָּמִיד

J. N. Andrews in his book on the 2,300 days, written about 1853,[19] in an extensive block quotation cites Apollos Hale's account of how Miller originally arrived at his conclusion that "the daily" must be Roman paganism.[20] Andrews obviously agreed with Miller, and

---

16. Miller, *Evidence* (1842), 23–25.

17. This definition of the earth as the "sanctuary" was standard in 1844 Millerism. It is also the identification which would be refuted by J. N. Andrews, Uriah Smith, and Ellen White as a mainstay of their argument that they got the date of October 22, 1844 correct, while merely mistaking the event.

18. Smith, *Daniel and the Revelation* (1897), 154–56.

19. Evidently published about spring of 1853, since later Uriah Smith wrote a book of the same title in 1854, and G. Valentine in his biography of Andrews mentions that Andrews wrote prior to this date. See Valentine, *J. N. Andrews*, 164.

20. Hale, *Second Advent Manual*, 66. Brackets in original and in J. N. Andrews's

then asked rhetorically: "Well, what is it which hinders popery from being revealed? Why, it is paganism; well, then, 'the daily' must mean paganism."[21] He goes on to argue that there are "two desolations" mentioned in Daniel. First is the "daily" desolation, which designates paganism. Second is the "abomination of desolation," which he stated designates popery. Thus, Andrews artificially createed twin "desolations," both proceeding from a satanic Rome. Henceforth Andrews refers to "continual desolation" when he references "the daily sacrifice" and wishes to evoke paganism, and the "abomination of desolation" when he wishes to evoke popery. In short, he gratuitously supplies the word "desolation" to the first term. This is ironic when it is well known that SDA interpreters from Uriah Smith to Ellen G. White made a major issue out of the fact that the KJV interpreters supplied the word "sacrifice" in the term "the daily sacrifice." Moreover, Smith's contention makes little sense when one returns to the original sequence of events in the immediate context, Daniel 8:9–12.

A hostile power, the little horn, attacks the "host," the prince of the host, "the daily," and the "sanctuary." These four make up a single inseparable targeted entity. These four elements, attacked by the hostile power, are symbols of positive, righteous things. They could not be symbols condemned by Yahweh. "The daily" is not a "desolation."

Andrews asserts that the word "sanctuary" (mentioned 145 times in the Bible according to him) in verse 11 is the "sanctuary of Satan," while the identical word, "sanctuary," mentioned twice in verses 13 and 14, is the "sanctuary of the Lord of hosts." This is a striking illustration of the extreme to which an SDA exegete will distort the literal, plain meaning of the text to justify a preconceived idea. In contrast to Miller, above, he denies that the "lively stones" of the Christian church could be the "sanctuary of the Lord of hosts." He states that "in almost every instance (of the 145 instances) in which the word does occur, it refers directly to the typical tabernacle." He cites Daniel 9:2, 17, showing his awareness that the immediate context of Daniel 8 demonstrates that the center of Daniel's attention was the "sanctuary that is desolate."[22] This was none other than Solomon's temple desolated

citation of the same text.

21. It is highly unlikely that Andrews, writing in 1853, would so unambiguously and vigorously assert that "the daily" was to be interpreted as Roman paganism if Ellen G. White was not in agreement with this.

22. Andrews, *Sanctuary and the 2300 Days*, 47–48, 67,

by the Babylonians. Ironically, Andrews never states that the "true" or "typical tabernacle" of God is not the "sanctuary" spoken of in Daniel 8! This would be difficult since Daniel 9:24 speaks of the "city of thy [Daniel's!] sanctuary" in reference to Jerusalem. In a lengthy section 15 of his book, what he does do is refute three other lexical possibilities: that the "sanctuary" is 1) the earth, 2) the church, or 3) the land of Canaan. He then traces this earthly sanctuary in its various modes: 1) the Mosaic tabernacle in the wilderness; 2) its location at Shiloh during the period of the judges; 3) its location at Nob in the days of Saul; 4) its location at Gibeon in the days of David, the Solomonic temple, and the rebuilt second temple. Neither does Andrews explicitly assert in sections 15–18 that the word "sanctuary" in Daniel 8 is a heavenly sanctuary. He ends section 18 with the assertion that the "old will never be rebuilt," which was a popular 1840s concept among his post-millennialist opponents.[23]

The word "host" is mentioned several times in Daniel 8:9–14. According to Andrews, there are two diametrically opposed hosts: satanic versus heavenly. Per Andrews, the word "host" in Daniel 8:12 is the "forces of Satan"; the word "host" in Daniel 8:10 is "the host of heaven." He also asserts that this same satanic host is mentioned in Daniel 11:31, where, he asserts, pagan Rome, "sanctuary of the daily desolation," is succeeded by papal Rome, the "abomination of desolation." Ironically, there is no "host" at all mentioned in Daniel 11:31. But this is the verse relied upon by Andrews for the purported transfer of pagan power, "the daily," to papal power, that occurred in the 508–538 interval.

In short, rather than a solid textual foundation for their assertions, both Miller and Andrews start with the presumption that "the daily" must be a Roman paganism succeeded by a Roman papacy that they have already presumed was dated to a 508–538 time frame.[24]

---

23. Andrews, *Sanctuary and the 2300 Days*, 76.

24. Andrews, *Sanctuary and the 2300 Days*, 40. Andrews evidently also accepted the Apocrypha as canonical as did Joseph Bates, Ellen Harmon, and James White, just as James and Ellen White tacitly endorsed the Wisdom of Solomon. On page 63 Andrews cited Wisdom of Solomon 9:8 in his exposition of the sanctuary alongside a myriad of other biblical texts without distinction between canonical and apocryphal.

Smith disputes translation of הַתָּמִיד

Smith's 1854 book on the sanctuary and the 2,300 days is not examined here because I was unable to obtain the 1854 edition. An 1877 edition was the latest I could examine. In his 1877 work Smith disputed the translators translating הַתָּמִיד (*hatamid*) as "the daily sacrifice." He asserted: "By him the daily (not sacrifice, as our translators have supplied, but daily desolation [which Smith supplied], which is paganism) was taken away, and the transgression of desolation, the papacy, was set up (Chap. 11:31)." In other sections of his book, Smith clearly was aware that הַתָּמִיד (*hatamid*) refers to twice-daily sacrifices, yet he was psychologically incapable of recognizing the connection.[25] Both Andrews and Smith had virtually no formal education. Neither were translators. Miller himself crudely disparaged Bible scholars as effete elitists, and saw no reason to seriously consider learning Hebrew or any biblical language. "Miller essentially ignored the literary and historical context of a passage and was totally unconcerned with the original author's intent for the original recipients." "Nor was Miller interested in reading the Scriptures in the original languages." Thus, George Bush in 1844 pointed out to Miller that his seven-times-of-the-Gentiles proof, based "mainly upon the reading of the English text of the Scriptures," was plainly in error because "seven times" plainly means that God was threatening Israel that he would punish them with sevenfold severity and was not an indication of a 2,520-year interval of time. Bush concluded that it "cannot be expected that intelligent men will receive any interpretation which is not sustained by the original." Miller blasted Bush with a withering, caustic reply absolutely denying the validity of his points. This was typical Miller. He also blasted other learned exegetes sarcastically on the basis that they were merely using fancy phrases "spotted over with a little Hebrew, Greek, & Latin, all obtained [from] . . . obscure writers, and classical blockheads."[26] Miller considered that the Bible would be plain to the most uneducated but sincere person. Miller, Smith, and Andrews

---

25. Smith, *Sanctuary*, 41–42. It is remarkable that Smith (page 240) noted that: "It was necessary for the priest of the house of Levi to offer up *sacrifices daily* . . . [for all] those who had transgressed." Yet he was incapable of considering these daily sacrifices as the proper referent for הַתָּמִיד (*hatamid*). He also referred (page 291) to the "daily morning and evening sacrifices [that] were offered in behalf of the whole people."

26. Crocombe, *Feast of Reason*, 83–84.

appear to have assumed that just because the Hebrew term had four consonants with a space on either side, it must represent a single noun in English. They did not consider that the first consonant is the equivalent to the English definite article, "the." Thus, the Hebrew already has two words in one word, or single unit. Furthermore, they did not consider that not infrequently a single word in one language requires two or even three words in another language, or perhaps even a longer phrase that is not the grammatical equivalent in another language. For example, an infinitive might replace a phrase with 1) an article, 2) an adjective, plus 3) a noun. In this particular case even their preferred English translation, "the daily," has a definite article followed by an adjective, and demands a noun which the article and adjective modify. In this case, given the obvious context of the same word in Numbers, it would have been clear to any Jew of Daniel's time that the term הַתָּמִיד (hatamid) refers to the twice-daily "perpetual holocaust" as ordered by Yahweh in Numbers. This divine service was central to the Jewish religion.

Smith also followed Andrews in a subtle manner concerning the "host." He said the little horn "took away the daily, cast down the place of his sanctuary, gathered to itself an overwhelming host by reason of transgression..."[27] He was not as blatant as Andrews in claiming that there are two hosts, one of which is satanic. He paraphrased the text "an host was given him against the daily sacrifice by reason of transgression" using the active voice ("gathered to itself") rather than the passive ("a host was given him"), and supplied the adjective "overwhelming" to convey the concept of a majority satanic host persecuting the minority church in the wilderness. Smith specifically identified this host as the barbarians that "became converts to that nominal Christianity," Roman Catholicism, and then supported its persecution of the church in the wilderness.[28] So the host was transformed from a positive entity being persecuted by the little horn into its willing henchmen.

There are three occurrences of the word "sanctuary" in Daniel 8. Smith asserted that in two of the occurrences it refers to the heavenly sanctuary, but in the third it refers to its opposite, the "city of Rome." He further asserted that this precisely fulfilled a day-year prophecy

27. Smith, *Sanctuary*, 41–42.
28. Smith, *Sanctuary*, 43.

covering the interval 31 BC to 330 AD. The city of Rome was "cast down" by Constantine's establishing a new Rome in the East.

> [T]he place where paganism had long had its sanctuary, Rome with its Pantheon, or temple of all the gods, was cast down, or degraded to the second rank, by removal of the seat of government to Constantinople, in A.D. 330.[29]

In Smith's 1897 *Daniel and Revelation*, he largely followed Andrews. He asserted that the little horn represents both pagan and papal Rome. He asserted that when "the daily sacrifice" occurs in the KJV, since "'sacrifice' is a supplied word," it is illegitimate and he preferred to supply a different word so that he translated "the daily sacrifice" by "daily (desolation) signifying the pagan form, and the transgression of desolation, the papal (See on verse 13.)". He further stated that the words "By him (the papal form) 'the daily' (the pagan form) was taken away" means "Pagan Rome was remodeled into papal Rome. And the place of his sanctuary, or worship, the city of Rome, was cast down. The seat of government was removed by Constantine in A. D. 330 to Constantinople." So, what Andrews termed the "sanctuary of Satan" of verse 11 became more prosaically the city of Rome; and when the papal form casts down this "sanctuary," it does so by Constantine establishing Constantinople. This gave Smith the opportunity to discern a day-year prophecy in which a 360-year interval occurs between 31 BC and 330 AD.[30] Moreover, Smith did not, like Miller, claim he could find no instance of "the daily" in his concordance. Rather, he claimed that he found it in his Hebrew concordance:

> one hundred and two times, and is in the great majority of instances, rendered continual or continually. The idea of sacrifice does not attach to the word at all. Nor is there any word in the text which signifies sacrifice; that is wholly a supplied word, the translators putting in that word which their

---

29. Smith, *Sanctuary*, 42.

30. See Smith, *Daniel and the Revelation*, 153–54, 253–55. To further support his contention that the "sanctuary" of Daniel 8:11 that was "cast down" was the city of Rome, Uriah Smith in his interpretation of Daniel 11:23–24 said that the "he" with the "small people" refers to Rome. Also, that his success "even for a *time*" is "doubtless a *prophetic time*, 360 [literal] years." This little-known application of the day-year principle Uriah Smith applied to the battle of Actium, fought September 2, 31 BC. When he added the requisite 360 years, he arrived at 330 AD when Rome was "cast down" and replaced by Constantinople as the new capital of the Roman Empire.

understanding of the text seemed to demand. But they *evidently entertained an erroneous view, the sacrifices of the Jews not being referred to at all* [emphasis added].³¹

Later Smith, in commenting on the same words in Daniel 11:31, further insisted that the translators were mistaken.

> It was shown, on Dan 8:13, that sacrifice is a word erroneously supplied; that it should be desolation; and that the expression denotes a desolating power, of which the abomination of desolation is but the counterpart, and to which it succeeds in point of time The "daily" desolation was paganism, the "abomination of desolation "is the papacy."³²

However, despite the absolute assurance demonstrated by both Andrews and Smith, they were both demonstrably wrong.

Numbers occurrences of הַתָּמִיד (*hatamid*)

Virtually every occurrence of this exact form, with the definite article, occurs in Numbers or in Daniel. The overwhelming majority occur in Numbers 28–29. (All the translations for Numbers 28–29 below are from the Jerusalem Bible.) Numbers 28 in the Jerusalem Bible has the heading: "Regulations for Sacrifices." There follow precise stipulations for the daily sacrifices, followed by stipulations for specific annual feast sacrifices. It is clear from this organization of the text that, in addition to the daily sacrifices, each special feast day has its own supplementary sacrifices. The daily sacrifice regulations begin with verse 3 as follows:

Daily

> Every day, two yearling lambs without blemish, as a perpetual holocaust ["the daily," הַתָּמִיד (*hatamid*)]. The first lamb you must offer in the morning, the second between the two evenings, together with an oblation of one-tenth of an ephah of fine flour mixed with one quarter of a hin of purest oil. This is the perpetual holocaust made long ago at Mount Sinai.

---

31. Smith, *Daniel and the Revelation* (1897), 154–56.
32. Smith, *Daniel and the Revelation* (1897), 254.

Monthly

The first feast that follows in verses 11–15 is the Feast of the New Moon. In it "two young bulls, one ram and seven yearling lambs without blemish" are to be offered along with designated cereals and libations. Then the text says: "This must be the monthly holocaust, month after month, every month of the years. In addition to the perpetual holocaust [דִּימָתָה [33] a he-goat must be offered to Yahweh as a sacrifice for sin, with its accompanying libation."

Feast of Unleavened Bread or Passover

Here again animal, vegetal, and drink offerings specific to this feast are ordered. Then the text says: "This must be done in addition to the morning holocaust which is a perpetual holocaust. You must do this every day for seven days . . . it is to be offered in addition to the perpetual holocaust and its accompanying libation."

Feast of Weeks

Here again specific sacrifices particular to this feast are ordered and then the rote phrase is repeated: "This must be done in addition to the perpetual holocaust and its accompanying oblation."

Feast of Acclamations

Again, specific sacrifices particular to this feast are ordered, then: "All this must be done in addition to the monthly holocaust and its oblation, the perpetual holocaust and its oblation . . ."

Day of Atonement

A young bull, one ram, and seven yearling lambs of your choice without blemish" must be offered. In addition, a he-goat must be offered for the sacrifice for sin. This is in addition to the victim for sin at the feast of Atonement, and to the perpetual holocaust with its accompanying oblation and libations.

---

33. In the Jerusalem Bible translation "the daily" is regularly translated as "perpetual holocaust."

Feast of Tabernacles

With the particulars of the sacrifices related to this feast, the following phrase is repeated at intervals eight times: "This is in addition to the perpetual holocaust with its accompanying oblation and libations."

Clearly, the concept of sacrifice is inextricably associated with the Hebrew word in question. Indeed, "the daily *sacrifice*" is most emphatically and repeatedly meant.

The SDA interpretation of הַתָּמִיד originated in William Miller's peculiar word association of the phrase "to be taken out of the way," which he found in both Daniel 8 and 2 Thessalonians 2. Then he concluded that הַתָּמִיד must be paganism, which from 508 to 538 was taken out of the way by popery. This provided him with specific dates to calculate exact prophetic periods. More importantly, it provided him with the two-phased Roman power which could extend two millennia from the pagan powers oppressing Israel to the papal powers oppressing the Christian church—to the end of time.

Andrews actually gave an exact quotation of Miller's explanation for concluding that הַתָּמִיד must be pagan Rome. Andrews built on Miller by then referring to "continual desolation" when he referenced "the daily" and wished to evoke paganism, and the "abomination of desolation" when he wished to evoke popery, gratuitously supplying the word "desolation" to the first term. He worsened Miller's already extreme eisegesis by arbitrarily asserting that both an evil and a good host and an evil and good sanctuary are meant. Uriah Smith then claimed that the KJV Bible interpreters were mistaken; that they gratuitously supply a noun, "the daily *sacrifice*." Ellen G. White put the capstone on this development by stating that she saw by direct revelation that fallible, foolish, finite human wisdom supplied the word "sacrifice," and that this was done erroneously.

However, Miller, Andrews, Smith, and White were all mistaken in their assessment of הַתָּמִיד. It was well attested in their concordance and does refer to daily sacrifices as demonstrated in the many occurrences of the exact word in the identical form in Numbers 28–29.[34] Thus, the SDA exegete faces a dilemma. One must either base one's

---

34. Gesenius, *Hebrew and English Lexicon*, 556 specifically notes that this means a "daily (morning and evening) burnt-offering," citing the five instances in Daniel, and taking notice of those in Numbers as well.

conclusion on actual grammatical and textual evidence in applying *sola Scriptura*, or allow *Millerite tradition*, as mediated via Ellen G. White, to stand above *sola Scriptura*. The first option requires that one acknowledge that Ellen G. White was mistaken.

On its face, Miller's indefensible justification for his teaching about pagan Rome and its transition period from 508 to 538 is textually untenable. Similarly, Smith's and White's assertion that they were more qualified translators than the KJV Bible translators, whether by prophetic gift or otherwise, is also factually incorrect. The history of interpretation of הַתָּמִיד, the "host," and the "sanctuary" further reinforces this conclusion.

To summarize, Miller's method of concluding that "the daily" must be Roman paganism is fatally flawed. This fatal flaw invalidates several of his interlocked prophetic intervals. The translation of the Hebrew word as "the daily sacrifice" by the KJV Bible translators is exquisitely appropriate—contrary to Ellen G. White's assertions to the contrary. In 1850–1851 Ellen G. White still believed and vigorously supported this fatally flawed conception of "the daily." Yet she believed that she had received a direct revelation affirming that the translation "the daily sacrifice" was itself fatally flawed. About fifty years later during the theological civil war over "the daily," she would claim that she had no light on the topic. As Gilbert Valentine has recounted in his biography on Prescott, S. N. Haskell, Uriah Smith, and other old pioneers insisted that Ellen G. White saw that "the daily" was pagan Rome. Fortunately we are not reliant upon the memories of Ellen G. White, S. N. Haskell, or Uriah Smith for what "the daily" meant in 1844 and 1850. There are still extant copies of the 1851 White/Nichols chart that Ellen G. White created in accord with visionary instruction in 1850. This chart is unequivocal about the identity of "the daily" and its prophetic significance.

XI

1851 Chart Perpetuates Erroneous "Daily" Concept

APOCALYPTIC CHARTS OF DANIEL and Revelation were celebrated in Millerite evangelism. The stupendous beasts of the 1840s were just as fascinating to Ellen Harmon as *Tyrannosaurus rex* dinosaurs are to twenty-first-century children. They were America's nineteenth-century analogy to the renowned stained glass windows of France's medieval cathedral of Chartres, an impressive visual representation of fabulous beasts, angels, and horsemen. They struck an emotional and intellectual chord in the eyes of their beholders, teaching Bible lessons about Daniel's and St. John's apocalyptic visions. In addition to stunning imagery, they included biblical mathematics proving undeniably that the second coming would occur "about 1843." Probably between fifty and one hundred thousand Americans had been enchanted by their appeal during the midnight-cry phase of the movement. By 1850 James and Ellen G. White's Little Flock had been decimated to a remnant of "torn and pealed" survivors numbering less than 1 percent of that number. The two founding fathers of the Sabbatarian Adventists, James White and Joseph Bates, were engaged in a disheartening dispute over methods of evangelism, and Ellen White was desperately seeking a means of uniting them and spreading her new battle cry of the Sabbath and the shut door. Suddenly, Samuel W. Rhodes, one of the few itinerate Sabbath and shut-door preachers, rode into Centerport, New York with a new and improved version of the 1843 Millerite chart. Ellen G. White, writing an August 15, 1850 letter to her dear friends Stockbridge and Louisa M. Howland, recorded her reaction to Rhodes's splendid new chart:

> Brother Rhodes came here last Tuesday which is just one week ago today. We were glad to see him. He has just got out a new chart. It is larger than any chart I ever saw; it is very clear. We [James and Ellen or the Imperial We?] like his chart much.[1]

This oversize and clear chart fired her imagination. It was replete with evangelistic possibilities. However, at that moment Ellen G. White was unable to initiate any new strategic initiatives. Her "babe [James Edson] had been very sick for about a week," so gravely ill that it seemed to Ellen "that Satan had stepped in and was troubling Edson. We found it even so; we found the child at the point of death."[2] Alarmed, Ellen and James concluded that only group prayer could save Edson. Brother Rhodes had parted. James rode his own horse at breakneck speed to overtake Rhodes, brought him back, and the three of them pleaded with God to save Edson from Satan's fiery darts. "When Satan found he could not take the life of the child, he tempted me that God had left me or the child would have been healed when we [she and James alone] first prayed for him." According to Ellen, Satan then attacked Clarissa M. Bonfoey, the White family nanny who cared for Henry White. (Henry also stayed at the Howland family for several years. In 1863, when he was a teenager, he also stayed with them, "employed at mounting prophetic charts on cloth backing for sale to Adventist evangelists," according to his biographical entry in the *Ellen G. White Encyclopedia*.) "At the same time James was taken with the *cholera morbus*."[3] Sister Lydia Harris, Clarissa M. Bonfoey, Sarah

---

1. White, *Ellen G. White Letters & Manuscripts*, 215.

2. Martin Luther, like Ellen G. White, did duel directly with the devil not infrequently. See, for example: https://www.thegreatcoursesdaily.com/luther-battle-devil/. He is quoted as reporting: "'The devil woke me up at night with this argument against me,' and then there's a five-page argument from the devil, deadpan." And again: "One time at the dinner table, he said: 'Earlier this morning, the devil was arguing with me about Zwingli.'" Less well attested is a report that he threw an inkwell at the devil. Did both Mrs. White and Luther corporealize their unconscious mental conceptions of the devil?

3. Mrs. White seemed to personify *cholera morbus* with Satan himself. For centuries Christians had believed that illnesses were caused directly by either God or the devil. They had little or no concept of secondary causes. At the time of this incident in Ellen White's life, germ theory was decades away from being discovered

B. Harmon, and Ellen White then engaged in intercessory prayer for James. Ellen "anointed his head and stomach and bowels in the name of the Lord." James was healed. But "when Satan found his power was completely broken upon him [James], he went to the child again. He waked us crying at the top of his voice. He seemed to have the colic and we went up to the chamber, anointed his stomach with oil and prayed over him, rebuked Satan and he had to flee."[4] Satan had also

---

and accepted. Even as late as 1863 Charles Darwin suspected that his own gastrointestinal symptoms might be caused by microorganisms. He sent a specimen of his GI tract to a Dr. John Goodsir for analysis. He had recently discovered that an organism he named *Sarcina goodsir* could be found in the vomitus of patients with symptoms similar to Darwin's. Dr. Goodsir found that Darwin's sample did not contain the suspected *Sarcina goodsir*. Where Darwin suspected microorganisms as being culpable, Ellen G. White thought the devil was directly involved. Similarly, where Ellen Harmon seemed to see God's supernatural intervention in smiting the sheriff who attempted to arrest Israel Dammon during the winter of 1845, the sheriff himself only saw persons engaging in mass passive resistance. See Hoyt, " Trial of Elder I. Dammon," 29–36. Also, several of Ellen G. White's letters concerning Elvira Hastings and her illness illustrate the same phenomenon. She said of Elvira Hastings: "Especially was the heart of sister Hastings knit with mine, as were David's and Jonathan's." On March 11, 1849 she wrote that an angel "shewed " her "a person who was short and thick." Then, "I saw Satan pouring upon this person a stream of darkness, as a sunbeam is poured forth from the sun, and as it came upon him he bloated. His head seemed larger than usual, and his face was red and much bloated." She asserted that Satan was using this agent to cause Sister Hastings' sickness, "and that the object of this person was to afflict unto death, so that his iniquity might be covered which might otherwise be exposed." Nonetheless, she also "saw that it was time for God to work and deliver her, . . . and that now his power is completely broken." See White, *Ellen G. White Letters & Manuscripts*, 156–57. On April 21, 1849 in another letter to the Hastings she said: "I saw that some of the agents of the devil were affecting the bodies of those they could not deceive and draw from the present truth. Some of them were even trying to afflict some of the saints unto death." No doubt she had in mind Elvira Hastings, to whom the letter was addressed. One inference was that the devil "could not deceive" Elvira Hastings. See White, *Ellen G. White Letters & Manuscripts*, 168. Finally, Elvira Hastings died February 1850. On March 18, 1850 Ellen G. White wrote her widower, Leonard W. Hastings. She recounted a very unique story. She claimed that she received a revelation from God that he had given Joseph Bates a dream. She also stated that Ezra L. H. Chamberlain had been with Bates at that time and suggested that he somehow dissuaded Bates from following the divine guidance of his dream. Otherwise, Bates would have "come directly to your house when Satan had got your wife in his grasp." Then God "would have wrenched her from the power of the enemy." See White, *Ellen G. White Letters & Manuscripts*, 199–200.

4. Like the COVID-19 virus, the symptoms can range from none to severe. Some cases might be fatal while other victims recover quite quickly. It is usually caused by unsafe water and/or food contaminated by feces containing the bacterium *Vibrio cholerae*. God had not seen fit to provide Ellen G. White with visionary

just smitten President Zachary Taylor with cholera morbus recently. Taylor was not as fortunate as James and Edson White. Just the month before, on July 9, 1850, the president died from gastrointestinal symptoms his personal physician diagnosed as cholera morbus. At this time, the Lord showed Ellen that James must republish what several of the leading Millerite preachers "had written in 1844, upon the truth, Satan would try to hinder us; but we must struggle for the victory and go on." Thus, Ellen focused upon James White's publishing strategy and the idea of a large and magnificent chart remained dormant in Ellen's mind for several months.[5] On September 1, 1850 she wrote Prudence M. Bates that the "enemy has tried hard to take some of our lives here of late. One after another of us has been afflicted almost unto death."[6]

The next month she wrote: "A vision the Lord gave me October 23, 1850, at the house of Bro Nichols in Dorchester, Mass. I saw that we must redouble our efforts now in this gathering time . . . I saw that efforts to spread the truth should now be made, such as were put forth in 1843 and '44." Thoughts of the tornado-like movements of 1843

---

information about infectious disease prevention regarding cholera or tuberculosis. As a result, many Adventists died of such preventable diseases, including several first-degree relatives of James White.

5. White, *Ellen G. White Letters & Manuscripts*, 216–17.

6. White, *Ellen G. White Letters & Manuscripts*, 232–33. For millennia primitive peoples believed that both physical and mental afflictions were directly caused by either satanic attacks or divine punishments. Similarly, natural phenomena like lightning, storms, earthquakes, and epidemics were believed to be supernaturally caused. This was based on biblical accounts. For example, when the bubonic plague appeared to have afflicted the Philistines after they captured the ark, it was considered to be divine punishment. When David attempted a census, he chose a divine plague when offered a multiple choice of appropriate divine punishment. The book of Revelation's seven last plagues and apocalyptic earthquakes solidified this conception in the world of Western Christianity. Further, Ellen White's contemporaries had no idea of effective treatments. The 1850 conceptional world of Ellen G. White regarding illnesses was not much advanced from the 1850 BC Bronze Age. The pathological effects of microscopic bacteria and viruses were just as invisible as evil spirits. The germ theory of disease was not a settled consensus among scientists until decades after the 1850 cholera-satanic attack on James White and his family. Not until 1876 did Robert Koch publish results of his experiments demonstrating that bacteria caused disease. But it was not until about 1890 that germ theory was widely accepted. For example, it was not until 1890 that Dr. William Howard introduced the idea of using rubber gloves during surgery. In the thought world of Ellen G. White, the germ theory of 1850 was equivalent to the theory of evolution in the 2021 thought world of most Seventh-Day Adventists.

and 1844 recalled to her mind the legendary 1843 charts of that time. It was no coincidence that just such a vision occurred in the home of Brother Nichols, who was an illustrator and engraver and would shortly thereafter create just such a chart and finance it with a contribution of seventy-five dollars.

> I saw that the truth should be made plain on tables, that the earth and the fullness thereof is the Lord's, and that necessary means should not be spared to make it plain. I saw that the angels' messages, made plain, would have effect. I saw that the old [1843] chart was directed by the Lord, and that not a peg[7] of it should be altered without inspiration.[8] I saw that the figures on the chart were as God wanted them, and that His hand was over and hid a mistake in some of the figures so that none could see it until His hand was removed.[9]

It was in this same October 23, 1850 vision that Ellen G. White made her celebrated commentary regarding "the daily":

> Then I saw the "daily," that the Lord gave the correct view of it to those who gave the first angel's message. When union existed before 1844, nearly all were united[10] on the correct view of the "daily," but since, in the confusion, other views have been embraced and darkness has followed. I saw that

---

7. The colloquial equivalent of "not a jot or a tittle."

8. As Ellen G. White was the only person who had the gift of inspiration, and as several aspects of the two charts differed, it is clear that Ellen G. White closely supervised the construction of the 1851 chart to ensure that "not a peg" of "the figures on the chart" were altered without her inspiration.

9. White, *Ellen G. White Letters & Manuscripts*, 242–44. This is the basis of the concept that God deliberately obscured from everyone's view their error in not accounting for the fact that there was no zero year in the transition from BC to AD. This is doubtless the basis for the fact that in Otis Nichols's 1851 chart in his lower right corner's "Explanation of the Time," he equivocated on many of the "figures." Mrs. White had said "not a peg" of the 1843 chart should be changed without "inspiration." Thus, Nichols did not engrave simply 508, 538, or 1798 but rather 508-9, 538-9, and 1798-9. This reveals some uncertainty about the exact dates and events that were to have occurred on these dates. Was "the daily" removed in 509, the papacy set up in 539, and did the "time of the end" begin in 1799?

10. Valentine, *W. W. Prescott*, 215 documents that the "old view" of "the daily" around which "nearly all were united" was the assertion that "the daily" was a prophetic symbol for pagan Rome. He states that "Joseph Bates, J. N. Andrews, and James White had all followed Miller in adopting the view [that "the daily" was pagan Rome], and Uriah Smith had set the interpretation in concrete . . . in his book *Daniel and Revelation*."

God had not made a test of time since 1844, and that time never again will be a test.[11]

White expressed the same material in a slightly different wording a few weeks later:

> Then I saw in relation to the "daily," that the word "sacrifice" was supplied by man's wisdom, and does not belong to the text;[12] and that the Lord gave the correct view of it to those who gave the judgment hour cry. When union existed, before 1844, nearly all were united on the correct view of the "daily"; but since 1844, in the confusion, other views have been embraced, and darkness and confusion has followed.[13]

Both the 1843 and the 1851 charts identify "the daily" as "Pagan Dominance."

In the 1843 chart, 508 is almost dead center with the notation "Taking away of the daily sacrifice Daniel 12:11, 12." This directly follows the date 490 and the notation "Division of Rome completed into ten kingdoms," with a citation of a specific historian's reference to justify that date.[14] There is seamless continuity between the 1843 and 1851 White/Nichols chart regarding the identity of "the daily."

In the 1851 White/Nichols chart, also in the middle, a reference to "the daily" occurs. It states that "Ten Horns arose 490; Pagan Dominance or **The DAILY** taken away Dan. 11:31 508" "Papacy set up, 538." "Sacrifice" is eliminated[15] after the word "**DAILY**."

Most significant is the chart's mishandling of its gloss on Daniel 8:13–14 in the top middle portion of the chart. It says, as if quoting

---

11. White, *Ellen G. White Letters and Manuscripts*, 246–47.

12. Nichols took Ellen G. White's comment seriously in constructing the 1851 chart. What would later be called the "old view" of "the daily" was concretized in this chart. For an excellent overview of this controversy see Valentine, *W. W. Prescott*, 214–37.

13. White, *Ellen G. White Letters & Manuscripts*, 246 n. 17. See E. G. White, "Dear Brothers and Sisters," 87.

14. This chart embodies two indispensable elements of historicist Millerism: a dated historian's reference and quotation matched with a biblical text, both of which are given a pictorial representation.

15. It was eliminated because Ellen G. White said she saw that "sacrifice" was incorrectly supplied by the KJV translators in harmony with what she had learned from William Miller.

the KJV Bible: "How long shall be the vision concerning the DAILY[16], and the TRANSGRESSION OF DESOLATION, to give both the Sanctuary and the host to be trampled underfoot?" Under the guidance of E. G. White's inspiration, Nichols felt free to eliminate the word "sacrifice" from his citation of the KJV version of Daniel 8:13–14.

These two interpretations and alterations of the actual biblical text demonstrate that when the White/Nichols chart came out in 1851, about six years after the Disappointment, "the daily" was still a vital theme of SDA chronology and theology. Ellen G. White was persuaded that "sacrifice" was improperly supplied by the KJV translators. Both charts contain the calculation which situated the elimination of "the daily" after the breakup of the Western Empire into ten barbarian tribes in 490.

1,290 years, 1,335 years, and 2,520 years in both 1843 and 1851 charts

The White/Nichols 1851 chart features the 1,290-day-year calculation as well. The chart asserts that "The pope's DOMINION over the [10] kings continued 1260 years. It was taken away by France A. D. 1798-9, just 1290 years after paganism lost its CIVIL POWER. Dan 12: 7, 11." Note that here also the 1,290-year calculation assumes a beginning date of 508 and and end in 1798–1799, when the "time of the end" began, according to Miller.

In a letter written on November 27, 1850 by Ellen G. White "To the Church in Bro. Hastings' house," she addressed a diversity of topics, including the necessity for Otis Nichols to create his 1851 White/Nichols chart. She encountered a Brother Hewit from Dead River (Maine) who was setting new dates for the second coming based on his understanding of the 1,335-year prophecy. Roland Karlman notes that Mrs. White's "Brother Hewit" was most likely Brother Oren Hewett from Dead River. He had written articles for the *Advent Herald* and the "*Bible Advocate* in 1847 that repeatedly set new times for the Second Advent, times often held to coincide with the ending of the 1335 days/years." For Brother Oren Hewett, the 1,335 day-year period was an imminent/future date. Ellen G. White, believing this prophecy had been fulfilled in 1844, wrote that she corrected this

---

16. The word "sacrifice" follows in the KJV.

error and informed him that "the 1335 days were ended . . ." Karlman observes that "The united position of Sabbatarian expositors during this and subsequent stages was that the 1335 day/year period had ended in 1843/1844."[17]

On November 1, 1850 from Paris, Maine, in a letter to the Lovelands, E. G. White stated she received a vision at Otis Nichols's home. "There in the night God gave me a very interesting vision, the most of which you will see in the paper. God shewed me the necessity of getting out a chart. I saw it was needed and that the truth made plain upon tables would effect much and would cause souls to come to the knowledge of the truth." Her vision led directly to the "first publication of a prophetic chart. Prepared by Otis Nichols, an edition of 300 copies was read for distribution by January 1851."[18]

When Brother Rhodes created a particularly large and striking prophetic chart in August of 1850, this inspired Ellen G. White with the thought of duplicating his accomplishment on a three-hundred-fold scale. At the home of the very person who could realize her dream, Otis Nichols, she envisioned the project. One of the novelties it contains is the assertion that the number 666 represents the number of Protestant sects—not the papacy. Below the engraving of a two-horned beast, it is identified as the "IMAGE OF PAPACY"—not the papacy but the "IMAGE OF PAPACY." There follows the explanation: "The two lamb like horns, (REPUBLICANISM & PROTESTANTISM,) whose names number 666."[19]

Another Millerite definite-time proof was the 2,520-year prophecy. It also appears on the 1843 Millerite chart, and it appears again on the Nichols 1851 chart.[20] It states in the top middle of the chart:

"Before Christ 677 Israel carried captive; 2 Chron. 33:11 The 7 Times commence. Lev. 26."

---

17. White, *Ellen G. White Letters & Manuscripts*, 255–56. This indicates that for Ellen G. White, Miller's prophetic 1,335-year interval was just as prophetic as his 2,300-year or 1,260-year prophetic period.

18. White, *Ellen G. White Letters & Manuscripts*, 243, 249.

19. At the same time Nichols confusingly conflated his engraving of a beast identified as "PAPAL ROME Rev. 13:11–17," which "had two horns like a lamb" and the beast below, which he also said had "two lamb like horns." The upper beast's image does not have two horns; the lower beast does.

20. Arasola, *End of Historicism*, 95–101 points out the several failures of this purported prophetic interval. Nichol, *Midnight Cry*, 507–10, Appendix L labels these prophetic intervals "fanciful and far-fetched."

In the lower right corner, there is a box featuring the following text:

> Explanation of the Time
>
> A prophetic year or time is 360 days denoting years. 7 Times is 7×360=2520 yrs ...
>
> The treading down of Israel by the gentiles commenced before Christ 677, 1843 years after Christ added to 677 make 2520 yrs, 7 Times
>
> The length of the daily, Dan 8:13 from B. C. 457 to A. D. 508-9[21] is 965 yrs.
>
> From the daily taken away, to papacy set up,—538-9 -30 yrs.

The chart has several other significant dates, chronologies, and explanations that have since been disconfirmed. One alludes to a vision Ellen G. White had on December 16, 1848. In this vision she saw the "open space in Orion" through which the "Holy City will come." At that time Joseph Bates asserted that the European revolutions of 1848 were "the shaking of the powers of heaven," just preceding the second coming. On December 16, 1848 Ellen G. White claimed to have a direct revelation in which God showed her the meaning and chronology of this phrase. She asserted that "the shaking of the powers in Europe is not (as some teach) the shaking of the powers of heaven, but it is the shaking of the angry nations."[22] The expression about "angry nations" is used in the White/Nichols 1851 chart to describe events following the seven last plagues, the third woe, and the sounding of the seventh angel's trumpet. When this happens the

---

21. The key point is that, according to the chart, "the daily," a pagan phase, lasted a total of 965 years, a very unique number found nowhere else in Millerite chronology to my knowledge; then from 508-1798 a papal phase would last 1,290 years with the 1,335 years extending from 508 to "about 1843." The rational of the printing "508-9" here is not certain. However, it appears to mean that the 508 date may in fact be 509; similarly, the "538-9" may indicate an uncertainty between 538-539 AD. The Millerites had had to acknowledge that their calculations may have been off a year. Thus, on the same chart the printing is not simply "1798" but "1798-9." It is known that Litch argued for a 1799 date for the captivity of the pope, for example. Thus, on this chart in the same box it printed "From 1798-9 to 1844." However, 1844, NOT 1843-44, stood in splendid isolation as the year Ellen Harmon's first vision asserted this fact.

22. White, *Ellen G. White Letters & Manuscripts*, 149–50. Interestingly there is no phrase in the KJV that refers to the "shaking of the nations." The "nations were angry," as in this chart, is evidently the essential equivalent.

chart quotes Revelation 11:15–19: "The kingdoms of this world are become of our Lord, and of his Christ, and he shall reign for ever and ever. And the nations were angry, and thy wrath is come, and the time of the dead that they should be JUDGED." In short, this was a phrase which denoted extreme imminence. The chart, like many of her statements between 1844 and 1851, demonstrates that Ellen Harmon expected the Parousia within months of January 1851, when the White/Nichols chart was first distributed.

One of Miller's proofs of "about 1843" was that he held that a 666-year prophetic interval stretched from 158 BC to 508 AD. He asserted that in 158 BC the Romans made a league with the Jews and this marked the beginning of the Romans being involved with the "people of God." The 1851 White/Nichols chart's chronological timeline still contains the note that "Time of the league between the Jews & Romans, B. C. 158."

August 11, 1840 collapse of Ottomans in both charts

The entire right-hand column, with a width of between one-third and one-fourth of the chart, is taken up with a purported detailed chronology of Muslim forces in prophecy. As demonstrated in chapter 2, this schema has been disconfirmed. Most significantly, the August 11, 1840 collapse of the Ottoman Empire is a collapse which never occurred. Otis Nichols, under Ellen G. White's direction, nevertheless included it.

The cliché is that a picture is worth a thousand words. The White/Nichols 1851 chart captures Ellen G. White's theology, chronology, and hermeneutical positions in pictorial form. The most significant change between the 1843 chart and the White/Nichols 1851 chart is that the latter chart adopted O. R. L. Crosier's two-compartment extended-atonement hypothesis. There is an image captioned: "The Most Holy." The Most Holy is engraved with a crowned High Priest with a "golden censer" and "burning incense" in his right hand. The golden censer was a new element that Ellen G. White first saw in her 1847 Sabbath vision, which, significantly, she did not see in her first vision.[23] Below, the Most Holy Place is engraved outside the

---

23. The golden censer was the symbolic incarnation of the new doctrine of the investigative judgment, just like the bright halo over the Sabbath commandment

"2nd Vail Heb 9:3," and below that "Sanctuary or Holy, Heb. 9:2." The explanatory text identifies three symbols pertaining to the Holy Place: "the Golden Candlestick, the Table and shewbread, and the Brazen Altar and Laver." The chart also includes the newly minted three-angels hypothesis, with images of feminine angels with flowing skirts and lengthy, well-coiffured hair and specific dates for each angel: first angel 1837, second angel 1843, and third angel 1844.

As 1845 and 1846 expired, a new test was needed before the second coming could happen. This occurred in 1846–1847, when Ellen White rebranded the Little Flock as the "Sabbath and shut door Adventists," the third angel of Revelation 14:9–12. This angel denounced Sunday worship and blessed Saturday Sabbatarians. Ellen White implicitly assumed that the fact that Seventh-Day Baptists had been preaching a Saturday Sabbath for two centuries had no chronological, biblical, eschatological, or soteriological significance. According to Ellen White's concept, the Sabbath angel of Revelation 14:9–12 could only be historically fulfilled after October 22, 1844.

In 1908 Ellen G. White was asked to decide which view of "the daily" was consistent with her 1850 vision. S. N. Haskell was quite certain that her 1850 vision guaranteed that "the daily" referred to paganism, while W. W. Prescott argued that it referred to Christ's mediatorial ministry. A. G. Daniells reported that when he stretched out Haskell's chart on her lap and tried to talk to her about the meaning of "the daily," she "'would go into that twilight zone right away.' She could not understand the points raised and stated that she had no light on the matter."[24] Mrs. White may have been in the "twilight zone" in 1908 and not have remembered what she meant by "the daily" in 1850. However, we do not have to rely on her octogenarian recollection to know what she meant by it. The White/Nichols 1851 chart plainly informs us what she thought at the time. Like the well-known 1843 chart, beastly images and apocalyptic symbols are visually dominate. Almost as striking are dates in bold print and mathematical calculations of exact prophetic intervals. Brief captions explain the beasts and mathematical calculations. The following is a significant caption associated with a date and text:

"Pagan Dominance or The DAILY taken away Dan. 11:31 508"

symbolized the "Sabbath and shut door" slogan adopted by James and Ellen White at this time.

24. Valentine, *W. W. Prescott*, 224.

"Papacy set up, 538."

Recall that Ellen G. White claimed: "Then I saw in relation to the 'daily,' that the word 'sacrifice' was supplied by man's wisdom, and does not belong to the text."[25] Clearly Otis Nichols was guided by this assertion. Thus, he excised the word "sacrifice" from the KJV text of Daniel 11:31 in this caption. Not only does the 1843 chart clearly teach what Haskell termed the "old view," but the contemporaneous chart of 1851 also supports Haskell's interpretation of Ellen G. White's original intent. Prescott's "new view" of "the daily" may have had the virtue in that it "focused on the gospel rather than on dates, forgotten nations, and questionable events in the past." Prescott was correct when he told Haskell "that your interpretation would make the Spirit of Prophecy contradict history,"[26] but that was no vice for those who believed that Ellen G. White spoke with the advantage of direct revelation. If the Spirit of Prophecy contradicted history, it was because the historians were in error, according to those holding the "old view." Whatever the case, the original 1850 statement alone, especially when put in the context of the 1851 White/Nichols chart, demonstrates that in 1850 Ellen G. White did support the "old view," which asserted that "the daily" was a symbol for "Pagan Dominance or The DAILY taken away Dan. 11:31 508." (Theologically, "Pagan Dominance" was equivalent to "The DAILY.")

Thus, two facts about "the daily" are beyond dispute. One, Ellen G. White's belief that the word "sacrifice" in the translated phrase "the daily sacrifice" was improperly inserted by the KJV translators is factually false—despite what she thought she saw. Two, Ellen G. White, claiming inspiration, supervised the 1851 White/Nichols chart containing the assertion that "the daily" was "pagan dominance" and had nothing to do with literal sacrifices.

There is considerable theological significance in Ellen G. White's assertion that "God was in" the "publishment" of White/Nichols 1851 chart. This is identical to her assertion that "God was in" the midnight-cry movement. Yet both the midnight cry and the 1851 White/Nichols chart contain erroneous eschatological concepts. One of the results of these errors was that between 1844 and 1851 Ellen G. White

---

25. White, *Ellen G. White Letters & Manuscripts*, 246.
26. Valentine, *W. W. Prescott*, 216, 223.

did believe that the door of probation was closed and that no genuine conversions could take place after October 22, 1844.

XII

Waldenses: Poster Children for Historical Sabbatarians

"If we have any point that is not fully, clearly defined and can [not] bear the test of criticism, don't be afraid or too proud to yield it."

"The truth can lose nothing by close investigation."

ELLEN G. WHITE

Apostolic, Waldensian Sabbath-keepers massacred by the millions?

The historicist Protestant interpretation of Daniel and the Apocalypse required that the appacy had persecuted members of the "church in the wilderness" for 1,260 years, from 538 to 1798. Joseph Bates, upon becoming a Sabbatarian, and Ellen G. White, upon developing her Great Controversy theme, asserted that the Waldenses especially represented the true, Sabbath-keeping church that had existed ever since apostolic times.

One of the widespread Protestant beliefs in the 1840s was that the papacy had for centuries persecuted and put to death millions of "pure" Christians who had not apostatized. It was one of those "facts" which Ellen G. White considered to be "well known and universally accepted by the Protestant world."¹ Among these pure, proto-Protestant Christians, Protestants identified such individuals as Hus and Jerome, movements such as the Lollards in England, but most especially the Waldenses and Albigenses. The charge that the papacy massacred millions was repeated frequently in the Millerite journals that Ellen Harmon was exposed to. For example, in a *Western Midnight Cry!!!* article asserting that the "Saviour designed in this chapter, to teach the time (i.e. the year)² of his second advent," the author, commenting on the 1,260-day period, said that "over 50,000,000 Christians, were martyred for their faith in Jesus," and more would have been except for the "shortening of those days"—meaning the "Papal civil rule."³ Similarly, the editors of *The Midnight Cry!!!* claimed that "the vallies [*sic*] of Piedmont, and mountains of Pyrenees" afforded the "church in the wilderness" some succor but nevertheless the toll was: "Destroyed under Papal rule, Innoc't Christians, 50,000,000."⁴ Again, commenting on the "mystery of iniquity," Millerite authorities charged: "It was Papal Rome, which during 1260 years destroyed 50,000,000 innocent unoffending Christians."⁵

Another example of a Protestant writer who considerably predated Ellen White is Brownlee.

> "In one word, the church of Rome has spent immense treasures and shed, in murder, the blood of sixty-eight millions and five hundred thousand of the human race, to establish before the astonished and disgusted world, her fixed determination to annihilate every claim set up by the human family to liberty, and the right of unbounded freedom of conscience."⁶

William Miller typified the conviction that the "millions" had been massacred by the papacy when he said: "The history of the

1. Ellen G. White, *Great Controversy*, (1888), xi.

2. The parenthesis containing "the year" is in the original. By this date Millerites united on an official platform that "sincere" Christians should and *must know* "the year" of the Second Advent. A literal reading of many texts restrained them from knowing "the day or hour," but as the text did not explicitly say the year could not be known, they insisted it could be.

3. Jacobs, "But of that Day and Hour Knoweth No Man," 6–7.

4. Jacobs, "Matthew, 24th and 25th Chapters," 59.

5. Jacobs, "2d Thess. 2:7–12," 74.

6. Brownlee, *Popery the Enemy of Civil and Religious Liberty*, 104–5.

church, in all ages of this present world, is but a history of persecution and blood." Specifically, in his interpretation of Revelation 12, he dated persecution to the time period 538–1798. This was the time when the "church in the wilderness" was hunted and slaughtered almost to extinction, but never quite disappeared. Rather, there had always been a minority of Christians who from apostolic times resisted the growing apostasy of the state church, the Roman Catholic Church. When the papacy became supreme, according to Miller in 538 AD, this pure, apostolic church sought refuge in the wilderness. Thus, about 538, due to their refusal to worship "departed saints" or submit to the "infallibility of the church at Rome," "many privately withdrew themselves," eventually settling in the "Piedmont and valleys of the Alps," "Where it is supposed the true worship of God[7] was retained during the dark ages of Papal ignorance, bigotry, and superstition." Then, said Miller, at the "beginning of the thirteenth century," papal Rome "sent forth his armies and inquisition to subdue the heretics, as he called them, who dwelt in the valleys of the Alps."[8]

In addition to finding the Waldenses in Revelation 12's "church in the wilderness," Miller also found them in his exegesis of Revelation 1 and the church of Sardis, which he calculated to run from "about the tenth century, and lasted until the Reformation under Luther, Calvin, and others." According to Miller, the KJV phrase "'I will come upon thee,' is *undoubtedly* a prophecy of the persecution of the Waldenses and Lollards, by the Papal authority," resulting in their eventual annihilation.[9]

Ellen White's prophetic endorsement of William Miller warrants repetition.

> I saw that God sent his angel to move upon the heart of a farmer who had not believed the Bible, and led him to search the prophecies. Angels of God repeatedly visited that chosen one, and guided his mind, and opened his understanding to prophecies which had ever been dark to God's people.[10]

---

7. Ellen G. White presumed "the true worship of God" must include Sabbath keeping. Miller's "it is supposed" betrays the tenuous nature of his assertion. Miller's tenuousness is transformed by Ellen G. White into certainty.

8. Miller, *Evidence* (1842), 124–29.

9. Miller, *Evidence* (1842), 85–88. Emphasis added.

10. White, *Spiritual Gifts*, 1:128.

She even likened him to three of the greatest prophets in the Bible; Elijah, Elisha, and John the Baptist. Indeed, William Miller was a modern-day John the Baptist, a pivotal personage whom Jesus said was greater than a prophet:

> As John the Baptist heralded the first advent of Jesus, and prepared the way for his coming, so also, Wm. Miller and those who joined him, proclaimed the second advent of the Son of God.[11]

She then gave a homily on how angels guided John the Revelator prior to a segue on how the same angels guided William Miller as he interpreted the Revelation of St. John.

SDA theology and eschatology depends upon her assumption that Miller was favored with divine insight. If Miller (and then Snow) were really justified in claiming that the years 1843 and 1844 fulfilled the first two angels' messages of Revelation 14, then Ellen White could retroactively claim that her movement fulfilled the third angel's message.

While Ellen G. White did not explicitly label Miller a prophet, neither did she claim this appellation for herself. Practically and operationally, nonetheless, she put him in the highest prophetic company, certainly surpassing any candidate for that office proposed by the best historical and contemporary SDA theologians for the period 100–1844 AD.[12]

In short, Ellen G. White likened Miller to John the Baptist, John the Revelator, and Elisha the prophet. It is easily comprehensible that this lofty conception of William Miller would have led Ellen Harmon to accept Miller's identification of the Waldenses as the bloodied and martyred "church in the wilderness."

---

11. White, *Spiritual Gifts*, 1:129–130.

12. See for example the collective work *The Gift of Prophecy in Scripture and History*, edited by Alberto R. Timm and Dwain N. Esmond. This consortium of authors, after much effort, are unable to unambiguously identify any person a prophet in the same league with Ellen G. White and protocanonical writers. Ellen G. White and her disciples insisted that the *perpetuity* of the "gift of prophecy" proved that this "gift" did not terminate about 95 AD with the Apocalypse of St. John. See White, *Spiritual Gifts*, 3:1–30. This was the consensus of Protestant theologians. It was considered that the canon of Scripture closed with the Apocalypse of St. John about 95 AD. The claim that Ellen G. White's two thousand visions were direct emanations of the divine mind after a two-millennia gap is quite extraordinary. How could the gift exist in perpetuity if there was a hiatus of two almost millennia?

Ellen Harmon's KJV family Bible informs her beliefs about Waldenses

An additional reason why Ellen White would claim that millions of "pure" Christians would be massacred during the period of papal supremacy of 538–1798, and that Waldenses were the prototypical representatives of the "church in the wilderness," is that she could read this assertion in her 1822 KJV family Bible.[13] Indeed, this KJV Bible anticipated William Miller and at least ten typical Millerite expositions of the apocalyptic books of the Bible. This particular Bible was a type of study Bible. That is, it exhibited a particular hermeneutic with explanatory footnotes that guided its readers to particular conclusions. An analogous example would be a Darby dispensational study Bible, or a Jehovah's Witness translation of the Bible. Even a *sola Scriptura* approach to either work would likely bring the reader to particular dogmatic conclusions.[14] A very particular point of view informed the printing and translation of the "pure" text. Just so, the footnote apparatus in Ellen Harmon's 1822 family Bible had an idiosyncratic, historicist set of presumptions. Most critically, it had already adopted two of Miller's prime assumptions. First is the day-year principle in which the word "day" in prophetic literature should be interpreted as a year in actual history. Second is that the intent of God in Revelation was to announce a sequence of exact prophecies that would, century by century, exactly predict major epochs in church history. In short, it foreshadowed many of Miller's continuous-historical interpretations. These included major military conquests and several of Miller's lesser known prophetic interpretations. One of the most famous of the Millerite predictions is the footnotes' interpretation of verses they believed referred to Muslims, the "Saracens," or the Ottoman Empire.

The author of the footnotes for Ellen Harmon's 1822 King James Bible had already anticipated Miller by a couple decades. The footnote

---

13. Citation from this Bible originate from xerox copies made at my request by James Hayward from the Ellen G. White family Bible, located in the Ellen G. White Estate vault, located at Andrews University. Graybill, *Visions*, 35 identifies this Bible as "a copy of Joseph Teal's *Columbian Family and Pulpit Bible*," which included the Apocrypha.

14. The Jehovah Witness translation of John stating that the Word was "a god" rather than "the Word was God," for example, is *sola Scriptura* support for Arian views favored by them and numerous pioneers like Joseph Bates, James White, and Uriah Smith.

for Revelation 9:1, 3 reads: "A star—locusts," "A star," "Mahomet, or Mahommed, who began his imposture in Arabia about A. D. 606. He shone with a conspicuous but pestiferous lustre. Locusts. The vast armies of Saracens, resembling locusts in numbers and in desolating effects." Is there really anything in the text that unambiguously designates Mahomet or Muslims?

The footnote to Revelation 9:5 explains: "Kill," "Not kill them as a state," meant that "[t]hey [the Muslims] could not wholly extirpate the Greek and Latin churches." Revelation 9:11's footnote interprets: "Apollyon," "Destroyer." This refers "to the caliphs or chief priests of their religion, in succession destroying both the bodies and souls of men." Revelation 9:16's footnote reads: "Two hundred" (and refers to one of the most notorious Millerite predictions), "A large definite put for an indefinite number of men, employed in the conquests of 391 years." According to Millerite calculations, Osman I began his invasion of the Byzantine Empire on July 27, 1299. The five (30-day) months of prophecy, or 150 years, brings one to 1449, when Constantine XI relinquished Byzantine political independence. Then the year, month, day, and hour of this verse (391 + 1449 = 1840), according to the year-day principle, brings one to August 11, 1840.

Missionary and Bible Societies predicted per 1822 KJV footnotes and Miller

According to the footnote to Revelation 11:11, "Three days and an half," this refers to:

> attempts to slay the witnesses, and subvert all religion in Europe generally, may refer to that period, when, in a certain stage of the French Revolution, the atheists, and other infidels, and abandoned persons of France and of Europe, threatened, by insurrection and military, and other violent power, to put down Christianity in every form. The fall of so many myriads in the contest, by the pretense of establishing civil and religious liberty, during the war of all European Christendom for twenty years or more, may possibly be here predicted. Perhaps the witnesses, whose testimony was to extend its influence eventually, with other concurring religious associations, over the world, revived, with the period of the establishment of the first and principal London Missionary

Society, 1793, and of the English Church Missionary Society, of similar evangelical aims, and of the British and Foreign Bible Society, 1804.

Miller copied this same interpretation. Ellen G. White then copied it from Miller.[15]

The Waldenses and other proto-Protestants figured prominently in the 1822 KJV Bible in three footnotes. William Miller made similar references to the Waldenses many times.[16] The Albigenses, conflated with the Waldenses by these footnotes, by William Miller, and by Ellen G. White, were notable and quite unorthodox dualists, like the Gnostics.[17]

The first footnote referring to the Waldenses is to Revelation 11:3. It comments on the words of the text, "Two witnesses." It explains that a "succession of witnesses suffered for . . . the continuance of a pure seed, perhaps from the eighth to eleventh century and onwards, as the Waldenses of Piedmont, the Lollards of England, the Bohemians and many faithful and suffering witnesses of the truth in France." Comparing with Miller's exposition above, one can see that he followed the same chronological framework. It was important for both writers to mark out prophetic time, century by century, predicted event after predicted event, right up until the period immediately preceding the Second Advent.

The second footnote referring to the Waldenses is linked to the words "To make war" in Revelation 13:7. It asserts that "A million of the Waldenses, &c. perished in France and Savoy; 900,000 of the orthodox were slain after the establishment of the Jesuits, A.D. 1540. The duke of Alva, the Spanish general of the Netherlands, boasted of killing 36,000 Protestants; and the Inquisition destroyed 150,000 within thirty years."

The third footnote placing the Waldenses in prophecy is linked to Revelation 14:6 and the words "Another angel." (This is the first angel of what SDAs would later call the three angels of Revelation 14.) The commentator asserted that this refers "to the Waldenses and Albigenses of Savoy and France, the Lollards of England, &c. or to the dawning, by their efforts, principles and example, of a reformation of

---

15. Miller, *Evidence*, 120.
16. Miller, *Evidence*, 85–88.
17. Casebolt, "Ellen White, the Waldenses, and Historical Interpretation," 37–43.

the church in the twelfth, thirteenth and fourteenth centuries." However, there is nothing specific in the text that would suggest a one-to-one relationship between this "another angel" and the Waldenses, Albigenses, or Lollards. But, following the commentator's entire sequence, one notes that it progresses from apostolic times right up until the last days following the French Revolution and 1798. Just in the verses concerning the Waldenses we've travelled from the eighth to the fourteenth century. This is another example of Miller taking a traditional identification of an apocalyptic symbol and speculating on a new and improved interpretation. Miller, followed by Ellen White, abandoned the Waldensian identification of the first angel of Revelation 14:6. They asserted that the Millerite movement of 1843 (or 1837 according to the 1851 White/Nichols chart), was the historical embodiment of the first angel. Nevertheless, they retained the general continuous-historical placement of the Waldenses as the martyred "church in the wilderness."

Having these "facts" about the Waldenses affirmed by the glosses in her 1822 KJV family Bible was like the near-universal glosses in the margins of KJV Bibles which stated as fact that the world was about six thousand years old. Indeed, one of Miller's proofs that the second coming would occur in 1843/1844 was that this was the six thousandth year of earth's history.[18] Miller asserted that the creation occurred in 4157 BC. Therefore, since the world would last only six thousand years, it would end exactly in 1843.[19] Twelve-year-old Ellen Harmon took both "facts" with equal seriousness.

White's novel assertion that Waldenses and Albigenses kept Sabbath

Neither Miller nor the author of the footnotes in Ellen Harmon's 1822 KJV Bible asserted that the Waldenses and/or Albigenses were Saturday Sabbatarians. To my knowledge, no author prior to Ellen Harmon ever made such a claim. However, Miller, the Millerites, and the author of the 1822 KJV footnotes depicted the Waldenses as an apostolically "pure" church that retained its most authentic Christian teachings from apostolic times. After being persuaded by Joseph

---

18. This was Miller's millennial-Sabbath hypothesis.
19. Miller, *Evidence* (1842), 166.

Bates that Sabbath was a "pure" apostolic doctrine, could Ellen White conceive of a "church in the wilderness" from 538 to 1798 AD that did not keep a Saturday Sabbath?

Did Ellen White receive a special direct revelation that revealed to her that the Waldenses and Albigenses did keep the Sabbath for centuries since apostolic times? If historians have unimpeachable documentary evidence that the Waldenses and Albigenses did not keep the Sabbath, must SDAs reject such historical conclusions as "science falsely so-called"? Or is it possible that Ellen White was mistaken? In which case, could SDA apologists concede that since the assertion that the Waldenses kept the Sabbath does not rise to the significance of a doctrinal error, it is possible to admit that she erroneously adopted the unbroken apostolic, proto-Protestant lineage from fallible Protestant historians? Certainly, W. C. White's reproof to S. N. Haskell is solid support for this interpretation: "Regarding Mother's writings, she has never wished our brethren to treat them as authority on history." Additionally, as Knight has astutely observed, the precedent for how Ellen G. White responded to the controversy over the "law" in Galatians and "the daily" in Daniel suggests that were Ellen G. White alive today she would refuse to be utilized as a historical authority regarding the Waldenses and Albigenses.[20]

Recently, an article was published demonstrating that Ellen G. White was intellectually dependent for material in her first vision on the pseudepigraphal book of 2 Esdras (4/5/6 Ezra), deuterocanonical books, and William Foy's vision.[21] Additionally, both James White and Joseph Bates considered 2 Esdras to be Scripture, containing prophecies which were being fulfilled during the period 1844–1849. If Ellen White, James White, and Joseph Bates could all mistake the pseudepigraphal 2 Esdras as Scripture, could not Ellen White also have been mistaken about the history of the Waldenses? Korpman documented that in 1849 Ellen White strongly endorsed the Apocrypha, calling it "pure and unadulterated," "pure and undefiled," and "The Word of God," but saying that a "part of the hidden book, a part of it is burned (the apocrypha)," and that it was in danger of being "cast out."[22] Thus, Ellen White urged witnesses to her vision of the Apocrypha to "bind

---

20. Knight, *Reading Ellen White*, 26–27, 109, 115.
21. Casebolt, "It Was Not Taught," 66–73.
22. Korpman, "Adventism's Hidden Book," 56–65.

it, bind it, bind it," "let not its pages be closed, read it carefully," "le[s]t everything be cast out."²³ He also documented a decades-long history of its citation and endorsement by famous SDA authorities such as Uriah Smith. Why she thought that "It was not taught me by man" in the particular case of 2 Esdras is probably because she thought 2 Esdras was "The Word of God," part of the "hidden book" reserved for the "wise" of the last days. Other material that she saw in her visions and believed "was not taught me by man," has also been demonstrated to have literary parallels with other fallible moral sources. This has been extensively documented by such researchers as McAdams and Veltman.²⁴ Several of her assertions regarding the *Great Controversy* originated from several inaccurate and partisan Protestant historians. That is, the "facts" she believed she obtained by direct revelation were actually obtained from mundane, fallible documents she read *prior* to her visions. Her statement that "millions" of Sabbath-keeping Waldensians, a "pure" version of the church that originated in apostolic times, were massacred by the Catholic church is a textbook example of this phenomenon. This is one of the "facts" which she understood to be universally acknowledge by the Protestant world; therefore, they played a prominent role in her depiction of the "church in the wilderness" existing for hundreds of years. This theme of a Sabbath-keeping, pure church that resisted the papacy's Sunday began in her earliest visions—after she was taught this concept by Bates and Preble. She made such a categorical, authoritative statement about seeing the pure, apostolic, Sabbath-keeping "church in the wilderness" that it is inconceivable to most SDAs that she could be mistaken.

Although the word "Waldenses" does not appear in *Spiritual Gifts*, it is there in a euphemistic, symbolic form and is currently read back into it from her later works such as the *Great Controversy*. In her later expansions on this theme she would specifically identify these "true and faithful witnesses keeping all of God's commandments," [i.e., the Sabbath], "through *all* this time of error and deception," as the Waldenses, the Albigenses, and Columba.²⁵ In her later expansion, Ellen White was specific and categorical:

---

23. White, *Letters & Manuscripts*, 183–84, 195.

24. McAdams, "Shifting Views of Inspiration," 27–41; Veltman, "Desire of Ages Project," 11–15.

25. Casebolt, "Ellen White, the Waldenses," 37–43. Emphasis added.

> The faith which for centuries was held and taught by the Waldensian Christians was in marked contrast to the false doctrines put forth from Rome.
>
> Among the leading causes that had led to the separation of the true church from Rome was the hatred of the latter toward the Bible Sabbath.[26]

In the decades since Donald Casebolt initially presented the historical facts concerning the Waldenses in 1981, even more overwhelming evidence has been published substantiating his original thesis. For example, Cameron has an excellent and well-documented demonstration of how the legend of the Waldenses originated and was propagated.[27] Nonetheless, a recent SDA scholar has attempted to reinterpret the evidence.[28] The present author was first alerted to this in reading *Focus*, the Andrews University alumni journal, in which Damsteegt claimed to have found evidence substantiating Ellen G. White's assertions about the Waldenses. Given Ellen White's apparently categorical statements about the Waldenses, combined with the current predominant concept of inspiration within the SDA church that Ellen White could make no "significant" errors, this is to be expected.

EGW not dependent on extra-biblical material for "information and ideas"?

Two of the crucial *a priori* assumptions of traditional orthodoxy are as follows. First, regardless of the amount and type of extra-biblical material Ellen White borrowed, all significant dogmas elucidated by her are essentially infallible in practice (if not in theory). The only possible exception to her practical infallibility regards trivia, according to denominational authors. Mueller, for example, after listing a number of biblical inaccuracies, concludes that these are insignificant because

---

26. White, *Great Controversy* (1888), 64–65. In other words, just as Sabbatarianism in the last days will be the major distinguishing factor between those with the Sabbath seal and those marked by the image of the Beast, Sabbath was not a marginal issue but *the major* issue in the history of the Waldenses.

27. Cameron, *Waldenses*, 285–297.

28. Damsteegt, "Decoding Ancient Waldensian Names," 237–58.

"all these historical inaccuracies are minor."[29] However, he does not include in his list major contradictions involving biological impossibilities.[30] Rodriquez similarly argues that since the Bible has "some minor discrepancies and difficulties," by implication, one should expect the same in Ellen White.[31] The stress is on "minor" However, this nuance at least avoids the insuperable difficulties involved in verbal inerrancy that other fundamentalists espouse. But the preponderance of denominationally published authors come right up to the border of verbal inerrancy. Lake makes the following characteristic assertion:[32]

> When Ellen White read her sources, she was not dependent on them for getting information and ideas as in reading-directed thinking. Rather, she came to her sources with a preunderstanding as in thinking-directed reading... The common knowledge Ellen White obtained from reading the Protestant religious authors was always subordinate to her inspired understanding.[33]

Lake's claim is that Ellen White could not have have made any significant errors in her borrowing from extra-biblical writers because she was not really "dependent on them for getting information and ideas." She had a "preunderstanding" which caused her to read only what fit in with that. She came to these sources with a divinely provided filter which eliminated all misconceptions and "important" inaccuracies. (What is the evidence for such a claim?) Another author in the same collective work asserts: "Can a biblical author mislead in doctrine...? My answer is categorically no; prophets do not make doctrinal mistakes... there are no examples that would convincingly demonstrate that prophets made mistakes in doctrines..."[34] Given

29. Mueller, "Prophetic Voice in the New Testament" 36.

30. For example, see Brown, *Birth of the Messiah*, 66–94 for unresolved contradictions noted in comparing Matthew's and Luke's genealogies.

31. Rodriquez, *Revelation/Inspiration and the Witness of Scripture*, 84–104.

32. Her description of the Waldenses is one of the clearest examples which disproves this. To the polemical distortions of typical Protestant narratives, she added the erroneous claim that they kept the Sabbath. She was subordinate to Protestant religious authors, not the reverse. Similarly, her erroneous assertions that self-abuse led to an epidemic of insanity, cancer, and a whole plethora of other serious diseases was clearly obtained from the exaggerated and erroneous misconceptions of some medical writers of her day.

33. Lake, "Ellen G. White's Use of Extrabiblical Sources," 326.

34. Moskala, "Prophetic Voice in the Old Testament," 40.

Ellen White's rather categorical assertions regarding the Waldenses, and given these denominationally promoted scholars' assumptions that she could make no "significant" errors, one can easily see that it would be almost impossible for any empirical evidence to convince them otherwise.

The position that no empirical evidence could persuade inerrantist Seventh-Day Adventist thought leaders to consider the possibility that Ellen G. White made significant errors was typified by S. N. Haskell's statement during the 1910 dispute over "the daily." He wrote to Ellen G. White that:

> There is no hope of these old people [adherents of the old view] who lived back in the early days of the Message being converted to this new light, even if they [the new-view proponents] bring volumes of histories to prove it. Because they [the old-view supporters] give more for one expression in your testimony than for *all the histories you could stack between here and Calcutta* [emphasis added]" (S. N. Haskell to EGW, May 30, 1910).[35]

If one starts, as denominationally supported authors generally do, with the *a priori* assumption that Ellen White's "thinking-directed" reading made her practically inerrant as regards the historiography of the Waldenses and Albigenses, no amount of evidence to the contrary could ever shake this conviction. "All the histories you could stack between here and Calcutta" would not make any difference! The absence of any evidence to support Ellen White's assertions that the Waldenses kept the Sabbath for centuries can always be justified by either of the two following alternatives. One, all such evidence has been destroyed by papists. Two, there still exists evidence which will demonstrate that Ellen White was correct; it has just not been located—yet.

A more empirically based explanation is that Ellen White simply adopted the typical nineteenth-century Protestant view of Latin Christianity and grafted Sabbatarianism into the metanarrative. The Waldenses were exhibit A in this regard. Despite a major collective *opus* created by SDA scholars trying their best to locate early (200–300 AD) historical evidence of Sabbath-keeping, they were unable to substantiate Ellen White's account. Notably, in regard to the Waldenses, they concede that the sect did not keep the Sabbath and that Peter

---

35. Moon, "Daily," 752.

Waldo was its founder.[36] In order to adopt this empirically based explanation, SDA theologians and parishioners would simply have to label this an "insignificant error." After all, even if the Waldenses did not keep the Sabbath, SDAs can, with much more reason, assert that the preponderance of the evidence from both the Old and New Testament support the doctrine that the fourth commandment was never abrogated. Thus, Ellen White's assertions regarding the Waldenses was a mere historical error, not a doctrinal error.

How the Waldensian legend originated

It is incontrovertible that the Waldenses did begin with a rich citizen of Lyon France called Valdesius around 1170; that he recognized the authority of the pope; that he was doctrinally in accord with the Catholic Church; that he was chiefly interested in being authorized to preach and teach as a layman and live in wandering, apostolic poverty.[37] The Waldenses became useful for disputes between Reformers and Catholics when the Counter-Reformation forced Reformers to agree that Christ had prophesied that his church would never fail; a prophecy that implied "that there must be a continuous, visible succession of the Church from the time of the apostles to the present." Given that the Reformation was no older than Luther, who other than the Catholic Church could this church be? Thus, Reformers were stimulated to identify a persecuted, hidden but not altogether invisible church that had existed since apostolic times. Protestant references to the Waldenses began about 1550 and, starting with the latest sources, began projecting them into a hoary past. Waldensian martyrological narratives multiplied and were incorporated into John Foxe's works, the official martyrology of the Church of England. The ultra-Lutheran theologian and church historian Matthias Flacius Illyricus, when incorporating them, had to "explain away elements of [ancient] text[s] which described the Waldenses as holding beliefs not shared by Protestants." But "the sources did not support the idea that the Waldenses were forerunners of the reformers." James Ussher and Jean-Paul Perrin then massaged the sources and gave tendentious interpretations to the earliest documents to create a pristine Waldensian church useful

---

36. Augsburger, "Sabbath and Lord's Day During the Middle Ages," 205–7.
37. Cameron, *Waldenses*, 1–34.

in debating Catholics. Modern scholars have reexamined the manuscripts and seen "marginal notes, excisions and deletions in the Dublin manuscripts [most likely in Perrin's hand]." The "clear purpose of the notes is to remove from the record pieces of evidence which were unhelpful to the argument that the Waldenses were really Protestants." One researcher bluntly stated: "I have no hesitation in saying that they were made with the dishonest intention of concealing the original difference in doctrine and discipline between the Vaudois and the reformed, and of representing the ancient state of the former as identical with that to which the reformers of Germany, at the beginning of the sixteenth century, were anxious to reduce the Church." Then in 1655 Ussher convinced Samuel Morland (an Ellen White source) to write what became *History of the Evangelical Churches of Piedmont*. In so doing, he back-dated sixteenth-century documents to 1120, "a date antecedent even to Valdesius himself." Then Piedmontese Waldensian pastor Jean Leger wrote his *L'Histoire Générale des Eglises Evangeliques des Vallées de Piemont* in 1669, by back-translating Morland's English account into French. This then "became the reference work of Waldensian history which appeared to derive authentically from the Piedmontese churches themselves."[38] Needless to say, from the beginning of the Reformation until 1669 and well beyond, Catholics were charged with slaughtering millions of Waldenses. William Miller incorporated this conception uncritically,[39] and was a major influence in inculcating Ellen White—not to mention that her 1822 KJV family Bible's footnotes alleged that millions of Waldenses were massacred. Furthermore, Enoch Jacobs, Ellen Harmon's first editor, edited several articles in *The Western Midnight Cry!!!*, asserting: "over 50,000,000 Christians, were martyred for their faith in Jesus"; "Destroyed under Papal rule, Innocent Christians, 50,000,000"; "It was Papal Rome which during 1260 years destroyed 50,000,000 innocent unoffending Christians."[40] Without discounting that there are later documented Catholic atrocities against the Waldenses, the Albigenses, and even other orthodox Christians,[41] the magnitude has been exaggerated and, more importantly, their doctrinal teachings over the decades

---

38. Cameron, *Waldenses*, 285–96.
39. Miller, *Evidence*, 85–89.
40. Jacobs, "2d Thess. 2:7–12," 74.
41. The Crusaders' rampage throughout eastern Christendom, for example.

have been well documented as not being proto-Reformation. And as concerns their "cornerstone" function in Ellen White's assertion of a hidden, apostolic, Sabbatarian church, this is simply inaccurate. This is just another myth grafted onto the general Ussher-Morland-Leger-Wylie tale.

Cameron summarizes:

> Between the sixteenth and the nineteenth centuries they [the Waldenses] were regularly cited by Protestant controversial writers as evidence that there had survived down the ages a counter-Church, or 'true Church' of orthodox but anti-Roman Christian believers detached from and opposed to the Roman 'Antichrist'. This apologetic stance *would not now be taken seriously by any modern scholarly historian.*[42]

Indeed, the entire calculation and conception of wholesale murderous persecution being practiced in Latin Christianity, with Waldenses being at its center, is a major misconception. During the half-millennium following 538, there were virtually no Catholic massacres of "heretics." "Although the burning of heretics is now commonly thought of as an ordinary, even routine, expedient in medieval society, it did not become so until late in the twelfth century." "The systemic, violent and large-scale repression brought to western Europe by the war on heresy of which these events in the 1160s were the opening shots had *no earlier parallel.*"[43]

Moore substantiates this: "No heretic had been executed in western Europe for almost 600 years after the end of the Roman empire until in 1022, about sixteen people were burned alive at Orleans by order of King Robert II of France." In the 140 years following 1028, "heretics, real or alleged, were burned on five other occasions we know of, but the numbers involved were much smaller."[44] Apart from the Albigensian Crusade and until the Reformation sparked religious wars, the historians' consensus is that the number of deaths due to religious violence was nowhere in the magnitude of the millions described by Brownlee, Miller, Jacobs, and White.

---

42. Cameron, *Waldenses*, 6. Emphasis added.
43. Gregory, *Salvation at Stake*, 75. Emphasis added.
44. Moore, *War on Heresy*, 2–4.

How one SDA scholar attempts to maintain the Waldensian legend

Ellen White's assertion was that the Waldenses kept the Sabbath since apostolic times. Damsteegt reaches the same conclusion in a more euphemistic fashion. He claims that the term "*sabbatati* also could have been used to describe some groups of Waldenses who followed the Jewish practice of resting on the Sabbath." His conclusion is not supported by his own citations. He does not address the historicity of Peter Waldo, who is universally acknowledged to be the founder of the Waldenses, but he asserts that the Waldenses "were not a new religious movement of the twelfth century as Catholics had argued," without providing any evidence that they existed prior to the twelfth century. He simply makes the nebulous claim that "the beliefs of the Waldenses had their spiritual roots in the apostolic faith as set forth in the Bible." He does admit that "there is no record that Waldo and his followers observed the seventh-day Sabbath."[45]

The evidence he presents to support his conclusion is centered on his discussion of the terms *insabbatati, sabbatati, sabatatos,* and other similar Waldensian appellations which he proposes to decode. He observes that the first time *insabbatati* occured was 1192. This would appear *prima fascie* evidence that the Waldenses originated in the twelfth century and are not apostolic as he and Ellen White have suggested. He disputes the general consensus of historians that this term had its origins in the distinctive footwear of the Waldenses. He acknowledges that several Waldensian groups who reconverted to Catholicism also wore this distinctive footwear, had similar beliefs, had similar lifestyles, and were easily confounded with them. This, he says, vitiates the "shoe theory." But he admits that Waldensian historian Emilio Comba (1839–1904) accepted the "shoe theory," and that today "most Waldenses have accepted the shoe interpretation originating with Waldo as the explanation of the names given them during the thirteenth century."

Why does Damsteegt propose a "holy days theory" in place of the "shoe theory?" Because, he claims, *four centuries after* Peter Waldo, a Waldensian pastor named Jean Perrin (1580–1648) said that the word *insabbatati* expresses a negation of the root word *sabbat*, indicating that the "Waldenses rejected Catholic holy or rest days, called

---

45. Damsteegt, "Decoding," 249.

sabbaths," and that they "observed no other day of rest than *Sunday*."[46] He also cites Huguenot historian Nicolas Vignier (1588), who said that Waldenses were called Insabathaires because they "observed no other day of rest or holiday, than Sunday"; Calvinist historian Friedrich Spanheim (1632–1701), who says they were called "*Sabbatati* because they rejected Papal feasts, only observing the Lord's Day"; a Bernard Gui, who said that Waldenses kept no days holy except "the Lord's Day and the feast of the Blessed Virgin Mary"; and Pope Pius II (1405–1464), who said they "cease from work on no day, except on the Lord's Day."[47] Noting these and multiple sources that refer to the Waldenses keeping Sunday in addition to the "feast of the Blessed Virgin Mary" is a peculiar way to support the conclusion that Waldenses were Sabbatarians from apostolic times. However, that the Waldenses kept Sunday is consonant with all the generally acknowledged facts about them. They did originate in the twelfth century with Peter Waldo, initially as a protest movement against a wealthy and corrupt ecclesiological hierarchy. Even then, they initially gave no hint of a Donatist argument; they simply asserted their right to preach without the authority of the hierarchy. They did doubt the doctrine of purgatory, the efficacy of prayer for the dead, the Catholic priesthood's monopoly regarding the sacraments of baptism and the Eucharist, and the validity of oaths and judicial execution, but were similar to Catholics in faith and practice in many respects.[48]

Even Damsteegt's assertions which best support his hypothesis are equivocal, late, and document Sunday-keeping rather than Sabbath-keeping. For example, he claims manuscripts of the fifteenth century from Moravia that may confuse a non-Waldensian group with the Waldenses and accuse them of Judaizing and of not celebrating any feasts "except the Lord's day. Not a few celebrate the Sabbath with the Jews."[49]

In sum, the Waldenses did originate in the twelfth century with Peter Waldo ,who did not keep the Sabbath. At best, a very poorly and ambiguously attested group (not demonstrated to be even Waldensian) three centuries after the well-attested Peter Waldo was accused

---

46. Damsteegt, "Decoding," 249. Emphasis added.
47. Damsteegt, "Decoding," 258, 254, 247, 249–51.
48. Cameron, *Waldenses*, 11–60.
49. Damsteegt, "Decoding," 254.

of celebrating Sabbath with the Jews. Such allegations may not even have been true since labelling dissident Christians as "Judaizers" was a common way of discrediting a religious opponent. Such groups could have spontaneously arisen without any continuous historical or ecclesiological pedigree stretching back to apostolic times, much as Seventh-Day Baptists and Seventh-Day Adventists originated centuries after apostolic times. Thus, even if accusations of Sabbath-keeping were authenticated for later centuries, this does not substantiate Ellen White's assertion that a Sabbath-keeping Waldensian church could be traced back to the apostolic age. Moreover, her sources, Preble and Bates, conceded that a Sunday celebration was kept by the apostles.[50] There is simply no clear historical record of how an originally Jewish Christian church of 30 AD morphed into a mainly Gentile, Sunday-keeping church. However, Sunday was widely celebrated by a date well prior to Constantine. Any attempt to depict the Christian church as "pure," meaning that it celebrated a Saturday Sabbath, until 313, at which time it suddenly became "corrupt" under the influence of Sunday legislation promulgated by Constantine (or even later by Pope Gregory in the seventh century), is not accurate. Nor is it accurate to portray the papacy as having corrupted the church by coercing, persecuting, and martyring Sabbath-keepers, especially when several Sunday-keeping popes were themselves martyred prior to the time of Constantine.

The fact that the Waldenses were "a new religious movement of the twelfth century" is so well attested that denying it comes perilously parallel to the historical negationism of Holocaust deniers.

Some SDAs find it so difficult to accept that Ellen White was at times dependent on erroneous, merely human sources for some of her significant historical assertions that they deny solidly substantiated historical and scientific facts. There are scholars with a (at least) semi-inerrantist view of inspiration, who cannot allow the cumulative, overwhelming "evidence beyond a reasonable doubt" to alter their *a priori* theological assumptions. They comb through historical and scientific evidence for even a semblance of evidence to fit their assumptions. They function as experts whom the untrained SDA laity can cite to buttress their shared assumptions. Unfortunately, this is a disservice to both faith and truth. As W. White observed, such rigid

---

50. Bates, *Seventh Day Sabbath*; Preble, *Tract*.

defense of Ellen White's prophetic gift has been the most effective way of destroying its influence. For example, he said: "I certainly think we will make a great mistake if we... endeavor to settle historical questions by the use of Mother's books as an authority..."[51] During the early 1900s "the daily" controversy, the General Conference president, A. G. Daniells, also repeatedly warned that Ellen White had been done a "great wrong" when her fundamentalist supporters "are arraying her against the plain text of the Scripture, and all the reliable history of the world." Such exegetes "make too great claims, and so we have gotten into difficulty," observed Daniells.[52]

In chapter 4 many of Miller's proofs that the second coming would occur "about 1843" have been deconstructed. This did not include the 1,260-year interval from 538 to 1798. Because of its association with the Waldenses, I analyze it here and in the following chapter. This was the crucial time period that for Miller initiated the "time of the end." Recall that the 1,290-year period spanned 508 to 1798 as well. To those unacquainted with the historical development of how historicists like Miller settled on 1798, the event associated with this date has a superficial plausibility. However, 1798 was never predicted in advance. Actually, Froom provides voluminous documentation that for decades the overwhelming majority of historicists proclaimed different dates, especially 606–1866.[53] For example, David Pareus (1548–1622) calculated the 1,260 years "from 606 to 1866—beginning with Phocas' recognition of the Roman pope, and ending in 1866, though for the elect's sake the Lord will shorten it."[54] George Downham (d. 1634), an English theologian, dated the 1,260 years as starting with "the round number" 600 AD, when "Phocas recognized the pope as universal bishop."[55] John Gill (1697–1771), an imminent Orientalist and Baptist expositor, made the remarkable assertion that for the wise who understood prophecy, it could be known when the

---

51. Knight, *Search for Identity*, 135.

52. McArthur, *A. G. Daniells*, 295–97, 395.

53. Froom, *Prophetic Faith of Our Fathers*, 3:798, 799. See the index on these pages for multiple entries regarding dates for the 1,260 years, especially the long-held, dominant view that it spanned 606–1866.

54. Froom, *Prophetic Faith of Our Fathers*, 2:519–20. Note the theme, two hundred years prior to the time that William Miller, Ellen White, and Uriah Smith copied it, that the 1,260 years of persecution would be shortened.

55. Froom, *Prophetic Faith of Our Fathers*, 2:536.

reign of the Antichrist began and, "it might be *exactly* known when his reign will end." He admitted of some uncertainty regarding the beginning of the reign of the Antichrist, "but seeing the time when he [Antichrist] was made universal bishop by Phocas, bids fair for the time of his open appearance, and the beginning of his reign, and of his blasphemy, which was in the year 606, to which if we add 1260, the expiration of his reign will fall in the year 1866 . . ."[56]

It was only after the French Revolution began that various expositors began to see prophetic significance in these events, eventually settling on the 1798 arrest of Pope Pius VI. Besides the 2,300-year interval, the 1,260-year interval was the most pivotal historicist calculation. Therefore, it is appropriate that special attention be given it.

---

56. Froom, *Prophetic Faith of Our Fathers*, 2:683–84. Emphasis added.

XIII

"Enslavement of the Papacy" (Caspar)—or "Supremacy" of the Papacy (White)?

WILLIAM MILLER ASSERTED THAT the Bible taught that a persecutory papacy was biblically predicted in Daniel 7:25 to exercise an absolutist supremacy for precisely 1,260 years, from 538 to 1798.[1] But if one reads Daniel 7 from beginning to end, it is impossible to show that the Bible provides anything remotely resembling an exact starting (or ending) date for this period. Moreover, the entire thrust of the chapter is to assure the saints that the end of the time period involved would extend not until 1798, now almost a quarter of a millennium in the past, but when the Son of Man comes on the clouds of heaven, and he rules with an "eternal sovereignty," "and the kingdom will be theirs for ever, for ever and ever" (Daniel 7:18, KJV).

Miller copied 1,260-day-year interpretation from tradition

Ellen White's exposition of the 1,260 day-years was dependent on William Miller. Despite claiming that no commentators influenced his conclusions, Miller did copy previous commentators' calculations of the 1,260-day-year theory. Froom documented scores of commentators who suggested both 606–1866 and 538–1798 as intervals fitting the 1,260-year calculation. Moreover, Ellen Harmon's 1822 family

---

1. Miller, *Evidence*, 57.

KJV Bible's footnotes also contained multiple elements upon which Miller was dependent, which Ellen G. White borrowed from Miller and which later became standard SDA interpretation. Commenting on Revelation 11:2's "42 months," the commentator stated: "If they mean twelve hundred and sixty years, (each day for a year Ezekiel), perhaps the period begins, not as is commonly supposed,[2] with the date of the high title conferred by Phocas on the bishop of Rome A. D. 606[3], but A. D. 533, (73 years before) when Justinian styled Pope John 'The Head of all the most holy churches and of all the most holy priests of God.' Christian Observer Perhaps millennial dawn commenced A.D. 1793 — twelve hundred and sixty years advance of 533." Both Miller and then Ellen G. White followed a timeworn, unoriginal tradition. It goes without saying that none of these commentators was inspired or inerrant. Such commentators, like Uriah Smith, emphasized the amazing exactitude with which the purported prediction was fulfilled.

> Did the Papacy possess dominion that length [1260 years] of time? The answer again is, Yes. The edict of the emperor Justinian, dated A. D. 533 made the bishop of Rome the head of all the churches. But this edict could not go into effect until ... A. D. 538 ... From this point did the papacy hold supremacy for twelve hundred and sixty years? —Exactly. For 538+1260 = 1798; and in 1798, Berthier ... entered Rome, proclaimed a republic, took the pope prisoner, and inflicted a deadly wound upon the papacy.[4]

Miller went into considerable historical detail to justify picking the dates of both 508 and 538 AD. Additionally, he said:

> In the beginning of the sixth century, about A.D. 538, Justinian, emperor of Constantinople, in his controversy with the Arians[5], and other schismatics in the Greek church,

---

2. Twenty-four years after 1798, when this KJV Bible was published in 1822, it was "commonly supposed" that the 1,260 began in 606, not in 538.

3. Note first that this is the date that Bates and Preble used to date not only the Papal supremacy but also the time when papacy substituted Sunday for Saturday; second, that the suggested dates (533-1793) vary by five years from the eventual 538-1798 period. To obtain an artificial exactitude, White argued that it took five years for the decree to go into effect during a specific military victory of Justinian.

4. Smith, *Daniel and the Revelation* (1944), 145.

5. Non-Trinitarians, whom Miller identified with the three uprooted powers.

constituted the bishop of Rome head over all others, both in the western and eastern churches, who, by his authority, suppressed the reading of the Bible by laymen, pretending that they could not read and understand without the assistance of the clergy.[6]

Ellen White did not go into as much detail but adopted Miller's scheme along with a vaguer version of his historical justification. For example, she said:

> In the sixth century the papacy had become firmly established. Its seat of power was fixed in the imperial city, and the bishop of Rome was declared to be the head over the entire church. Paganism had given place to the papacy. The dragon had given to the beast "his power, and his seat, and great authority. Revelation 13:2.[7]

While Miller linked very particular events to pagan Rome in 508, morphing into papal Rome's supremacy in 538, White was more ambiguous in citing the "sixth century" as the period during which "Paganism had given place to the papacy." The *Ellen G. White Encyclopedia* in its article on "Prophetic Interpretation" cites the 1,260 day-year, 42 months, and the August 11, 1840 prediction of the fall of the Ottoman Empire as key examples of Ellen White's endorsement and application of the day-year principle.[8]

White, in her *Great Controversy* chapter on the French Revolution, explicitly proclaimed her adherence to Miller's 1,260-year scheme. She wrote: "Said the angel of the Lord: 'The holy city shall they tread underfoot forty and two months. And I will give power unto My two witnesses, and they shall prophesy a thousand two hundred and threescore days, clothed in sackcloth.'" Then she commented:

> The periods here mentioned—"forty and two months," and "a thousand two hundred and threescore days"—are the same, alike representing the time in which the church of Christ was to suffer oppression from Rome. The 1260 years

---

Note the unsubstantiated charge of suppressed Bible reading repeated by White.

6. Miller, *Evidence (1842)*, 169, 120.

7. White, *Great Controversy* (1888), 795.

8. The *Ellen G. White Encyclopedia* cites both the 1,260-day/year and Ottoman Empire calculation as evidences of exactly fulfilled prophecy. See Damsteegt, "Prophetic Interpretation," 1061–63.

of papal supremacy began in A.D. 538, and would therefore terminate in 1798. At that time a French army entered Rome and made the pope a prisoner, and he died in exile. Though a new pope was soon afterward elected, the papal hierarchy has never since been able to wield the power which it before possessed.[9]

Like Miller, she equated the 42 months with the 1,260 days just below: "They shall prophecy a thousand two hundred and three-score days, clothed in sackcloth." Then she commented again:

> During the greater part of this period, God's witnesses remained in a state of obscurity. The papal power sought to hide from the people the word of truth, and set before them false witnesses to contradict its testimony. (See Appendix.) When the Bible was proscribed by religious and secular authority; when its testimony was perverted, and every effort made that men and demons could invent to turn the minds of the people from it; when those who dared proclaim its sacred truths were hunted, betrayed, tortured, buried in dungeon cells, martyred for their faith, or compelled to flee to mountain fastnesses, and to dens and caves of the earth—then the faithful witnesses prophesied in sackcloth. Yet they continued their testimony throughout the entire period of 1260 years.[10]

"This [1,260 day-year] prophecy has received a *most exact and striking* [emphasis added] fulfillment in the history of France. During the Revolution, in 1793," said Ellen White.

She continued by making a specific application to France: "According to the words of the prophet, then, a little before the year 1798 some power of satanic origin and character would rise to make war upon the Bible. And in the land where the testimony of God's two witnesses should thus be silenced, there would be manifest the atheism of the Pharaoh and the licentiousness of Sodom."

She identified the "church in the wilderness" very specifically with the Waldenses and Albigenses.

> Century after century the blood of the saints had been shed. While the Waldenses laid down their lives upon the mountains of Piedmont "for the word of God, and for the testimony

---

9. White, *Great Controversy* (1888), 266.
10. White, *Great Controversy* (1888), 267.

of Jesus Christ," similar witness to the truth had been borne by their brethren, the Albigenses of France.[11]

The "Church in the Desert," "the few descendants of the ancient Christians that still lingered in France in the eighteenth century, hiding away in the mountains of the south, still cherished the faith of their fathers. As they ventured to meet by night on mountainside or lonely moor, they were chased by dragoons and dragged away to lifelong slavery in the galleys. The purest, the most refined, and the most intelligent of the French were chained, in horrible torture, amidst robbers and assassins. (See Wylie, b. 22, ch. 6.)."[12] Notably, she relied on Wylie, whom we now know to be unreliable concerning the Waldenses, the Albigenses, and the magnitude of the persecution in general.

Arbitrary choice of 538

What happened in 538 that justified White's assertion that this year marked the beginning of papal supremacy? Miller, Smith, and White claimed that it was a 533 edict of Justinian making the pope the head of the Catholic Church, but that this edict only went into effect in March 538 when Justinian's forces lifted the Gothic-Arian siege of Rome.[13] In other words, political control by orthodox Catholic forces opposed to heretical anti-Trinitarian tribes was the determinant factor. However, such control alternated many times in this epoch—making the March 538 lifting of a Gothic siege an arbitrary choice.

For example, White could have as easily chosen December 10, 536, when Justinian's army under Belisarius entered Rome, or 553, which, by Smith's own admission, was when the Ostrogoths (another Arian power) were "finally plucked up."[14] The control of Rome fluctuated between the Ostrogoths and the emperors several times between these two dates, and any one of these events could just as well have been chosen. Adventist expositors could not agree on the time for the 1,260 days. Nor could they agree on the identity of the three kings who were plucked up by the little horn. W. W. Prescott, for example, favored

---

11. White, *Great Controversy* (1888), 271.
12. White, *Great Controversy* (1888), 265–89.
13. Smith, *Daniel and the Revelation* (1944), 278.
14. Smith, *Daniel and the Revelation* (1944), 277, 128.

533–1793.[15] Only the passage of time and Ellen G. White's prophetic endorsement of 538–1798 made the dates 538–1798 sacrosanct.

How arbitrary the 538 date is can be noted from the information in the following details. The Ostrogoths were disunited when Belisarius first arrived and inflicted his initial defeats upon them. However, a new king, Totilla, began his reign in 541 and

> ... wielded the Ostrogothic scepter for eleven years, a longer period than any of his predecessors since the great Theodoric. Coming to the aid of his countrymen when their cause seemed sunk below hope, he succeeded in raising it to a height of glory such as even under Theodoric himself it had scarcely surpassed.[16]

In 546 the Goths retook Rome by the Asinarian Gate under Totilla, who demolished one-third of its walls and then evacuated it, retaking it once more in 546. If Justinian's lifting of an Arian siege of Rome in 538 established the supremacy of the pope, would not an Arian power reconquering Rome in 546 terminate it?

The first biblical occurrence for the expressions equivalent to 1,260 days is in Daniel 7:25. Even a fleeting glance at the context reveals major objections to White's interpretation. A horn power "making war" on the saints is pictured and Daniel is assured that its hegemony will only be temporary, for a "time, two times, and half a time" (assumed to be 1,260 years in Millerite interpretation), until God will end the reign of this power. At the end of the 1,260 years, according to Daniel 7:26–28 (KJV), God will judge the horn power, "his power will be stripped from him, consumed, and utterly destroyed. And sovereignty and kingship and the splendours of all the kingdoms under heaven will be given to the people of the saints of the Most High." It is clear that these verses envision God's everlasting kingdom being set up at the end of this period. Obviously, this did not occur in 1798.

A parallel scenario is given where the same expression is mentioned in Daniel 12:7. A power warring with the saints will be crushed when Michael will stand up for the saints. This is immediately followed by the 1,290-day-year and 1,335-day-year figures, suggesting that perhaps the saints will have to endure a somewhat longer period

---

15. Olson, "Ellen G. White's Use of Historical Sources," 3.
16. Hodgkin, *Italy and Her Invaders* (8 vols.), 4:438–39, 557, 566–68, 573, 675.

than 1,260 day-years, more in the neighborhood of 1,290–1,335 day-years. This expression is taken up in Revelation 11:2, 3; 12:6, 14; and 13:5. Here "pagans" will trample Jerusalem, the sanctuary, and its worshippers for 1,260 days or 42 months. But these worshippers are assured that at the end of this period Yahweh will establish his *eternal* kingdom. In short, the terminus of the 1,260 days or 42 months will be marked by a *cosmic—not merely historical—*event. More troubling for White's and Smith's interpretation, there is not the slightest indication that this period started in 538. The *purely speculative* nature of such dating schemes is exposed by simply listing some of the many competing conjectures. Froom gives the following sampling.[17] One exegete proposed 312–1572, justifying the choice of these dates by asserting that the Battle of the Milvian Bridge/Vision of Constantine in 312 represented the beginning of Caesaropapism while the St. Bartholomew's Day Massacre of the Huguenots in 1572 marked the high point of Catholic persecution; a second suggestion was 756, marked by the Donation of Pepin to a presumed fall of the papacy projected to happen in 2016. "Robert Fleming writing in 1701 (The Rise and Fall of Rome Papal) stated that the 1260-year period should commence with Pope Paul I becoming a temporal pope in AD 758 with the period expiring in 2018."[18] Such unfettered speculation hardly comports with Miller's supposed criteria, whereby each word must be exactly matched by a plain Bible verse. But what is the evidence that the 538–1798 hypothesis is any less arbitrary than 312–1572, 606–1866, 756–2016, or 758–2018? Particularly since it should never be forgotten that 1798 was never predicted in advance; it was only "predicted" after 1798.

Arian, anti-Trinitarian bias in interpretation

A subsidiary part of Smith's argumentation that is of some note is the emphasis which he gave to the fact that the Heruli, Vandals, and Ostrogoths were Arian rather than Catholic. (The emphasis on the Arian or anti-Trinitarian beliefs of the tribes "plucked up" by the Trinitarian Catholic church is a tradition which was found in Ellen Harmon's 1822 KJV Bible's marginal notes and in William Miller's writings as

17. Froom, *Prophetic Faith*, 2:784; 3:744–45; 4:392–400.
18. See https://en.wikipedia.org/wiki/Day-year_principle.

well. Isaac Newton was also virulently anti-Trinitarian well before Miller. Ellen White's two cofounders, James White and Joseph Bates, had very strong anti-Trinitarian beliefs. This shared anti-Catholic and anti-Trinitarian belief was a determinative factor in the interpretive roots of the nascent SDA church.) According to Smith, "the possession of Italy and its renowned capital by a people of the Arian persuasion would be fatal to the supremacy of a Catholic bishop." Thus, he went to some lengths to demonstrate that the Arian powers were hostile and unfair to the popes. In particular, he charged the Arian king Theodoric with severely abusing a pope.[19] However, one authority characterizes Theodoric's relationship with the Catholic Church as being just the opposite. He stated that "even orthodox bishops loudly praised his [Theodoric's] fairness and moderation," and cited as an example of his fairness that when blood flowed between rival popes Festus and Symmachus, he made a fair decision supporting Symmachus, whereas political considerations would have inclined him to support Festus.[20] Fliche and Martin state that Theodoric "had demonstrated the greatest religious tolerance toward the Catholic church."[21]

As to the hindrance which Arians posed to the pope's supremacy, Smith conveniently neglected to mention the fact that scarcely had Justinian been dead three years when the Arian Lombards began their conquest of Italy, wreaking havoc everywhere:

> The Lombardish conquest damaged the Roman Catholic church even more than the Empire. For the new tribe ... saw Romans as the enemy, the Catholic bishops as enemy priests and the pope as the head of an enemy religion.[22]

Erich Caspar describes the relationship between the Lombards and the Catholic Church as follows: "The Lombards, already feared because of their barbaric ferocity, ... came, in distinction to Theodoric's Goths, as enemies of the Empire, and treated the Catholic church also as an enemy."[23]

In 574 the Lombards surrounded the Eternal City. Communications with Constantinople were severed. Ten months passed after

---

19. Smith, *Daniel and the Revelation* (1897), 131–33.
20. Hodgkin, *Italy and Her Invaders*, 3:489, 495.
21. Fliche and Martin, *Histoire de l'Eglise*, 4:434.
22. Haller, *Das Papsttum*, 285. All German translations are mine.
23. Caspar, *Geschichte des Papsttums*, 2:351.

Pope John III died on July 13 before Benedict I could be chosen. There was famine. Again in 579 the Lombards were besieging Rome so that another pope had to be picked without consultation with Constantinople. In the 580, popes still complained about "insults offered to the Catholic faith by these [Lombard] idolaters." As late as 590 Authari, a Lombard king, forbade the sons of Lombards to be baptized according to Catholic rite.[24]

Pope Pelagius II complained bitterly in 580 to a Frankish bishop (whose countrymen stood passively by during the Lombardian invasion) that:

> Almost before your very eyes is so much innocent blood being spilled, so many holy altars desecrated by idolaters, that it would have been more seemly to have offered brotherly help.[25]

Thus, one must ask, if "possession of Italy and its renowned capital by a people of Arian persuasion" was such a hindrance to papal supremacy before 538, why not in the decades following 538?

In 538 popes were humiliated and anathematized, not supreme!

Another factor undermining Smith's explanation of the 1,260-day-year prediction is that the pope in 538, and in the following decades, was hardly treated with supreme regard personally. The first pope in 538 was Silverius. On a charge of treasonable correspondence with the Goths, he was deposed and exiled to the desolate island of Palmaria, where he died on June 21, 538. Hodgkin summarizes the affair thusly:

> That a Pope, the son of a Pope and a great Roman noble, should have the pallium torn from him and be thrust forth into obscure exile at the bidding of a woman, and that woman the daughter of an actress and a circus-rider, was a degradation to which the Arian Theodoric and his successors had never subjected the representative of St. Peter.[26]

---

24. Hodgkin, *Italy and Her Invaders*, 5:286.
25. Caspar, *Geschichte des Papsttums*, 2:352.
26. Hodgkin, *Italy and Her Invaders*, 4:254.

Vigilius, who had bribed the empress with two hundred pounds of gold and promised to reinstate Anthimus, the Byzantine patriarch of the heretical Monophysite heresy, became the next pope and fared even worse than Silverius.[27]

First, Vigilius refused to publicly recognize Anthimus, and so was charged with the homicide of Silverius. Then, in a scandal known as the "Three-Chapter Controversy," he refused to obey Justinian's demands to condemn them. Thus, on November 22, 545 he was arrested and put onboard a ship to Constantinople. By 548 the court had coerced him, by a combination of threats of imprisonment and flattery, to contradict his own previously issued papal pronouncements. Therefore, he then issued the *judicatum* condemning the "Three Chapters." Opposition to the *judicatum* was fierce and a significant portion of the pope's own retinue refused him their obedience. Because of this, Vigilius was forced to dismiss and ban eight of his own staff. Worse yet, opposition spread to include virtually the entire Western half of the empire. In 550 the African bishops excommunicated the pope! Moreover, the Western bishops refused to attend a general council called by Saint Peter's successor.[28]

Therefore, Vigilius was forced to reverse his position yet again. He went to the extreme of excommunicating Mennas and Theodore of Caesarea for celebrating mass in a church where Justinian's decree concerning the "Three Chapters" was publicly displayed. In attempting to escape Justinian's wrath, he took asylum in a church only to be routed out by Urbanus, head of the city police. The scene, as Hodgkin describes it, was a real tragicomedy.

> This Praetor [Urbanus], the head of the City police, "to whom," as the adherents of Vigilius indignantly asserted, "thieves and murderers rightly belonged," came with a large number of soldiers bearing naked swords and bows ready strung in their hands. When he beheld them Vigilius fled to the altar, and clung to the columns on which it was supported. The deacons and other ecclesiastics who surrounded the Pope were first dragged away by the hair of their heads, and then the soldiers seized Vigilius himself, some by the legs, some by the hair and some by the beard, and endeavoured to pull him from the altar. Still, however, with convulsive grasp

---

27. Hodgkin, *Italy and Her Invaders*, 4:486.
28. Hodgkin, *Italy and Her Invaders*, 4:665–67.

the Pope clung to the pillars and still the soldiers strove to drag his tall and portly form away from the place of refuge. In the scuffle the pillars of the altar were broken, and the altar itself was only prevented by the interposed hands of the ecclesiastics from falling on the Pope's head and ending his Pontificate and his sorrows at one blow.[29]

Such was the high esteem bestowed upon the "supremacy of the Pope!" Still, Vigilius had not yet drunk his full cup of woe. He was finally persuaded to return to his residence by oaths proffered for his safety—but had to flee once again. Then the council, absent the pope, condemned the "Three Chapters," whereupon Pope Vigilius in his *constitutum* defended them. He was repudiated by the council and banned and anathematized. After suffering a six-month banishment, he reversed himself yet again. On February 23, 554 he issued a new papal encyclical repudiating his own *constitutum*. For this act of abject subservience, he was released from banishment and allowed to leave for Italy, but he died in route in Sicily on January 7, 555.

Hodgkin summarizes the shambles this left the papacy in:

> Travelling as he did at least four times from one point to the diametrically opposite point of the theological compass, he deeply injured the credit of the Roman See, which now passed through half a century of obscurity till the arising of the first and greatest Gregory.[30]

Hodgkin further notes that the ignominious pontificate of Vigilius was "a calamity for the pontifical arms as great ... as that which befell the Roman legions on the disastrous day of Caudium."[31]

Uriah Smith and Ellen White attempted to characterize the period beginning in 538 with the arrival of imperial rule as marking the beginning of papal supremacy. Virtually all other disinterested historians describe it quite differently. Lot gives the following assessment:

> [T]he Bishops of Rome never had to submit to such a despotic and brutal regime as after the recapture of Rome by the Empire ... The position of the Pope seemed to be equally

---

29. Hodgkin, *Italy and Her Invaders*, 4:671–72.
30. Hodgkin, *Italy and Her Invaders*, 4:685.
31. Hodgkin, *Italy and Her Invaders*, 4:486. The Battle of Caudine Forks, 321 BC, was a decisive event of the Second Samnite War in which the Romans were trapped without water and ignominiously forced to surrender.

weakened from the point of view of outward honour and even in matters concerning the faith, by the re-establishment of the Imperial authority.[32]

538: period of "catastrophic decline" for the papacy

Caspar calls it a period of "catastrophic decline," and adds that "the enslavement of the Papacy to the Byzantine Empire, which characterizes this its second world period, reached its highpoint with Vigilius' pontificate," and terms the popes of 537–565 as "vassals of Caesaro-Papism."[33]

Haller characterizes this era as one of "deep decay." The results of this papal catastrophe were, he says, "deep and long lasting." He further states that:

> In the West, the Popes were long regarded with distrust. Only by following Pelagius' example of intentionally spreading disinformation as to their actual position were they able to prevent a broadening, open revolt from spreading. More than forty years later Gregory I had to defend himself against the accusation that he had fallen away [apostatized] from Chalcedon and Leo, because of his fellowship with the Eastern Church, by resorting to misrepresentation, concealment and disavowals; and more than one of his successors had to put up with bitter recriminations from admirers of Rome in the Lombardian Empire, because he did not meet the suspicion that he had fallen into heresy with a clear explanation.[34]

Inseparable from affronts to the personage of the pope was the centuries-long damage the Three-Chapter Controversy caused to the moral prestige and teaching authority of the Roman Church. For example, the authority of Rome had been renounced in upper Italy in 556. Thus, even after the Lombards broke from Arianism and professed the Catholic form of Christianity, it took decades before the authority of Rome was again recognized by them. In Italy, during the Synod of 595, only twenty-three bishops, most of them only from

---

32. Lot, *End of the Ancient World*, 297–98.
33. Caspar, *Geschichte des Papsttums*, 2:216, 234.
34. Haller, *Das Papsttum*, 1:283.

bishoprics adjacent to Rome, attended, as compared to three or four times that many a hundred years earlier.

The connection between Rome and Spain was severed even earlier and more completely. The Spanish church, therefore, never recognized the Fifth Synod. And when the Gothic kingdom converted from Arianism to Roman Catholicism in 586, this took place without any participation from Rome whatsoever. Previously mentioned was the fact that the African churches had excommunicated Pope Vigilius, even though they had to endure persecution from the emperor for their stand. Strained relations between Africa and Rome also lasted for decades.[35]

For two centuries following 538 the papacy had to suffer many serious indignities. For example, Pope Martin I suffered a fate quite similar to Pope Silverious for opposing the theological wishes of the emperor as embodied in the *Type*. In 653 Emperor Constans had him arrested and deported to Constantinople. For his offense he was originally sentenced to death, but this was later commuted to a sentence of exile. So, after eighty-four days in a prison at Diomede, he was put onboard a ship and finally allowed to land two months later at Cherson. Worn out by disease, he died there four months later in September of 655. "Yielding to Imperial pressure, the Roman clergy had acquiesced in his deposition and [had already] elected another pope, Eugenius I." Eugenius would have met a similar fate had not the empire been fully occupied in its own defense after the emperor's fleet was defeated by the Arabs, and the next pope, Vitalianus, reigned fifteen years "in total dependence on the Empire's power."

The papacy had to suffer still more humiliations at the Council of 692 in Trullo (*Quinisextine*). At this council, a number of ecclesiastical practices and peculiar forms of discipline in the churches of Africa and Rome were condemned. The aim of the church at Constantinople was to extend Byzantine practices over the church at large, thus overtaking the authority of the Roman Church. The Roman legates, under the pressure of Justinian II, were "obliged to accept and to subscribe."[36]

Schatz agrees with the global assessment of both Caspar and Haller when they state that the "Three Chapters" dispute and the fate of Pope Vigilius (537–555) marked a historical nadir in the authority

---

35. Haller, *Das Papsttum*, 2:284, 291–300.
36. Lot, *End of the Ancient World*, 299.

of the papacy—far from 538 marking the beginning of papal supremacy. He states that the Three-Chapter Controversy "led to an unexampled low point in papal authority not only in the East but even more in the West."[37]

Pope retrospectively anathematized

Yet probably the most serious blow to the teaching authority of the pope came during the Sixth Ecumenical Council (Constantinople, 681 AD), which included a retrospective anathema of Pope Honorius (625–628). Thus, Rome and the papacy were fallible. Honorious' name was included as a condemned monotheletist because he admitted to agreeing with the heretical Sergius and had supported his "godless" teachings.[38] Over one thousand years later, this incident was one of the greatest stumbling blocks to the official proclamation of papal infallibility in 1870. This is how Haller summarizes this anathema's tremendous historic importance:

> In a historical perspective it was a matter... above all of how the Church of the seventh century; namely the worldwide church in so far as it was orthodox, viewed the possibility that a Roman bishop could lapse into heresy. It had unhesitatingly affirmed this possibility by anathemizing a Roman bishop on grounds of heresy, and Rome itself had not objected. Rome had underscored the verdict, promulgated it and even made it its own... [Leo II, the next pope, dedicated in August 682] even underscored the decree against Honorius "who," he said, "did not undertake to illuminate the apostolic church by the teachings of apostolic tradition, but rather allowed the spotless [Church] to be sullied by an unholy betrayal..." When Leo II and the long succession of his followers over perhaps 350 years—because just this long, until the middle of the 11th century, was this confession of faith with its anathematizing of Honorius most likely in use—when they all took no exception to the fact that one of their predecessors, an undoubted successor of St. Peter's, was solemnly abandoned as a promoter of heresy, we know just how much worth to place on the sonorous proclamations of

---

37. Schatz, *Papal Primacy*, 52.
38. Caspar, *Geschichte des Papsttums*, 2:602.

a Leo I or Gelasius, and on the self-assured outspoken claims of Agathos.[39]

Finally, an examination of the letters and decrees of Justinian upon which White and Smith built their arguments does not support their interpretation. Long prior to Justinian's rule and decrees, the papacy commanded greater prestige and rank, both in form and in substance, compared to any other church.[40]

> The Council of Constantinople in 381, by ruling that the bishop of Constantinople should have precedence of honor next to the Bishop of Rome, gave formal if indirect recognition to the precedence *already granted by general consent* . . . The emperor himself recognized the precedence of the Roman church when he accorded the Roman delegates the right to preside at the Council of Chalcedon in 451 and gave the Roman bishop the title of *princeps episcopalis* coronae, "chief wearer of the episcopal crown."[41]

An examination of novella 131 (collection 9, title 6) confirms that Justinian was not setting a new precedent by acknowledging the preeminence of the bishop of Rome. He was merely *reaffirming long-accepted ecclesiological tradition*. After enumerating the first four ecumenical councils, he stated: "Hence, in accordance with the provisions of these Councils, We order that the Most Holy Pope of ancient Rome shall hold the first rank of all the pontiffs." And the 533 imperial letter to John II stated that Justinian was enlisting the pope's authority because he was "the head of all the Holy Churches." Emperor Justinian was not *creating* the authority of the papacy; he was *confessing* it.

Thus, regarding the date 538, we may summarize as follows.

First, it is a date arbitrarily arrived at *post hoc*. No prediction was involved. It was a postdiction arrived at by capriciously singling out 1798 and then subtracting 1,260. Expositors like William Miller, Ellen White, and others jiggered the data around 538 to construct a patina of plausibility for their foreordained conclusions. Even then, Adventist expositors could not agree, with some choosing 533–1793 in place of 538–1798.

---

39. Haller, *Das Papsttum*, 1:338, 341.
40. Caspar, *Geschichte des Papsttums*, 1:85.
41. Bruce, *Spreading Flame*, 340–41. Emphasis added.

Second, far from ushering in an epoch of glory, authority, and "supremacy," 538 marked the beginning of an era in which the popes were personally humiliated, imprisoned, and exiled. During this period they were excommunicated, their teaching authority was rejected, and they were anathematized as heretics, even while speaking *ex cathedra*.

When and why, then, did Miller and Ellen G. White chose 538?

First, because ever since the Protestant Reformation, and even prior, the critics of the papacy had branded it as the Antichrist. The period of 1,260 day-years was associated with a persecuting sacrilegious power that would fall after these time frames had ended. Such an interpretation could not be created until around 1560. This is because it would take at least 1,260-years plus 200–300 years for an apostasy to develop. Then all that remained was a *post hoc* linkage of the 1,260 day-years with the Catholic Church by tinkering with dates and facts to work out a mathematically exact interval, a method analogous to postdating a check or legal document.

Arbitrary "prediction" of 1798 made after the fact

Second, the age of Napoleon and the French Revolution was epochal, but not cosmically or biblically more significant than the grand revolutions and battles of various Chinese dynasties. When general Berthier took Pius VI prisoner in 1798, this event captured the Western world's imagination as a symbol of the indignities to which the papacy was having to become accustomed to as a temporal ruler. Moreover, this was a battle between the revolutionary ideals of egalitarian democracy versus the traditional hierarchical, divine-right-of-kings ideology. However, for decades prior to this, the pope, so far as his temporal powers were concerned, was viewed as only a petty Italian prince. Long gone were the days when the papacy had been one of the major European powers. The Protestant Reformation and the long religious wars that had devastated Europe severely curtailed papal influence. The Age of Enlightenment and the epoch of nationalism eroded the prestige of the papacy enormously. The fate of the Jesuits best illustrates the papacy's impotence vis-à-vis the major European powers. A jealous nationalism was manifested in the resentment that even Catholic kingdoms felt regarding papal interference in their national affairs generally and their national churches specifically. Thus, in 1759 Portugal banished the Jesuits from its realm. In France, the eldest daughter of the Catholic Church, the parliament of Paris evicted the Jesuits from their domains, while the Spanish king brutally suppressed them both in Spain and in the Spanish colonies. Finally, in July 1773 Pope Clement XIV was forced to sign the document *Dominus ac Redemptor*, dissolving the Jesuit order.[42]

This was certainly a severe blow to the papacy; and if one wished to construe this as a "deadly wound," a certain amount of plausibility could doubtless be established. However, even though several popes had suffered imprisonment and exile, the imprisonment and exile of Pius VI in 1798 was promoted as if it was a unique fulfillment of prophecy.

How arbitrary the choice of dates was can be seen in how Josiah Litch manipulated the dates retrospectively. For years premillennial historicists had calculated that Justinian's *Novallae* had been issued in 533 and that the 1,260-year interval would end in 1793. Only after a pope had been toppled by Napoléon's general Berthier in 1798 did they subtract 1,260 years from 1798. They then had to adjust the 533 *Novallae* by five years to arrive at 538 retroactively. Thus, they argued that the *Novallae* may have been issued in 533 but had only gone into effect in 538. The mathematical precision of 538 + 1,260 = 1798 replaced the traditional precision of 533 + 1,260 = 1793. Similarly, just as he had recalculated the dates and precise event for the fall of the Ottoman Empire in 1840, Josiah Litch found a justification for delaying the second coming a year when this did not occur in March 1844.[43] Litch still affirmed that February 5, 1798 was the day when the "papal government was abolished." But now that the Parousia had been delayed, Litch found significance that "the pope was not led into captivity until [March 27] 1799." Thus, perhaps the second coming had been programmed for 1845 rather than 1844. Litch did not explain the supposed difference between "abolished" and "led into captivity." Like beauty, the exactitude of prophetic prediction was in the eye of the expositor. (This hair-splitting of terms is reminiscent of O. R. L. Crosier's semantic gymnastics regarding the terminology of "forgiving" and "blotting out" sins.) Thus, on April 20, 1844 Litch conceded:

---

42. Latreille, *L'Eglise Catholique*, 4:16–17. All French translations are mine.
43. Anderson, "Millerite Use of Prophecy," 78–91.

> I have looked with great interest for some months past, to the anniversary of the captivity of the pope, which took place March 27th, A. D. 1799. The papal government was abolished Feb. 15, 1798; but the pope was not led into captivity until 1799. I have thought that might have been the end of the 1290 days as 1798 was of the 1260. But the day has gone by, and I have no more time to count. I do, however, expect, if we have time to hear from Europe, that the anniversary of that captivity is marked by some important event.[44]

He further confessed: "I have looked upon the 1335 days of Dan. 12:12, as extending beyond the 2300 days and reaching to the resurrection. Their termination cannot be far distant." Thus, splitting hairs in distinguishing the abolishment of the papal government from the captivity of the pope could give Millerites another year's time to buffer their "exact" calculations while preserving their all-encompassing continuous-historical system. Litch's exposition is a textbook example of confirmation bias.

A marked similarity in several SDA/EGW interpretations of historical events is the fact that their superficial impressiveness rests on ignorance of comparable historical events. Being unaware of similar events, the typical catechumen is unable to even conceive of the criteria for why one such event has been chosen as being significant and not another. In his limited perspective, it seems that something unique has indeed happened on a given date. (Was not Pope Pius VI indeed imprisoned in 1798?) In the typical parishioner's perspective, this fortuitous coincidence apparently confirms the choice of said dates and rapidly justifies the entire interpretive system. Only by being exposed to all the data, several competing hypotheses, and their various merits can the candid seeker after truth truly be said to have reached an informed conclusion. This seldom if ever occurs within the confines of a given religious body's religious instruction or evangelism. Very few are aware of the indignities and persecutions that the popes following 538 had to suffer. Thus, they never have to ponder how it could be that a papacy, supposedly supreme, powerful, and persecutory, could be suffering persecution itself. They are also totally unaware that Pius VII, Pius VI's successor, suffered at least as badly, if not worse, than Pius VI. Thus, they never have to wonder why some

---

44. Litch, "Where Are We?," 46.

date during Pius VII's pontificate would not have been better chosen as the time of the "deadly wound."

All that Uriah Smith had to tell about Pius VII was the following:

> In 1800 another pope was elected, his palace and his temporal dominion over the Papal States were restored, and, as George Croly, noted British commentator, says, every prerogative except that of a systematic persecutor was again his, for the "deadly wound" was beginning to be healed.[45]

Several remarkable things are revealed in this statement. First, it is noteworthy that Smith admitted that "every prerogative" (save one) was restored the papacy. Yet even in his and Ellen White's interpretation of papal powers, both insisted that the persecutory powers had been greatly hobbled years prior. In other words, they could not identify any discernable demarcation or date or event between the supremacy pre-1798 or the supremacy post-1798. Furthermore, more than two centuries have past since the "deadly wound" was healed. Has any discernable development in the papacy occurred since?

Second, it is remarkable that it took a mere two years for the "deadly wound" to be healed; or as Smith tellingly phrases it, "was *beginning* [emphasis added] to be healed." Within two years a remarkably rapid recovery from the so-called "deadly wound" was affected. By July 16, 1801 a new concordat between France and Rome had been signed by Pius VII and Napoleon. Within a month after the signing of the Treaty of Amiens on March 25, 1802, a great celebration was held in the Cathedral of Notre Dame to mark the reconciliation of France with the Roman Catholic Church. Some prerogatives were won by the new pope that the papacy never had before.

> The absence of any specific provisions concerning monastic orders and the reestablishment of religious congregations was a notable victory for the papal cause. By giving the pope the right to demand the resignation of all the bishops Bonaparte all but rendered illusory his own right to nominate new ones, for never before had the French state or the French clergy attributed such sweeping power to Rome.[46]

---

45. Smith, *Daniel and the Revelation* (1897), 143.
46. Gershoy, *The French Revolution and Napoleon*, 365–369.

Pius VII achieved with Napoleon "a coup like none other in history before or since, but it was also a brilliant demonstration of papal power over the entire Church," summarizes Schatz.[47]

Additionally, the label "systematic persecutor" needs to be examined briefly. Naturally, it would be a bit absurd for anyone to formally give someone else the title of "systematic persecutor." The pope had for some time been quite impotent of being a "systematic persecutor." Thus, this supposed exception is vacuous. Mrs. White, closely following William Miller, herself made the statement that a "quarter of a century prior to 1798" "persecution had almost wholly ceased."[48] Furthermore, it was not until years after the arrest of Pius VII, in 1809, that Napoleon abolished the office of the Sacred Inquisition.[49]

In any case, with the signing of the new concordat, the symbiotic relationship between Napoleon and the papacy seemed mutually beneficial. Napoleon needed Pius VII and Pius VII needed Napoleon. Thus, after Napoleon was proclaimed emperor on May 4, 1804, he invited the pope to crown him as such. Pius VII then went to France, where he stayed from November 1804 through April 1805. However, their relationship rapidly soured.

By February 2, 1808 things had deteriorated to the extent that French troops forced an entrance to Rome, disarmed the papal guard, surrounded the residence of the pope, and put him under house arrest. Whereupon Pius VII complained to intimates that the Roman Catholic Church suffered the same persecution under Diocletian, to whom he compared Napoleon. On May 17, 1809 Napoleon pronounced the end of the temporal sovereignty of the pope. Finally, during the night of July 6, 1809, General Radet drove in the gates to the pope's residence at the Quirinal, entered the personal apartment of the pope, and took him away.[50] Thus, some comparison of the arrest and imprisonment of Pius VII with that of the highly touted 1798 arrest of Pius VI is called for.

In many respects the tragicomedy of Pope Vigilius in the sixth century is mirrored in the ride which Pius VII was forced to take in

---

47. Schatz, *Papal Primacy*, 145. Schatz provides a magistral, nuanced, and comprehensive history of Papal Primacy. It is indispensable to anyone wishing to have a broad historical comprehension of the secular development of the papacy.

48. White, *Great Controversy* (1950), 306.

49. Latreille, *L'Eglise Catholique*, 4:172.

50. Latreille, *L'Eglise Catholique*, 4:157–64.

the nineteenth century. While being taken from the Quirinal in a coach, Pius VII suffered an episode of dysentery, then the bumpy road provoked a crisis of "strangurie"[51] even more troubling and painful, especially as his prison warden hadn't any intention of either moderating the speed or multiplying rest stops. To top it off, near Poggibonsi the coach overturned on a sharp curve and broke into pieces. While Radet was thrown into a pond, from which he pulled himself out all covered with ooze, Cardinal Pacca had collapsed onto the pope, where they were stuck in the interior of the smashed-up coach, and it was only with great difficulty that they were eventually extracted.[52]

Pius VII's imprisonment "more harsh" than that of Pius VI

Pius VII made an explicit comparison of his fate with the more notorious Pius VI of 1798. He described it as being "more harsh than that of Pius VI during the excesses of a shameless Jacobinism," since the 1798 government had at least allowed a cardinal, some prelates, secretaries, and a minister of Spain to accompany his predecessor. And, after this, Napoleon gave an order to tighten his captivity. Thus, the hapless pope was deprived of paper, pens, and a beautifully engraved golden inkstand. No means of writing was left to anyone in his entourage. Pope Pius VII's jailer interpreted Napoleon's command so strictly that he removed the chaplain Soglia, the valet Morelli, and the prelate Coria; he even disputed the pope's request that he be allowed a personal confessor for Lent.[53]

Pope Pius VII compared himself with all his predecessors thusly:

> We have sworn to defend the temporal power *usque ad effusionem sanguinis* and, having no means other than spiritual, we must use them as did our predecessors. *None of which have been reduced to the same point as we have.*[54]

---

51. Painful, spasmodic, urgent urination.

52. Fliche and Martin, *Histoire de l'Eglise*, 20:252. All French translations are mine.

53. Fliche and Martin, *Histoire de l'Eglise*, 20:254.

54. Latreille, *L'Eglise Catholique*, 4:170. Emphasis added. The Latin expresses the idea that Pope Pius VII said he would defend his prerogatives even if he would have to spill his own blood.

Thus, after earlier noting that the papacy post-538 was more "enslaved" than supreme, we have now seen how easily Pius VII might have been chosen as candidate for receiving the "deadly wound" in 1809, rather than Pius VI in 1798. This makes the traditional interpretation of the 1,260-day-year prediction doubly dubious. Aside from this factor, is there any consistency in an interpretation that emphasizes the ecclesiological headship of the Roman bishop in 538, yet never mentions how secular events of 1798 impacted the ecclesiological supremacy of the Roman bishop in 1798 and afterward? And why this convenient silence? Because the ecclesiological supremacy of the Roman bishop was far too well and too long established by 1798 to have been significantly diminished. In 538, the 1870 dogma of papal infallibility was a millennium in the future. Indeed, we've seen that a pope was formally anathematized for hundreds of years after 538. Indeed, the French Revolution paradoxically strengthened an ultramontanism[55] which shortly led to the historic, novel pronouncement of the dogma of papal infallibility in 1870.

538–1798 a postdiction, not a prediction

A large dose of confirmation bias is necessary to construct the purportedly mathematically exact fulfillment of a 1,260-day-year prediction. This speculative construct is a postdiction. No historicist commentator ever made an accurate, specific prediction based on the biblical figure of 1,260. Even after the supposed *terminus ad quem* in 1798, there has been a surfeit of contradictory hypotheses, none of which can be supported with any degree of conviction or evidence. The same observation can be made about the *terminus a quo* of 538.

This same fundamental observation can be just as validly made of every single supposedly day-year calculation. All the *terminus a quo* and *terminus ad quem* which have been advanced as demonstrating some sort of wondrous supernatural foreknowledge collapse upon closer inspection. I have provided a detailed analysis regarding 538–1798 for two reasons. First, because the 1,260-day-year speculations are more ubiquitous; second, because they serve as a fulcrum for several other

---

55. The very word means an extreme support of papal authority on the other side of the French Alps in Italy, as opposed to a conception of conciliar authority or Gallicanism.

year-day "predictions." Specifically, the fact is that the 1,290- and 1,335-day-year calculations are directly based on the mathematics of the 1,260-day-year equation. The respective difference between 1,290 − 1260 = 30 and 1335 − 1290 = 45 is used to piggyback both forward and backward from 538 to 1798. 538 − 30 = 508 and 1798 + 45 = 1843. Both these calculations are found in the 1843 chart that Ellen White asserted was endorsed by God. Both 508 and 1843 were supposedly key dates in salvation history according to the 1843 chart.

The continuous-historical hypothesis depends upon several critical presumptions. First, that God intended to communicate a long series of sequential, predictive (historical) time prophecies extending from the Assyrian Empire in 677 BC, over 2,520 years, to almost two millennia into the Christian Era until 1844. Second, that one of the main purposes of this series of sequential predictive prophecies was to enable William Miller to use them as precedents so that he might accurately predict October 22, 1844 as the *very day* of the second coming (and retroactively so that the proto-SDA "Little Flock" could calculate the very day of the beginning of the investigative judgment). Third, that the 1,260-, 1,290-, and 1,335-day-year periods could accurately mark out 1798–1843 as the "time of the end," only after which other previously "sealed" predictive prophecies would be understood by the "wise" Millerites. Fourth, that the *terminus a quo* and the *terminus ad quem* for the 1,260-, 1,290-, and 1,335-day-year periods could be unambiguously and accurately identified by a meticulous reading of the historic events of 508, 538, and 1798.

Allegorical-typological historicism requires its practitioners to be able to accurately evaluate *remote, poorly attested, ambiguous historical events* and wed them accurately to *inherently ambiguous symbolic entities* found in specific verses. This necessitates considerable historic perspicacity and exegetical dexterity to convincingly link a specific biblical phrase to a specific historical event. The internecine battle within the SDA church over the identity of "the daily" in 1910 illustrates the dubious nature of such an enterprise. As George Knight documented in several of his books, Ellen White declined to fill the role of the ultimate historical expert who would decide whether a Prescott or a S. N. Haskell was correct in matching text to history.[56]

56. Knight, *Search for Identity*, 135.

A further difficulty is that to arrive at exact times, typological arguments replaced syntactical exegesis. As Arasola points out, "Millerites never realized that they were no longer interpreting Daniel" when they started attempting to get exact autumn dates for the second coming based on Levitical typologies. "Leviticus 16 was presented as the primary interpreter of Daniel 8." This typological method of ascertaining an exact time in the autumn of the Jewish year 1844 was reinforced by importing a precise day-year principle into the parable of Matthew 25. The tarrying time of the bridegroom was calculated using even fractions of the day-year. George Storrs, on October 9, 1844, asserted that "the tarrying time is just half a year," which had to start in spring 1844, "March or April," and that "July would bring us to midnight." This was when S. S. Snow preached the midnight cry.[57] After October 22, 1844, Matthew 25's parable continued to be historicized in the same mathematically precise manner. In sum, interpretation of the 2,300 day-years and the 1,260 day-years were both made based on thoroughgoing chronologizing of a parable and chronologizing OT typologies without regard to the syntactical context of Daniel 8:14 itself.

So certain was S. S. Snow that God was an "exact timekeeper" that he induced a reluctant Miller to agree with him that "Jesus will certainly come" on October 22, 1844.[58]

Schatz outline of historical development of papal primacy

Above I have documented two major historical difficulties with the traditional Millerite interpretation of the 1,260 day-years. Both dates have been demonstrated to be arbitrary. However, an even more fundamental problem is present.

Depending upon any act of Justinian, the Byzantine emperor, for establishing the spiritual or ecclesiastical authority of the papacy is a fundamentally erroneous paradigm. A secular ruler cannot establish the religious authority of an ecclesiological position. It was the general assent of the Christian laity and clergy developed *over centuries* that gave the bishop of Rome authority. That is, the *bishop of Rome*

---

57. Arasola, *End of Historicism*, 156, 160.
58. Arasola, *End of Historicism*, 151, 157.

had authority only in so far as it was generally acknowledged by the church—its masses, its clergy, its theologians, and its councils. Historically, papal authority imperceptibly expanded, first informally, then juridically, and in an absolute sense over centuries. In a process of gradual accretion, it reached its apogee in 1870 Vatican I's pronouncement of papal infallibility. The following is an abbreviated summary of this historical process based on Schatz.[59] The pope's spiritual authority was not dispensed by a political actor. The pope's spiritual authority resulted from a papal self-perception that it was a repository of apostolic tradition; popes acted on this self-perception, and it was ratified by actual practice, custom, and general consent. The organization that Ellen G. White eventually inspired experienced similar development. Initially, the "Little Flock" was, a Joseph Bates phrased it, a torn and peeled, disorganized band in which James and Ellen White exercised informal and charismatic control. There was no clergy, excepting for a sprinkling of self-called itinerate evangelists. It took almost two decades before any sort of legal ecclesiological organization was structured. It then took several more decades before it evolved from a more congregational style with the Bible only for a creed until is solidified into a steeply graded hierarchy with a painstakingly refined and meticulous twenty-eight-point creed.

Just as the SDA church gradually formalized a hierarchical ecclesiology—for many of the same practical reasons: a locus of unity was felt to be necessary when lower levels of church organizations like bishops, regional synods, and even ecumenical councils could not agree.

SDAs may be surprised to know that the papacy could not have replaced Sabbath with Sunday for the simple reason that Sunday was venerated *prior* to a pope even existing.

> The title "pope" itself first appears in the fourth century, initially for a number of individual bishops including the bishop of Alexandria; it has been reserved for the bishop of Rome since the fifth century.[60]

---

59. Schatz, *Papal Primacy*, 1–59. Rather than merely demonstrate that the SDA paradigm of the supremacy of the papacy is historically untenable, I offer a brief historical outline of how and when the Roman bishops' prestigious papal position actually evolved.

60. Schatz, *Papal Primacy*, 28–29.

There is abundant documentation that Sunday was venerated centuries prior to the fifth century.

However, the Roman bishops were accorded a position of deference from the early second century. This was because Rome was *generally believed* to be a duel apostolic see (Peter and Paul) beginning about the same time as John is reputed to have composed the book of Revelation. The Letter of Clement of about year 95 attests this; the 110 letter of Ignatius of Antioch to the Romans does as well. Clement speaks in the voice of Rome as if it was speaking for God. Indeed, it was considered canonical (Word of God) by some Christian communities. Ignatius lauds the Roman church and advised: "Do nothing without the bishop." It is clear from the earliest post-apostolic times that an aura of sanctity surrounded the Roman church (Romans 1:8) as the apostolic seat *par excellence* of both Peter and Paul. This authoritative position was reinforced during struggles against the Gnostics.

Tradition *(paradosis)* and *(sedes apostolicae)* apostolic sees, like Antioch, Philippi, Ephesus, Corinth, and Rome, were seen as public repositories of reputable, generally acknowledged apostolic traditions as opposed to the mystical, "secret" gospels of the Gnostics. Irenaeus of Lyons' *Adversus Haereses*, written in 180, testified to this dynamic. Rome was the only Latin *sedes apostolicae* (as opposed to Greek), thus becoming the *de facto* locus of *(communio)* communion for Latin Gaul and North Africa. The Jewish Christian Hegesippus and Tertullian (ca. 200) both praised Rome in special terms. In the Quartodeciman dispute over the proper day to celebrate Easter (160–195), the bishops of Rome, Anicetus and Victor, exercised (Irenaeus of Lyons would say) an excessive, intolerant rigidity in supporting a Latin, Sunday-only rather than a Jewish-Christian method of reckoning Easter which could fall on any day of the week. In 255–256, Bishop Stephen of Rome insisted rebaptism was not needed for those becoming orthodox who had grown up in heretical sects—in opposition to Cyprian of Carthage. After the Decian persecution, bishop Cornelius of Rome's position on lapsed Christians won out over the rigorism of Novatian.

The concept of communion was a central notion that determined who was an authentic Christian. As Christians travelled throughout the vast Roman Empire, say from Carthage, Alexandria, Antioch, or Jerusalem to Rome, how would membership be transferred or recognized, particularly during periods when christological disputes could split the church communion, or as heretics arose claiming to be orthodox, or after periods of persecution when lapsed Christians requested readmission to communion? Only bishops could certify such communion, communicating Christian membership lists to fellow bishops whom they considered orthodox. Thus, for example, the bishop of Carthage was the center of a network of North African bishops, Alexandria played the same role for Egypt, and Rome for the entire Latin church. Rome communicated directly with Alexandria, Carthage, Antioch, and other provincial or apostolic centers.

If two bishops quarreled and excommunicated each other, where did genuine communion rest? From about 200 onward, determinations were made by regional episcopal synods. By the third century, Rome, Alexandria, and Antioch had acquired a species of normative status. The Arian controversy in the fourth century revealed the inadequacy of merely regional synods. A higher universal authority was required to decide such major theological issues for the universal church. In actual historical practice, the Roman bishop increasingly was called upon to fill such a role. Thus, for example, when the bishop Marcian of Arles (Gaul-Europe) in 255 was seen as unduly harsh in refusing to readmit Christians lapsed in the Decian persecution, bishop Cyprian of Carthage (Africa) requested the Roman bishop Stephen to depose him, appoint a replacement, and communicate the identity of the new bishop in communion to Cyprian. Bishop Faustinius of Lyon, France (near Arles) had previously written to both Latin bishops (of Rome and Carthage). Both Faustinius and Cyprian had the implicit expectation that Stephen should act. A few years previous, when Cornelius had been elected bishop of Rome, Cyprian had written him describing the Roman church as the "matrix and root of the catholic church" and as the *cathedra Petri* (chair of Peter). In short, by general consent, Rome came to be considered preeminent both because it was the apostolic church of Peter and Paul and, only secondarily, because it was the capital of the empire.

What to do if not merely two bishops quarreled, but when one synod proposed to annul what another synod had approved? When Constantine transferred the imperial capital from Rome to Constantinople, the bishop of Rome escaped the fate of becoming the "court bishop" like the bishop of Constantinople often became. Previously fluid and informal relations between regional synods and principal churches became institutionalized. Provincial churches (usually mirroring imperial provinces) headed by metropolitans were topped by bishops of the three chief bishoprics recognized by the Council of Nicaea: Rome, Alexandria, Antioch—soon joined by Constantinople. The bishops of these were called "patriarchs" beginning in the fifth century and had formal supervisory functions over large regions. The dilemma was: what to do if two of these patriarchs had irreconcilable differences of faith?

The Arian controversy demonstrated the difficulty of determining an ultimate authority when two patriarchs differed: Athanasius of Alexandria and Eustations of Antioch. This escalated into a battle of synods. Neighboring Eastern bishops asserted that the regional synod (Tyre 335) sufficed to determine the conflict, enunciating the principle of autocephaly. But a Roman synod (341) and the Roman bishop, Julius, simultaneously supported the person and position of Athanasius and the necessity of the whole church's participation, (especially Rome's), based on the concept of universal communion, especially since Alexandria was involved. Julius asserted that the "customary law" was to obtain written consultation with Rome before making a decision that impacted the entire church. He asserted this based on generally accepted ecclesiological custom.

In 342 a universal synod was convoked by both emperors at Sardica. It decreed that bishops deposed by a synod could appeal to the bishop of Rome, who could decide to have a new (different) synod review such an appeal and potentially reverse it. In 380 when Emperor Theodosius made Christianity the state religion (not Constantine earlier), he decreed that the faith preached to the Romans by St. Peter as promulgated by Rome and Alexandria, the primary sees in West and East, was normative.

> From the Roman council of 382 onward it was taken for granted that the Roman church outranked other churches not by conciliar decree, but by divine institution.[61]

Thus, by 382 there was a sentiment that the Roman bishop "had a position independent of and superior to councils." This was in the aftermath of the double synod at Seleucia and Rimini in 359–360, which, under imperial pressure, had adopted a semi-Arian dogma. The prime objective of the emperor in this was to force the adoption of a theological formula which could unite the empire politically,

---

61. Schatz, *Papal Primacy*, 30.

irrespective of theological considerations. Given that Rome insisted on an older Trinitarian formula, and given that Arian and semi-Arian formulations are regarded as unorthodox by both contemporary SDAs and Catholics, the Roman bishop can be seen to have been correct in insisting that orthodox Trinitarianism should be upheld as a top priority regardless of its political divisiveness. In the historical context of the late fourth century, this could only be done by asserting that since the Roman bishop disapproved of the formula adopted by the double synod of Seleucia and Rimini, it was a false council. Thus, a precedent was set that the bishop of Rome was practically and theologically superior to councils.

Augustine of Hippo's (396–430) dictum "Rome has spoken, the matter is settled" illustrates other churches' deference toward Rome—even if the African church still strongly maintained its right to independent thinking. Rome's imprimatur, if not sufficient in itself, became more and more indispensable to any consensus position. Rome's increasingly authoritative aura was based on theological considerations, not political ones. The crucial inspiration motivating the Roman bishop went counter to imperial concerns. The emperor did not confer spiritual authority upon the Roman bishops; rather, internal ecclesiastical considerations and self-understanding determined Rome's view of its spiritual prerogatives. Its self-concept became more and more tacitly accepted by other centers of power within the universal church.

The sixth canon of the Council of Niceae (325), a "super council," explicitly confirmed the "*ancient custom*" (emphasis added) that the three bishops of Rome, Alexandria, and Antioch enjoyed ecclesiastical jurisdiction over their regions. Constantine did not confer this authority upon these sees; he recognized an "ancient" reality and formalized it within the structures of the empire. This ratification of ancient custom contributed to the growing authority of the Roman bishop but it did not create papal supremacy. Rome, Alexandria, and Antioch morphed into patriarchates and, with a newly minted Constantinople joining their august rank, the patriarchates became fixed usage by the sixth century. Constantinople's growing weight in the East would gradually diminish the authority of Alexandria; and the fact that these two eastern counterweights competed tended to diminish their relative spiritual authority vis-à-vis Rome, particularly when Rome was called on to decide controversies that divided Constantinople and Alexandria.

In the 431 Council of Ephesus, Constantinople supported an unorthodox Nestorianism. Alexandria in the person of Cyril allied with Rome in the person of Celestine to oppose Nestorius. At the "Robber Synod" of 449 (Ephesus II) Eutychus of Constantinople denied that Christ had two natures (a divine and human nature), refused to allow Pope Leo's Tome to be read at the council, and excommunicated Leo. The question was: what to do with a council that was not merely without Rome but explicitly against Rome? In 451 a new emperor, not so attached to Eutychus of Constantinople or a Nestorian Christology, sponsored a new council at Chalcedon. In contradistinction to Ephesus II, it affirmed a Roman-Alexandrian Christology. Thus, Chalcedon was not only a pivot point in Christology; it was crucial to a growing Roman primacy in the East. As a consolation prize, Chalcedon's famous canon 28 replaced Alexandria with Constantinople in second place within the hierarchy, because it was the "new Rome." Naturally, this formulation tended to increase the prestige of Rome. Leo protested that the eternal Nicean order of Rome, Alexandria, and Antioch could not be abrogated—on the basis that Scripture and custom proclaimed that all three were Petrine sees: Peter died in Rome; Peter worked in Antioch (Galatians 2:11); and in Alexandria in the person of his disciple Mark. Leo was not successful in preserving Alexandria's position, but the political dynamics of Chalcedon worked in the long run to cement and increase Rome's prestige. After Chalcedon, the emperor's political imperatives would not infrequently split him from the Roman bishop's theological imperatives. The Byzantine emperors' first priority was to obtain the allegiance of the non-Hellenized Eastern peoples, who tended to be opponents to Chalcedon's christological formula, which posited that Christ had two natures, human and divine. In contrast, these opponents, who were termed "Monophysites," insisted on only one divine nature in Christ. When the Persians in 613 and the Arabs in 639 invaded, these Monophysites tended to welcome the invaders as liberators. It was then in the emperor's interest to conciliate the Monophysites by pressuring Rome to accept christological compromises amenable to the Monophysites. As champion of Chalcedonian orthodoxy, the Roman bishop won prestige not merely in the Latin West but the Greek East for defending the independence of the church from the state and for defending Nicean and Chalcedonian formulas of orthodoxy.

The Acacian schism (484–519) illustrates how the Monophysite dispute developed to reinforce papal prestige. To gain Monophysite loyalty, the emperor persuaded Patriarch Acacius to agree to a christological formula, the *Henoticon*, amenable to the heretical Monophysites. Thereupon, the pope excommunicated the Constantinople patriarch, starting a thirty-five-year schism. The fact that Rome was then ruled by benevolent Arian kings facilitated the 494 letter of Pope Galasius to the emperor, called the great "magna carta of Western church freedom." When union with the Monophysites failed, Emperor Justin I renounced the *Henoticon*. Not only this, but in 519 he signed the pope's Hormisdas Formula, making Rome the "only ultimate norm for ecclesial communion and true faith." Also, in 519 the Hormisdas Formula was signed by the Constantinople patriarch and some two hundred bishops.

Ironically for the hypothesis that 538 signified some sort of pinnacle in papal supremacy, the foregoing illustrates that Roman bishops already customarily exercised a commanding position in the universal church well before the oft-cited *Novellae* of Emperor Justinian. Even more ironically, the events surrounding 538, specifically the Three-Chapter Controversy, spiritually and literally trampled the prestige of the Roman bishops into the dust. The Roman bishops had had more freedom of action, but in 536 Rome came under Byzantine rule. Emperor Justinian was determined to consolidate this power by a forced theological union between a Chalcedonian pope (Vigilius) and the Monophysites. The emperor constrained Vigilius in 548 to condemn three theological opponents to the Monophysites. For this Vigilius was condemned by his own constituency for heresy against the Chalcedonian formula. Therefore, in 553 in his *Constitutum* he retracted his condemnation of the "Three Chapters." Whereupon, in the Second Council of Constantinople, 553, the emperor arranged to have Vigilius excommunicated. This conciliar excommunication of a pope—a unique case—was even recognized by future popes as valid! The excommunication achieved the emperor's purpose. Vigilius reversed himself yet again and reinstated his condemnation of the "Three Chapters." Thereupon, a North African synod of bishops excommunicated the pope and extensive areas of Latin Christianity were estranged from the Roman bishops for centuries. When

Emperor Heraclius I (610–641) tried to establish union with the Monophysites via monothelitism (the concept that Christ had only one will), Pope Honorius I (625–638) accepted it and was condemned by the Third Council of Constantinople (680–681) as a heretic. As Schatz observes, the problem posed by the 553 Council of Constantinople to the prestige of the papacy "has not really been resolved to this day." Significantly, the related problem of having Pope Honorius I officially declared a heretic by the Third Council of Constantinople (680–681) is "one of the principal historical arguments against papal infallibility" that Vatican I had to face. This "council and the subsequent popes clearly condemned Honorius as a heretic. In other words, they formally ruled that a pope could fall into heresy."[62] Given the disastrous consequences of the Three-Chapter Controversy, the assertion that 538 marked a high point in papal authority cannot be maintained. Emperor Justinian's savage treatment of the papacy during the pontificate of Vigilius (537–555), leading to the pope being excommunicated and physically maltreated, demonstrates that, far from elevating the pope in 538, the total impact of Justinian's actions toward the papacy denigrated it rather than enhancing it—in spite of what was written in his 533 *Novellae*.

In summary, the hypothesis that the 1,260 day-years extended from 538 to 1798 fails for multiple reasons. First, according to Daniel 7:22, at the end of this period the malevolent little horn would be destroyed, and all earthly kingdoms would be given to the people of the saints of the Most High. This did not happen in 1798. Second, the 1798 date was not obtained by interpreting a predictive prophecy in advance of the events there described. This date was proposed only afterwards. Third, even inveterate Millerite interpreters like Litch were ready to shift this date when the event they expected in 1843/1844 did not occur on schedule. A French general's capture of Pope Pius VI in 1798 (or deposition in 1799 per Litch) was an arbitrary choice after the fact. The tragicomedy of Pope Pius VII could just as easily be proposed. Fourth, the date of 538 was obtained only by retrospectively subtracting 1,260 from the presumed 1798 date. Only then, and with difficulty, was an event settled on to fit that date. Fifth, it has been demonstrated that Justinian's *Novellae* did not establish papal prestige. Multiple historians have documented that the pontificate

---

62. Schatz, *Papal Primacy*, 54–55.

of Vigilius, the pope during 538, marked a spectacular nadir in the history of the papacy. Sixth, the special prestige and authority that was associated with the bishop of Rome was not bestowed upon the papacy by a secular ruler like Justinian. Rather, it was the result of an organic ecclesiastical self-concept of Rome as the *cathedra Petri* which *originated in apostolic and immediately post-apostolic times* and was well entrenched in "ancient custom" long before Justinian wrote his *Novellae*. This conception of the special authority of the Roman bishop was received by *general assent* of Christian laity, clergy, synods, and councils. It was not merely an empty, arrogant boast of Rome itself. Finally, 538 did not mark the onset of a period of persecution during which millions of proto-Protestants were massacred by a persecuting papacy. There were essentially no judicial killings of anti-Catholic heretics for the next six hundred years. The targets of the Albigensian crusades were not orthodox proto-Protestants but Gnostic-like dualists. The Waldenses did not keep Sabbath, nor did they exist from apostolic times. Anything like the magnitude of the purported millions of victims slaughtered by Catholics because they were considered heretics did not occur until the wars of religion that occurred after the Protestant Reformation.

Rather the 1,260 days/42 months/3.5 times are not to be taken as literal, historical, exact dates. Rather, these symbolic figures denote a temporary, indeterminate time during which God allows demonic powers to persecute his saints, whether these be saints of the Old Testament times that lived in the "Land of Splendor" (Daniel 8:9) or saints of the New Testament in Revelation. Both groups are advised that they must have patience because Yahweh will eventually give them the majesty of all the kingdoms under heaven (Daniel 7:27).

Did Pope Gregory change Sabbath to Sunday in 603?

In a July 13, 1847 letter from Gorham, Maine to Joseph Bates, Ellen White explained the circumstances of both her midnight-cry vision of December 1844 and the bridegroom vision of February 1845. She took great pains to emphasize that the information that she announced to "the band" from these visions was independent of any human influence. She specifically denied getting information about the bridegroom vision from Joseph Turner, although she admitted that he had put out a broadside regarding it and that "one was in the house." She further admitted that she had conversations with him prior to revealing her vision on the topic, and that he had given an exposition of his views in her house but that "not a word was said by any of the family about the meeting." She concluded by saying: "I know the light I received came from God, it was not taught me by man. I knew not how to write so that others could read it till God gave me my visions." From that time forward, Ellen White categorically denied any human influences in her writings. After her death, the White Estate continued to deny that Ellen White was dependent on mere human influences for her spiritual teachings. Since 1919, and despite mounting evidence since the 1960s that many pages had been borrowed and paraphrased, the White Estate claimed that she just filled in unimportant historical details into her visionary framework, or that she had a photographic memory, or that she misinterpreted her visions—in cases in which human influence and errors could not be denied.

EGW "is the only infallible interpreter of Bible principles" —GC President Irwin

Simultaneously, however, the custodians at the White Estate and the General Conference were quite sensitive that the religious public not get the idea that the SDA church was a cult; one of the chief characteristics of a cult being that a non-canonical entity in the form of a prophet is the source of authority for church dogma. Therefore, they were at pains to also assert that none of the distinctive teachings of the SDA church originated in Ellen White's visions. Although in theory Ellen G. White was the "lesser [non-canonical] light," shining light onto the "greater [canonical] light," the Bible, in practice and in intramural discussions, Ellen G. White was asserted to be both canonical and infallible. For example, George A. Irwin, president of the Adventist General Conference from 1897 to 1901, stated that "the Spirit of Prophecy is the only infallible interpreter of Bible principles, since it is Christ through this agency giving the real meaning of His own words." And Arthur Delafield, associate secretary and a lifetime trustee of the Ellen G. White Estate, said that since Ellen White had the Spirit of Prophecy, "she was canonical insofar as doctrinal interpretation authority is concerned."[63]

However, there are several instances in which Ellen Harmon did utilize (consciously or unconsciously) human material that she claimed to have seen in vision. This began with her earliest vision. This case is unique in that she obliquely admitted that she did duplicate the material in William Foy's visions. However, since she claimed that the reason for the similarity was that God decommissioned the earlier prophets, William Foy and Hazen Foss, and gave her the same message, we leave that to one side.

Bates: EGW's source for idea that pope changed the Sabbath in 603

It is the vision that she first announced pertaining to the Sabbath truth that can be demonstrated to have come from human sources, specifically her interactions with Joseph Bates. In an April 7, 1847 letter addressed to Bates from Topsham, Maine, she first gave a long preamble describing how she went first to the Holy City, then passed into the Holy Place, and finally passed into the Most Holy Pace, where she saw that the Sabbath commandment "shone above them all" and was "not nailed to the cross." "I saw that God had not changed the Sabbath, for He never changes. [Malachi 3:6.] But the Pope had changed it from the seventh to the first day of the week; for he was to change times and laws. [Daniel 7:25.]" She went on to say that keeping the Sabbath "enraged the church, and nominal Adventists." She then cited two passages from the pseudepigraphal book of 2 Esdras to assert that the aforementioned "wicked" would attempt to "rid the earth of us." Her paradigm that her Millerite 144,000 was threatened by death from what she termed the "Synagogue of Satan," had its origin in the hostility that arose between the Millerites and the Protestant churches that refuted Miller's date-setting theory. Miller condemned the Protestant "sects" for having joined the Papal Beast and become "Babylon" themselves. This was the original kernel of The Great Controversy. In the White/Nichols chart, not only the Pope but also Protestantism, was accused of being 666. She then identified the pope with the Beast, the image of the Beast, and the number 666:

63. Rea, *White Lie*, 59, 96.

> I saw all that 'would not receive the mark of the Beast, and of his Image, in their foreheads or in their hands,' could not buy or sell. [Revelation 13:15–17.] I saw that the number (666) of the Image Beast was made up; [Revelation 13:18.] and that it was the Beast that changed the Sabbath, and the Image Beast had followed on after, and kept the Pope's, and not God's Sabbath. And all we were required to do, was to give up God's Sabbath, and keep the Pope's, and then we should have the mark of the Beast, and of his image.[64]

In what is called the "open- and shut-door vision," which Ellen White stated she had on March 24, 1849 she wrote:

> I saw that the present test on the Sabbath could not come until the mediation of Jesus in the Holy Place was finished, and he had passed within the second vail;[65] therefore, Christians who fell asleep before the door was opened in the Most Holy,[66] when the midnight cry was finished, at the seventh month 1844, and had not kept the true Sabbath, now rest in hope, for they had not the light, and the test on the Sabbath, which we now have since that door was opened. I saw that Satan was tempting some of God's people on this point. Because so many good Christians have fallen asleep in the triumphs of faith, and have not kept the true Sabbath, they were doubting about it being a test for us now.[67]

In a vision dated January 5, 1849, entitled "The Sealing," Ellen White referred to the devil and the Beast's decree to slay the (Sabbath-keeping) saints; she contrasted their eventual triumph and contrasted their fate with persons who were enthusiastic shut-door Millerite

---

64. White, *Sketch of the Christian Experience*, 16.

65. There is no scriptural basis for this. In a violation of *sola Scriptura*, SDAs must *a priori* accept Ellen G. White's assertion that the Sabbath was relevant only after 1844, ignoring the Adventist reliance on the Seventh-Day Baptist history and practice of this doctrine. Ellen G. White was also violating her own historiography of the Sabbath. She portrayed a Saturday Sabbath as a life-and-death issue for the Waldenses and Albigenses from apostolic days until sometime after the Reformation when Catholic forces massacred them. She implied that for some vague period following this, Saturday Sabbath lost its existential character during the time in which Seventh-Day Baptists revered it, and that it only again became relevant after her faction of ex-Millerites adopted it about 1847.

66. Ellen Harmon was perhaps unaware of it, but William Miller wrote a detailed refutation of keeping Saturday rather than Sunday in the 1840s.

67. White, *Sketch of the Christian Experience*, 25.

Adventists but had given up the Sabbath and ended up in hell, "howling in agony." When they protested that they had vigorously preached the midnight cry, they were told that with the Sabbath being the new final test, this was no longer enough.[68]

Taken together, these visions were the nucleus of what would later become the Great Controversy theme and series. The controversy pivoted around the Sabbath. Keeping it seals the Sabbatarians. Disregarding it results in receiving the mark of the Beast. Only after October 22, 1844 could the Sabbath be the final test: 1) Christians who had died not keeping it (would this include the popes martyred during the Decian, Valerian, and Diocletian persecutions?) would still be saved; but 2) even the staunchest shut-door Adventists would be damned if they did not keep the Sabbath.

She later continued the same theme under direct angelic guidance and in the context that it is Sabbath-keeping which will enrage the wicked and cause them to attempt to massacre Sabbath-keepers.

> The Pope has changed the day of rest from the seventh to the first day, and has thought to change the very commandment that was given to cause man to remember his Creator, so that the nations might not forget God. He has thought to change the greatest commandment in the decalogue, and thus make himself equal with God, or even exalt himself above God. I saw that God is unchangeable, therefore his law is immutable; but the Pope had exalted himself above God, in seeking to change his immutable precepts of holiness, justice and goodness. He has trampled under foot God's Sanctified Day, and put in its place one of the six laboring days, on his own authority. And the whole nation has followed after the beast, and every week they "rob God" of his Holy Time. The Pope has made a breach in the holy law of God, but I saw that the time had fully come for this breach to be made up by the people of God, and the waste places built up.[69]

These historical assertions that the pope had changed the Sabbath to Sunday were transmitted to Ellen Harmon via the human influence of Joseph Bates, who in turn received them from a T. M. Preble, who in turn received them from a Frederick Wheeler, who began keeping the seventh day as the Sabbath after personally studying

68. White, *Sketch of the Christian Experience*, 19–20.
69. White, *Sketch of the Christian Experience*, 53–54.

the issue in March 1844 following a conversation with Rachel Preston, according to his later report. Ellen Harmon even admitted that when Bates initially exposed her to the Sabbath, she thought he was exaggerating the significance of the Sabbath to the detriment of the remainder of the Decalogue. Bates, she said, was keeping the Sabbath and "urged its importance. I did not feel its importance, and thought that Bro. B. erred in dwelling upon the fourth commandment more than the other nine."[70] During the late summer or fall of 1846, Bates had travelled to Port Gibson, New York, met Hiram Edson, Owen R. L. Crosier, and Dr. F. B. Hahn, and convinced them all to keep the Sabbath. He convinced Ellen and James White of the Sabbath's centrality about the same time.

"The disciples evidently kept the first day of the week as a festival"

T. M. Preble had published a document on the Sabbath in which he asserted:

> The disciples evidently kept the first day of the week as a festival, in commemoration of the resurrection of Christ, but never as the Sabbath. A controversy however commenced toward the close of the first century to see whether both days should be kept, or only one; and if one should be given up, which one, the first day, or the seventh. This controversy increased century after century till A. D. 603, when Pope Gregory passed a law abolishing the seventh day Sabbath, and establishing the first day.[71]

Preble's commentary originated the narrative that Bates and Ellen White adopted. First, he asserted that Pope Gregory made a decisive change "abolishing the seventh day and establishing the first day." Second, that this change occurred "A. D. 603." Preble did not provide any of the text of this legislation. Additionally, there is the curious coincidence that the date of 603 AD which Preble supplied happens to be the same number that he had marked in a footnote, "*Baronius' Councils, 603," where 603 appears to be suspiciously

---

70. Knight, *Joseph Bates*, 95.

71. Preble, "Tract," 9–10, citing Baronius' Councils, 603, in a footnote marked by a *.

more like a page number reference and not a historical date. Furthermore, Daniel Augsburger's analysis of Pope Gregory's actions does not support Preble's description. Augsburger states: "Although Pope Gregory had upheld a spiritual rest, he demanded that all secular activities should stop to allow the people to devote their time to prayer." He also cites Gregory as fulminating against some "teaching that all work must be interrupted on the Sabbath. Whom could I call them but preachers of the Antichrist?" Augsburger's comprehensive and meticulous documentation of Gregory and numerous ecclesiological authorities for the entire Middle Ages does not cite any such pivotal legislation. Augsburger's introductory topic sentence is: "The early Middle Ages as a whole accepted without questioning the Lord's day of the great Church Fathers and their spiritualized interpretation of the Sabbath rest."[72] Preble, copied by Bates, misconstrued the actual events and the role of Pope Gregory in legislation "changing times and laws." Thus, the supposed date of 603 for a momentous change in the Sabbath is likely traceable to Preble's conflation of a date with a page number. Bates slavishly copied the 603 "date" from Preble.

Preble went on to cite Eusebius and Constantine: "Eusebius says of Constantine that he commanded, through all the Roman Empire, that the first day of the week should be observed as a Sabbath day." Then he commented: "Thus we see Dan. 7:25 fulfilled, the 'little horn' changing 'times and laws.'"[73]

Bates, borrowing from Preble, informed Ellen Harmon that 1) the pope was responsible for replacing Sabbath with Sunday; that 2) this change was prophesied in Daniel; that 3) Sunday was the "mark of the Beast;" that 4) the devil was the ultimate beast sponsoring the papal power; that 5) the devil in an end-times battle would make war on the "living saints" specifically because they kept Sabbath. In other words, although previous generations of "dead saints" did not need to keep Sabbath, in the last days the Sabbath as a distinguishing mark would have to be preached to all the world and kept by a remnant who "had the testimony of Jesus" and kept *all* the commandments of God, especially the Fourth. In Bates's *The Opening Heavens* (May

72. Augsburger, "Sabbath and Lord's Day During the Middle Ages," 193, 194, 190.

73. Preble, "Tract," 9–10. Although White stated that Daniel 7:25 was "exactly" fulfilled, there was no exact date which Preble, Bates, or Ellen Harmon pointed to—except 603.

1846), he already was asserting that the "Papacy had sought to change the worship day to the first day of the week." Bates went on to assert that Sunday was the devil's Sabbath:

> Is it not clear that the first day of the week for the Sabbath or holy day is a mark of the beast [which changed the Sabbath according to Daniel 7:25]. It surely will be admitted that the Devil was and is the father of all the wicked deeds of Imperial and papal Rome. It is clear then from this history that Sunday, or first day, is his Sabbath throughout Christendom.[74]

Furthermore, "keeping of the seventh day Sabbath has been made void by the working of satan [sic], and is to be restored . . . before Jesus can come."[75] As Knight observed, Bates's exposition of the Sabbath, the mark of the Beast, the remnant, and the devil's eschatological warfare against Sabbatarians "preceded Ellen White's vision on the topic by three months."[76]

Bates added to the minimalist sketch of Preble, enhancing it with several eschatological or apocalyptic aspects which were repeated by Ellen White in several of her visions dated between 1847 to June 27, 1850.

Her later writings, like *Spiritual Gifts* and *The Great Controversy* merely added more details, largely borrowed from Protestant historians, and modified stylistically by Fanny Bolton and other of E. G. White's "bookmakers" to fit this basic schema. For example, she said:

> Eusebius, a bishop who sought the favor of princes, and who was the special friend and flatterer of Constantine,[77] advanced the claim that Christ had transferred the Sabbath to Sunday. Not a single testimony of the Scriptures was produced in proof of the new doctrine. Eusebius himself unwittingly acknowledges its falsity, and points to the real authors of the change. "All things," he says, "whatsoever that it was duty to do on the Sabbath, these we have transferred to the Lord's day." But the Sunday argument, groundless as it was, served to embolden men in trampling upon the Sabbath of

---

74. Knight, *Joseph Bates*, 108, 115.

75. Thus, a plausible explanation for the delay of the Parousia is offered.

76. Knight, *Joseph Bates*, 116–17.

77. Note that Ellen White had also borrowed the narrative concerning Eusebius and Constantine from Preble and Bates.

the Lord. All who desired to be honored by the world accepted the popular festival.

The Pope has attempted to change the law of God. The second commandment, forbidding image worship, has been dropped from the law, and the fourth commandment has been so changed as to authorize the observance of the first instead of the seventh day as the Sabbath. But papists urge, as a reason for omitting the second commandment, that it is unnecessary, being included in the first, and that they are giving the law exactly as God designed it to be understood. This cannot be the change foretold by the prophet. An intentional, deliberate change is presented: "He shall *think* to change the times and the law." The change in the fourth commandment exactly[78] fulfills the prophecy. For this the only authority claimed is that of the church. Here the papal power openly sets itself above God.[79]

In 603 Pope Gregory changed the Sabbath per Bates

In 1846, in a work mainly speaking of Orion and a literal second coming, Bates specifically identified which pope and on what date the Sabbath was changed:

> I wish here to ask a few questions on one of the greatest errors that the world ever embraced, first[80] established by Pope Gregory, A. D. 603. I mean the changing of God's seventh day, Sabbath . . .[81]

---

78. This claim that a prophecy has been fulfilled "exactly" was a consistent part of Millerite practice.

79. White, *Great Controversy* (1888), 574, 446.

80. It appears that Bates contradicted himself, here stating that Sunday was "first" established in 603 while elsewhere stating that Sunday had been instituted "since the days of the apostles."

81. Bates, *Opening Heavens*, 35.

Popes, "since the days of the Apostles, have changed the seventh day Sabbath to the first day of the week!" —Bates, 1847

In his 1847 revised edition of *Seventh Day Sabbath: A Perpetual Sign*, Bates wrote: "[T]he Imperial and Papal power of Rome, since the days of the Apostles, have changed the seventh day Sabbath to the first day of the week!" He further stated in his historical section entitled "Word Respecting the History" that:

> At the close of the first century a controversy arose, whether both days should be kept or only one, which continued until the reign of Constantine the Great. By his laws, made in A. D. 321, it was decreed for the future that Sunday should be kept a day of rest in all the cities and towns … The controversy still continued down to A. D. 603, when Pope Gregory passed a law abolishing the seventh day Sabbath, and establishing the first day of the week … While Daniel beheld the little horn, (popery) he said, among other things, he would 'think to change times and laws'". "Is it not clear that the first day of the week for the Sabbath or holy day is a mark of the beast. It surely will be admitted that the Devil was and is the father of all the wicked deeds of Imperial and papal Rome.[82]

Therefore, the devil would make war on "those who keep God's Sabbath holy." He then distinguished the dead saints from the "living saints" because the Sabbath "would save the living saints only at the coming of Jesus." In a final eschatological battle, "it is evident the devil is making war on all such [Sabbath-keepers]."[83]

It is no coincidence that Preble and Bates shared the obscure reference to Pope Gregory while citing "Baronius' Councils, 603." Protestants like Preble and Bates had a long tradition of castigating the papacy for everything that was wrong with Christendom. When Sabbatarianism became a contentious issue, responsibility for its desecration was merely tacked onto the pope's previously established catalogue of errors. Ellen White followed general Protestant historiography in charging the papacy with slaughtering millions of Protestants. She claimed to have seen "torrents" of blood flowing in her visions. It is significant that Preble and Bates relied on this Baronius

---

82. Bates, *Seventh Day Sabbath*, ii, 45, 58-60.
83. Bates, *Seventh Day Sabbath*, ii, 45, 58-60.

for a specific date and pope. Baronius was the leading source for Anabaptists' martyrologies[84] of the medieval period. "Baronius" is "the monumental Counter-Reformation church history, the Ecclesiastical Annals of Caesar Baronius."[85] Ellen White, as she did with J. N. Andrew's depiction of Columba, was reliant on faulty Protestant historiography.[86]

Only after told by Bates does EGW have vision confirming popes changed Sabbath

The central thesis of this chapter contains three points: 1) there are primary documents demonstrating that Sabbatarians made both written and oral arguments to Ellen White asserting it to be a historical fact that the pope had changed Sabbath to Sunday; 2) she only subsequently had a vision in which she saw that this was so; and 3) a meticulous examination of the history of the entirety of Christendom (rather than just Western Christendom) demonstrates that Sunday diffused very early and without specific attribution to the papacy.

Indeed, T. M. Preble had conceded that the very disciples "kept the first day of the week as a festival":

> The *disciples evidently kept the first day of the week as a festival, in commemoration of the resurrection of Christ*, but never as the Sabbath. A controversy however commenced toward the close of the first century to see whether both days should be kept, or only one; and if one should be given up, which one, the first day, or the seventh.[87]

Bates copied this almost verbatim:

> At the close of the first century a controversy arose, whether both days should be kept or only one, which continued until the reign of Constantine the Great. By his laws, made in A. D. 321, it was decreed for the future that Sunday should be kept a day of rest in all the cities and towns.[88]

---

84. Rachel Oaks was a Seventh-Day Baptist. The Anabaptists were thus the natural source for SDAs' historiography of the Sabbath.
85. Gregory, *Salvation at Stake*, 243.
86. Casebolt, "Ellen White, the Waldenses, and Historical Interpretation," 37–43.
87. Preble, "Tract," 9–10. Emphasis added.
88. Bates, *Seventh Day Sabbath*, ii, 45.

This indicates, at minimum, that the disciples honored both Saturday and Sunday; that a blurring of the distinction between the two days existed since apostolic times, long before the bishops of Rome had the ability to single-handedly change Sabbath to Sunday.

There is no controversy about whether Bates-Preble was Ellen Harmon's intellectual source for the Sabbath issue. However, to document the inaccuracies of Bates's summary requires painstakingly combing through several centuries of data in multiple languages.

Both Ellen Harmon and James White repeatedly asserted that the information that Ellen received from visions was *ex nihilo*, regardless of whether the topic was the history of the Sabbath or masturbation. Despite clear evidence that she paraphrased erroneous preconceptions of the 1860s, her publishers claimed that "she had read nothing from the authors here quoted and had read no other works on this subject, previous to putting into our hands what she has written. She is not, therefore, a copyist . . ."[89] In other theological discussions, she said that after listening intently to her brethren debate a pivotal theological point, her brain simply could begin to grasp the issues; then, shortly afterward, she would receive a divine communication to authoritatively settle the issue. This was the dynamic surrounding the Sabbath also. She initially could fathom the importance of Joseph Bates's new pet issue; then suddenly she was able to enunciate not only a biblical argument for it, but a historical polemic in its favor.

Sunday-keeping popes and Christians martyrs

Ellen Harmon asserted that for over 1,260 years the papacy had persecuted and massacred Sabbath-keeping groups like the Waldenses and the Albigenses. A novel accusation she formulated was that just prior to the second coming the papacy would again attempt to exterminate Sabbath-keepers. This is ironic because one of the chief difficulties of the Bates-Harmon historical schema is that the very entities that she said would martyr Sabbatarian Adventists "in the time of trouble" were themselves martyrs. For example, the very SDA scholars who have spent decades in attempting to buttress Ellen White's historical paradigm have reluctantly admitted that one of the earliest and vehement supporters of Sunday is known to us as Justin Martyr, who

---

89. Numbers, *Prophetess of Health,* 206–18.

lived circa 100–162 AD. This historical personage demonstrates that Sunday was venerated in the immediate post-apostolic period, long before Roman bishops developed the institutional power to impose Sunday on Sabbath-keepers. Furthermore, reportedly the first Roman bishop to follow St. Peter was a man named Linus, who was also martyred circa 66 AD. Linus was presented by Jerome as "the first after Peter to be in charge of the Roman Church" and by Eusebius as "the first to receive the episcopate of the church at Rome, after the martyrdom of Paul and Peter." "A man named Linus is mentioned in the closing greeting of the Second Epistle to Timothy. In that epistle, Linus is noted as being with Paul in Rome near the end of Paul's life. Irenæus stated that this is the same Linus who became Bishop of Rome, a view that is generally still accepted." Now, according to ancient traditions, many of the bishops of Rome were martyrs for their faith.[90] In general, the historical thumbnail sketch that the vast majority of SDAs have is that Sabbath was kept until Constantine in 321, when he colluded with the pope to abruptly abolish Sabbath and replace it with a Sunday law enforced by the state. Given that the well-known persecutions of a pristine, pure, primitive Christianity preceded Constantine, it was imagined that it was Sabbath-keeping believers who were beheaded and thrown to the lions in the first three centuries. Then the semi-pagan, nominally Christian emperor, and a newly born, official state church which he coopted, caused a great apostasy associated with the "mark of the Beast. However, evidence points to the conclusion that several of the "evil" popes and probably hundreds of common Christian parishioners throughout the Roman Empire who suffered persecution and martyrdom were Sunday-keepers.

---

90. See, for example, *Wikipedia* articles on both the entire list of popes as well as the entries on each individual bishop. See also the *Wikipedia* article entitled: "Persecution of Christians in the Roman Empire." Today's scholars note that Christian institutions had motive for retrospectively exaggerating the scope of persecution they suffered, that there were only four general periods of persecution separated by decades of calm, that most anti-Christian violence was local and regional in nature and not promulgated by imperial policy, and that during the first three centuries of the Christian era only about 5,500–6,500 Christians were executed. Similarly, Protestants made exaggerated claims, asserting Catholics made millions of martyrs. Ellen G. White built on this foundation.

Decius martyrs the Roman pope in 250

Notably, Emperor Decius (249–251) ordered a severe systematic persecution during which the bishops of Rome (the pope), Antioch, and Jerusalem were all martyred, and Bishops Cyprian of Carthage and Dionysius of Alexandria barely escaped by going into hiding. "Pope Fabian was seized, tried before the Emperor himself and executed on 10 or 21st January 250."[91] This led to a schism in the church as Cyprian's flight was considered an apostasy by rigorists. Those who had been punished for being "confessors" (or near martyrs) disputed Cyprian's authority. To reconquer his authority, he had to promulgate a rigorist position initially but then endorsed a lax position. Thus, Stephen, a new bishop of Rome, called him an antichrist and in so doing made the first formal appeal to Petrine primacy. Cyprian was eventually martyred by Valerian but not before he wrote *On the Unity of the Church*, stating that all the apostles and bishops "were of equal rank." After the martyrdom of Pope Fabian during the Decian persecution, a Roman priest, Novatian, opposed the election of Pope Cornelius in 251 on the grounds that Cornelius was too liberal in accepting lapsed Christians. The Novatianists did not recognize the authority of the Roman bishops and became widespread and numerous throughout the empire. In the fourth and fifth centuries, the Donatists of North Africa maintained a similar belief about Christians who had lapsed under the pressures of persecution. This was an existential crisis for the church within the entire Roman Empire. Paradoxically, these persecutions and martyrdoms led to ecclesiological pressures which eventually led to Roman bishops having more jurisdictional authority. To avoid anarchy a unified response was critical, and this led to a centralization of power to enforce unity. In retrospect, the jockeying among the bishops is easily understood without attributing satanic motives to either the bishop of Rome or other bishops. Both rigorist and laxist bishops made reasonable arguments. On the one hand, lenient bishops argued that the church was for sinners and therefore should be lax and forgiving. The rigorist bishops argued that the church must uphold high standards (a church for saints) and not readmit the insincere who had apostatized under persecution. It was impractical and impolitic for the church in one location to be a church for sinners while the other was a church for saints. Thus,

---

91. Frend, *Martyrdom and Persecution*, 406.

each competing side tried to force a uniformity of doctrine on other jurisdictions for understandable reasons.[92] When local or regional bishops differed, it became customary to appeal decisions to Rome.

How such conflicts developed is illustrated in the career of Hippolytus, presbyter of Rome, who wrote the first Christian commentary on any OT book, Daniel. Hippolytus accused Pope Zephyrinus (199–217) of modalism. He accused Pope Callixtus I (217–222) of laxity toward Christians who had lapsed under persecution. He continued to attack Pope Urban I (222–230) and Pope Pontian (230–235). However, under persecution from Emperor Maximinus Thrax, both Pope Pontian and Hippolytus were exiled at hard labor to Sardinian mines. It appears that they reconciled before dying there. Under Pope Fabian their bodies were brought back to Rome for an honorable interment.[93]

Sixtus II, twenty-fourth pope, martyred by Emperor Valerian in 258

The reputed twenty-fourth bishop of Rome, Sixtus II (died August 6, 258) was martyred in the persecutions promulgated by the Emperor Valerian. During this time, numerous bishops, priests, and deacons were put to death. Sixtus himself was beheaded.

Marcellinus, twenty-ninth pope, martyred by Emperor Diocletian in 304

Marcellinus (died 304) was the twenty-ninth bishop of Rome from June 30, 296 to his death in 304. Reportedly, due to persecution by Emperor Diocletian, he at first surrendered the sacred books (as did Mensurius, bishop of Carthage), but repented shortly afterwards and suffered martyrdom along with several of his deacons.[94]

The nomenclature "the pope" was used by Preble, Bates, and Harmon in an anachronistic manner. From their later prospective as nineteenth-century Protestants, they projected back into an earlier

---

92. Chadwick, *Early Church*, 118–23.

93. Schmidt, *Hippolytus of Rome*, 1–20, 157–87. Despite his well-documented conflict with Roman bishops, Hippolytus considered it obvious that Antiochus Epiphanes, not the papacy, was the little horn of Daniel.

94. Frend, *Martyrdom and Persecution*, 504.

period what does not actually apply. For most of the Roman bishops prior to 300 we only have sketchy information. Certainly prior to Constantine the Roman bishops had neither the power nor jurisdiction to impose Sunday to replace Saturday. When the title "pope" first came into usage in the early third century, it was applied generically to all bishops. Thus, the earliest extant record of the word *papa* being used in reference to a bishop of Rome dates to the late third century, when it was applied to Pope Marcellinus. Projecting this honorific title backwards to 90–110, as the Bates and Preble assertions imply, is to invest the primitive Roman bishops with a power and primacy that did not exist initially. (It's well known that to support an "ultramontane" conception of the papacy, forged decretals and documents were manufactured out of whole cloth at a much later date. It follows that genuine documents proving the primacy of the papacy did not exist in earlier centuries.) As Christianity spread across the Roman and Persian Empires, certain large metropolitan church districts acquired more prestige and authority. This was formalized centuries later; but early on the very human nature of seeking preeminence led to multiple jurisdictional disputes between the most well-known archbishops. "Between the Third Ecumenical Council of Ephesus (431 AD) and the Fourth Ecumenical Council of Chalcedon (451 AD), the archbishops of the Eastern and Western Roman Empires (i.e. the archbishops of Alexandria, Antioch, Rome, Constantinople, and Jerusalem, also known as the Archbishops of the Ancient Apostolic Thrones), were given the title of patriarch. These titles were ratified at the Fourth Ecumenical Council of Chalcedon (451 AD), and henceforth were known historically as the Ancient Patriarchates of the Holy Catholic and Apostolic Orthodox Church or otherwise as the Pentarchy." Furthermore, there were also large, prestigious Christian centers, even in addition to these five, which often quite zealously defended their ecclesiological and dogmatic prerogatives. (For example, the bishops of Edessa that were Syriac or Jacobite and later the Nestorian bishops within the Persian Empire.) Also, there were Monophysite Christians, some in the area of Egypt, who would vigorously dispute the authority of both the Roman bishops and the bishops located in Constantinople. These Coptic Christians did not recognize the Roman bishop's religious authority over them.

Sunday-keeping Christians exist outside the Roman Empire and papal jurisdiction

The bishops of Constantinople and Rome, in their roles as locations of the old and new capitals of the Roman Empire, were especially zealous rivals. After Constantine adopted Christianity, the state (via the emperor) obviously was a major formative factor in church polity as well. (Given that the emperor located at Constantinople exercised more power than any political power in Italy for several hundred years, and given that the bishop of Constantinople was geographically closer to the emperor, the bishop of Constantinople was often more politically powerful than the Roman bishop.) Furthermore, Christianity did exist outside the Roman Empire—and therefore *outside the jurisdiction of any Roman pontiff or Roman emperor* attempting to mandate a Sunday Sabbath. For example, Nestorian Christians were not dictated to by the Roman bishop. They became increasingly identified with the Persian Empire and were considered heretical by Rome and Constantinople. After the Council of Chalcedon, the Monophysite controversy (together with institutional, political, and growing nationalistic factors) led to a lasting schism between the Oriental Orthodox churches, on the one hand, and the Western and the Eastern Orthodox churches on the other. A variant of Monophysites, the Miaphysite Oriental Orthodox Churches, today include the Ethiopian Orthodox Tewahedo Church, the Eritrean Orthodox Tewahedo Church, the Coptic Orthodox Church of Alexandria, the Armenian Apostolic Church, the Syriac Orthodox Church, and the Malankara Orthodox Church of India. Christian churches outside the Roman Empire and considered unorthodox by both the bishops of Constantinople and Rome could not have had Sunday imposed on them by the papacy.

The rather fierce independence of various Orthodox churches and their rejection of the Roman bishop's jurisdiction even today is palpable in the following citation. A congregant has demanded to know why they "refuse to accept the Pope." The spiritual guide responds thus:

> The bottom line is that, during its 2000-year existence, the Orthodox Church had not been subject to the administrative authority of the Pope of Rome, and this is borne out in the extant decrees of the early Church councils. These councils, while acknowledging the Pope as the "first among equals," in

no way envision the Bishop of Rome's "primacy of honor" as a "supremacy of jurisdiction." The papal claims to supremacy are of much later origin, and there are many who would argue that such claims have done far more damage to the unity of Christendom than anything else.[95]

Therefore, for vast geographical areas beyond the Roman bishop's control, one has to identify someone other than the Roman bishop as the instigator of Sunday. In a macro-ecclesiological sense, the above two schisms and the Muslim conquest of Jerusalem, Antioch, and Alexandria had the practical effect of leaving only two of the five patriarchates, Rome and Constantinople; or the Western Latin church and the Eastern Greek church. Both claimed to be *primus inter pares.* When the Reformation fractured Christendom, it split only the Western Latin church and rejected the Roman bishop's claim to primacy rather than that of the Eastern patriarchies—simply by geographical default. The Roman pontiff, as *de facto* head of any Christianity with which Luther concerned himself, was (in his view) primarily responsible for all the ills of Christendom. Now, of course, as concerns Sabbath, Luther and other Reformers did not consider Sunday-keeping a heresy and naturally did not blame Rome; if anything, they considered Sabbatarians as Judaizers. Similarly, Nestorians, Russian Orthodox, Ethiopian churches et al. were non-existent in the mental and theological universe of North American Protestants in 1844. On the other hand, centuries of Protestant tradition and historiography had concluded that the Latin pope was the origin of all the ills of Christendom. Therefore, nothing could be more logical than that the pope should be responsible for yet one additional heresy, Sunday-keeping.

But even asking the simple what, where, when, and how questions in addition to the who question would reveal the hollowness of pinning the responsibility to a nebulous "the pope." Exactly with what proclamation, in what location, on what date did what pope establish Sunday? Second, given the pope's limited jurisdiction, how could Ellen G. White explain the widespread custom of Sunday-keeping in churches outside of Roman Catholicism?

---

95. From the Orthodox Church in America's website: https://oca.org/questions/romancatholicism/the-pope-christian-unity.

"The disciples evidently kept the first day of the week" per Preble and Bates

As noted above, Preble made an unexpected statement linking the twelve disciples to Sunday, stating: "The *disciples evidently kept the first day of the week* [emphasis added] as a festival, in commemoration of the resurrection of Christ, but never as the Sabbath." Bates did not link Sunday to the disciples so explicitly. He said in his preface: "I understand that the SEVENTH day Sabbath is not the LEAST one, among the ALL things that are to be restored before the second advent of Jesus Christ, seeing that the Imperial and Papal power of Rome, *since the days of the Apostles*, have changed the seventh day Sabbath to the first day of the week!"[96] Could Bates really believe that during the apostles' lifetime a Roman pope had already "changed the seventh day Sabbath to the first day of the week"? As previously quoted, after an extensive forty-five-page biblical exegesis, he abruptly returned to his historical analysis: "At the close of the first century a controversy arose, whether both days should be kept or only one, which continued until the reign of Constantine the Great. By his laws, made in A. D. 321, it was decreed for the future that Sunday should be kept a day of rest in all the cities and towns."[97] In sum, Bates not only stated that "since the days of the Apostles" Rome changed the Sabbath to Sunday, but also that as early as "the close of the first century" Sunday as well as Saturday was venerated. These time frames are well before a Roman papacy became powerful enough to impose Sunday on the universal church.

Popes responsible for disciples who "kept" the first day?

The phrase "toward the close of the first century" is shockingly close to the date given for the publishing of the book of Revelation. This was during the lifetime of the original apostles and prior to the close of the New Testament. Then, if one examines which pope or popes theoretically would have been involved, one finds nothing but the vague accusation that "the pope did it." In short, this is significantly before

---

96. Bates, *Seventh Day Sabbath*, ii. Emphasis added.
97. Bates, *Seventh Day Sabbath*, 45, 58–60.

any Roman bishop established a primacy and enforced it on all of Christendom. Then, by the time one passes to 603 and Pope Gregory the Great (540–604), referred to by Preble and Bates, one must explain how he could have imposed Sunday on Nestorians, Eritreans, Ethiopians, Armenians, and assorted Eastern Orthodox.

SDA scholars find no evidence that the pope changed the Sabbath

Even a large team of SDA scholars have failed in answering all the problems that Ellen G. White's blanket statements raise. They have been forced to admit that Sunday-keeping was very early and very widespread and certainly not limited to the Roman sphere of influence. Even Bacchiocchi struggles to tie Sunday to a pope.[98] Further, he admits a difficulty. Namely, Justin Martyr, was an early (ca. 150) and staunch Sunday-keeper. Bacchiocchi implicitly suggests that because Justin Martyr was in Rome for a time, this makes the Roman pope responsible for the imposition of Sunday on Sabbatarians. How does one explain a martyr dying on behalf of the mark of the Beast? Just because Justin was at one time in Rome, how does that even tenuously implicate the papacy, as Bacchiocchi extrapolates?

Moreover, Justin Martyr is not the only martyr that one will have to credit with supporting the mark of the Beast. As noted elsewhere, several popes and many Sunday-keeping Romans, and hundreds of other Sunday-keeping Christians, were martyred prior to Constantine, precisely when the mark of the Beast was supposed to be the most virulent at Rome. Even Bacchiocchi must admit that the most obvious Sabbath-keepers were Ebionites and Nazarenes, whose Christology made them arguably more Jewish than Christian. In short, the tome edited by Strand does a very convincing job of demonstrating that Sunday was widely diffused prior to Constantine; it does a very unconvincing job of demonstrating that "the [generic] pope" initiated the mark of the Beast. Only three chapters deal with the history of the Sabbath prior to the Middle Ages. One chapter by Bacchiocchi centers narrowly on Rome. Two chapters by Vyhmeister deal only with Asia, Egypt, and Ethiopia, from the "fourth to the seventeenth centuries." And Vyhmeister concedes that during these early centuries Sunday

---

98. Bacchiocchi, "Rise of Sunday Observance in Early Christianity," 132–50.

was overwhelmingly predominate and that virtually every reference to the Sabbath was linked either clearly with Judaizers or with fasting controversies. Thus, the consensus of the best of SDA scholarship is that Sunday had replaced Saturday worship very early and very diffusely.

In fact, to illustrate this, one should take the most prolific and most strenuous proponent for the Bates-Harmon paradigm of the pope replacing Sabbath with Sunday, Samuele Bacchiocchi. Chapter 6 of his book *From Sabbath to Sunday* is entitled "Rome and the Origin of Sunday." The entire fifty pages that he devotes to the thesis that if not "the pope," then Rome was responsible for Sunday is riddled with "may haves," "we would assumes," "this suggests," and many other such phrases which demonstrate the tenuous nature of his evidence and argumentation. I will cite a comprehensive list that shows an average of about one equivocating expression per every three pages. 1) Arguing that Rome had a predominance of Gentile Christians as distinguished from Judeo-Christians, and therefore Rome may have originated Sunday, he says: these demographic proportions "*may have* indeed contributed to an earlier break from Judaism in Rome" (emphasis added). (But Gentiles soon outnumbered Jewish Christians virtually everywhere except Jerusalem.) 2) Arguing that in Palestine sooner than at Rome Christians were distinguished from Jews, he says: "This *suggests the possibility* that the abandonment of the Sabbath and adoption of Sunday as a new day of worship *may have occurred first* in Rome." 3) He argues that "introduction of Sunday worship" "*could well* represent a measure taken by the leaders of the Church of Rome" to differentiate themselves from Jews. (Christians of non-Jewish origins could have done the same anywhere). 4) "We *would presume* therefore that the Church" at Rome would "discourage Sabbath observance." 5) After admitting that Justin Martyr demonstrated extremely early (circa 135 AD) Sunday worship, he tries to link Justin's coincidental, temporary location in Rome to the conclusion that Justin was the vicar of Rome theologically. But he is forced to admit, "[s]omeone could argue that Justin's position does not necessarily reflect the attitude of the whole Church of Rome," given that Rome was the crossroads of the entire empire. Exactly. Just as tenuous is his link between Justin Martyr and Marcion. 6) He says: "*It seems* more likely that some, at least, already practiced Sabbath fasting in Rome prior to Marcion's arrival." 7) He says: "Since Easter-Sunday . . . was apparently introduced first in Rome, . . . it is possible that the weekly Sabbath fast arose contemporaneously . . ." 8) He says: "it would be reasonable to *assume* that the very hierarchy of the Roman Church was responsible" for Sabbath fasting. 9) He says: "The fact that the Sabbath fast *seemingly* originated in Rome . . ." (Is this a "fact" or simply a "seemingly"?) 9) He argues that there is a "close nexus existing between the annual Paschal Sabbath fast and the weekly one"; therefore, "it is reasonable to conclude that the latter originated in Rome . . ." 10) The non-existence of eucharistic celebrations on Sabbath should "allow us to *suppose* that the celebration of mass and injunction of fasting *"may well have* originated" "early in the second century." (Calculating this to be 120 AD, he "supposes" that the two customs originated within the lifetimes of the writers of the New Testament.) 11) Discussing the quartodeciman Easter controversy about 135 AD and asserting that Roman Christians had just started celebrating a Sunday Easter rather than a fourteenth Nisan Easter, he argues that "Sixtus [Roman bishop ca. 115–124 AD] could very well have been the initiator of the new [?] custom . . ." 12) He then tries to bootstrap his own argument that his hypothetical "birthplace of Easter-Sunday *could well be* also the place of the origin of the weekly Sunday observance . . ." 13) He then admits a key difficulty in his hypothesis for making "the pope" responsible for weekly Sunday observance; namely, that the "primacy of the Bishop and of the Church of Rome in the early Church is difficult to trace" because it's virtually impossible to define its "jurisdictional authority." 14) Finally, he, as briefly as possible, alludes to the occasions when "some churches rejected his instructions."[99]

The historiography of the Sabbath demonstrates Ellen White was intellectually and literarily dependent on Joseph Bates and T. Preble for her vision that a generic "the pope" legislated the replacement of Sabbath for Sunday. They erred in their assertion that it was "the pope" who changed the Sabbath to Sunday. The historical evidence demonstrates that Sunday resulted from extremely diffuse, widespread, and very early influences that simply cannot be pinned down to any single person, institution, or location—much less "the pope" or papacy. These practices started very, very early in Palestine, not Rome, when, as Preble says: "The [Palestinian] disciples evidently kept the first day of the week as a festival." Surely it takes a remarkable metamorphosis to transform a festival that the disciples celebrated into the "mark of

---

99. Bacchiocchi, *From Sabbath to Sunday*, 167–211. Emphasis added.

the [papal] Beast" and make it the centerpiece of a cosmological Great Controversy.

Thus far I have focused on theological and historical misconceptions that Ellen G. White promoted. She entertained such faulty interpretations because of her dependence on Miller's method of biblical interpretation. However, Ellen G. White did not merely expound about the theological world; she expounded almost like the Talmud on a multiplicity of themes. One of her chief preoccupations for several decades was the fatal physiological effects of "solitary vice " or masturbation.

XIV

I saw "Solitary vice is killing tens of thousands."

IN A SWEEPING STATEMENT in 1876 Ellen G. White asserted: "Solitary vice is killing thousands and tens of thousands." Medical authorities which both she and James cited made virtually identical assertions—that thousands were dying due to solitary vice. James White echoed his wife's concern for mass fatalities, especially for babies: "Babies die by thousands before they are born, and one fifth of those born alive are laid away in their graves before they reach the age of seven."[1] Curiously, both recounted an anecdote claiming that they, "the writer," in the fall of 1844, visited the Massachusetts State Lunatic Hospital. There they were witness to a large number of persons whose insanity was attributed to their practice of solitary vice. They closed the anecdote with a quote from Deslandes, one of their medical authorities, that solitary vice results in "stupidity, phthisis, marasmus, and death."[2] She also wrote that it could "damage the eyes and muscles, causing fatigue, headache, and diseases of almost every description (2T 402, 404, 481; CG 444)."[3] Ellen White, along with many medical and religious authorities of her time, was convinced that masturbation (also called "self-abuse" or "solitary vice") caused countless serious diseases

---

1. James White, *Solemn Appeal*, 81.

2. James White, *Solemn Appeal*, 19. Compare with Ellen White, *Appeal to Mothers*, 42. This visit could not have been far removed from the fatidic date of October 22, 1844.

3. Lake and Moon, "Current Science and Ellen White," 234.

for numerous persons. This belief was supported by the notable Swiss physician Samuel-Auguste Tissot, who wrote *L'Onanism: Dissertation sur les Maladies Produites par la Masturbation* in 1760. In it he stated that seminal fluid was critical to health and that the "loss of one ounce of it, enfeebles more than forty ounces of blood." He warned of the "many bad consequences with which the emission of so precious a fluid must be attended," and alluded to the "author of Genesis" who "left us the history of the crime of Onan." Thus, he conflated masturbation with *coitus interruptus* and the crime of Onan in not fulfilling the Hebrew custom of levirate marriage. He also argued that loss of semen by "natural" means not only "causes very serious symptoms," but that this great evil is compounded "when the same amount has been discharged by unnatural means."[4] Several writers during Ellen White's time cited a whole litany of similar evils. When Ellen White published her identical descriptions of the evils of solitary vice, they were so indistinguishable from her contemporaries' writings that she had to issue a denial that she had previously read such works. Yet multiple close paraphrases (almost word for word in several cases) have been documented.[5] Nonetheless, she claimed to have received this information from direct divine revelations.

Masturbation: chief cause of an epidemic of imbecility

God had revealed to her that masturbation was "the great, crying sin of our time." "Everywhere I looked, I saw imbecility, dwarfed forms, crippled limbs, misshapen heads, and deformity of every description." This was not a rare phenomenon or limited to extreme excesses of "self-abuse." Masturbation and its pernicious effects were so universal that it impacted "a large share of the youth now living." This was such an existential threat that Ellen White labelled those who practice solitary vice as "self-murders." They "defile their own bodies and commit self-murder." She went on to expound that those who murder themselves slowly via solitary vice are just as guilty as persons who commit suicide rapidly. They have no more chance of being "admitted into Heaven hereafter, . . . than the one who destroys life instantly."[6]

4. Females, having no semen, had less vital force.
5. Numbers, *Prophetess of Health*, 207–18.
6. Ellen White, *Solemn Appeal*, 72, 80.

Moreover, even next door, she claimed that her sons' two playmates, Samuel and Charles Daigneau, had "gone to great lengths in this crime of self-abuse." The result, she asserted, was that Charles was losing his intellect and eyesight. Yet Charles managed to exceed the biblical three-score and ten without going either blind or insane, while Samuel served "two terms in the Michigan state senate and died at age 82," in "remarkably good health."[7] The ubiquity of "self-abuse" and the immensity of its ill effects is illustrated in the title Ellen White chose in 1864 for her first "health message" book, written after her health vision of June 6, 1863: *Appeal to Mothers Relative to the Great Cause of the Physical, Mental, and Moral Ruin of Many of the Children of Our Time.*[8] This was such a critical subject that she reemphasized its criticality in her 1870 title: *A Solemn Appeal Relative to Solitary Vice and Abuses and Excesses of the Marriage Relation.*[9] To persuade her readers that medical authorities supported her, she also cited many popular authors on the subject. Yet again in the 1890s she reworked much of her material from the 1860s and 1870s to produce materials for the Australian public in a pamphlet entitled *A Solemn Appeal*. Her fixation on the topic continued posthumously. In the 1950s and 1960s the White Estate again reworked much of the material into *The Adventist Home* and *Child Guidance*. Thus, the connection between masturbation, sin, and insanity deeply penetrated the collective SDA consciousness; yet it always remained a repressed, unmentionable subject. Many parents wordlessly handed tomes on sexuality, based on Ellen White's divine admonitions, to their teenagers. Other teenagers were only apprised by their peers and had to furtively rummage through the index of Ellen White's writings under "M for masturbation,"[10] "S for Self-abuse" or "Solitary Vice," or was it "O for

---

7. Numbers, "Science and Medicine," 200.

8. White, *Appeal to Mothers*, 17, 24–25.

9. Ellen White, *Solemn Appeal*. James White published that same year a book with the same title, *A Solemn Appeal*. He duplicated some of Ellen White's words and included even more testimonies from "men of high standing and authority in the medical world," several of whom Ellen White also cited. See James White, *Solemn Appeal*, 84.

10. Some SDA apologists have noted that Ellen White did not use the precise term "masturbation" or "masturbator." They suggest that there may be some difference between solitary vice and masturbation. However, it is clear that the terms are interchangeable. See James White, *Solemn Appeal*, 85, where he specifically states that "hired servants" may initiate "the little masturbators" into the "practice of

Onanism"—to receive medical and spiritual enlightenment regarding their burgeoning bodies. The longevity of the belief that masturbation is the chief cause of a plethora of physical and mental illnesses only faltered a half-century after Ellen G. White was dead. Thus, no one in her lifetime was likely to suggest that Ellen White was mistaken in her belief that God had shown her this vital truth; although they might have wondered why a divine revelation was necessary to support a dogma which seemed universally supported by medical authorities. However, since about the 1960s–1970s, the idea that masturbation causes a whole host of diseases, especially insanity and cancer, has been considered an outdated, superstition misconception.[11] Thus, the question arises: how could God have revealed to her in vision something that is blatantly erroneous and whose origin is clearly rooted in misconceptions that Ellen White shared with most of the medical authorities of 1864?

Sylvester Graham was one of the most agitated and earliest of Ellen White's contemporaries to wax eloquent on the subject. Ellen White may not have been solely dependent on Graham, but she displayed the most intellectual affinity for him. McMahon notes that Ellen White signed Graham's *Lectures on the Science of Human Life*, suggesting she had studied it. Yet there was a great overlap with several of her predecessors and her copies of Alcott's *The Laws of Health* and Dr. Cole's *Philosophy of Health* (and Graham's lectures) were underlined and marginally marked. Moreover, while Graham's *Lecture to Young Men* mainly displayed his fixation with "self-pollution," he associated many other health "principles" with his central theme, which Ellen White also borrowed. The relation between Graham, White, Alcott, and others is illustrated by the fact that in the publicity blurb to Graham's second edition of *A Lecture*, Dr. Alcott endorsed the crying need for Graham's book with the observation that "solitary vice is rapidly gaining ground among us." It was in note A, however, that Graham made what was to Ellen White the most persuasive argument

---

self-pollution." He simultaneously repeated Ellen White's suggestion that hired girls would initiate innocent children into the practice of solitary vice.

11. Nonetheless, Lake and Moon, "Current Science and Ellen White, 234 struggled valiantly to construct some sort of explanation that distances Ellen G. White's pronouncements regarding masturbation from the contemporary medical authorities whom she held in such high esteem.

that masturbation was a multiheaded hydra which needed to be slain at all costs.

Graham's appeal to mothers like Ellen G. White

Graham evoked the experience of a young, pious Christian mother who had employed every means at her disposal to give her children, daughters as it happens, a perfect Christian upbringing. Her daughters were "taught to pray as soon as their lisping lips could utter articular sounds"; they were inculcated with pious doctrines at Sunday school; they were provided private tutors, yet there was one massive, unsuspected "radical defect" in their upbringing.

> Highly seasoned flesh-meat, rich pastry, and every other kind of rich and savory food, and condiments in abundance, together with strong coffee and tea, and perhaps occasionally a glass of wine, were set before these children for their ordinary fare.[12]

The result was that all the daughters exhibited "excessive lasciviousness," and defiantly affirmed their dedication to "self-pollution." Furthermore, when Graham admonished them, he found it "impossible to awaken any moral sensibility." They had "no remorse, no compunction on the subject." He then wrote the phrase which would pierce Ellen White's heart: "Here, then, would seem to be a case in which the very best efforts of a pious mother had entirely failed of their object."[13] Both Graham and Ellen White were convinced that a diet of flesh, spice, tea, and coffee was at the epicenter of an epidemic of insanity and a whole host of "loathsome diseases." Per Graham: "[V]enereal excesses occasion the most loathsome, and horrible, and calamitous diseases that human nature is capable of suffering."

To drive his point home Graham cited a Dr. Woodward, superintendent of a lunatic hospital, who stated: "No cause is more influential in producing insanity, and in a special manner, perpetuating the disease, than self-pollution." "[T]he victim of self-pollution passes from one degree of imbecility to another, till all the powers of the system, mental, physical and moral, are blotted out forever." Graham cited one such victim who confirmed Dr. Woodward's testimony and illustrated

---

12. Graham, *Lecture to Young Men on Chastity*, 149–52.
13. Graham, *Lecture to Young Men on Chastity*, 149–52.

Graham's contention that should a young man engage in masturbation while a teen, even after years of later abstinence, he could relapse. Thus, one informant stated that "he was perfectly certain that he had committed the unpardonable sin," crying out in desperation, "my soul is sealed to eternal perdition!" Thus, "the early forming of the habit of self-pollution is one of the most alarming evils in our land." It was near universal.[14] Such testimony no doubt convinced many readers, including Ellen White, that a national emergency of eternal consequence was crying out for action.

Best established principles of science prove masturbation causes insanity

Besides Graham's claims regarding the soul- and body-destroying effects of self-pollution, he cited a chaplain from a state prison who witnessed that "even an atheist" would see the force of Graham's arguments because a "man must deny many of the best established principles of science, before he can deny most of the conclusions to which the lecturer [Graham] comes." Graham claimed to be "as purely scientific as possible." No doubt the unanimity of medical experts and their absolute claims that their assertions were established upon the most solid "principles of science" caused Ellen White to issue similar categorical claims.

Masturbation's diseases transmigrate to the masturbator's progeny

Graham assured his readers that "the body of man has become a living volcano of unclean propensities and passions," that man would "sink himself in degeneracy below the brutes," that the earth had become a "mighty sepulcher, for those who prematurely fall the victims of the *innumerable* diseases [emphasis added] which result from" masturbation. Every system of the body is attacked, according to Graham, "but in this extensive mischief, the NERVOUS SYSTEM, all along leads the way in suffering." "Numb palsy" results. The senses of smell, hearing, and sight are all damaged. The eyes are the "greatest sufferers from venereal abuses." The spinal marrow "becomes the focal point

14. Graham, *Lecture to Young Men on Chastity*, 149, 185, 186, 179, 173.

of mischief," leading to "loathsome termination in death." Apoplexy, epilepsy, and paralysis result. The memory decays. The masturbator "becomes a confirmed and degraded idiot, whose deeply sunken and vacant, glossy eye, and livid, shriveled countenance" repels all. Masturbators have "ulcerous, toothless gums, and foetid breath, and feeble broken voice, and emaciated and dwarfish and crooked bod[ies], ... head-covered, perhaps, with suppurating blisters and running sores—denot[ing] a premature old age—a blighted body—and a ruined soul!" These victims said they "would give worlds to be annihilated. His life is intolerable, and he often determines, and still fears to throw it off. Amidst this dreadful conflict, reason is frequently dethroned, and terrible insanity usurps its place."[15] This resembles Dante's innermost circle of hell. Yet, it became worse. Graham assured masturbators that "there is no door of mercy open for his escape!—inevitable and utter ruin lies before him!" Yet worse was yet to come: the effects of solitary vice would "transmigrate" to his progeny, resulting in "early death, in the offspring of the transgressor!"[16] In an epoch with immense neonatal and early childhood mortality, no doubt this caused an immense amount of inexpressible parental guilt and shame.

Tuberculosis is caused by solitary vice

According to Graham, virtually every disease known to man is caused by solitary vice. In addition to the above-mentioned diseases of the nervous system, Graham continued systematically through every single body system (for about twenty pages), comprehensively listing an almost endless compendium of loathsome diseases. He began with the gastrointestinal system since the stomach is the "grand central organ." Thence, his and Ellen White's single-mindedness regarding diet. He advanced to the intestines, which suffer "diarrhea, cholics, spasmodic disorders" and "purulent discharges from the anus." The heart and circulatory system are next. Graham assured his readers that heart, arteries, and capillaries suffer. More gravely, orgasmic paroxysms "often cause spasms in the heart," "causing sudden death, in the unclean act." He proceeded to the pulmonary system, about which he asserted that "pulmonary consumption" is "hastened on" in

---

15. Graham, *Lecture to Young Men on Chastity*, 33, 102–10.
16. Graham, *Lecture to Young Men on Chastity*, 120–23.

"thousands of instances." This assertion is of particular significance. Before Robert Koch discovered the causative microbe, *Mycobacterium tuberculosis*, in 1882, and Wilhelm Roentgen's 1895 discovery of x-rays allowed physicians to track it on chest x-rays, tuberculosis was commonly known as "consumption." It was historically called this due to the weight loss. These discoveries were well after Ellen White's 1864, 1870, and 1876 assertions that solitary vice was the *chief cause of consumption*. Most notably, White asserted that masturbation caused all manner of loathsome diseases. "*But the most common of these is consumption.*"[17] White was unambiguously asserting that solitary vice is the most common cause of what we now know as *Mycobacterium tuberculosis*. Ellen White thought she knew something via her visions which is completely erroneous. She made a testable assertion that has been falsified. Namely, she asserted that solitary vice is the chief cause of *Mycobacterium tuberculosis*, known to Ellen White as "consumption," and today colloquially known as "TB."

White made another dubious assertion about another type of mycobacteria that contained misinformation about scrofula combined with misinformation about its transmission. She asserted that "many women" have "blood filled with scrofula, transmitted to them from their parents..."[18] What was anciently called "scrofula" is now known as mycobacterial cervical lymphadenitis, legendarily known also as "king's evil," because medieval societies believed it could be healed by the touch of a king. In adults almost all of scrofula cases are caused by *Mycobacterium tuberculosis*. However, in children it is often caused by atypical mycobacteria (*Mycobacterium scrofulaceum*)

---

17. Ellen White, *Solemn Appeal*, 74. Emphasis added. See also White, *Appeal to Mothers*, 128. White's *Solemn Appeal* of 1870 was largely a repetition of her 1864 *Appeal to Mothers*, where she said: "The practice of secret habits surely destroys the vital forces of the system . . . Among the young, the vital capital, the brain, is so severely taxed at an early age, that there is a deficiency, and great exhaustion, which leaves the system exposed to disease of various kinds. But the most common of these is consumption." In addition to her belief that solitary vice caused TB (consumption), White also believed that shade trees close to houses and the accumulation of dead leaves caused TB (consumption). "Shade trees and shrubbery too close and dense around a house are unhealthful; for they prevent a free circulation of air and shut out the rays of the sun. In consequence of this, dampness gathers in the house. Especially in wet seasons the sleeping rooms become damp, and those who occupy them are troubled with rheumatism, neuralgia, and lung complaints which generally end in consumption." See White, *Counsels*, 58.

18. Ellen White, *Solemn Appeal*, 12.2.

and other non-tuberculous mycobacteria (NTM). The name scrofula comes from the medieval Latin *scrofula*, meaning brood sow, because swine were purported to be affected by this problem.[19] Of all the foods considered unclean by Jews and Muslims, pork is considered the most abhorrent. Antiochus Epiphanes considered that he was making the supreme insult to the Jews when he sacrificed a pig on the altar in Jerusalem. Ellen White became convinced that pork was the ultimate in unclean foods according to the codes in the Pentateuch. Thus she wrote: "The eating of pork has produced scrofula, leprosy and cancerous humors."[20]

Graham also alleged that the liver and kidneys, because they are]"peculiarly associated with the stomach [that grand central organ] are affected causing fatal diabetes." The urinary system is afflicted with "renal calculi," resulting in premature death. The external skin, he averred, is impeded such that "insensible perspiration is greatly diminished; impurities are accumulated." These poisons are then reabsorbed, causing "distressing chilliness" continually "in the region of the spine," resulting in itching like "myriads of ants." Moreover, "permanent fistulas, of a cancerous character" continue "for years, to discharge great quantities of foetid, loathsome pus, and not unfrequently terminate in death." These beliefs about the dermatological system led Graham and White to emphasize "cleanliness"[21] via frequent bathing. The musculoskeletal system is not spared. Masturbation causes weak muscles, drooping of the head, "palsy," bones become "dry and brittle," and teeth decay and drop out. The GU system is afflicted by "ulceration of the testicles" and impotence.[22]

White was in lockstep with Graham in his assertion that masturbation causes a vast plethora of diseases. Solitary vice, she said, is the "great cause of these physical, mental, and moral evils," because it predisposes the young to "disease of almost every description." "Many sink into an early grave" "by numerous pains in the system, and various diseases, such as affection of the liver and lungs, neuralgia, rheumatism, affection of the spine, diseased kidneys, and cancerous

---

19. Wikipedia, "Mycobacterial cervical lymphadenitis," https://en.wikipedia.org/wiki/Mycobacterial_cervical_lymphadenitis.

20. White, *Spiritual Gifts*, vol 4a, 146.

21. An extremely malleable term of many meanings for White and McMahon.

22. Graham, *Lecture to Young Men on Chastity*, 90–112.

humors."²³ Apologists for Ellen White have heroically struggled to find a reasonable scientific basis to support Ellen White's claim that masturbation is the primary cause of insanity. *None* have dared to assert that masturbation causes the encyclopedic number of loathsome diseases and tens of thousands of deaths claimed by White.²⁴

Even stranger is the fact that White concurred with Graham when he said that the maleficent effects of solitary vice "transmigrate" from the masturbator to his or her progeny, resulting in the "early death, in the offspring, of the transgressor."²⁵ White paraphrased Graham's thought as follows: "Disease had been transmitted from parent to children from generation to generation. Infants in their cradle are miserably afflicted because of the sins of their parents, which have lessened their vital force."²⁶ White said a carnivorous diet after Noah's flood was the proximate cause for humanity becoming rapidly and progressively degenerate both mentally and physically. She averred that the habit of indulging the "animal passions" is genetically inheritable. In numerous sections of her tome on solitary vice she asserted that: "This is one great cause of the degeneracy of the race." Those who practice solitary vice will beget "offspring [who] are compelled to be sufferers by disease transmitted to them. Thus disease has been perpetuated from generation to generation." She asserted that the offspring of masturbators are "compelled to receive a miserable inheritance of disease and debility, before their birth, occasioned by the wrong habits of their parents . . ." "The offspring, before its birth, has had transmitted to it disease and an unhealthy appetite."²⁷

---

23. Ellen White, *Solemn Appeal*, 63–64.

24. If they were confident in E. G. White's scientific credibility in this matter, the Ellen G. White Estate authorities should commission a blue-ribbon panel of medical experts from the denomination's medical school at Loma Linda to examine the evidence for such claims and publish their conclusions.

25. Graham, *Lecture to Young Men on Chastity*, 123.

26. White, *Christian Education*, 8–12. Originally published in 1873 in "Testimony" no. 22.

27. Ellen White, *Solemn Appeal*, 105, 108, 112, 122.

Solitary vice depletes "vital forces" of semen; females have none to lose!

White had adopted Graham's notion of humanity being endowed with a specific amount of "vital force" that is especially exhausted by the practice of solitary vice. Both she and Graham repeatedly used this supposition regarding infants, whose own vital force had been reduced because a parent masturbated. White even expanded on this idea, claiming that "females possess less vital force than the other sex."[28] Ellen White borrowed this concept from her contemporaries. It has an ancient lineage. Her sources claimed that there is forty times the amount of vital force in a drop of semen compared to a drop of blood. Men lose vital force with each ejaculation. Current apologists claim that losing zinc in the semen may lead to insanity. However, White and her contemporaries claimed that male masturbation before the age of puberty was especially health destroying because prepubescent "males have no semen to lose, and females have none at any age."[29] Females have less vital force than males simply because they have no semen, White and her contemporaries believed.

White echoed Graham's entire constellation of ideas. She repeated Graham's conception that seasonings and fatty foods are a chief incitement to masturbate. Graham said:

> All kinds of stimulating and heating substances, high-seasoned food, rich dishes, the free use of flesh, and even the excess of aliment, all, more or less—and some to a very great degree—increase the concupiscent excitability and sensibility of the genital organs.[30]

While White wrote in almost identical language:

> Our food should be prepared free from spices. Mince pies, cakes, preserves, and highly-seasoned meats, with gravies, create a feverish condition in the system, and inflame the animal passions. We must dispense with animal food, and use grains, vegetables, and fruits, as articles of food.[31]

---

28. Ellen White, *Solemn Appeal*, 73.
29. James White, *Solemn Appeal*, 83.
30. Graham, *Lecture to Young Men on Chastity*, 40.
31. White, *Appeal to Mothers*.

Graham and White were in harmony asserting that the above "inflammatory" types of foods are transformed by the great central organ of the body, the stomach, resulting in "corrupt" and "impure" blood. For example, in *Spiritual Gifts* she said: "Indulging in eating too frequently, and in too large quantities, over-taxes the digestive organs, and produces a feverish state of the system. The blood becomes impure, and then diseases of various kinds occur."[32]

Both authors seemed to tepidly acknowledge the validity of phrenology and its hypothesis of the organ of amativeness; however, both assured their readers that, far from excusing men in exercising their animal lusts, a knowledge of phrenology should restrain them. Both also suggested that "excess" marital sex is a major health risk, but nothing in comparison to self-pollution. Both associated hypochondriacs with masturbation. Graham said that "hypochondriacs . . . are generally morbidly lecherous."[33] White alluded to hypochondriacs always complaining about a myriad of symptoms when their only real problem was that masturbation had made them languid and innervated.

White echoed Graham as both recommend vigorous exercise to combat and counteract the stimulants causing solitary vice. Both writers were quite convinced that when parents allowed their children to be indolent, shielded them from physical labor, and emphasized intellectual exercises, particularly at a younger age, that this stimulated and irritated the brain, making them more likely to indulge in solitary vice.[34] They both expressed this concept in such a singular turn of phrase that the proposition that White borrowed this concept directly from Graham seems quite reasonable. Graham wrote:

> [W]e are threatened with all the horrors of an over-exercised brain and cerebral irritation and nervous derangement, &c. &c., if we do not abandon our attempts at early education, and turn our children loose, to develop their bodies like calves and colts.—(See Note N.)[35]

White wrote:

---

32. White, *Spiritual Gifts*, vol. 4a, ch. 39, p. 8. See https://egwwritings-a.akamaihd.net/pdf/en_4aSG.pdf.
33. Graham, *Lecture to Young Men on Chastity*, 39.
34. Graham, *Lecture to Young Men on Chastity*, 53, 134, 138–39.
35. Graham, *Lecture to Young Men on Chastity*, 145.

> Many children have been ruined for life by urging the intellect, and neglecting to strengthen the physical powers. Many have died in childhood because of the course pursued by injudicious parents and school-teachers in forcing their young intellects, by flattery or fear, when they were too young to see the inside of a school-room. Their minds have been taxed with lessons, when they should not have been called out, but kept back until the physical constitution was strong enough to endure mental effort. Small children should be left as free as lambs to run out-of-doors . . ."[36]

Similarly, both authors evinced a prejudice that it is the brutish underclass who are more likely to spread the contagion of self-pollution. Graham forewarned that "servants, and other laboring people of loose morals" are the most likely to insinuate themselves into decent homes and surreptitiously introduce masturbation.[37] White echoed this suspicion, intimating that there is "much evil, which a hired girl may bring into a family," clearly alluding to masturbation.[38]

In 2005 an SDA physician, McMahon, wrote *Acquired or Inspired*, his analysis of Ellen White's assertions regarding the health principles she claimed to have received in vision. As his title suggests, he implies that either her information was acquired from fallible nineteenth-century health reformers or it was inspired via direct revelation. Ironically, he appears to conclude that her statements were a hybrid, half inspired and half acquired. He pleads with his readers that his purpose is "not to prove her to be fallible," even when he is constrained by medical science to concede that an impressive percentage of her health statements "are totally rejected today" because they are "unlikely to ever be verified by future investigations." He also concedes that "it seems Ellen White copied heavily from Graham, Alcott, Coles, and Jackson," and that it is even "possible Ellen White copied all her medical and health statements, both whats and whys," from them. The "whats and whys" are two categories McMahon discerns in Ellen White's health assertions. He believes that the "whys" are more probably uninspired and so more likely to have been copied from Graham, Alcott, Coles, and Jacksob, whereas the "whats" seem less derivative and therefore are more probably inspired. Per

---

36. White, *Christian Education*, 8–12.
37. Graham, *Lecture to Young Men on Chastity*, 82.
38. Ellen White, *Solemn Appeal*, 61.

McMahon, the "why" statements that are "unlikely to ever be verified by future investigation" include: 1) the fallacy that persons are born with a specific amount of "vital force," the expenditure of which, via solitary vice, results in premature death, insanity, and cancers; 2) that "fallen leaves" around dwellings poison the air, leading to "many an epidemic of fever"; 3) that the skin is the main excretory organ, resulting in accumulation of impurities that would "be reabsorbed." The skin's "millions of pores are quickly clogged unless kept clean by frequent bathing."[39] Additionally: 4) that certain foods make the "blood feverish and impure," leading directly to sexual depravity and masturbation; 5) that the digestion in the small bowel transforms food into blood. "It is a wonderful process that transforms the food into blood," but by "eating highly seasoned foods, especially flesh-meats . . . the blood . . . becomes impure." Finally, 5) White accepted the idea that it is is vital to equalize circulation so that the "blood will remain healthy and pure."[40]

Apologists traditionally offer two justifications for Ellen White's assertions about masturbation. One, they cite very rare, atypical associations between masturbation and insanity. Apologists have sifted through medical literature to find even a scintilla of support for her depiction of the evils of masturbation. Thus, for example, they cite an article by E. H. Hare, "Masturbatory Insanity: The History of an Idea," (*Journal of Mental Science* 108:1, January 1962). Hare cited a single ambiguous study by Malamud and Palmer in which purportedly 1 percent of persons suffering from insanity had masturbation as "apparently the most important cause of disorder." Hare himself observed that this is the sole study which even attempted to test the "masturbatory hypothesis." He concluded that if there is even an "association," it is "weak and inconstant" and "therefore, if masturbation is a causal factor, it is probably not a very important one." White apologists comfort themselves that at least Hare did "not dismiss it altogether." Apologists cite another 1965 source which labelled masturbation a "perversion" whose effects "are not fully known."[41] These

---

39. This belief conflated with Old Testament concepts of purity/impurity resulted in a frequent emphasis on cleanliness. McMahon augments this confusion by further conflating Ellen White's and the Old Testament's concept of cleanliness with the World Health Organization's category of cleanliness.

40. McMahon, *Acquired or Inspired*, 25, 30, 52, 114–20.

41. Lake and Moon, "Current Science and Ellen White," 234.

two sources likely originated from authorities like Graham and Ellen White, whose beliefs never became completely extinct. Since Ellen White reinforced primeval and shame-based beliefs, and claimed her assertions had divine authority, these visceral dogmas have remarkable longevity.

Zinc hypothesis for female insanity due to masturbation

Their second tactic consisted in citing persons who hypothesized that loss of zinc in the semen by "excess" masturbation may lead to insanity. For example, they cited a Carl C. Pfeiffer, who wrote a book entitled *Zinc and Other Micro-Nutrients* (1978) and who said: "We hate to say it, but in a zinc-deficient adolescent, sexual excitement and excessive masturbation might precipitate insanity."[42] This is the identical hypothesis I received in a personal letter in the 1980s from the then-secretary of the White Estate when I inquired as to whether the official position of the White Estate and the SDA church in general is that Ellen White's statements regarding masturbation are reliable. Thirty-five years later, *The Ellen G. White Encyclopedia* of 2013 has dredged up the same Carl C. Pfeiffer article on zinc to suggest that losing zinc in seminal fluid causes the insanity that Ellen G. White spoke so passionately about.

I would suggest to the reader the two following observations: 1) The sources the White apologists cite are extremely weak; and even they implicitly acknowledge that they are clutching at straws. Namely, the less than one in 100,000 cases in which a *bona fide* zinc deficiency exists; and even then, it only "might" precipitate insanity. 2) Given that females do not ejaculate zinc in semen and that Ellen White said that females, having less vital force, are even more susceptible to insanity, cancer, and many other diseases, how does the zinc hypothesis aid apologists' cause?[43] Furthermore, it is clarion clear in Ellen White's

---

42. Lake and Moon, "Current Science and Ellen White," 234. See also "Testimonies on Sexual Behavior, Adultery, and Divorce: Appendix A: Masturbation and Insanity" at website EGWWritings.org: https://m.egwwritings.org/en/book/122.1406.

43. "Females possess *less vital force* than the other sex. . . . The result of self-abuse in them is seen in various diseases, such as catarrh, dropsy, headache, loss of memory and sight, great weakness in the back and loins, affections of the spine, and *frequently* inward decay of the head. Cancerous humor, which would lie dormant in the system their lifetime, is inflamed, and commences its eating, destructive work. The mind is

writings that she was asserting that insanity, cancer, and multiple other diseases are rampant, not rare, and that masturbation is the chief cause of all these maladies—not a rare, marginal phenomenon. Yet it is upon the rare, marginal cases from fringe authors that White apologists rely.

In short, there are so many parallels in thought and word between Graham and White that McMahon's suggestion that this is simply coincidence is highly unlikely. But McMahon does perceptively note that there may have been a unique dependence of White upon Dr. Jackson in one of Jackson's peculiar notions. He thought that a disequilibrium in blood distribution causes disease. Cold extremities force the blood to the central organs, causing inflammation and impure blood. Thus, Jackson's recommended treatment was to "equalize the circulation," forcing the blood back to the extremities. Following Jackson's notions, White advised warming the extremities so that "the circulation will be equalized, and the blood will remain healthy and pure." Too much blood in the core of the body, White said, produces "congestion. Headache, cough, palpitation of the heart, or indigestion is often the result."[44] Graham also believed in a similar hypothesis. He theorized that too much brain work irritates the brain and should be equalized with physical exercise, which would direct more blood to the muscles and keep it pure. In addition to a meatless, no-spice, no-fat diet to prevent masturbation, Graham prescribed "proper exercise to promote the equal distribution of the blood."[45] After her comments saying that young children should be "left as free as lambs to run out-of-doors," that from "eight to ten years of age" the only school for children should be "the open air," White further asserted:

> Children and youth who are kept at school, and confined to books, cannot have sound physical constitutions. The exercise of the brain in study, without corresponding physical exercise, has a tendency to attract the blood to the brain, and the circulation of the blood through the system becomes unbalanced. The brain has too much blood, and the extremities too little.[46]

---

often utterly ruined, and insanity supervenes [emphasis added]" See White, Ellen, *A Solemn Appeal*, 73.

44. McMahon, *Acquired*, 118–19.
45. Graham, *Lecture to Young Men on Chastity*, 138.
46. White, *Christian Education*, 8–12.

Perhaps Ellen White amalgamated two of her favorite medical authorities on this point.

Above I have attempted to make an inductive argument. I have documented many cases where statements considered prophetic, authoritative, and accurate can readily be shown to be both incorrect and themselves derived from other, oftentimes even more obviously erroneous sources. For example, would a twenty-million-strong denomination spend millions of dollars and hundreds of man-hours attempting to prove that Dr. Graham's statements about masturbation are scientifically defensible? Not likely. It is only because someone considered a prophetic authority repeated Graham that an ecclesiological organization has felt constrained to defend it. Similarly, would an ecclesiological institution mount an immense apologetic effort, like the encyclopedic tomes of Froom and F. D. Nichol, to defend the exegetical positions of William Miller and S. S. Snow? Not likely. So because Ellen G. White copied what Miller and Snow wrote, why should that merit such an apologetic defense? Because the "light" that Ellen Harmon received from Snow and Miller she believed "came from God, it was not taught me by man." It requires ignoring a considerable amount of inductive evidence to defend such an assertion. A more reasonable explanation is that twelve-year-old Ellen Harmon, with a shattered central nervous system and a morbid fear of hellfire, became convinced of a non-scriptural dogma, and that four additional years of being exposed to intense propaganda within an isolated, cultic social environment did not disabuse her of her error. Rather, it reinforced her prepubescent judgments so that from seventeen to eighty-seven she could not disassociate herself from her age-twelve convictions.

XV

Summary of Evidence

IN MAY OF 1847 Ellen G. White asserted: "I know the light I received came from God, it was not taught me by man."[1] She asserted this with reference to her first vision and bridegroom vision. However, since 1847 both she and SDA apologists have interpreted this as a universal principle applying to any "light" she believed she saw. Ellen G. White's critics and defenders have framed the issue in terms of polar opposites. Both they and Ellen G. White have suggested that her work was either entirely of God or of the devil. In other terms, her utterances were either a result of devilish mesmerism or the unmediated expression of the Holy Spirit. The expansive latter doctrine was officially adopted at the November 1855 General Conference held in Battle Creek, Michigan. This marked a tipping point for Sabbatarian Adventists regarding their public promotion of Ellen White. A General Conference committee consisting of Joseph Bates, J. H. Waggoner, and M. E. Cornell proclaimed to the assembly that they held Ellen White's visions and views "as emanating from the divine mind." The visions were "messages from God."[2]

As SDA scholarship matured, however, even the most loyal and orthodox apologists had to admit that Ellen White borrowed large swathes of material—even if one accepts the General Conference's legal team's assertion that the material was not "plagiarized" in a technical, legal sense. Even while conceding that Ellen G. White

1. Casebolt, "'It Was Not Taught Me by Man,'" 66–73.
2. Levterov, *Development*, 71–73.

had appropriated historical, scientific, and theological "facts" from others, the dominate SDA corporate position is that either all Ellen G. White's borrowings were accurate or an insignificant number of trivial errors *may* have been borrowed. However, for generations an obvious source upon which Ellen Harmon was most dependent was almost entirely overlooked. This was Father Miller, Ellen Harmon's spiritual father. Additionally, it has never been recognized that Miller was so heavily dependent on discredited historicism and that Miller's methods and results were as fatally flawed as they are. Ellen Harmon was dependent upon Miller for immense amounts of detailed eschatological minutiae, calculations, basic assumptions, method, and his global paradigm. Most egregious of all was Miller's and Snow's practice of setting specific dates for the second coming. Historicists like these had a seemingly irresistible fondness for claiming that the Bible provided *exact* dates. There is no evidence for this assertion and much evidence against it. This is true whether one is predicting an exact date for the second coming or an invisible divine movement in a heavenly sanctuary. Strangely, Ellen Harmon's appropriation of Miller's entire overarching scheme remained an interpretive blind spot both because it was so obvious and because of Ellen G. White's own description of Miller's inspiration. The collective, unconscious presumption was that since Ellen G. White claimed that Miller got all his interpretations and calculations directly from divine guidance, it did not matter that Ellen Harmon was entirely dependent on Miller (and Snow) for her personal eschatological doctrines. Ellen G. White portrayed herself and Miller as receiving all their "light" from literal, plain, commonsense readings of the prophecies of Daniel and Revelation (and Leviticus, Ezekiel, Jeremiah, Matthew, and others). *Their only tools were the Bible and a concordance, both mediated via either angelic or direct visionary guidance.* According to Ellen G. White, for centuries, multiple mathematically precise, eschatological periods had been hidden from humanity's view until God unveiled them for the first time to the untaught, backwoods, gentleman farmer William Miller.

Now, if Miller's only inspiration really was angelic guidance, plain Scripture, and a concordance, Ellen Harmon's foundational dependence on Miller might be considered an arcane triviality. However, William Miller systematically made an enormous number of outlandish, stunning misinterpretations of Scripture. Not only was he erroneous in numerous detailed verse-by-verse cases, but his global approach and faulty methodology made such errors predictably and inevitably numerous. To make matters worse, S. S. Snow made plentiful non-sensical prophetic miscalculations compounding Miller's misinterpretations. *It was Snow* who originated the midnight cry, which Ellen Harmon adamantly confirmed in her first vision. Both Miller and Snow were distant echoes of Reformation Era historicists. These Reformation Era commentators themselves had made numerous, purportedly mathematically precise interpretations, based on their presumption that God had provided them a roadmap of precise historical events that had a one-to-one relationship with unambiguous biblical texts. The dustbin of history is liberally littered with their interpretations, retrospectively proven to be utterly false. Their predictions failed—failed spectacularly and undeniably. Ironically, because Miller imagined his findings as virtually *ex nihilo, de nouveau* results, the significance of Miller's massive reliance upon Reformation Era historicists was initially overlooked. However, Froom's nearly four-thousand-page *magnus opus, The Prophetic Faith of Our Fathers*, seeking to normalize and justify Miller, paradoxically proved repeatedly just how dependent Miller was on his historicist predecessors, and just how speculative, fanciful, and demonstrably erroneous these predecessors had been. They were like blind men shooting buckshot into a midnight darkness. Even though the mathematics of Reformation Era historicists, Miller, and Snow were flagrantly false, Ellen Harmon believed that Miller and Snow (and Crosier) were led to their conclusions due to direct divine guidance.

Ellen Harmon believed that she had not been "taught by man" regarding eschatological calculations. She was mistaken. The term one uses to describe her relationship to Miller is not as critical as the recognition that she was undeniably intellectually dependent on his faulty practices. Did she copy, borrow, echo, plagiarize, or merely appropriate material from Miller? The fact is that she was intellectually dependent on Miller (Snow, Turner, Crosier) *et al.* Yet, Ellen White seems to have been incapable of realizing her dependence on these commentators. To the contrary, she had a penchant for characterizing their speculations as "true light." Like William Foy, she considered her out-of-body experiences to be irrefutable evidence that she was the object of a divine imperative. She related several incidences which convinced her that she had to either accept a divine commission of Messenger or be eternally lost. As a result, she confabulated when confronted with the choice of being eternally lost or being God's eschatological Messenger. However, the evidence that she was "taught by man" and that these men were erroneous has been demonstrated beyond a reasonable doubt. It will be extremely difficult for the SDA community to admit such facts. But it is the only intellectually honest thing to do. And a commitment to tthe Truth is a very important moral value for Seventh-day Adventism.

Miller was not only demonstrably wrong; he was *systematically and consistently* wrong. I have documented, in excruciating, granular detail, at times, overwhelming evidence to this effect. Similarly, I have documented Ellen G. White's intellectual dependence on several other erroneous sources for topics as disparate as the misshapen heads driven to insanity by masturbation, supernatural Dark Days, miraculous meteorite showers, the collapsing Ottoman Empire, the "old view" of "the daily," and purportedly Sabbath-keeping, apostolically pure Waldensians that were slaughtered by the millions by the Dark Ages papacy for 1,260 years.

Conceptions about the nature of the material that Ellen G. White claimed she saw must be based on the empirical facts. It is no longer possible to presume that whatever she said she saw is an accurate view of reality.

The ultimate locus of authority

Seventh-day Adventism is analogous to Islam in the most critical theological aspect possible: the ultimate locus of authority. The founding confession of Islam is: Allah is One and Mohammad is his prophet. Once these two premises are admitted, one becomes a Muslim and necessarily submits to all the words of Mohammad as the words of Allah. If Mohammad is Allah's Messenger, everything he says in the Koran carries divine authority. The same dynamic is inherent in SDA theology. Its equivalent is: Ellen G. White is God's Prophetess; consequently, everything she says she saw must be submitted to. The thesis of the scores of apologetic books and articles about her writings can be distilled as follows: if Ellen G. White saw it and wrote it, it has to be true. Regardless of empirical evidence to the contrary, there exists an *a priori* presumption that whatever she saw is authoritative. Although the SDA church has always denied that she is inerrant, for all practical purposes she is at least semi-canonical.

Yet it can be empirically demonstrated that she did err in significant respects historically, medically, scientifically, biblically, and theologically. Whereas she was adamant that whatever she saw was untainted by fallible human influences, it can be demonstrated that in multiple instances she was "taught by man," preeminently William Miller. But S. S. Snow, Joseph Turner and Apollos Hall, O. R. L. Crosier, William Foy, Sylvester Graham, and Joseph Bates also "taught" Ellen Harmon a great deal. Since these men and Ellen Harmon were almost wholly consumed with eschatology, and both William Miller's and Ellen Harmon's authority were based on their claim to divine insight into Daniel and Revelation, Ellen White's personal authority and Millerite eschatology have been inextricably intertwined since the immediate aftermath of the 1844 Great Disappointment.

Epilogue

Love not Logarithms

MILLERITES PERCEIVED THEIR DATE-SETTING proclamation as a *necessary* saving truth. Ellen Harmon became convinced that she was saved through Miller's date-setting proofs—not through Methodism.[1] Her dream of a temple of Millerism that must be entered she considered a divine omen and instruction.[2] In 1858 she specifically referred to the "preaching of definite time" and the exact year when Millerites "believed the prophetic periods would run out." Here she refers about a dozen times to "prophecies" or "prophetic periods" which "proved that they [the prophetic periods] would terminate in 1844" and calls this a "*saving message* [emphasis added]."[3] A saving message? This is a paradigm of the "gift of prophecy" as the gift of exact prediction. Prophecy as time predictions. Miller believed that this gift of prediction disproved deism and proved the foreknowledge of a personal God. This was the "good news" of Millerism. Ellen Harmon subjectively experienced Millerism as responsible for her salvation, but its date-setting does not survive objective textual or historical scrutiny. The Millerite proclamation of "definite time" is based on a fundamental misconception of the gift of prophecy.

The prophetic word is not an eschatological, mathematical series of prophetic periods all simultaneously ending in 1843–44. The prophetic word is the incarnate Christ. The prophetic word is God is love and his law is a law of love. Love God with your entire soul and your neighbor as yourself. There is no polar opposition between love

---

1. Casebolt, *Child of the Apocalypse*, 26.
2. Casebolt, *Child of the Apocalypse*, 23.
3. White, *Spiritual Gifts*, 1:128–139.

and law, between law and grace. The law and its specific regulations are intended to concretize love in action. "All you need is Love" is true but it can masquerade as a pious, fraudulent, platitude. Like James 2:15–16 KJV admonishes: "If a brother or sister be naked, and destitute of daily food, and one of you say unto them, 'Depart in peace, be ye warmed and filled'; notwithstanding ye give them not those things which are needful to the body; what doth it profit?" Is not this the opposite of Christ's parable—in a discourse upon *the law*—of the Good Samaritan?

The biblical equation derived from obscure textual (hapax legomenon) and archaeological data, 457 BC +2300-years = 1844, and fourteen similar proofs, are only superficially impressive. But by 2022 its exact predictions have revealed themselves to be as dry as the hills of Gilboa and as obsolete as a model-T Ford. In 1844 its claim to have predicted the exact day of the second coming failed spectacularly. In its remodeled form, originating with O. R. L. Crosier, Joseph Turner, and Apollos Hale, it claims to have predicted the exact day when Christ invisibly moved from one apartment of a heavenly sanctuary to another one. But why is this missing from Ellen Harmon's December 1844 vision? And why would God mark an invisible event with such obscure and arcane proofs? When without exception all of Christ's teachings about time are prohibitions about attempting such time calculations? It hardly resembles a liberating good news. For example, it is nothing like the *triumphant and ecstatic* day the Israelites were freed from Egyptian slavery—marked by the celebration of *Seventh-day* Sabbath. It is nothing like June 19th, the jubilant day when slavery in the United States was extirpated. It stands in stark contrast with authentic good news, illustrated by the parable of the prodigal son and the parable of the good Samaritan. The Father of the prodigal son has liberating and loving qualities of unearned grace which can penetrate even the most hardened cynic. The story of the good Samaritan captures the essence of one of the "hard sayings" of Jesus: Love your enemies. Sometimes your coreligionists are your enemies, and your enemies show unmerited mercy.

It was a Jew travelling from Jerusalem who was attacked, stripped naked, robbed, and left for dead *by his tribal fellows*, other Jews. His neighbor, the abominable Samaritan, not only unstintingly gave him acute care but graciously provided him chronic financial support as well. What an astounding and shocking concept: The abominable Samaritan incarnated God's love in action!

A purportedly predicted 1755 Lisbon earthquake, a Dark Day of 1780, a meteorite shower of 1833, an exact August 11, 1840 collapse of the Ottoman Empire, and an exact date of October 22, 1844 for the midnight cry are simply not good news gospel. Moving from an invisible heavenly holy place to an invisible most holy place is not the everlasting gospel. The acceptable year of the Lord is not 1844. No. The good news, the everlasting gospel, is not fifteen, farfetched, fanciful, historicist calculations. The prophetic word is: "The Spirit of the LORD is upon me, because he hath anointed me to preach the gospel to the poor, he hath sent me to heal the broken hearted, to preach deliverance to the captives, and recovery of sight to the blind, to set at liberty them that are bruised, to preach the acceptable year of the Lord." Luke 4:18-19 KJV When Christians embody this vision, then non-Christians will be convinced and convicted that God is Love. Like the Nazarenes, astounded and stupefied at the gracious words which proceeded out of Christ's mouth.

The Spirit of Prophecy cares for the poor, heals the broken hearted, delivers the captives, liberates the bruised, restores vision to the blind. Apologists for the Spirit of Prophecy need to be as zealous in promulgating this good news as they have been zealous in promoting Ellen White's quasi-canonical, quasi-inerrant authority. The gifts of the spirit incarnate a Father's love for a profligate son and a Samaritan's love for a Jew. A love not found in ill-fitting, historically poorly attested, biblical equations. Is one required to interpret obscure, apocalyptic passages—"prophecies which had ever been dark to God's people?"

"He hath shewed thee, O man, what is good; and what doth the Lord require of thee, but to do justly, and to love mercy, and to walk humbly with thy God?" Micah 6:8 KJV

Bibliography

Aamodt, Terrie Dopp. "The Hardest Question." *Spectrum* 49 (2021) 63–72.
Arain, M., et al. "Maturation of the Adolescent Brain." *Neuropsychiatry Disease and Treatment* 9 (2013) 449–61.
Anderson, Eric. "The Millerite Use of Prophecy: A Case Study of a 'Striking Fulfilment.'" In *The Disappointed: Millerism and Millenarianism in the Nineteenth Century*, edited by Ronald L. Numbers and Jonathan M. Butler, 78–91. Bloomington: Indiana University Press, 1987.
Andrews, Evans. "Remembering New England's 'Dark Day.'" https://www.history.com/news/remembering-new-englandsdark-day.
Andrews, John. *The Sanctuary and the 2300 Days*. San Bernadino, CA: Waymark, 2012.
Arasola, Kai. *The End of Historicism: Millerite Hermeneutic of Time Prophecies in the Old Testament*. Sigtuna: Datem, 1990.
Augsburger, Daniel. "The Sabbath and Lord's Day During the Middle Ages." In *The Sabbath in Scripture and History*, edited by Kenneth Strand, 190–214. Washington, DC: Review and Herald, 1982.
Bacchiocchi, Samuele. *From Sabbath to Sunday: A Historical Investigation of the Rise of Sunday Observance in Early Christianity*. Rome: Pontifical Gregorian University Press, 1977.
———. "The Rise of Sunday Observance in Early Christianity." In *The Sabbath in Scripture and History*, edited by Kenneth Strand, 132–50. Washington DC: Review and Herald, 1982.
Bailey, Mark L. "Guidelines for Interpreting Jesus' Parables." *Bibliotheca Sacra* 617 (1998) 29–38. https://biblicalstudies.org.uk/article_parables_bailey.html.
Baker, Benjamin. "They Lived Near the Bridge Where We Went Over." *Spectrum* 42 (2014) 45–51.
Baker, Delbert W. *The Unknown Prophet: Before Ellen White, God Used William Ellis Foy*. Washington, DC: Review and Herald, 1987.
Bates, Joseph. *The Opening Heavens*. New Bedford, MA: Benjamin Lindsey, 1846.
———. *A Seal of the Living God*. Fairhaven, MA: Benjamin Lindsey, 1849.
———. *Second Advent Way Marks and High Heaps: Or a Connected View of the Fulfilment of Prophecy by God's Peculiar People, From the Year 1840 to 1847*. New Bedford, MA: Benjamin Lindsey, 1847.
———. *Seventh Day Sabbath: A Perpetual Sign from the Beginning, to the Entering into the Gates of the Holy City According to the Commandment*. 2nd ed. New Bedford, MA: Benjamin Lindsey, 1847.

———. "A Tract, Showing that the Seventh Day Should Be Observed as the Sabbath, Instead of the First Day, 'According to the Commandment.'" 1845.

Bright, John. *Jeremiah*. Anchor Bible 21. Garden City, NY: Doubleday, 1978.

Brown, Jerrod, et al. "Confabulation: A Guide for Mental Health Professionals." *International Journal of Neurology and Neurotherapy* 9 (2017) 1–2. https://clinmedjournals.org/articles/ijnn/international-journal-of-neurology-and-neurotherapy-ijnn-4-070.pdf.

Brown, Raymond E. *The Birth of the Messiah*. New Haven, CT: Yale University Press, 1993.

Brownlee, W. C. *Popery an Enemy of Civil and Religious Liberty*. New York: J. S. Taylor, 1836.

Bruce, F. F. *The Spreading Flame: The Rise and Progress of Christianity*. Grand Rapids: Eerdmans, 1973.

Burgeson, Ruth Elizabeth. "A Comparative Study of the Fall of Man as Treated by John Milton and Ellen G. White." Masters thesis, 1957. https://www.nonegw.org/egw102.shtml.

Burleigh, Michael. *Earthly Powers: The Clash of Religion and Politics in Europe*. New York: HarperCollins, 2006.

Burt, Merlin D. "The Day-Dawn of Canandaigua, New York: Reprint of a Significant Millerite Adventist Journal." *Andrews University Seminary Studies* (2006) 317–30.

———. "Elizabeth Haines." In *The Ellen G. White Encyclopedia*, edited by Denis Fortin and Jerry Moon, 393–94. Hagerstown, MD: Review and Herald, 2013.

———. "The Extended Atonement View in the Day-Dawn and the Emergence of Sabbatarian Adventism." *Andrews University Seminary Studies* 44 (2006) 331–39.

———. "The Historical Background, Interconnected Development, and Integration of the Doctrines of the Sanctuary, the Sabbath, and Ellen G. White's Role in Sabbatarian Adventism from 1844–1849." PhD diss., Andrews University, 2002.

———. "The 'Shut Door' and Ellen White's Visions." In *The Ellen G. White Letters & Manuscripts with Annotations: 1845–1859*, annotated by Roland Karlman, 41–61. Hagerstown, MD: Review and Herald, 2014.

Cameron, Euan. *Waldenses: Rejections of Holy Church in Medieval Europe*. Oxford: Wiley-Blackwell, 2001.

Casebolt, Donald. *Child of the Apocalypse: Ellen G. White*. Eugene, OR: Wipf & Stock, 2021.

———. "Ellen White, the Waldenses, and Historical Interpretation." *Spectrum* 11 (1981) 37–43.

———. "Is Ellen White's Interpretation of Biblical Prophecy Final?" *Spectrum* 12 (1982) 2–9.

———. "'It Was Not Taught Me by Man': Ellen White's Visions and 2 Esdras." *Spectrum* 46 (2018) 66–73.

Caspar, Erich. *Geschichte des Papsttums*. Tubingen: Mohr, 1930–33.

Chadwick, Henry. *The Early Church*. New York: Dorset, 1967.

Coon, Roger W. *The Great Visions of Ellen G. White*. Hagerstown, MD: Review and Herald, 1992.

Cottrell, Raymond F. "Sanctuary Debate: A Question of Method." *Spectrum* 10 (1980) 16–26.

Crocombe, Jeff. "'A Feast of Reason': The Roots of William Miller's Biblical Interpretation and Its Influence on the Seventh-Day Adventist Church." PhD diss., University of Queensland, 2011.
Crosier, O. R. L. "Dear Bro. Jacobs." *Day-Star* (1845) 23.
———. "'The Law of Moses'" The Sanctuary." *Day-Star Extra*, February, 7, 1846, 37–44.
Crosier, O. R. L., and F. B. Hahn. "Reprint of 1845 Day-Dawn." *Ontario Messenger*, March 26, 1845, back cover.
Damsteegt, P. Gerard. "Decoding Ancient Waldensian Names: New Discoveries." *Andrews University Seminary Studies* 54 (2016) 237–58.
———. "Early Adventist Timesettings and Their Implications for Today." *Journal of the Adventist Theological Society* 4 (1993) 151–68.
———. *Foundations of the Seventh-Day Adventist Message and Mission*. Berrien Springs, MI: Andrews University Press, 1977.
———. "Prophetic Interpretation." In *The Ellen G. White Encyclopedia*, edited by Denis Fortin and Jerry Moon, 1061–63. Hagerstown, MD: Review and Herald, 2013.
"Exposition of Matthew, 24th Chapter." *Signs of the Times*, June 21, 1843, 121–28.
Firth, Katharin R. *The Apocalyptic Tradition in Reformation Britain, 1530–1645*. Oxford: Oxford University Press, 1979.
Fliche, Augustine, and Victor Martin. *Histoire de l'Eglise*. 20 vols. Paris: Bloud & Gay, 1934–1964.
Ford, Desmond. *Daniel 8:14: The Day of Atonement and the Investigative Judgment*. Casselberry, FL: Euangelion, 1980.
Fortin, Denis. "Visions of Ellen G. White." In *The Ellen G. White Encyclopedia*, edited by Denis Fortin and Jerry Moon, 1249–53. Hagerstown, MD: Review and Herald, 2013.
Foy, William E. *The Christian Experience of William E. Foy: Together with the Two Visions He Received Jan. and Feb. 1842*. Portland, ME: John and Charles Pearson, 2011.
Frend, W. H. C. *Martyrdom and Persecution in the Early Church*. Grand Rapids: Baker, 1965.
Froom, Leroy Edwin. *The Prophetic Faith of Our Fathers*. Vol. 1. Washington, DC: Review and Herald, 1954.
———. *The Prophetic Faith of Our Fathers*. Vol. 2, *PreReformation and Reformation, Restoration, and Second Departure*. Washington, DC: Review and Herald, 1948.
———. *The Prophetic Faith of Our Fathers*. Vol. 3, *The Historical Development of Prophetic Interpretation*. Washington, DC: Review and Herald, 1946.
Gershoy, Leo. *The French Revolution and Napoleon*. New York: F. S. Crofts, 1933.
Gesenius, William. *A Hebrew and English Lexicon of the Old Testament*. Oxford: Clarendon, 1997.
Graham, Sylvester. *A Lecture to Young Men on Chastity*. Boston: Light & Stearns, Crocker & Brewster, 1837.
Graybill, Ron. "How Did Ellen White Chose and Use Historical Sources? The French Revolution Chapter of the Great Controversy." *Spectrum* 4 (1972) 49–53.
———. "The Last Secrets of the White Estate." *Spectrum* 49 (2021) 73–76.
———. "Under the Triple Eagle: Early Adventist Use of the Apocrypha." *Adventist Heritage* 2 (1987) 25–33.
———. *Visions & Revisions: A Textual History of Ellen G. White's Writings*. Westlake Village, CA: Oak & Acorn, 2019.

———. "Visions and Revisions—Part 1" *Ministry Magazine* (1993) 1–8.
Gregory, Brad S. *Salvation at Stake: Christian Martyrdom in Early Modern Europe.* Cambridge, MA: Harvard University Press, 1999.
Hale, Apollos. *The Second Advent Manual.* Boston: J. V. Himes, 1843.
Haller, Johannes. *Das Papsttum: Idee und Wirklichkeit.* Esslingen am Neckar: Port, 1962.
Harmon, Ellen. "Letter from Sister Harmon, Portland, Maine, Dec. 20, 1845." *The Day-Star* 9, January 24, 1846, 31–32.
Harris, Ruth. *Lourdes: Body and Spirit in the Secular Age.* London: Penguin, 1999.
Harrison, Kathryn. *Joan of Arc: A Life Transfigured.* New York: Doubleday, 2014.
Hartman, Louis F., and Alexander A Di Lella. *The Book of Daniel.* Garden City, NY: Doubleday, 1978.
Himes, J. V. "Fundamental Principles on which the Second Advent Cause Is Based." *Signs of the Times*, July 17, 1844, 185–92.
Hodgkin, Thomas. *Italy and Her Invaders.* New York: Atheneum House, 1967.
Hoyt, Frederick. "Trial of Elder I. Dammon Reported for the Piscataquis Farmer." *Spectrum* 17 (1987) 29–36.
———. "We Lifted Up Our Voices Like a Trumpet: Millerites in Portland, Maine." *Spectrum* 17 (1987) 15–22.
Iliffe, Rob. *Priest of Nature: The Religious Words of Isaac Newton.* Oxford: Oxford University Press, 2017.
Jacobs, Enoch, "2nd Thess." *The Western Midnight Cry!!!*, May 18, 1844, 74.
———. "But of that Day and Hour Knoweth No Man." *The Western Midnight Cry!!!*, December 9, 1843, 1–8.
———. "Extract of 2 Esdras." *The Western Midnight Cry!!!*, April 13, 1844, 33–40.
———. "A Glimpse of Paradise." *The Western Midnight Cry!!!*, April 13, 1844, 33–40.
———. "If the Vision Tarry, Wait for It." *The Western Midnight Cry!!!*, April 13, 1844, 33–40.
———. "Matthew 24th and 25th Chapters." *The Western Midnight Cry!!!*, April 13, 1844, 57–61.
———. "Prophetic Time." *The Western Midnight Cry!!!*, March 9, 1844, 1–8.
———. "Scriptural Test of Saving Faith." *The Western Midnight Cry!!!*, March 23, 1844, 17–24.
———. "The Time." *The Western Midnight Cry!!!*, November 29, 1844, 1–4.
———. "Tour to New York." *The Western Midnight Cry!!!*, June 22, 1844, 89–96.
———. "The Watches." *Day Star*, September 20, 1845, 38.
Jennisken, Peter. *Meteorite Showers and Their Parent Comets.* Cambridge: Cambridge University Press, 2006.
Jones, Henry. "Fearful Sights, Great Signs." *Signs of the Times*, February 15, 1843, 169–77.
———. "Fearful Sights, Great Signs, &c." *The Midnight Cry*, November 22, 1842, 177–85.
Kaiser, Denis. "The History of the Adventist Interpretation of the 'Daily' in the Book of Daniel from 1831 to 2008." Masters thesis, Andrews University, 2009. https://digitalcommons.andrews.edu/theses/45/.
———. *Trust and Doubt: Perceptions of Divine Inspiration in Seventh-Day Adventist History.* St. Peter am Har, Austria: Seminar Schloss Bogenhofen, 2019.

Kaiser, Denis, and Jerry Moon. "For Jesus and Scripture: The Life of Ellen G. White." In *The Ellen G. White Encyclopedia*, edited by Denis Fortin and Jerry Moon, 18–95. Hagerstown, MD: Review and Herald, 2013.

Keith, Alexander. *Evidence of the Truth of the Christian Religion Derived from the Literal Fulfillment of Prophecy*. New York: Harper, 1839.

Knight, George R. *Joseph Bates: The Real Founder of Seventh-Day Adventism*. Hagerstown, MD: Review and Herald, 2004.

———. *Millennial Fever and the End of the World*. Boise, ID: Pacific, 1993.

———. *Walking with Ellen White*. Hagerstown, MD: Review and Herald, 1999.

Korpman, Matthew J. "Adventism's Hidden Book: A Brief History of the Apocrypha." *Spectrum* 46 (2018) 56–65.

Lake, Jud. "Ellen G. White's Use of Extrabiblical Sources." In *The Gift of Prophecy*, edited by Alberto R. Timm and Dwain N. Esmond, 320–36. Silver Springs, MD: Review and Herald, 2013.

Lake, Jud, and Jerry Moon. "Current Science and Ellen White: Twelve Controversial Statements." In *The Ellen G. White Encyclopedia*, edited by Denis Fortin and Jerry Moon, 234–40. Hagerstown, MD: Review and Herald, 2013.

Latreille, Andre. *L'Eglise Catholique et La Revolution Française* Paris: Editions du Cerf, 1970.

Levterov, Theodore N. *The Development of the Seventh-Day Adventist Understanding of Ellen G. White's Prophetic Gift*. New York: Peter Lang, 2015.

Litch, Josiah. "Where Are We?" *The Western Midnight Cry!!!*, April 20, 1844, 41–48.

Loftus, E. "The Formation of False Memories." *Psychiatric Annals* 25 (1995) 720–25.

Lot, Ferdinand. *The End of the Ancient World and the Beginning of the Middle Ages*. London: Kegan Paul, Trench, Trubner, 1931.

Lovejoy, David S. *Religious Enthusiasm in the New World: Heresy to Revolution*. Cambridge, MA: Harvard University Press, 1985.

Marini, Stephen A. *Radical Sects of Revolutionary New England*. Cambridge, MA: Harvard University Press, 1982.

McAdams, Donald R. "Shifting Views of Inspiration: Ellen G. White Studies in the 1970s." *Spectrum* 10 (1980) 27–41.

McArthur, Benjamin. *A. G. Daniells: Shaper of Twentieth-Century Adventism*. Nampa, ID: Pacific, 2015.

McMahon, Don S. *Acquired or Inspired?: Exploring the Origins of the Adventist Lifestyle*. Nampa, ID: Pacific, 2005.

McMurry, et al. "Fire Scars Reveal Source of New England's 1780 Dark Day." *International Journal of Wildland Fire* 16 (2007) 266–70.

Miller, William. *Evidence from Scripture and History of the Second Coming of Christ*. Boston: Himes, 1842.

———. *Evidences from Scripture and History of the Second Coming of Christ about the Year A.D. 1843*. 3rd ed. Syracuse, NY: T. A. and S. F. Smith, 1835.

———. *Evidences from Scripture and History of the Second Coming of Christ About the Year A.D. 1843, and of His Personal Eeign of 1000 Years*. Brandon, VT: Vermont Telegraph Office, 1833.

———. "A Lecture on the Signs of the Present Times." *Signs of the Times*, March 20, 1840, 1–8.

———. "Mr. Miller's Letters No. 5." *Signs of the Times*, May 15, 1840.

———. "A New Year's Address." *Signs of the Times*, January 25, 1843, 145–52.

———. "A Synopsis of Miller's Views." *Signs of the Times*, January 25, 1843, 145–52.

Ministerial Association. *Seventh-Day Adventists Believe*. Boise, ID: Pacific, 2006.

Misson, Maximillien. *A Cry from the Desert: Or Testimonials of the Miraculous Things Lately Come to Pass in the Cevennes, Verified upon Oath, and by Other Proofs*. London: Paternoster-Row, 1707.

Moon, Jerry. "'The Daily.'" In *The Ellen G. White Encyclopedia*, edited by Denis Fortin and Jerry Moon, 752. Hagerstown, MD: Review and Herald, 2013.

Moore, R. I. *The War on Heresy*. London: Profile, 2014.

Moskala, Jiri. "The Prophetic Voice in the Old Testament: An Overview." In *The Gift of Prophecy*, edited by Alberto R. Timm and Dwain N. Esmond, 13–45. Silver Springs, MD: Review and Herald, 2013.

Mueller, Ekkehardt. "The Prophetic Voice in the New Testament: An Overview." In *The Gift of Prophecy*, edited by Alberto R. Timm and Dwain N. Esmond, 46–83. Silver Springs, MD: Review and Herald, 2013.

Nichol, Francis D. *The Midnight Cry*. Washington, DC: Review and Herald, 1944.

Numbers, Ronald. *Prophetess of Health: A Study of Ellen G. White*. New York: Harper & Row, 1976.

———. "Science and Medicine." In *Ellen Harmon White: American Prophet*, edited by Terrie Dopp Aamodt, Gary Land, and Ronald L. Numbers, 196–223. New York: Oxford University Press, 2014.

Olson, Robert W. "The 'Shut Door' Documents: Statements Relating to the 'Shut Door,' the Door of Mercy, and the Salvation of Souls, by Ellen G. White and Other Early Adventists." https://whiteestate.org/legacy/issues-shutdoor-html/.

———. "Ellen G. White's Use of Historical Sources in the Great Controversy." *Adventist Review*, February 23, 1984, 1–3.

Olson, Robert W., and Roger W. Coon. "Ellen G. White: A Chronology." In *The Ellen G. White Encyclopedia*, edited by Denis Fortin and Jerry Moon, 112–14. Hagerstown, MD: Review and Herald, 2013.

Peterson, Donald I. *Visions or Seizures: Was Ellen White the Victim of Epilepsy?* Boise, ID: Pacific, 1988. https://whiteestate.org/legacy/issues-visions-html/.

Phillips, Campbell. "Earthquakes: The 10 Biggest in History." *Australian Geographic*, March 14, 2011. https://www.australiangeographic.com.au/topics/science-environment/2011/03/earthquakes-the-10-biggest-in-history/.

Poirier, Tim. "Black Forerunner to Ellen White: William E. Foy." *Spectrum* 17 (1987) 23–28.

Preble, T. M. "*A Tract, Showing that the Seventh Day Should Be Observed as the Sabbath, Instead of the First Day; 'According to the Commandment.'*" Nashua: Murry & Kimball, 1845. http://www.aloha.net/~mikesch/tract.htm.

Rea, Walter T. *The White Lie*. Turlock, CA: M&R, 1982.

Rowe, David L. *God's Strange Work: William Miller and the End of the World*. Grand Rapids: Eerdmans, 2008.

Schatz, Klaus. *Papal Primacy: From Its Origins to the Present*. Collegeville, MN: Liturgical, 1996.

Schmidt, T. C. *Hippolytus of Rome: Commentary on Daniel and "Chronicon"*. Piscataway, NH: Gorgias, 2017.

Smith, Uriah. *Daniel and Revelation: Response of History to the Voice of Prophecy*. Battle Creek, MI: Review and Herald, 1897.

———. *Daniel and the Revelation*. Nashville: Southern, 1944.

———. *Daniel and the Revelation*. Jasper, OR: Adventist Pioneer Library, 2016.
Snow, S. S. "Behold, the Bridegroom Cometh; Go Ye Out to Meet Him." *The True Midnight Cry*, August 22, 1844.
———. "Letter from S. S. Snow." *The Midnight Cry*, February 22, 1844.
———. "Letter from S. S. Snow." *The Midnight Cry*, June 27, 1844.
Spitzer, Robert L., et al. "Silent Sister." In *A Learning Companion to DSM III Case Book*, 158–59. Washington, DC: American Psychiatric Association, 1981.
Storrs, George. "Go Ye Out to Meet Him: The Tenth Day of the Seventh Month." *The Advent Herald, and Signs of the Times Reporter*, October 16, 1844.
Strayer, Brian E. *J. N. Loughborough: The Last of the Adventist Pioneers*. Hagerstown, MD: Review and Herald, 2014.
Timm, Alberto. "Sola Scriptura and Ellen G. White: Historical Reflections." In *The Gift of Prophecy*, edited by Alberto R. Timm and Dwain N. Esmond, 289–300. Silver Springs, MD: Review and Herald, 2013.
Turner, Theodore. *The Three Angels' Messages Source Book*. https://www.academia.edu/34595991/The_Three_Angels_Messages_Source_Book.pdf.
Valentine, Gilbert. *J. N. Andrews: Mission Pioneer, Evangelist, and Thought Leader*. Nampa, ID: Pacific, 2020.
———. *W. W. Prescott: Forgotten Giant of Adventism's Second Generation*. Hagerstown, MD: Review and Herald, 2005.
Veltman, Fred. "The Desire of Ages Project: The Conclusions." *Ministry Magazine*, December 1990, 11–15. https://www.ministrymagazine.org/archive/1990/12/the-desire-of-ages-project-the-conclusions.
———. " The Desire of Ages Project: The Data." *Ministry Magazine*, October 1990, 4–7. https://cdn.ministrymagazine.org/issues/1990/issues/MIN1990-10.pdf.
Walters, Kathie. *Child Prophets of the Huguenots*. Translated by Claire Uyttebrouck. Macon, GA: Good News Fellowship Ministries, 2016.
Wheeler, Gerald. *James White: Innovator and Overcomer*. Hagerstown, MD: Review and Herald, 2003.
Whiston, William. *The Literal Accomplishment of Scripture Prophecies, Being a Full Answer to a Late Discourse, of the Grounds and Reasons of the Christian Religion*. London: J. Senex, 1724.
White, Arthur. *Ellen G. White: The Early Years, 1827–1862*. Vol. 1. Washington, DC: Review and Herald, 1985.
White, Ellen G. *Appeal to Mothers Relative to the Great Cause of the Physical, Mental, and Moral Ruin of Many of the Children of Our Time*. Battle Creek, MI: Steam Press, 1864.
———. "Christ Our Hope." *Advent Review and Sabbath Herald*, December 20, 1892, 785.
———. *Christian Education*. Battle Creek, MI: International Tract Society, 1894.
———. *Christian Experience and Teaching of Ellen G. White*. Mountain View, CA: Pacific, 1940.
———. "Communications: Dear Young Friends." *The Youth's Instructor*, December 1852, 20–22.
———. *Counsels on Health*. Mountain View: CA, Pacific, 1923.
———. "Dear Brothers and Sisters." *Present Truth*, November, 1850, 87.
———. *Early Writings: Experience and Views and Spiritual Gifts*. Vol 1. Battle Creek, MI: Review and Herald, 1882.

---. *Ellen G. White: Letters & Manuscripts with Annotations, 1845–1859*. Hagerstown, MD: Review and Herald, 2014.

---. *The Great Controversy*. Oakland, CA: Pacific, 1888.

---. *The Great Controversy*. Mountain View, CA: Review and Herald, 1911.

---. *The Great Controversy*. Mountain View, CA: Pacific, 1950.

---. *The Great Controversy*. Altamont, TN: Harvestime, 1998.

---. *Life Sketches*. Mountain View, CA: Pacific, 1915.

---. *Selected Messages*. Vol. 1. Washington, DC: Review and Herald, 1958.

---. *A Sketch of the Christian Experience and Views of Ellen G. White*. Saratoga Springs, NY: James White, 1851.

---. *A Solemn Appeal Relative to Solitary Vice and Abuses and Excesses of the Marriage Relation*. Battle Creek, MI: Steam Press, 1870.

---. *Spirit of Prophecy*. Vol 4. Oakland, CA: Pacific, 1884.

---. *Spiritual Gifts*. Vol. 2. Washington, DC: Review and Herald, 1945.

---. *Spiritual Gifts*. Vol. 1. Battle Creek, MI: Review and Herald, 1858.

---. *Spiritual Gifts*. Vol. 3. Tellico Plains, TN: Digital Inspiration, 2020.

---. *Spiritual Gifts*. Vol. 4a. Ellen G. White Estate. https://egwwritings-a.akamaihd.net/pdf/en_4aSG.pdf.

White, James S. *A Solemn Appeal*. Battle Creek, MI: Steam Press, 1870.

---. "Watchman, What of the Night?" *Day Star*, September 20, 1845, 256.

---. "A Word to the "'Little Flock.'" Brunswick, ME: James White, 1847.

---. "A Word to the "'Little Flock.'" Ringgold, GA: Teach Services, 2014.

White, James S., and Ellen G. White. *Life Sketches: Ancestry, Early Life, Christian Experience, and Extensive Labors of Elder James White, and His Wife Mrs. Ellen G. White*. Battle Creek, MI: Steam Press, 1880.

Wigger, John H. *Taking Heaven by Storm: Methodism and the Rise of Popular Christianity in America*. Urbana, IL: University of Illinois Press, 2001.

Winship, Michael P. *Making Heretics*. Princeton, NJ: Princeton University Press, 2002.

Index

Acacian schism, 243
Acquired or Inspired (McMahon), 280–81
Adult Teachers Sabbath School Bible Study Guide, 42–43
The Adventist Home and *Child Guidance*, 270
Advent Mirror, 116
Adversus Haereses (Irenaeus), 238
African churches, 225
Age of Enlightenment, 228–29
Albany Conference, 138
Albigenses, 198–201, 204–7, 216–17, 245, 256
Alcott, William, 271, 280
Alexandria, 238–42, 262
allegorical-typological historicism
   biblical authority, 99
   Crosier's extended atonement, 104
   and Damsteegt, 97
   Daniel and Revelation, 69–75
   EGW's dependence on Millerism, 1–3, 165
   four watches, 141–42
   Gog and Magog proof, 55–56
   Great Disappointment, 111–12
   Habakkuk, 86–90, 91
   historicists' method, 31
   interpreting Scripture, 112
   Jeremiah, 85
   and Litch, 230
   Matthew 25, 119
   Parable of the Bridegroom and the Ten Virgins, 10–12
   post-Great Disappointment events, 12–13
   requirements of, 235

   Scriptural interpretation, 7–10, 77, 86–87, 95
   shut-door Adventists, 131
   three categories of proofs, 62
   Waldenses, 199
   White/Nichols 1851 chart, 161
analogy of Scripture, 138
Andrews, J. N., 16, 119n9, 163–64, 169–75, 177, 255
angelic guidance, 81, 97, 194–95, 286
Angers, France, 67–68
angry nations, 187–88
anosognosia, 120
Anthimus, 222
Antichrist, 44, 49, 168n15, 212, 228
Antioch, 238–42, 258, 262
Apocalypse, 192
apocalyptic signs and symbols, 33–34, 61–63, 62n25, 112–13, 113n30, 189, 199
Apocrypha, 200–201
apostasy, 228
apostolic sees *(sedes apostolicae)*, 238
apostolic traditions, 237–38
Appeal to Mothers (White), 270, 275n17
Arasola, Kai, 2n4, 236
arbitrary choices, 70, 74, 217–19, 228–33
Arian controversy, 239–41
Arian or anti-Trinitarian beliefs, 219–21
ark, 148–49, 151–52, 154, 156–57
Athanasius of Alexandria, 240
Augsburger, Daniel, 251
Augustine of Hippo, 241
Authari, 221

autocephaly, 240

Babylon, 10, 29, 84–86, 247
Bacchiocchi, Samuele, 264–66
Bailey, Mark L., 104–5
Baronius, Caesar, 254–55
Bates, Joseph
   allegorical-typological-historicism, 161
   allegorical-typological historicism for post-Great Disappointment events, 12
   anti-Trinitarian beliefs, 220
   Apocrypha as canonical, 171n24
   breastplate, 152n10
   the daily, 164
   disciples keeping the first day of the week, 210
   EGW's dependence on Turner and Hale, 117–18
   endorsement of Crosier, 130, 141, 153
   European revolutions of 1848, 187
   evangelism, 179
   General Conference committee, 285
   intellectual dependence of EGW on, 289
   Little Flock document of 1847, 151
   papal supremacy, 214n3
   Pope Gregory, 251, 253–54
   pope nomenclature, 259–60
   repudiation of the midnight cry, 127
   Sabbath, 14, 122, 158
   Sabbath as "pure" apostolic doctrine, 199–201
   Sabbath change to Sunday, 247–52, 254, 255–56, 263–66
   second coming, 98
   three angels of Revelation, 96
   2 Esdras, 95n60, 147
   Waldenses, 192
Battle of the Milvian Bridge/Vision of Constantine, 219
Benedict I (pope), 221
Bible, literal reading of, 99
Bible and continuous historical sequences, 86–87
Bible and definite time, 79–80
Bible prophecy, 159
Bible societies, 47n73, 71–72, 197–99
biblical proofs, 41n52, 51, 59, 77, 82
Bolton, Fanny, 252
Bonfoey, Clarissa M., 180–81
bridegroom concept, 115–19, 122, 147, 165, 236, 245–46
Bridegroom Parable. *See* Parable of the Bridegroom and the Ten Virgins
Brightman, Thomas, 6–8
Brown, Jerrod, 120
Brownlee, W. C., 193, 207
Burt, Merlin, 12, 98, 103, 104, 114, 130, 135, 138–40
Bush, George, 172
Byzantine Empire, 197, 224–26

Caesaropapism, 219
Callixtus I (pope), 259
Cameron, Euan, 202, 207
captivity of the pope, 187n21, 229–30, 233–34
Casco street church, 77
Casebolt, Donald, 202
Caspar, Erich, 220, 224
catastrophic decline for the papacy, 223–26
censer. *See* golden censer
charts. *See* 1843 chart; White/Nichols 1851 chart
Christ, two-chamber process with, 12–14, 103–4, 114, 128, 146, 152n10, 153, 292
Christianity, 240, 260, 261
Christology, 242
chronology of the parable, 103, 104, 108–9, 114
churches of Revelation. *See* seven churches of Revelation
church in the wilderness, 173, 192–96, 199, 200–201, 216–17
circulation, 281, 283
citation of Scripture, 39–42
Clavis Apocalyptica (Mede), 26

cleanliness, 276, 281n39
Clement XIV (pope), 229
Clemons, Emily, 153
close of probation
  acceptance of the midnight cry, 18, 123, 131
  Crosier's theory, 106
  EGW's first vision, 128, 137
  erroneous eschatological concepts, 140, 191
  and Miller, 115
  Ottoman Empire's collapse, 22–25, 22n2, 30
Coles, J. B., 81, 280
Comba, Emilio, 208
"comeouterism" sermon (Fitch), 85
communion, 238–39
confabulation, 119–21, 287–88
Conradi, Louis R., 15–16
Constantine, 174, 210, 239–41, 251, 257, 263
Constantinople, 28, 174, 220–22, 225, 239–44, 260–62
Constitutum (Vigilius), 223, 243
consumption. *See* tuberculosis
continual desolation, 170, 177
continuous-historical hypothesis. *See* allegorical-typological historicism
conversions, 13, 24–25, 110–11, 130–31, 132, 138n47, 191
Coptic Christians, 260
Cornelius (pope), 258
Cornelius of Rome, 238
Cornell, M. E., 285
correction, 139–40
Council of 692 in Trullo *(Quinisextine)*, 225
Council of Chalcedon, 242–43, 260, 261
Council of Ephesus, 242
Council of Nicea, 240–41
Counter-Reformation, 205
Cranmer, Thomas, 6
Cromwell, Thomas, 6
Crosier, O. R. L.

allegorical-typological historicism for post-Great Disappointment events, 12–13
allegorical-typological-historicist assumptions, 161
  and Bates, 250
close of probation, 123
EGW's endorsement of, 141
extended atonement, 10–11, 14, 98–99, 102–14, 143, 152–53, 165, 188
intellectual dependence of EGW on, 14, 289
movement of Christ to the Most Holy Place, 146
true light, 130
two "great signs," 87–88, 89
cults, 246–47
Cyprian of Carthage, 258

Daigneau, Samuel and Charles, 270
the daily
  allegorical-typological historicism, 235
  Andrews on, 169–75
  EGW's 1850 visions, 183–84, 189–90
  1843 chart, 15, 57, 161, 184
  empirical evidence, 204
  historical assertions, 211
  in Millerism, 162–69
  Numbers occurrences of, 175–79
  overview, 15–16
  pagan Rome, 57, 177–78
  Smith's disputes of translation, 172–75
Dammon, Israel, 117, 143, 181n3
Damsteegt, P. Gerard
  EGW'S dependence on Miller's allegorical historicism, 97
  midnight cry, 138–39
  prophetic periods, 141–44
  shut-door views, 124–25, 135
  two-abominations motif, 164
  Waldenses, 202, 208–9
Daniel
  allegorical-typological historicism, 69

(Daniel continued)
   the daily, 164–65, 166–71, 173–75, 177
   divine guidance, 286
   evangelism, 179
   Habakkuk, 89–90
   historicist Protestant interpretation of, 192
   Miller's Evidences, 42–48
   1,335-year prophecy, 56–57
   1,260 day-year equation, 218, 244
   Ottoman Empire collapse, 24–25
   persecutory papacy, 213
   Sabbath change to Sunday, 251
   sacrifice, 190
   sanctuary, 163
   White/Nichols 1851 chart, 184–85
Daniel 8:14, 160
Daniel 12:12, 230
Daniel and Revelation (Smith), 46, 174
Daniells, A. G., 189, 211
Dark Day of 1780, 61n20, 64–66, 89, 105, 108, 112, 293
day = 1000 years principle, 32, 34, 36–39, 40n50, 41, 41n51, 97
Day-Dawn (Crosier), 115, 153
Day of Atonement, 14, 100n79, 143, 147, 151, 153–55, 176
Day-Star, 115, 126, 127, 136–37, 142
day-year principle, 40n50, 57, 65, 174n30, 196, 215, 234–37
deadly wound, 25, 99, 214, 229, 231, 234
Decius, 258–59
definite time
   apocalyptic expostulations, 22
   biblical prophetic periods, 60, 61, 82
   Crosier's modification or midnight cry, 114
   as God, 62
   and Jacobs, 106
   Millerite struggle with doubt, 92n47
   Miller's prophecy, 40, 40nn47–48
   misconception of the gift of prophecy, 291
   parables, 109
   proclamation of, 79–80
   tarrying time, 76–77
   2,520-year prophecy, 186
   as untenable, 112
deism, 8, 71, 291
Delafield, Arthur, 246–47
delay. *See* tarrying time
desolation, 170–71, 172–75, 177
deuterocanonical books, 200
Deuteronomy, 54–55
diet, 272, 274, 276–77, 278–81, 283
Diocletian, 232, 259–60
Dionysius of Alexandria, 258
disciples keeping the first day of the week, 250–53, 255–56, 263
divine guidance and revelation
   Bates, 181n3
   from charts, 51
   conclusions, 285–89
   "the daily," 178
   endorsement of Miller, 2–3, 81, 83, 97, 195
   faulty premises, 113–14, 140
   human sources, 122
   "I saw" statements of EGW, 18, 20, 163
   masturbation, 269–71
   old view, 190
   parable of Matthew 25, 109
   Sabbath, 200–201, 256
   shaking of the powers of heaven, 187
divine punishment/retribution, 121, 182n6
Document 19, 127
Dominus ac Redempto, 229
Donation of Pepin, 219
Donatists of North Africa, 258
door of probation. *See* close of probation
Dorchester, Massachusetts, 160–61, 182
Downham, George, 211

earthquake in Revelation, 72–75. *See also* Lisbon earthquake of 1755
Easter, 238, 265–66

INDEX

ecclesiastical authority of the papacy, 236–45
Edict of Nantes, 56
Edson, Hiram, 153, 250
1843/1844 predictions, 58–60, 83, 85–86, 87, 100, 107, 108, 109n17, 110n21, 113–14, 182–83, 195, 199, 244, 291
1843 chart, 28n13
   change with White/Nichols 1851 chart, 16–17, 151–52, 188–90
   and Fitch, 89n41, 159
   identity of the daily, 15, 57, 161, 184
   1,335 day-year, 15–17, 57, 80n13, 160–61, 187n21, 235
   1,260 day-year, 57, 95, 235
   proclamation of time in 1843, 80
   production of, 58–59
   prophetic interval, 52
   and Rhodes, 179–80
   seven times of the Gentiles, 159–61
   2,300 day-year, 15
   2,520 day-year, 16–17, 51, 160, 186–87
eisegesis, 35, 44–45, 99, 104, 112, 168, 177
Elisha the prophet, 81, 195
Elizabethan vials, 6–7
Ellen G. White Encyclopedia, 30n23, 121, 180, 215, 215n8, 282
Ellen G. White Letters & Manuscripts (White), 114
empirical evidence, 8, 204, 288
The End of Historicism (Arasola), 2n4
end of sin, 48
Eusebius, 251–53, 257
Eustations of Antioch, 240
Eutychus of Constantinople, 242
Evidence from Scripture and History of the Second Coming of Christ (Miller), 8, 42, 62
Evidence of the Truth of the Christian Religion (Keith), 8
exercise, 279, 283
Exeter camp meeting, 78–79
extended atonement, 11–12, 14, 88, 99, 103, 104, 105, 106–7, 110, 111, 129, 130, 133, 141, 143, 152, 152n11, 165
extra-biblical material, 149, 202–3
Ezekiel, 9–10, 55–56, 77, 82–84, 86, 99–100

Fabian (pope), 258
fake conversions, 110–11
Feast of Acclamations, 176
Feast of Tabernacles, 177
Feast of the New Moon, 176
Feast of Unleavened Bread or Passover, 176
Feast of Weeks, 176
Festus, 220
fifteen proofs of Miller, 2, 2n4, 9–11, 20, 31–32, 42, 51, 58–60, 69, 76–82, 86–87, 97–99, 105, 106–7, 108, 113
Fifth Synod, 225
fifth trumpet, 7, 27
first angel of Revelation, 9, 57n8, 95n63, 96, 153, 183, 189, 198–99
first resurrection
   collapse of the Ottoman Empire, 24, 25, 30, 98n75
   Crosier's extended atonement, 111
   EGW's first vision, 123–24
   Miller's historicist predictions, 2, 48, 50n83, 114
   as visible event, 22n2
first vision, December 1844, 14, 18, 22, 94, 108, 117–19, 121–22, 123–24, 126, 128–29, 132, 135–38, 140, 143, 146–58, 188, 200–201, 245, 285, 287, 292
Fitch, Charles, 85, 89n41, 96n67, 151–52, 159
538 to 1798 interval, 17, 50, 56–57, 63, 70, 162, 192, 194, 196, 200, 211, 213–21, 223, 224–26, 227–28, 229–30, 234–36, 243–45
508 to 538 interval, 57, 164, 166, 168, 171, 177–78, 215
Fliche, Augustine, 220
Focus (journal), 202
Ford, Desmond, 98
forty days, 106–7, 123

forty-ninth jubilee trumpet, 107
Foss, Hazen, 247
four beasts, 69–70
four watches, 87n33, 98, 141–45
Foxe, John, 205
Foy, William, 22, 200, 247, 287–88, 289
French Revolution, 43–46, 73–74, 216–17, 228–34
From Sabbath to Sunday (Bacchiocchi), 265–66
Froom, Leroy Edwin, 58, 211, 213, 219, 287
fulfilled prophecies, 8, 25
Fuller, Andrew, 28
Fuller, Isaac, 30
functional date-setting, 133–40

Galasius (pope), 243
General Conference, 22, 60, 79–80, 246, 285
geopolitical identification, 75
Gill, John, 211–12
Gnostics, 198, 238
Gog and Magog proof of 1843, 55–56
golden censer, 14, 147–48, 150–58, 161, 188
Graham, Sylvester, 271–84, 289
grammatical-historical method, 34, 42–51
Graybill, Ron, 73
Great Controversy, 192, 247, 249
The Great Controversy (White), 29, 73, 89n41, 201, 215, 252
Great Disappointment, 10–13, 20, 23, 87, 98, 111, 114, 116, 120, 123–24
Great Jubilee, 59, 142–43
great signs, 11, 87, 89, 104–5, 108
Gregory (pope), 245–46, 250–51, 253–54
Gregory the Great (pope), 264
Gui, Bernard, 209
"Guidelines for Interpreting Jesus' Parables" (Bailey), 104–5

Habakkuk, 9–10, 77–82, 83–84, 86–95, 99–100, 151–52, 160

Hahn, F. B., 153, 250
Haines, Elizabeth, 121–22
Hale, Apollos
    allegorical-typological historicism for post-Great Disappointment events, 12
    bridegroom explanation, 116–17
    coreligionists' protests, 60
    the daily, 164, 169
    historicist traditions, 20
    intellectual dependence of EGW on, 289
    midnight-cry movement, 129
    movement of Christ to the Most Holy Place, 146, 153
    Second Advent Manual, 166
    and Snow, 78
Haller, Johannes, 224–27
halo, Sabbath, 14, 147, 152n11, 154, 156–58, 188n23
Hare, E.H., 281–82
Harmon, Ellen. *See* White, Ellen G. (née Harmon)
Harmon, Sarah B., 180–81
Harris, Lydia, 180–81
Haskell, S. N., 15, 178, 189–90, 200, 204, 235
health principles, 270–71, 280
Hebrew word for "the daily," 16, 164n8, 166–69, 173–78
Henoticon, 243
Heraclius I, 244
heresy, 133, 207, 224, 226–28, 243–45, 262
Heruli, 219
Hewett, Oren, 185–86
High Priest and censer, 12, 14, 103, 130, 147–48, 151–54, 158, 161, 188
Himes, J. V., 59, 78nn4–5, 116, 124, 125n19, 129, 131, 138
Hippolytus, 259, 259n93
historicism, 2n5. *See also* allegorical-typological historicism
History of the Evangelical Churches of Piedmont (Morland), 206
Hodgkin, Thomas, 221–23
Holy Alliance, 46–47

Holy Place/Most Holy Place, 128, 129,
    147, 154, 189
  EGW's first vision, 147, 152–54,
    157–58
  missing cultic objects, 14
  movement of Christ to, 153–54
  theological importance of, 154–55
  type-antitype parallels, 149–50
  White/Nichols 1851 chart, 152–53,
    161, 188–89
Honorius I (pope), 226, 244
Hormisdas Formula, 243
Hosea, 4, 10n22, 32, 35–42, 40n47,
  41n52, 50–51, 141
host
  the daily, 173
  in Daniel, 171
  little horn, 170
human sources, 20, 122, 145, 210, 247
hypochondriacs, 279. *See also*
  masturbation

Ignatius of Antioch, 238
Illyricus, Matthias Flacius, 205
imminence rhetoric, 113, 133–40, 188
imprisonments of Pius VI and VII,
  229, 232, 233–34
infallibility
  of EGW, 166n11
  of EGW according to Irwin,
    246–47
  EGW borrowing from extra-
    biblical writers, 202–5
  papal, 226
  papal infallibility, 234, 237
insabbatati, 208–9
insanity, 18–19, 268, 270–83. *See also*
  masturbation
investigative judgment, 12, 113,
  152n11, 153–55, 188n23, 235
Irenaeus of Lyons, 238, 257
Irwin, George A., 246–47
Islam, 288–89
Israel Dammon trial, 117, 143
"'It Was Not Taught Me by Man'"
  (Casebolt), 140

Jackson, Michigan, 159

Jacobs, Enoch, 90–91, 93n50, 106,
  123, 142, 154, 206–7
Jeremiah, 9–10, 53, 55, 77, 82–86,
  99–100
Jerome, 257
Jerusalem, 219, 258, 262
Jerusalem Bible, 175, 176n33
Jesus' parables, 104–5, 112
Jewish Christian Hegesippus, 238
Jews, 35–36, 173, 188, 209–10, 265,
  276
John III (pope), 221
John the Baptist, 3, 33, 81, 102, 195
John the Revelator, 81, 195
Jones, A. T., 113
jubilee trumpet, 107, 109
Jude, 126–27
judicatum, 222. *See also* Three-
  Chapter Controversy
Julius, 240
Justin I, 243
Justinian, 214, 214n3, 217–18, 222,
  227, 229, 236, 243–45
Justinian II, 225
Justin Martyr, 256–57, 264–65

Kaiser, Denis, 15, 125
Karaite interpretation, 77–78, 82,
  124n18
Karlman, Roland, 101n81, 159n27,
  185–86
Keith, Alexander, 8
king of the north and king of the
  south, 42–44
KJV family Bible, 1822, 27, 94,
  196–99, 206, 213–14
Knight, George R., 66, 137, 200, 235,
  252
Koch, Robert, 20, 182n6, 275
Korpman, Matthew J., 200

Lake, Jud, 203
Laodicean church, 7, 113
lapsed Christians, 238–39
last woe of Revelation, 30
Latin Christianity, 207, 243
Latter Rain and the Sealing, 113, 134

Lectures on the Science of Human Life (Graham), 271
A Lecture to Young Men on Chastity (Graham), 271
Leger, Jean, 206
Leo (pope), 242
Letter of Clement, 238
letter of Ignatius of Antioch, 238
levirate marriage, 269
Leviticus, 3, 50, 52–55, 141, 151, 164n8, 236
Levterov, Theodore N., 137
L'Histoire Générale des Eglises Evangeliques des Vallées de Piemon (Leger), 206
Linus, 257
Lisbon earthquake of 1755, 61n20, 62–65, 112, 293
Litch, Josiah, 22n2, 23, 25, 26, 27–30, 57, 87n33, 187n21, 229–30, 244
The Literal Accomplishment of Scripture Prophecies (Whiston), 8
Little Flock, 96, 111, 132, 151, 163, 179, 189, 237
little horn, 3, 26, 165, 170, 173–74, 217, 244, 254, 259n93
Lombards, 220–21
L'Onanism (Tissot), 269
lost prophecies of Miller, 33–35
Lot, Ferdinand, 223–24
Luke, 10n22, 32, 34, 35–38, 41n52, 42, 50–51, 61, 141, 293
Luther, Martin, 3, 26, 180n2, 262. *See also* Reformation Era

Malamud and Palmer study, 281
Manasseh, 53
Marcellinus (pope), 259–60
March 21, 1844, 3, 9, 11–12, 20, 22–23, 29–31, 40n47, 58–60, 76–82, 83–84, 85–88, 89–93, 94n54, 98–99, 104, 108–9, 142, 165, 176
Marcion, 265–66
Mark, 9, 34, 76, 122n15, 141, 143, 242
mark of the Beast, 95n61, 248–49, 251–52, 257, 264

marriage, chronology of four important events, 104, 110
Martin, Victor, 220
Martin I (pope), 225
martyrdom, 158n24, 193, 205–6, 210, 256–60, 264
Massachusetts State Lunatic Hospital, 268
masturbation, 18–19, 268–84
"Masturbatory Insanity" (Hare), 281–82
mathematical proofs. *See* fifteen proofs of Miller
Matthew 25. *See* Parable of the Bridegroom and the Ten Virgins
Maximinus Thrax, 259
McAdams, Donald R., 201
McMahon, Don, 271, 280–81, 283
Mede, Joseph, 26–29
Mediator and Priest in the Holy Place, 106
Mennas, 222
meteorite shower of 1833, 61n20, 66, 67–68, 89, 105, 108
midnight cry, 8–9, 11–12, 14, 18, 22, 31, 39, 57, 66, 78–79, 82, 87–88, 99, 103, 108, 109, 110, 113, 114, 117, 123, 124, 127–33, 135–38, 139, 140, 143, 147, 190, 236, 249, 287. *See also* Snow, S. S.
Midnight Cry (Snow), 58
Miller, William
  allegorical-typological-historicist method, 13
  Brightman's identifications, 7–8
  collapse of the Ottoman Empire, 21–32
  and Crosier, 105, 106
  the daily, 15–16, 162–69, 171–73, 177–78
  and Damsteegt, 139, 141
  and Daniel, 42–51
  Daniel and Revelation, 69–75
  dependence of EGW on, 1–3, 140, 165, 286–89
  EGW's endorsements of, 102–3, 195–96
  EGW's first vision, 132, 138

538, 217–19, 227–28
historicist predictions, 8–12
and Hosea, 39–42
Justinian, 217
KJV family Bible, 1822, 196
lost prophecies, 33–35
and Luke, 36–39
March 21, 1844 prediction, 3, 9, 76–101, 160
midnight cry, 129, 133, 236
and Nichol, 112–13
October 22, 1844, 235–36
1,290 day-year, 185
1,260 day-year, 213–17
prophetic periods, 108–9
Protestant churches, 247
religious violence, 193–94, 206–7
repudiation, 127–28
1798 prediction, 211
seven times of the Gentiles, 52–68
shut-door teaching, 115–16
666-year prophecy, 15, 32, 35–36, 48–50, 80n13, 186–88, 247–48
universal proclamation, 123–25
Waldenses, 198–99, 206
Millerite chart. *See* 1843 chart
Monophysites, 242–44, 260, 261
monothelitism, 244
Moore, R. I., 207
Morland, Samuel, 206
mothers, 272–73. *See also* progeny
motivated reasoning, 166
Mueller, Ekkehardt, 202–3
Muslims, 3, 7, 26–27, 188, 196–97, 262, 276, 288

Napoleon, 47
Napoleon Bonaparte, 24, 43, 43n57, 57, 231–32, 233
nationalism, 228–29
Nestorians/Nestorianism, 242, 261–62, 264
Newton, Issac, 28, 220
Nicean order, 242–43
Nichol, F. D., 42, 50–51, 53n3, 79, 97–98, 112–13, 160, 284

Nichols, Otis, 83–84, 138, 182–83, 185, 186, 188, 190. *See also* White/Nichols 1851 chart
Nigrinus, Georg, 26
Novatian, 258
Novatianists, 258
Novellae (Justinian), 229, 244–45
Numbers, 149, 164n8, 169, 173, 175–79

October 22, 1844, 3n7, 10–12, 14, 17, 22–23, 30–31, 66, 75, 78n4, 79, 80n11, 82, 85, 86n29, 87n33, 89, 96, 98–99, 103–7, 112, 117, 123–24, 125, 128–31, 138–39, 142, 146–47, 152–54, 165, 169n17, 189–91, 235–36, 249, 268n2, 293
October 23, 1844, 14, 85, 114, 131, 154
October 23, 1850, 151, 160–61, 182–84
Old Testament concepts of purity/impurity, 281n39
Old Testament prophets, 140
Old Testament sacrificial system, 163
old view of the daily, 190
Olson, Robert, 125–28, 135, 139
1,260 day-year equation, 211–12, 213–19, 221, 228, 229, 234–35, 244
1,335-year prophecy, 86n29
according to charts, 16, 80n13, 185–88, 187n21
analysis regarding 538–1798, 38n43, 235
background of, 56–57
as calculated backwards, 49n78
1843 chart, 15–17, 57, 80n13, 160–61, 187n21, 235
four watches eschatology of James White, 143
as main period, 61
saints, 218–19
1,290 day-year, 15, 16, 38n43, 48n77, 49n78, 51, 56–57, 59, 61, 80n13, 95, 185–88, 211, 218–19, 235

On the Unity of the Church (Cyprian), 258
open- and shut-door vision, 248
open-door Adventism, 13, 15, 110–11, 113n30, 124, 130–31
The Opening Heavens (Bates), 251–52
Orthodox churches, 261–62
Osman I, 197
Ostrogoths, 217–19
Ottoman Empire's collapse, 3–4, 21–32, 38n42, 87n33, 98n75, 160n30, 165, 188–91, 215

Pacca (cardinal), 233
pagan dominance, 189–90
pagan Rome, 15–17, 35–36, 49, 57, 162, 164, 166–68, 170–71, 174, 177–78, 183n10, 215, 219. *See also* papacy/papal Rome
Palmaria, 221
papacy/papal Rome, 16, 35n32, 49n81, 57, 71, 162, 164, 166, 171, 174, 192–94, 206, 210, 215, 288
  anathema, 221–28
  historical development of primacy, 236–45
  nomenclature, 259–60
  papal catastrophe, 223–26
  papal supremacy, 17, 56, 196, 214–15, 217–18, 220–21, 223, 226, 228–34, 241–45
  post-538, 234
  responsible for changing to Sunday, 263–67
  Sunday-keeping, 247–50, 253–57, 261, 263–67
  Three-Chapter Controversy, 224–26
Parable of the Bridegroom and the Ten Virgins, 10–12, 87, 96n68, 103, 104–5, 108, 110–11, 113, 115–16, 119, 128–29, 132, 236
parables, 104–5, 106, 108–9, 112–14, 116, 236
Pareus, David, 211
Passover, 143, 145, 176
Patriarch Acacius, 243
patriarchates, 240–41

Paul, 257
Peavy, G. W., 153
Pelagius II (pope), 221
Perrin, Jean-Paul, 205–6, 208–9
persecutory papacy, 63, 64–65, 192–94, 213
Persian Empire, 260–61
Pfeiffer, Carl C., 282
Phillips, Anna, 113
Phocas, 214
phrenology, 279
Pius II (pope), 209
Pius VI (pope), 17, 24, 212, 228–30, 233–34, 244
Pius VII (pope), 17, 230–34, 244
Plummer, F. G., 66
Pontian (pope), 259
pork, 276
Portland, Maine, 3, 22, 77, 118
Preble, T. M.
  disciples keeping the first day of the week, 210, 250–53, 255–56
  EGW's dependence on, 122
  papal supremacy, 214n3
  pope nomenclature, 259–60
  Sabbath change to Sunday, 201, 249–52, 263–64, 266–67
predictive prophecies, 55, 235, 244
Prescott, W. W., 15–16, 113, 178, 189–90, 217–18
present truth, 159–60, 181n3
Present Truth (journal), 159
Preston, Rachel, 250
Priestly, Joseph, 73
prince of the host, 170
proclamation of the time in 1843, 80–82
progeny, 273–74, 277
pronouns, 42–44, 50
proofs. *See* fifteen proofs of Miller prophecies
  continuous-historical interpretations, 196
  correction or growth, 140
  and Damsteegt, 97
  Daniel 11–12., 42–48
  doctrinal mistakes, 203–4

EGW's endorsement of Miller, 194–95
exact fulfillment of, 30, 49n79, 73, 101
French Revolution, 72–75
Habakkuk, 90, 91–93
Hosea 6: 1–3, 39–42
imprisonment of Pius VI, 228–29
infallibility, 246–47
lost prophecies of Miller, 33–35
Luke 13:32–3, 35–39
Matthew 25, 103, 110
Muslims in, 26–27, 188
papacy, 229
predictive, 235, 244
prophetic time, 52–54, 198
reign of the Antichrist, 211–12
Revelation, 196–97
2 Esdras, 200
Waldenses, 198–99, 205
in Whiston, 8
See also fifteen proofs of Miller; midnight cry
prophetic authority, 66, 103, 143, 284
prophetic endorsement, 3
The Prophetic Faith of Our Fathers (Froom), 58, 287
prophetic intervals, 9, 111–12, 178, 189–90
prophetic periods, 50, 52–68, 77, 80n12, 108–9, 114, 291–93. *See also* 1,335-year prophecy; 1,290 day-year; seven times of the Gentiles
prophetic predictions, Miller's, 29, 112
prophetic significance of October 22, 1844, 11
prophetic year, 26–27
Protestant historiography, 26, 71, 168n15
Great Controversy, 201
vs. Millerites, 247
papacy, 254–55
religious violence, 192–93
Sunday-keeping, 262
Waldensians, 204–6
Protestant Reformation. *See* Reformation Era

provincial churches, 239–40
purity. *See* cleanliness

Quartodeciman dispute, 238, 266

rebaptism, 238–39
Reformation churches, 29, 99
Reformation Era, 2, 7–8, 13, 28–29, 205–7, 262, 287
regional synod (Tyre 335), 240
religious violence, 196–97, 206–7
"Remarks in Vision" (White), 134
repudiation of the midnight cry, 18, 127–28
resurrection. *See* first resurrection
Revelation, 24–25, 26, 27–28, 35, 62–63, 69–70, 70–71, 72–75, 83–84, 85, 87, 96, 115, 179, 188, 194, 195, 197–99, 214, 219, 263, 286
Revelation of St. John, 81, 195
Rhodes, Samuel W., 119n9, 179–80, 186
Robber Synod of 449, 242
Rodriquez, Angel, 203
Roentgen, Wilhelm, 275
Roman bishops, 236–45, 256–62
Roman Catholic Church, 99, 194, 205–9, 228, 231–32. *See also* papacy
Roman synod (341), 240
Rome
concordat of 1801, 231–32
Council of Nicea, 240
fallibility, 226
letter of Ignatius, 238
papal catastrophe, 224–26
papal supremacy, 241–45
sanctuary, 173–74
spiritual authority vis-à-vis, 241–42
Sunday-keeping, 261–62, 263–66
two-phased entity, 162

Sabbatati, 209
Sabbath, 20, 131, 247–50
angels of Revelation, 189
disciples keeping the first day of the week, 250–53, 255–56, 263

(Sabbath continued)
  1847 vision, 14, 150, 152
  halo, 147
  historiography of, 122
  missing from first vision, 149
  papacy, 237–38
  Pope Gregory, 245–46, 250–51, 253–54
  popes responsible for changing to Sunday, 247–50, 254–56, 263–67
  shut door, 132
  Sunday-keeping as heresy, 262
  Sunday-keeping popes and Christians martyrs, 256–57
  within the veil, 156–58
  Waldenses, 192–95, 199–202, 204–5, 208–10
Sabbath Adventists. *See* Little Flock
sacrifice as inappropriately supplied, 15–16, 162, 163–64, 169, 170, 174–75, 178, 184–85, 190. *See also* the daily
sanctuary
  allegorical definition, 168–69
  Andrews on, 170–71
  in Daniel 8, 173–74
Sardica, 240
Sardis church, 194
Satan. *See* synagogue of Satan
Saturday. *See* Sabbath
Schatz, Klaus, 225–26, 232, 232n47, 236–45
schizophrenia, 119–20
Scripture, interpretation of, 2, 42, 50–51, 112, 114, 145
scrofula, 275–76
SDA Bible Commentary, 90
The Sealing vision, 248–49
Second Advent. *See* second coming predictions
Second Advent Conference, 59–60
Second Advent Manual (Hale), 166
second coming, 16, 22, 28, 31, 34, 36–39, 48, 57, 58, 60, 76–79, 81–82, 84–86, 93, 98, 99, 103, 105, 106, 109, 112, 113, 114, 116, 117–18, 120, 123–24, 132–33, 134–35, 137, 141, 143, 144, 165, 211, 245, 256, 264, 285, 286
  angels of Revelation, 189
  apocalyptic charts of Daniel and Revelation, 179
  creation, 199
  Day of Atonement, 151
  and Litch, 229
  Miller's historicist predictions, 2–3, 8–12
  October 22, 1844, 235–36
  1,335-year prophecy, 185
  prophetic time, 198
  typological arguments, 236
  White/Nichols 1851 chart, 161
Second Council of Constantinople, 243
Second Epistle to Timothy, 257
Seleucia and Rimini synods, 240–41
self-abuse. *See* solitary vices
self-pollution, 271–73, 271n10, 279–80. *See also* masturbation; solitary vices
selling time, 113–14
semen, 18–19, 269, 278–82. *See also* masturbation
sequential predictive prophecies, 235
seven churches of Revelation, 2, 7, 70, 113
seven forms of Roman government, 35
1798 date, 219, 229, 235, 244
Seventh Day Sabbath (Bates), 254
seventh-month movement. *See* midnight cry
seven thousand slain, 63n27, 72–73
seven times of the Gentiles, 51, 52–54, 60–61, 80n13, 159–61, 186
seven trumpets of Revelation, 2, 6–7, 26–28
seven years, 54–56
ship transit analogy, 123
shoe theory, 208
shut door, 10, 12–13, 15, 16, 18, 110–11, 113, 114–16, 123–25, 127, 128–29, 130–31, 132, 135, 138, 140, 147, 189, 248–49. *See also* Little Flock

"The 'Shut Door' Documents" (Olson), 125–26
signs. *See* great signs
Signs of the Times (journal), 58
Silverious (pope), 225
Silverius (pope), 221–22
Sitz im Leben, 85
666-year prophecy, 15, 32, 35–36, 48–50, 80n13, 186–88, 247–48
sixth canon of the Council of Niceae, 241
Sixth Ecumenical Council, 226
6,000 years, 59, 143
Sixtus II, 259
Smith, Uriah, 46
   anti-Trinitarian beliefs, 220
   Apocrypha, 201
   changing identifications, 43n56
   Christ's compartment, 128
   the daily, 163, 164, 166, 172–75, 177–78
   538, 219, 223
   French Revolution, 73–74
   Justinian, 217, 227
   "old view," 15–16
   1,260 day-year equation, 214, 221
   Pius VII, 231
   sacrifice, 169
   seven churches, 70
   seven times of gentiles, 52–53
Snow, S. S., 8–10, 31, 77–79, 82–86, 99, 107, 112, 114, 115, 130, 144, 284, 287–89. *See also* midnight cry; tarrying time
sola Scriptura, 34, 100, 166, 178, 196, 248n65
Solemn Appeal (White), 270, 275n17
solitary vices, 17–19, 268–84. *See also* masturbation
Spanheim, Friedrich, 209
speculative periodizations, 10, 10n22, 70, 219
spiritual authority, 236–45. *See also* papacy
Spiritual Gifts (White), 80, 201, 252–53, 279
standing up of Michael, 25, 47n73, 49n78

St. Bartholomew's Day Massacre of the Huguenots, 219
Stephen of Rome, 238–39
Stockman, Levi, 22, 89n41, 132, 148
Storrs, George, 78n4, 92–93, 236
Strand, Kenneth, 264
stream-of-consciousness mode of interpretation, 7, 34–35, 42. *See also* eisegesis
Sunday as the devil's Sabbath, 251–52
Sunday-keeping, 209–10, 237–38, 255–57, 261–62, 264–67
supernatural events, 64–68, 182n6
superstitious beliefs, 67–68
symbol and interpretation relationship, 70
Symmachus, 220
synagogue of Satan, 147, 150, 154–55, 155n17, 170–71, 174, 247–48
Synod of 595, 224–25
syntactical exegesis, 236
systematic persecutor title, 232

tablets of stone, 147, 149–50, 156–57
tarring vision in Daniel and Habakkuk, 89–91
tarrying time, 3, 9, 12, 23, 76–82, 87–88, 89–93, 95, 98–100, 108–9, 110, 165, 236
TB. *See* tuberculosis
Ten Commandments. *See* tablets of stone
terminus a quo, 234–35
Tertullian, 238
Theodore of Caesare, 222
Theodoric, 220
Theodosius, 240
The Prophetic Faith of Our Fathers (Froom), 2–3n6, 287
Third Council of Constantinople, 244
three angels of Revelation, 49n78, 83, 87, 95, 96, 141, 153, 189, 195, 198–99. *See also* angelic guidance
Three-Chapter Controversy, 222–26, 243–44
throne of God, 148, 154
time of trouble, 24–25, 25n6, 47, 48n74, 134–35, 157, 256

time prophecies, 52–54, 234–36
Tissot, Samuel-Auguste, 269
Totilla, 218
tradition *(paradosis)*, 238
Treaty of Amiens, 231
Trinitarianism, 241
true light, 12–13, 88, 100, 112, 113, 130, 142n55, 287
trumpets. *See* seven trumpets of Revelation
Trust and Doubt (Kaiser), 125
tuberculosis, 18–19, 182n4, 274–77
Turkey, 24, 25, 29
Turner, Joseph, 10, 12–13, 102, 115–19, 121–22, 129, 140, 146, 153, 161, 165, 245–46, 289. *See also* Hale, Apollos; Parable of the Bridegroom and the Ten Virgins
28 Fundamental Beliefs, 65–66
2 Esdras, 10, 77, 82, 93–95, 116, 140, 146–47, 200–201, 247
2 Thessalonians, 167–68, 177
two-phased atonement. *See* extended atonement
two-stage coming. *See* extended atonement
2,300 day-year, 10n22, 15, 34, 40n49, 54, 59, 60–61, 86n29, 91, 114, 160, 169, 172, 186n17, 236
2,520-year prophecy. *See* seven times of the Gentiles
two witnesses of Revelation, 36n36, 50, 70–71, 72, 198, 215
Type, 225
type-antitype parallels, 149–50
typological arguments, 236

ultimate locus of authority, 288–89
ultra-montanism, 234
underclass, 280
universal synod (342), 240
University of Missouri, 66
Urbanus, 222
Ussher, James, 205–7

Valdesius, 205–6
Valentine, Gilbert, 164, 178
Valerian, 258–59

Vandals, 219
Vatican I, 237
Veltman, Fred, 201
verbal inerrancy, 203
vials of Revelation, 11, 28, 95
Vigilius (pope), 222–23, 225–26, 232–33, 243–44
Vignier, Nicolas, 209
vital force, 19, 269n4, 277, 278–82, 282n43
Vyhmeister, Werner, 264–65

Waggoner, J. H., 285
Waldenses
  arbitrary equivalences, 74
  church in the wilderness, 192–95
  empirical evidence, 204–5
  KJV family Bible, 1822, 196–99
  1,260 day-year equation, 216–17
  origin of legend, 205–7
  persecuting papacy, 245
  persecutions of, 256
  Sabbath-keeping, 208–11
  Saturday Sabbath, 248n65
  verbal inerrancy, 203n32
Waldo, Peter, 204–5, 208–10
War in the Vendée, 44n61
The Western Midnight Cry!!!, 86, 88, 91, 94, 193, 206
Wheeler, Frederick, 137, 249–50
Whiston, William, 8
White, Ellen G. (née Harmon)
  allegorical-typological historicism for post-Great Disappointment events, 10–13
  "apparent" tarrying of the vision, 88
  Bible societies concept, 72
  church in the wilderness, 216–17
  citation of Scripture in Miller, 39, 50, 55
  close of probation, 123–25
  confabulation, 119–22, 287–88
  correction, 140
  the daily, 15–16, 162–65, 177–78, 183–84, 189–91
  Dark Day of 1780, 64–66
  December 1848 vision, 187

dependence on Miller, 1–3, 96–97, 140, 165, 286, 287
door of probation, 18, 106, 128, 191
earthquake of Revelation as figurative, 62–65, 72–75
1843 chart, 80, 235
elements brought to visionary experience, 146–49
endorsement of Crosier, 102–3, 104, 165
ex nihilo visions, 256
extended atonement, 12–13
extra-biblical material, 202–5
functional date-setting, 133–40
Great Controversy, 192
Great Disappointment, 98, 123–24
greater light, 114
and Hale, 117–19
health principles, 280–81
historical misconceptions, 188–91, 264–67
human influence and errors, 245–47
imminence rhetoric, 113, 133–40, 188
infallibility of, 246–47
influence of Miller, 34
intellectual dependence, 289
interpreting Scripture, 112
and James Edson, 180–82
and James White, 1n1, 143–44
Justinian, 227
KJV family Bible, 213–14
KJV family Bible, 1822, 196–99
Lisbon earthquake, 61n20, 62–64
Little Flock, 179, 237
Little Flock document, 151
March 24, 1849 open- and shut-door vision, 132
masturbation, 18–19, 268–84
maximalist claims, 140
meteor shower of 1833, 67–68
midnight cry, 131, 132
Miller, 81, 83, 97
Miller's proofs, 76–82
and Nichols, 138
October 22, 1844, 11–12
1,260 day-year equation, 213–17

open- and shut-door vision, 248
Ottoman Empire's collapse, 21–32, 188
on papal powers, 231
Parable of the Bridegroom, 103, 116–17
persecution, 232
pope nomenclature, 259–60
proclamation of the time in 1843, 80–82
prophetic endorsement of Miller, 3, 194–95
prophetic periods as definite, 61–62
Protestant historiography, 254–55
reformations, 138–39
religious violence, 196–97, 207
on revolutionary France, 73
and Rhodes, 179–80
Sabbath, 131, 132
Sabbath change to Sunday, 247–50, 252–53, 255–56, 264–67
Sabbath historiography, 122
Sabbath vision of 1847, 14, 150, 152, 156–58, 188
The Sealing vision, 248–49
seven times of the Gentiles, 159–61
shut door of Matthew 25, 132–33
shut-door teaching, 115–16, 124–27, 128–29
sleigh ride, 117–19
and Snow, 14, 18, 75, 78–82, 102–3, 114, 140, 286–89
solitary vices, 17–19, 268–84
summary of evidence, 285–89
tarrying vision referred to in Habakkuk, 89
third group, 139
three angels, 96
throne of God, 154
time of trouble, 135
true light endorsement, 87–88, 130
and Turner, 10, 102, 115–19, 121–22, 129, 146, 165, 245–46, 289
2 Esdras, 82, 93–95, 140, 146–47, 200–201, 247
two-phased coming, 103–4

(White, Ellen G. continued)
  visions of 1850, 151–54, 182–83, 186, 189–90
  Waldenses, 17, 192–95, 199–205, 207–11
  See also first vision, December 1844; White/Nichols 1851 chart
White, James
  allegorical-typological historicism for post-Great Disappointment events, 12, 107n13
  anti-Trinitarian beliefs, 220
  apocalyptic symbols, 113n30
  Apocrypha as canonical, 171n24
  and Bates, 250
  continuous-historical method, 87n33
  the daily, 164
  ex nihilo visions, 256
  four watches eschatology, 87n33, 98, 141–45, 143
  and James Edson, 180–82
  last watch of the night, 127n24
  Little Flock, 237
  Little Flock document, 151
  Miller's repudiation, 127–28
  and Nichols, 138
  Olson on, 126
  Sabbath observation, 95n63
  Sabbath vision, 14, 135–37, 158
  solitary vices, 19, 268
  three angels of Revelation, 96
  time of trouble, 25n6
  2 Esdras, 95n60, 147, 200
  visions as foundation of a novel doctrine, 129–30
  White/Nichols 1851 chart, 159
White, W., 210–11
White, W. C., 200
White/Nichols 1851 chart
  angels of Revelation, 95n63
  collapse of Ottoman Empire, 160n30
  cultic objects, 14
  the daily, 178, 188–91
  EGW's intellectual dependence on Millerism, 165
  High Priest and censer, 14, 151–54, 161, 188
  Muslims' 391-year rule, 28n13
  prophetic interval, 52
  Sabbath truth, 247
  within the veil, 14, 94, 146–49, 151, 153–54, 156–58

year of release proof of 1843, 4, 54–55

Zephyrinus (pope), 259
Zinc and Other Micro-Nutrients (Pfeiffer), 282
zinc hypothesis, 19, 278, 282–84

www.ingramcontent.com/pod-product-compliance
Lightning Source LLC
Chambersburg PA
CBHW050616300426
44112CB00012B/1534